D1595909

Stephen Girard
America's First Tycoon

Stephen Girard
America's First Tycoon

George Wilson

COMBINED BOOKS
Pennsylvania

PUBLISHER'S NOTE

Combined Books, Inc., is dedicated to publishing books of distinction in history and military history. We are proud of the quality of writing and the quantity of information found in our books. Our books are manufactured with style and durability and are printed on acid-free paper. Our logo reflects our commitment to the modern and yet historic art of bookmaking.

We call ourselves Combined Books because we view the publishing enterprise as a "combined" effort of authors, publishers and readers. And we promise to bridge the gap between us—a gap which is all too seldom closed in contemporary publishing.

We would like to hear from our readers and invite you to write to us at our offices in Pennsylvania with your reactions, queries, comments, even complaints. All of our correspondence will be answered directly by a member of the Editorial Board or by the author.

We encourage all of our readers to purchase our books from their local booksellers, and we hope that you let us know of booksellers in your area that might be interested in carrying our books. If you are unable to find a book in your area, please write us.

For information, address:
COMBINED BOOKS, INC.
151 East 10th Avenue
Conshohocken, PA 19428

Library of Congress Cataloging-in-Publication Data
Wilson, George.
    Stephen Girard: America's first tycoon. / George Wilson.
            p.   cm.
    "Signpost books."
    Includes bibliographical references and index.
    ISBN 0-938289-56-X
        1. Girard, Stephen, 1750-1831.   2. Bankers—United States—Biography.
    3. Merchants—United States—Biography.   I. Title.
HG2463.G56W55   1995
332.1'23'092—dc20
    [B]   95-42257
                                                                 CIP

Printed in the United States of America.

To My Mother,
Eva Frear Wilson

Contents

Preface to the Signpost Biography Series

BIOGRAPHY is the soul of history—the stories of individual lives that give meaning and life to the past, and allow the reader to share vicariously in the drama of other times and places. It is the classic form of historical narrative, for it is through the lives of individual men and women that we can best come to comprehend the complexities of other ages. At the same time, good biography does not reduce the past to "Great Men and Women." Rather, it appreciates the limits we all face in defining our lives, whether imposed by social forces beyond our control, the framework in which we interpret reality and opportunity, or our own limited experience and knowledge. Biography reflects the human condition: our actions, our decisions, our thinking have consequences. Biography also reflects and illuminates the world in which its subjects lived, an expression of another time and place.

Signpost Biographies are designed to bring the past alive through the stories of individuals whose lives have helped make their world, and whose lives provide the modern reader with an opportunity to be part of that world. Biographies in the series will reflect the best in contemporary historical scholarship while never forgetting that the essence of history is storytelling, and that good history is also good literature. The subjects of Signpost Biographies will be men and women whose lives were inherently interesting, often spanning a broad range of endeavors, and whose stories provide insight into their world. They will include men and women from different cultures and social positions, those who protested their age as well as those who guided

9

it. Our authors will include both professional historians and compelling writers with a love of historical scholarship.

In recent decades professional historians have vastly increased our understanding of the past and the processes of change through the insights of the social sciences, statistics, and linguistic analysis. Often, however, it has seemed as if historians were writing only for other historians, and that their rigorous analyses of process neglected the stories of the individuals and the texture of everyday life. It is our hope that Signpost Biographies will bridge the gap between academic analyses and good storytelling, and between the professional historian and the broad audience of readers fascinated by the past.

It is appropriate that George Wilson's biography of Stephen Girard is the first in the Signpost series. Stephen Girard reflects the early American republic in which he prospered—brash, daring, compassionate, hardworking. Arriving penniless in Philadelphia at the outbreak of the Revolution, his is the stereotypical success story: when he died, he was the richest person in America, a man determined to leave his mark on his adopted city and nation. He participated in the major events of his day, advised national leaders, and all but single-handedly saved his country from bankruptcy. Despite his success in business, his personal life was marked by disappointment and idiosyncrasy. Philadelphia was his heir, Girard College his legacy, where his vision for the future has endured to the present.

George Wilson is uniquely qualified to tell the story of Stephen Girard. Civic leader, journalist, editorial writer, and author, Wilson, like Girard, loves the sea and loves Philadelphia, and possesses an intimate knowledge of both. He understands the complex relationship between fate and individual initiative in the human condition. His vivid biography, based on extensive original research, not only tells the story of Stephen Girard without undue awe or cynicism, but also brings alive in rich detail the texture of everyday life in nineteenth-century Philadelphia.

Stephen Girard was a vital participant in our nation's early history who left a special imprint on Philadelphia. Wilson's biography of Girard makes available his compelling story for the contemporary reader.

Michael E. Burke
Editor, Signpost Biography

Preface

THIS BIOGRAPHY of Stephen Girard was a long time in the making. It was in 1974, while writing a book about Philadelphia, that I first became aware of how little has been written about this fascinating but almost forgotten figure who played several important roles, some of them heroically, in early American history. I resolved then and there to write an in-depth account of his life, but only when I was able to take on such a demanding project in a thorough and credible manner.

The opportunity came in 1987 when I retired as chief editorial writer of the *Philadelphia Inquirer*, concluding a forty-year career as a newspaperman. I devoted the next seven years, working full time, to researching and writing this book. It is the first biography of Girard to be published in the United States in more than fifty years.

The principal source of information about Girard is a collection of his personal and business files known as the Girard Papers. They consist of letters, bills, receipts, business records, bank records, farm records, household accounts, ships' logs, maps, official documents, newspapers, memoranda, laundry lists and miscellaneous material in numerous other categories. There are approximately a million items. Apparently Girard almost never threw anything away.

The Girard Papers are in Founder's Hall at Girard College in Philadelphia. The main entrance to the campus is at the intersection of Girard and Corinthian Avenues. Girard College, founded and funded by Girard, is a boarding school for orphans that, the name notwithstanding, serves students in elementary grades through high school.

The Library of the American Philosophical Society has the Girard

Papers on microfilm. The library is at 105 South Fifth Street in Philadelphia, about a hundred yards east of Independence Hall.

Seven biographies of Girard, including two with fewer than sixty pages each, have been published previously in the United States. One of the seven was written anonymously. Five of the remaining six were written by persons who were related to Girard or had been employed by him or had ties with Girard College.

I am not related to Girard and have no connection, financial or otherwise, with Girard College. Nevertheless, I had complete cooperation from the college in doing research for this book.

Biographies of Girard written in French have been published in France, most recently in 1977 and 1981. Girard was born in France.

There is temptation in writing biography to try to gather up all loose ends and to leave nothing hanging, nothing unanswered, nothing in doubt. I have vigorously resisted such temptation. Mystery is a part of history. No one's life is entirely and absolutely open to scrutiny in every respect. Truth is not served by pretending to know for sure what cannot be known for sure.

I have begun every chapter in this biography with a brief introductory comment, printed in italics, that helps to set the stage for what follows. All of these epigraphs are personal observations expressing my own thoughts in my own words.

This book was written in the Pocono Mountains in northeastern Pennsylvania. My wife and I live in a township with more deer than people and an ample supply of bears as well. It is a good locale for a writer who enjoys being close to Mother Nature but wants to maintain convenient access to research material in Philadelphia, a two-hour drive. There is nothing like a walk in the woods or a row on the lake (when it is not frozen) to get creative juices flowing.

I want to acknowledge, with thanks and gratitude, the valuable assistance given to me by many individuals and institutions while this book was being researched and written:

Phyllis Abrams, curator of the Girard Papers and the Stephen Girard Collection (furniture, works of art and other memorabilia) and a former librarian at Girard College, extended numerous courtesies and kindnesses to me on a continuing basis going back to the first week of my research. She allowed me to examine not only Girard's papers and other possessions but also a rich lode of private files and unpublished material pertinent to Girard. She spent many hours of unhurried conversation with me over the years, face to face or by telephone, answering my questions and sharing with me her own vast knowledge of Girard. I am grateful also to Jamesena Faulk, Girard College Librarian, and to others at the college who were helpful to me in my research and who took the time to talk with me and to share with me their thoughts about Girard and the college.

Elizabeth Carroll-Horrocks, associate librarian and manuscripts librarian at the Library of the American Philosophical Society, was extremely helpful to me in many aspects of my research. Martin L. Levitt, associate librarian, and Martha Harrison, manuscripts assistant, and others on the library staff also provided assistance that is much appreciated.

Walter Stock, outreach librarian for the Monroe County Public Library in Stroudsburg, Pennsylvania, served on a bookmobile that made two stops every week at locations ten miles from my house, bringing to me books that I had requested and that he had obtained from public libraries and from college and university libraries all over the state. The libraries are connected by computer through an interlibrary loan network called Access Pennsylvania. Thanks also to Barbara Keiser, interlibrary loan librarian for the Monroe County Public Library, and to all others who assisted her in book searches in my behalf, saving me much time and travel. (The Monroe County Public Library subsequently changed its name to the Eastern Monroe Public Library.)

E. Ann Wilcox, librarian at the Philadelphia Maritime Museum, and H. Ben Thomas, a volunteer researcher in the library, and others on the library staff were cooperative and resourceful in providing information about sailing ships and the Port of Philadelphia. (The Philadelphia Maritime Museum changed its name to the Independence Seaport Museum in 1995.)

Numerous staff members gave various kinds of help, efficiently and cheerfully, during my research at many other institutions including, especially, the Historical Society of Pennsylvania, the Free Library of Philadelphia, the Atwater Kent Museum, the Independence National Historical Park and the Pennsylvania Hospital, all in Philadelphia; the

Dimmick Memorial Library in Jim Thorpe, Pennsylvania, the Historical Society of Schuylkill County in Pottsville, Pennsylvania, the Museum of Anthracite Mining in Ashland, Pennsylvania, and the Public Library and the Historical Society in Mount Holly, New Jersey.

Marie Louise McDonald, a retired high school English teacher and librarian, read portions of the manuscript in early drafts and gave many suggestions that were discerning and useful.

Raymond Taub, an optometrist, provided pertinent information about functions and afflictions of the eye.

Anne Messersmith, who has some very old books about the history of Pennsylvania in her private library, graciously let me borrow several volumes.

Richard Wasson, a friend and neighbor, spent many hours over a span of seven years, often at the kitchen table or on the back deck, listening patiently as I ruminated aloud about Girard. Wasson's insightful responses, whether they were questions or comments, helped me get a clearer perspective on Girard and his times.

Lynn Gossett, a nephew, and his wife, Mary, who has book-editing experience, read part of a rough draft and gave constructive suggestions and criticisms.

Lee, a son and a high school English teacher, read early drafts of all the chapters and gave sound advice on many aspects of organization, substance and style.

Neva, my wife, a former newspaperwoman who is my severest critic and my greatest inspiration, read multiple drafts of every chapter and made well-reasoned recommendations for deletions, additions and revisions.

George Wilson

CHAPTER 1

Growing Up in France
1750-1764

There is nothing more unpredictable than the
future of a newborn baby. Never underestimate the
potential of a life not yet lived.

WHEN STEPHEN GIRARD was born in Bordeaux, France, on May 20, 1750, there was nothing to suggest that he was to become the richest person in the United States of America, a nation that did not yet exist.

Girard's journey on earth would span oceans and eras, wars and revolutions, an Old World and a New World. It would be a roller-coaster ride of ups and downs, twists and turns, accidents and ironies. His life would be one part soap opera, two parts melodrama and three parts epic.

He was, for several decades, a major player on the American scene and the world stage, but that was long ago. With the passage of years this eccentric and self-made multi-millionaire faded into anonymity. His exploits have been forgotten largely because he does not fit into the usual categories of important historical figures, i.e., he never held high public office, he did not invent or discover anything, and he was not a notorious tyrant or scoundrel.

Stephen Girard was a man of many parts, a man of derring-do. He bailed out the government of the United States when it ran out of money in the middle of a war. He put his life on the line to save the lives of others during one of the worst catastrophes ever to befall an American city. He was a philanthropist on a scale unprecedented in America, and its most powerful banker. In the heyday of masts and sails he was a visionary in the development of U.S. maritime trade and

15

an aggressive defender of America's sovereign right to freedom of navigation on the high seas. He was among the first to mobilize organized protests against policies of American presidents. He supplied arms to revolutionaries in far-away places long before foreign aid and covert action became fashionable. He invested a fortune in coal when skeptics were saying it would never replace firewood. He built railroads when others were still sinking money into canals. He was on the cutting edge of America's transition from a mercantile society to the Industrial Age. He was a farmer who, even when he was wealthier than any other American had ever been, would rather toil and sweat in honest labor than fritter away his time in the drawing rooms of high society. His private life ranged from pinnacles of pleasure to depths of despair.

If he were a fictional character in a novel, his adventures and misadventures might seem too far-fetched, and sometimes too bizarre, to be believable. Nonetheless, let there be no mistake: Stephen Girard was a real person, an extraordinary person in an extraordinary era.

On that day in 1750 when he was born, Girard did not get off to an auspicious start. He was star-crossed from the beginning. He had a defective right eye. It may have been entirely inoperative at birth, or the sight may have been lost at a very early age. In any case he would go through life blind in one eye.

The eye was not just unsighted; it was also unsightly. Many people who are blind in one eye have a normal appearance; it is hard to tell, at least at first, that there is an eye without sight. Girard had no such luck. His blind eye was grotesque. It was a walleye. The larger-than-normal eyeball was in the extreme right portion of the eye socket, as though it had rolled outward as far as it could go. The unseeing eyeball projected an illusion of a fixed stare. There was an unmistakable resemblance to the eye of a fish, an unhappy fact that Girard's playmates noted with glee when he was a child. They teased and ridiculed the "fish-eyed" boy unmercifully, as small children are wont to do. Their cruelty would make Girard shy and withdrawn, and he would often choose to stay to himself rather than suffer their taunts.

A contemporary of Girard, who knew him well, said: "He has, himself, confessed that the ridicule of the boys hurt him much."[1] Girard also said the blind and deformed eye was further damaged, after he had grown up, when it was struck by a snowball as he was walking on a street.[2]

The eye would badger and bedevil Girard all of his life. Even as an old man, he would be forever trying salves and ointments in the hope they would improve the eye's appearance.

As he grew to manhood, and then older, the eye gradually changed. An abnormal growth resembling a layer of skin stretched across the eyeball, concealing it partly and giving him a fearsome look. "A severe and harsh expression" was a description given by one observer.[3] Very late in life the eyelid came down, eventually closing the eye entirely. Portraits and sculptures created after his death showed the eye closed.

According to a story told by a nineteenth century biographer of Girard, which apparently has no basis in fact, the blindness in Girard's right eye was the result of an accident that happened when he was seven years old. It was said that someone threw wet oyster shells into a bonfire and the heat forcibly splintered them, whereupon "a fragment entered Stephen's right eye, at once destroying the sight in it beyond the hope of restoration."[4]

If Girard had suffered so devastating an accident at the age of seven, he surely would have remembered it. If there had been an accident of such magnitude when he was too young to remember, it is reasonable to assume that his parents or someone else would have told him about it when he was old enough to understand.

As an adult, Girard said on a number of occasions he could not recall ever having sight in the eye and had no recollection or knowledge of any accident or illness that could have resulted in loss of sight. He was nearly eighty when he said in a letter to an oculist in Paris: "I do not remember when I lost sight in that eye, indeed if it is since I was born, and I must have been very young."[5]

The defective eye in a roundabout way was not entirely a liability. It became a source of inner strength—posing a challenge, right from the start. Girard learned not only to live with a highly visible deformity but to rise above it.

Girard was born in the largest seaport in southwestern France. His birthplace, which was also the house where he lived while he was growing up, was in Chartrons. Officially a separate town in 1750, it was in fact an integral part of the City of Bordeaux and its port. Chartrons later ceased to be a separate municipality and became incorporated into the City of Bordeaux.

The small three-story brick house where Girard was born (it no longer stands) was on Rue Ramonet, a narrow street near the waterfront, and a convenient location for the home of his seafaring father, Pierre. Other Girards also had gone to sea, although the family's ancestral roots were in a farming area around Perigueux, about sixty-five miles east of Bordeaux. Stephen's mother, whose maiden name was Anne Odette Lafargue, was the daughter of a Chartrons maritime merchant and his wife, who also lived near the waterfront.

Thus Stephen Girard had, from birth, the sea and the soil in his blood. He had, from earliest memory, relatives in or near both Bordeaux and Perigueux. Some Girards had plowed the earth; others had plowed the ocean. Stephen would do both. His life would be attuned to land and to water. He would be, among many other things, a farmer and a sailor.

Pierre Girard, Stephen's father, had gone to sea at thirteen. He had become a ship's captain while still in his twenties. He had sailed frequently between his home port of Bordeaux and the West Indies. Each of these nautical details in the life of Pierre Girard were later repeated by Stephen Girard. He was a chip off the old block.

That is what Pierre had been, too. He had become a seasoned salt by heredity as well as by experience. His father (Stephen's grandfather) had gone to sea at ten. So Stephen, when he became a seafaring man, was doing more than just following in the footsteps of his father. Stephen was a part of a family tradition.

Pierre had been a naval hero in the War of the Austrian Succession (1740-1748), one of the innumerable wars between Great Britain and France, with other countries also involved. In 1744 a British fleet attacked Brest, a seaport in France, and tried to destroy French warships stationed there. The ship on which Pierre was serving caught fire and might have been destroyed were it not for his swift and heroic action. He risked his life to contain and extinguish the flames. King Louis XV, in recognition of Pierre's gallantry, had a gold medal struck in his honor and conferred upon him the Cross of the Royal and Military Order of Saint Louis, a high tribute reserved for exceptional bravery. Stephen

Girard's father, therefore, was a certified and decorated hero of naval combat before Stephen was born. Pierre was the kind of a father that a son, especially the oldest son, was expected to look up to and emulate.

Pierre Girard was thirty-one at the time of his marriage to Anne Lafargue in 1748. She was twenty-two. Their first child, a daughter, was born a few weeks after the wedding and died in infancy. Stephen was their second child. Eight other children, four sons and four daughters, followed in a span of eleven years. Stephen grew up as the oldest child in a large family in a crowded house.

Bordeaux at the time of Girard's birth was a major port of call on the trade routes of the world. Its inland location, on the Garonne River about sixty miles upstream from the Atlantic Ocean, was no handicap. The river was seven hundred yards wide at Bordeaux, providing ample room for ships to maneuver. Yet it was a quiet river, providing smooth sailing for ships of all sizes.

Little Stephen, in infancy and childhood, knew the Bordeaux harbor well. He knew the smells of the ships and the crews, the sights and sounds of cargoes being loaded and unloaded, the romance of vessels arriving and departing, coming from or going to distant places with strange-sounding names. The siren call of the sea was Stephen's lullaby. Each rock of his cradle was like the soothing roll of a gentle ocean wave. Even before he could walk, he was a young salt.

Girard had no formal schooling, a fact he would acknowledge in his later years.[6] He was educated by his parents and by tutors. A comprehensive system of public education was not established in France until after the French Revolution. In the middle of the eighteenth century there were no schools in Bordeaux for children under ten years of age. The schools for children ten and older were for boys only and were often called colleges. They usually were operated by the Roman Catholic Church and provided a curriculum with strong emphasis on religious indoctrination. Stephen's parents were Roman Catholics and he was baptized in the Catholic faith when he was one day old.

Stephen had close relationships with his mother and father as a child. They not only gave him much of his education but they also were there when he needed them, to talk with and to share his dreams with. They knew early that he had his heart set on going to sea. His mother, having baby after baby in rapid succession, was at home much of the time—and so was her shy, one-eyed oldest son. Stephen received much of his early learning literally at his mother's knee. He was comfortable and comforted in the presence of this kind and patient woman. She did not taunt him about his optic deformity as his playmates did, sometimes including his own siblings. She was his rudder and his anchor—keeping him on course and holding him steady. She was his guiding light. She was his safe harbor. He could not imagine having to get along without her. He could not know how soon he would have to.

Stephen's father, a bit more brusque that Stephen's mother, but good company nonetheless, was also home much of the time. Pierre's sailing days were over. He was sufficiently prosperous, although by no means rich, to be the owner of several vessels of modest size and to hire other captains to take command on voyages to the West Indies. His counting-room (his office and place of business) was on the first floor of his house, a convenient arrangement that Stephen, many years later, would imitate. Pierre taught Stephen the ropes, actually and figuratively, about being a seafaring man, but only in a detached way, without taking him to sea. More importantly for Stephen in the long run, his father taught him the business of maritime trade: buying and selling cargoes, giving instructions to captains embarking on long voyages, collecting accounts receivable in ports thousands of miles away.

By the time Stephen went to sea he was ready. He had proficiency in the rudiments of reading, writing and arithmetic. Beyond that, he had command of the French language in a degree sufficient to communicate in writing with clarity of expression and legibility in penmanship, essential skills in keeping ships' logs and preparing reports. He knew bookkeeping at a level necessary to maintain accounts of ships' stores and cargoes, and knew enough geometry to begin shipboard training in navigation.

No less significantly, young Stephen had acquired a taste for learning and a thirst for knowledge that lasted a lifetime. He would build on the foundations of his early education with an ongoing program of self-education. He would branch out into fields that went beyond basic learning, including architecture and philosophy. Stephen had, from the outset, a head for business and a heart for adventure, a combination

that would serve him well. He was practical-minded and action-ori-
ented. He was also contemplative. At an early age he began to reflect
on aspects of the society in which he lived. He developed serious
concerns about inequities in human relationships that he witnessed or
read about. He became an avid reader of the works of eighteenth
century French philosophers, and embraced many of their views on
the need for political and economic reforms and for an end to social
injustices and religious discrimination and persecution. Men like
Voltaire, Rousseau, Helvetius and Montesquieu stood on the leading
edge of new thinking in a golden era of philosophy in the Western
world. They were humanitarians as well as philosophers, and all of
them lived part of their lives when Girard was alive. Each of them left
a mark on him.

After he had completed the first decade of his life and was not yet
far into his second, Girard got an early taste of tragedy. It struck with
startling swiftness. In April of 1762, when he was eleven and coming
up on twelve, he was dealt a blow that would test his mettle. His mother
died. She was only thirty-six.

Young Stephen mourned the loss of his mother and was shattered
by the deprivation of her love and affection, but he knew he had to
pick up the pieces and make his life whole again as quickly as possible.
That is what she would have wanted him to do.

For anyone who has not gone through the experience, it is hard to
comprehend the devastation of a boy or a girl after the demise of a
mother or a father.[7] The initial shock is followed by after-shocks.
Children can only cope rationally with the loss of a loved one after a
long time because they lack the emotional equanimity that comes with
maturity.

When his mother died, Stephen had seven surviving brothers and
sisters ranging in age from ten years to eight months. A sister born in
1755 (as the one born in 1748) had died in infancy. In a span of
thirteen years, from 1748 to 1761, his mother had given birth ten
times and had been pregnant more than fifty percent of the time. In
the middle of the eighteenth century, when health care was as primitive
in France as it was in the rest of Europe and in America, it was not
unusual for a woman to die young after having a large number of

children. Death for a mother sometimes came immediately after a difficult childbirth or, as may have been the case with Stephen's mother, from the cumulative draining effect of many childbearings in rapid succession coupled with the strains of rearing a large family.

Pierre Girard, left with eight children and no woman to care for them, met the emergency in a manner that minimized the inconvenience to himself. He was able to persuade a twenty-eight-year-old unmarried half-sister of his deceased wife to become a live-in housekeeper and surrogate mother. Consequently the daily routine in the Girard household got back to normal rather quickly despite the difficult emotional adjustments that Pierre and the children had to make.

Early in 1764 Stephen Girard began his seafaring days at the age of thirteen.[8] He sailed out of Bordeaux headed for the West Indies as a *pilotin* aboard the brig *Pelerin*, owned by his father. A *pilotin* was an apprentice officer. It was the responsibility of the ship's captain, John Courteau, to begin training young Girard in all the skills required to command an ocean-going vessel on a long voyage. That would include rigorous training on many ships with many captains for many years, and be sufficiently demanding to test the courage and the endurance of the toughest youth.

Stephen had never been to sea before. As the *Pelerin* eased out of the harbor at Bordeaux and moved down the Garonne River toward the Atlantic Ocean, Stephen began to realize that he was a nautical neophyte, notwithstanding all of the instruction he had received from his father. Stephen had no real comprehension of what living on a ship was like except in very general terms. Being told about it was not the same as doing it. The only way to know what going to sea was like was to go to sea.

When the brig reached the mouth of the river and headed into the Atlantic, Girard's first challenge was to conquer seasickness. No one venturing into rough waters for the first time in the eighteenth century was likely to escape this malady. The only questions in most cases were how bad it would be and how long it would last. There were no stabilizers on the ships of that era. They pitched and tossed with every movement of the waves. Even an iron stomach needed time to adjust. The French, having sailed in the turbulent North Atlantic for centuries, were distressingly familiar with the sickness of the sea—so much so that they did not have just a word for it. They had three words for it. They called it *mal de mer*. If a *pilotin* could not overcome *mal de mer*, he could forget about taking the rest of the training to become a captain.

CHAPTER 2

A Whole New World Out There
1764-1774

*An ocean is an awesome thing. To sail upon it is
to be exhilarated and humbled in equal parts.*

NO ONE who has crossed an ocean in a ship ever forgets the experience. People who do it many times never forget the first time. The thrill is all the greater when a ship sails alone rather than in company of other ships.[1] The sea stretches to the horizon in all directions—no land in sight, no intrusions upon the rhythm of the waves, nothing to spoil the majesty of a piece of the world that has not changed for millions of years. The sky overhead, lighted by day and darkened by night, is a canopy that reaches down and touches the ocean full circle, 360 degrees. The sun in some miraculous manner seems to rise out of the ocean and set back into it, managing, strangely, not to get wet. So does the moon. Planets look down with a steady gaze while stars sparkle. All are reminders of the infinity of the universe and the infinitesimal nature of a human being, most particularly a human being on the deck of a solitary ship in the middle of an ocean. Such were the experiences of Girard on his first voyage that he would never forget. The thrill of sailing across an ocean was a dream coming true.

He was going to a New World in more ways than one. He was beginning not just a career but an adventure. Still scarcely more than a boy, barely into his teens, his eye scanning the horizon and groping for a future he could not yet see and could not possibly imagine, he was sailing west into the sunset. For him, the sun was also rising.

There were many *pilotins* who failed to complete training and never became captains. Some were dismissed because they could not master the skills, others because of a lack of leadership qualities. Some did not have the stamina to stay the course, no matter how hard they tried. Not everyone had what it took to be a sea captain.

For many reasons, therefore, to enter training as a *pilotin* was by no means a guarantee of success. Girard could not help but be aware that failure was a possibility. Having a father who owned the ship might help, but not necessarily. There is no evidence that Pierre told the captain to go easy on Stephen. It is far more likely the captain was instructed to be stern with the lad and to avoid giving him special treatment because he was the shipowner's son.

A *pilotin* had to learn all the chores performed by ordinary seamen, from the lowliest of the crew to the most able. Duties included dangerous work aloft on the masts, high in the rigging, where sails had to be handled, where repairs had to be made, where knots had to be tied, where one slip in a careless moment could mean the loss of a limb or a life. Work had to be done in fair weather or foul, under a boiling sun or in bone-numbing cold, in snow or sleet, in icy gales or torrential rains.

A *pilotin* not only had to acquire the skills of sailors but he also had to learn and to master the functions of officers, including the one in command. A captain had wide-ranging responsibilities whether in port or at sea. He had to navigate with a sure aim, precise enough to avoid dangerous shoals and reach a small island. He had to keep logs and other reports and records, financial books (income and expenditures) and stay within budget. If he did not operate at a profit he would not be a captain for long. He had to purchase food and other provisions for voyages. He had to monitor carefully—and, if necessary, to ration in small portions—supplies of everything, including fresh water, during long passages. He had to be a businessman, an administrator, a chief executive officer and a chief financial officer while at the same time maintaining discipline and being the kind of leader who not only demanded respect but earned it. He had to do whatever necessary to keep law and order. He had to make tough decisions and make them stick—decisions that could determine success or failure for a voyage and even life or death for all on board.

In the eighteenth century it was commonplace for ships to be at sea months at a time and to stay in ports many weeks. Round-trip voyages sometimes took a year or two, or several years. Once under way, a ship was out of touch with home port except for hand-written messages delivered via other ships, a hit-or-miss means of communication at best. To be master of a ship required being resourceful in the face of the unforeseen. Any number of things could go wrong and often did.

There was more. A *pilotin* also had to learn the intricacies of buying and selling cargoes in ports far from home, making and collecting payments with specie or currency or by barter, utilizing international exchange and credit where available, dealing with customs and health officers, quarantine officers and other bureaucracy, and offering bribes discreetly where they were customary or even mandatory. Some ships, especially large ones with high-value products on board, had a special officer who was responsible for buying and selling cargoes at ports of call. He was called a supercargo. However, many ships did not have a supercargo. The captain did it all. *Pilotins*, as part of their training, were required to become competent in all of the duties of a supercargo. They would then be qualified to serve as captain on any ship. They had to become expert in all facets of acquisition and disposal of cargo. They had to learn how to be both a mariner and a merchant. They had to learn how to be not only master of a ship but master of a ship's payload.

In addition, a captain (and also a *pilotin*) had to know the rudiments of medicine and surgery. There were no doctors on merchant ships. A surgical kit was kept in the captain's cabin.[2] The primary tool was a saw for amputations. The only anesthesia was an extra-large ration of rum or, if the patient was really lucky, a bottle of whiskey. A captain, if the need arose, could not be squeamish about inflicting pain. He could not let the screaming distract him or deter him from doing what had to be done.

A passage on the *Pelerin* was well suited for an introduction to the responsibilities of a *pilotin*. It was not too large and not too small. As cargo-carrying vessels went, in the middle of the eighteenth century, a brig was mid-sized. Typically, a brig was no more than ninety feet long and might be eighty feet or less. It would normally carry a crew of no more than ten—eight sailors and two officers (the captain and a first mate). Cost-conscious shipowners employed a bare minimum of crew members, not just to hold down operating expenses, but to save maximum space for revenue-producing cargo. The number of people on board determined how much space had to be devoted to sleeping quarters and to storage of food and water.[3]

A brig had two masts, the taller of which might soar seventy feet or more above the deck. Sailing vessels were called tall ships—some were taller than they were long, with masts of 130 feet or more, on large ships a spectacular sight.[4] Both masts on a brig were square-rigged, with sails hung from horizontal wooden beams called yards, three yards normally on each mast.[5] Brave and well muscled nimble men climbed up the masts to furl or unfurl the sails by hand, a feat that no doubt was a common experience for Girard.

The ends of the yards were called yardarms. They served handily as gallows, especially on warships. On a cargo ship a person accused of a capital offense, such as mutiny or murder, was brought to shore for trial if that was feasible. However, the captain had wide discretion in an emergency and could summarily execute an offender while at sea if deemed necessary to maintain order and authority.

Many types of vessels smaller than a brig (such as schooners and sloops) had triangular sails that could be raised or lowered by a person on the deck much as a flag is pulled up or down a flag pole. Smaller crews could handle sails of that kind, and the work was not as demanding or as dangerous. Sloops, engaged in coastal trade, sailing on an ocean but not across it, sometimes had only four people on board.

Merchant vessels larger than a brig commonly had three masts, sometimes more, and were usually called ships. However, any vessel could be called a ship if it had been designed and built large enough and rugged enough to travel regularly on oceans for long distances. Definitions of different types of sailing vessels in the eighteenth century were imprecise and varied from country to country.[6]

Girard's first voyage was to Port-au-Prince in the French colony known as St-Domingue on the western third of the island of Hispaniola. It was a thriving port when young Stephen arrived there in 1764 aboard the *Pelerin*.

France had acquired the western third of Hispaniola from Spain in 1697 under terms of the Peace of Ryswich, a treaty that ended one of France's many wars during the reign of Louis XIV. With Hispaniola divided, the western third of the island under French rule became known as St-Domingue while the eastern two-thirds of the island under Spanish control was called Santo Domingo. St-Domingue, with its highly productive sugar plantations worked by African slaves, was one of the most valuable pieces of real estate in the Western Hemisphere. In the nineteenth century St-Domingue would become Haiti, and Santo Domingo would become the Dominican Republic.

When Girard first saw St-Domingue (an area of a little over ten thousand square miles, about the size of Maryland) there were seven hundred thousand African slaves held in subjugation by only forty thousand French. There also were more than twenty-five thousand mulattoes, highly visible evidence that masters sometimes did more to their black female slaves than just put them to work. A severe shortage of white women was chronic in St-Domingue. Some Frenchmen dealt with the problem by purchasing slaves for bedroom duty, young black females who were required to give their masters sexual satisfaction. John Girard, a brother of Stephen, would own that kind of slave in St-Domingue for many years. Through a series of strange events, which will be detailed in a later chapter, Stephen became the slave's owner.

Slaves in St-Domingue, with little protection from governing authorities, were largely at the mercy of their masters and suffered unspeakable horrors. Laws known collectively as the *Code Noir* ostensibly provided modest safeguards for slaves but were seldom enforced. Whippings were routine. Another form of punishment for male slaves was castration. Masters summarily executed slaves, males and females, by various means including burning, sometimes letting them roast slowly on a banked fire.[7]

The French in St-Domingue, because of their proportionally small number in a relatively small space heavily populated by enslaved blacks, lived in fear and insecurity. Girard could see, in 1764, that there was widespread uneasiness about the possibility of a slave rebellion with potentially disastrous consequences for the white inhabitants.

Hispaniola and other islands in the West Indies that produced sugar as a major crop for export were known collectively as the Sugar Islands. French inhabitants of St-Domingue, consisting largely of prosperous plantation owners and merchants, used revenues from a sugar-based economy to buy a variety of goods from France: food, clothing, furniture, tools, pots and pans, cutlery, bric-a-brac—whatever would serve to sustain some semblance of the French way of life on a tropical island. Ships such as the one Girard had sailed on from Bordeaux could find a profitable market in St-Domingue for French products and then realize another profit from a cargo of sugar, sometimes in the form of molasses, on the return voyage to France. Europeans, particularly the French, had developed a "sweet tooth." Exploitation of the New World had made sugar available in Europe in abundant quantities and at affordable prices, which were low mainly because slaves did the work on the sugar plantations.

Cheap and plentiful sugar enlivened the taste of many traditional dishes and gave birth to delectable new confections. Syrups sweetened with sugar had almost magical qualities, enhancing the flavor of what formerly had been humdrum foods. Rum, a spirited by-product of sugar cane, was a popular beverage, especially among seafaring folk. Daily rations of rum helped sailors get through long voyages.

Simply put, Europeans (and Americans, too) were hooked on sugar and concoctions made with it. Sugar, like oil in later centuries, was something that nations would go to war over. Protecting sources of supply was a first priority in the foreign policies of many countries.

By the time of Girard's first voyage, sugar was beginning to have a role in fermenting revolution in America. Some of the Sugar Islands, notably Jamaica and Barbados, were under British domination. However, English colonies in America were buying much of their sugar and molasses from French and Spanish plantation owners on islands, such as Hispaniola, that were not as far away. In 1764, the same year that Girard sailed to the Sugar Islands for the first time, the British Parliament passed the Sugar Act. It intensified efforts to stop smuggling and increased the duties that colonists in America were required to pay when sugar or molasses was imported from any place not under British control. Great Britain thus began using sugar as a weapon of economic intimidation in the American colonies. In doing so, the British were pushing Americans closer and closer to a revolution. Girard, quite unintentionally, would wind up in the thick of it.

Girard's first sea voyage, round trip, lasted ten months. After arriving back in Bordeaux early in 1765 at age fourteen, he continued his education with a tutor while helping his father in his counting-house and learning more from him about doing business as a maritime merchant. Early in 1766, at fifteen, after a year at home, Stephen left Bordeaux on his second voyage to the West Indies as a *pilotin*. He was aboard the *Gloire*, with Jean Belso as captain, headed for Martinique, a sugar island under French control.

Like St-Domingue, Martinique was more than four thousand miles from Bordeaux. A small island with an area of a little over four hundred square miles (about one-third the size of Rhode Island), Martinique was eight hundred miles southeast of St-Domingue in a group of islands called the Windwards. The largest city and principal port in Martinique at the time of Girard's arrival was Saint Pierre. (Many years later, in 1902, Saint Pierre would be destroyed, with a loss of thirty thousand lives, when a volcano erupted.) No one knew it at the time but Martinique had a resident in 1766 who would become world famous. Three years old and named Josephine, she grew up to be Napoleon's first wife and the empress of France after her first husband died on the guillotine during the Reign of Terror.

Martinique, like St-Domingue, was a French colonial outpost where black slaves from Africa did grueling labor on sugar plantations while their French masters reaped the profits and were eager buyers of goods from France. In Martinique, as in St-Domingue, a bad case of homesickness was common among French inhabitants who had lived in France. They yearned for French things—furniture, dishes, anything—to help simulate life in the old country.

Girard's voyage to Martinique and back to Bordeaux spanned thirteen months, with more time spent in port than at sea. It typically took about two months, each way, for a sailing vessel to travel between France and the West Indies in the middle of the eighteenth century. That was at an average speed of about seventy miles a day. However, the trip might take much longer, depending on the weather.

Bad weather could take several forms. A long calm spell with little
or no wind could leave a ship stalled for days. Strong head winds could
slow it to a crawl or force excessive tacking that could add many miles
to the journey. Big storms could blow a craft far off course and inflict
heavy damage to masts, rigging and sails. An unscheduled stop might
be required to make repairs and take on new supplies of food and
water.

When ships from Europe arrived at destinations in the West Indies,
such as St-Domingue or Martinique, they sometimes stayed in port
many months for economic reasons. There might be little demand for
the goods that were to be sold, and prices could be depressed below
the profit level, because other ships with similar cargoes had recently
arrived. In such circumstances it would be prudent to wait for market
conditions to improve before selling a cargo. Similarly, when buying
cargo for the return trip, it sometimes was advisable to wait for
favorable supplies and prices. Consequently, as happened with Girard
on the voyage to Martinique, a round trip from France to the West
Indies could drag on for more than a year when supply and demand
and price were not right. The captain of the ship had to play it by
ear—evaluating market conditions from week to week and month to
month, exercising his own best judgment on when was the best time
to sell and when was the best time to buy. It was better to sail back
home belatedly with a profit than to hurry home with a loss.

Upon his return to Bordeaux from Martinique early in 1767, at the
age of sixteen, Girard found a significant change in conditions at home.
His father was a married man again. He had taken as his second wife
a widow, Marie Jeanne Geraud. She had been born in the West Indies,
the daughter of a prosperous French merchant, and had four children
from her first marriage. Pierre and Marie had lost no time starting a
family of their own. Their first child, a son, had been born seven weeks
before their wedding. After their marriage they had two more children,
both daughters, one born in 1768 and the other in 1769. Thus Stephen
Girard, while still in his teens, had a bewildering array of brothers and
sisters in three categories: full, half and step.

Following several months at home, studying with a tutor again and learning more about the merchant business from his father, Stephen set off on his third voyage to the West Indies early in 1768. He was gone eight months. There was a fourth voyage of eleven months starting in 1769. A fifth round trip of ten months followed. On this voyage, at the age of twenty-one, he was still technically a *pilotin* undergoing officer training but he also served as second mate. This was an important step toward completion of training and certification as a captain.

Girard's education in non-maritime fields of study was not interrupted while he was at sea. On all of his training voyages his regimen did not consist entirely of learning how to sail and command a ship and buy and sell cargo. He was encouraged to broaden and stretch his intellect and to develop an enduring dedication to self-improvement. Books in the captain's cabin were available to him. Despite a demanding work schedule he found time to continue reading Voltaire, Rousseau, Helvetius and Montesquieu. The latter, who died when Girard was five, had been the president judge of a court in Bordeaux and was revered with neighborly affection in Girard's home port.

On a sixth round trip to the West Indies, lasting ten months in 1772 and 1773, Girard was still a *pilotin* but served dual roles as first mate and supercargo on the outward-bound leg from Bordeaux to Port-au-Prince. Also on board as a *pilotin*, for his maiden voyage, was John Girard.[8] He was fifteen months younger than his brother and, unlike Stephen, had received extensive formal schooling in Bordeaux.[9] Impressively skilled in mathematics, John was able to perform complex exercises in navigation during his first weeks at sea.[10] Upon arrival in Port-au-Prince John left the ship and continued his training as a *pilotin* on another vessel bound for New Orleans.[11]

On the journey from Bordeaux to Port-au-Prince in 1772 the captain was John Petiteau, who had also been in command on one of Stephen Girard's earlier voyages. Petiteau could see that Stephen not only had matured but also had become highly skilled in all aspects of sailing and was fully capable of taking charge. When it was time to leave Port-au-Prince on the return trip to Bordeaux, Petiteau and local authorities were engaged in a dispute that seemed unlikely to be resolved quickly. He decided to stay behind and let Girard take his place. Petiteau ordered Girard to assume command of the ship and sail back to Bordeaux without him.

Although, officially, he was still a *pilotin*, this was Girard's maiden voyage as a captain. He was completely and unequivocally the master, with all of the authority and responsibility entailed in that role. He had taken the wheel and given orders before, but always under a captain's watchful eye. This time there was no one at Girard's side to correct his mistakes or to take control if he faltered. He was on his own, enjoying what would be the grand finale of his training.

On this voyage Girard was crossing the Atlantic for the twelfth time (six times in each direction). He had sailed on a variety of ships, some owned by his father, but each having characteristics not found in the others. He had served under several captains, each with a distinctive style and personality. The captains had tested him with oral lessons and written assignments, in addition to giving him practical experience and, when appropriate, parental advice. The captain-*pilotin* shipboard relationship had been not only teacher-student and master-apprentice but also father-son.

The ship Girard was commanding on his first voyage as a captain was a brigantine, which should not be confused with a brig, described earlier. A brig, such as the one that took Girard on his maiden voyage at the age of thirteen, was heftier than a brigantine—but a brigantine was spunkier. Often described as half brig and half schooner, a brigantine had two masts (like a brig) but the mainsail was not square-rigged. It was rigged so that the boom could be swung laterally to port or starboard to adjust for the wind. Brigantines were exceptionally fast and highly maneuverable. They were often used by pirates, who were commonly called brigands. The brigantine that was Girard's first command was named *Sally*. That also would be the name of the first of his long-term mistresses many years later. History has odd coincidences.

There was bad weather, including a spring storm with hurricane-force winds, for Captain Girard and his shipmates on their way back to Bordeaux, but the voyage was completed in two months despite rough waters. That was an impressive time for a first passage as master. Girard's exultation glowed in entries in the ship's log, as when he noted that the North Star looked "as large as a full moon."[12]

Girard observed his twenty-third birthday one day after he reached

Bordeaux. A lot of water had flowed over the rudder since he had first gone to sea shortly before his fourteenth birthday. The boy had become a man. He was not tall—just five feet six inches—but he was muscular, strong-voiced and impressive in such qualities as leadership and self-confidence. One eye was all he needed to stare down any shipmate who might be thinking about testing the captain's authority. His hair was redder than ever—fiery red, a match for his gung-ho spirit. He had lost his boyhood shyness, but he still was not one to engage in witty repartee. He was a no-nonsense captain. He did not waste words, nor did he mince them.

In October of 1773, several months after his arrival in Bordeaux after his first voyage in command of a ship, Girard was formally certified as a captain in the French merchant marine and received his license from the French government. It was a valuable document, entitling him to sign on as master of any merchant ship under the French flag, or under the flag of any nation that accepted the license, and to sail that ship to any port in the world. The license was tantamount to international certification, for France was highly regarded by seafaring people of the eighteenth century as a nation that did not confer a captain's license lightly. If France said a man was qualified to be a captain, there could be no doubt that he was qualified and that he had gone through long and rigorous training to prove it.

In Girard's case, his training had consisted of six round-trip transAtlantic voyages in a span of nine years, totaling more than fifty thousand miles. Each round trip had lasted no less than eight months and no more than thirteen months. He had been at sea or in New World ports for periods of time adding up to more than five years. His on-the-ocean time had been in excess of two years. He had become an old salt. He had his sea legs.[13]

Licensed captains were in demand not only to command ships but also to serve as supercargoes and first mates. When a licensed captain went to sea in a subordinate position—as a supercargo and/or a first mate—it was like having a co-captain on board. There was an extra measure of security in knowing that the second-in-command was fully qualified and formally licensed to take charge if the captain became incapacitated by illness or injury or died while the ship was at sea.

Girard's first voyage after being licensed as a captain was as super-cargo and first mate on the *Julie*, which sailed from Bordeaux in February of 1774 bound for St-Domingue. For young Stephen, at twenty-three, it was a far more significant departure than he realized. Although he did not know it at the time, he would never see Bordeaux again. He would never see his father again. He would never see his sisters again. Except for one, John, he would never see his brothers again. This was goodbye. This was farewell. This was adieu.

The parting was not painful because no one had any inkling that it would be forever. Stephen had every reason to believe, and so did his family, that he would be home again in about a year, probably sooner. No one, Stephen least of all, could have imagined it would be otherwise. If someone had told Girard, as the ship pulled away from the dock, that he would never return to Bordeaux, he would have considered that to be the most absurd thing he had ever heard anyone say.

Leaving Bordeaux for the last time—without knowing it was the last time—would be not only a major turning point in Girard's life but also part of a pattern. Over and over again in his life he would see one thing lead to another in some odd and unpredictable way. Over and over again in his life a chance happening would set off a chain of unforeseen and unexpected events. His time on earth was not to be just a journey, but a series of detours.

Girard had sailed out of Bordeaux for the first time, in 1764, without having the foggiest notion of what life held in store for him. Now he was sailing out of Bordeaux for the last time, in 1774, and he still did not have a clue. He may have thought he would follow in the wake of his father, plying the trade routes between France and the West Indies and then settling down in a counting-house in Bordeaux, but it was not to be. There were rumblings in the distance—far, far away. They came from beyond the horizon, from across the ocean, from a place called America. They were the rumblings of a revolution that would change the course of history. It also would change the course of Stephen Girard.

CHAPTER 3

Starting to Build a Fortune:
How It All Began
1774-1776

Sometimes the difference between opportunity and
opportunism is a very thin line.

STEPHEN GIRARD'S plans for a career as a seafaring man based in Bordeaux began to unravel soon after the *Julie* arrived in Port-au-Prince. He was unable to sell an important part of the cargo at a profit. It was a part that he owned, a part that he had purchased with borrowed money. He had gone heavily into debt to obtain a significant financial interest in his first voyage after receiving his captain's license.

It was not unusual for a supercargo to be given a "piece of the action" before a ship left port. A typical arrangement was for him to be allotted a portion of the cargo space, free of transport charge, for his own goods, whatever kinds of goods he wanted to carry. He would be free to sell his personally owned cargo whenever and wherever an attractive opportunity arose, and he could pocket all of the profit. Girard had that kind of arrangement, but he was operating on an exceedingly thin shoestring. Since he did not have much cash, he had bought a variety of goods from Bordeaux merchants on short-term credit. He had planned to sell the goods at a profit in Port-au-Prince and pay off his debts to the merchants upon his return to Bordeaux.

The plan went awry. There was no ready market for his goods in Port-au-Prince. He had handkerchiefs, hats and parasols, which usually sold well on a tropical island where fair-skinned French were forever mopping their brows and trying to shield their faces from the blazing sun. He had whips, which seemed always to be big sellers in countries with slaves. He had pistols, which slave-owners fearful of revolt usually stockpiled in large quantities. He had saddle cloths, silverware, snuff boxes and sundry other items that were generally useful.[1] The trouble was that other ships with similar cargoes were already in the harbor or had recently been there. Oversupply had dried up demand and forced prices down.

Buying and selling in the international trade in the eighteenth century, with long travel times and slow communications, always involved a high degree of risk. Supply and demand were constantly fluctuating, and so were prices. It was unrealistic to expect a profit on every voyage. Occasional losses were inevitable. Established merchants with adequate working capital and good credit could ride out periodic setbacks as long as profits exceeded losses over the long haul. Girard, however, had no cushion of operating capital, and his problem was compounded by his short-term debt. When the *Julie* got back to Bordeaux, or soon thereafter, the principal and interest on his promissory notes to the merchants would be due. He would not be able to pay the notes on time unless he sold his cargo promptly at a profit. It was in this situation that Girard made a momentous decision—although it could not have seemed so momentous to him at the time. It was a decision that would alter the remainder of his life in ways he could not have foreseen.

The decision was a simple and straightforward one in the circumstances. He decided not to go back to Bordeaux on the *Julie*. It was a rational choice that seemed to serve the best interests of his creditors. By staying in Port-au-Prince with his goods in storage in a waterfront warehouse, he could wait for the market to improve and prices to go up. Then he could sell the goods at a profit, go back to Bordeaux on another ship and pay the merchants what he owed them, in full and with interest. That would be better than selling the goods hastily at a loss and going home on the *Julie* to tell his creditors he could not pay his debts in full. He would not be doing them a favor by hurrying home with a tale of woe. He knew they would want a settling of accounts, not excuses. They would not be satisfied with partial payments.

There were other considerations. Stephen might have gone back to

Bordeaux and prevailed upon his father to bail him out by paying his creditors what they were owed, but that would have been an unwarranted imposition on the father and an extreme embarrassment for the son. Stephen had been working hard for a decade to gain personal and financial independence. He had taken pride, since the age of thirteen, in not having to rely on his father for support. Asking him for money would be all the more humiliating if the request was rejected. Moreover, France had harsh laws that could send debtors to prison. Stephen, besides not wanting to risk imprisonment, also did not want to put his father in a situation that would make him feel obligated to pay off a son's debts to keep him out of prison.

Thus it was for several reasons that seemed to him fair and reasonable that Stephen did not go back to Bordeaux on the *Julie*. His departure from the ship and his shipmates was amicable. He had discharged his duties as supercargo responsibly, disposing of the goods that he did not own himself at the best available prices over a period of several weeks. These goods, different kinds of items from the ones he owned, had sold reasonably well. So it came to pass that in early June of 1774, a time that would be a watershed in the life of Stephen Girard, he packed his personal belongings, said goodbye to others aboard the *Julie*, and went ashore. He had already put his cargo in storage in Port-au-Prince. The ship sailed for home without him. At the age of twenty-four, Stephen was alone and on his own for the first time, and he was in a New World, more than four thousand miles from Bordeaux.

Girard waited several weeks for the market to improve in Port-au-Prince, but it did not improve enough to enable him to sell his goods at a profit. In the meantime he received an offer that was too good to refuse. A ship being readied for a voyage to New York, about sixteen hundred miles away, was in need of a first mate. A cargo of sugar and coffee was on board. As an incentive to serve as first mate, Girard was offered a generous amount of space for his own personal cargo.

Having no cash of any consequence, and knowing that the items he had in a warehouse were not likely to bring higher prices in New York than in Port-au-Prince, Girard chose a course that seemed to give the best hope for the kind of profit he would need to settle accounts with his creditors in Bordeaux. He signed on as first mate, sold his goods at a loss, and used proceeds from the sale to buy sugar and coffee to take to New York on his own account. That was the seed of Girard's wealth. From that start would grow the largest fortune in America.

He collected twelve thousand French livres from the sale of his goods in Port-au-Prince. That was approximately seventy-five percent of the total of his debts to merchants in Bordeaux. He owed them close to sixteen thousand livres (a little under $3,000).[2] He would sell the sugar and coffee for a profit in New York and use the proceeds to buy another cargo to take on another voyage and sell for another profit. And so on, and so on. The nest egg would grow and grow.

Becoming wealthy would not be all that simple, of course. Girard would have to weather many reverses and overcome many obstacles. He would have to make shrewd judgments and daring moves on countless occasions. He would have to scratch and claw and persevere. It would be a long, long road to riches, but it was in Port-au-Prince, in the summer of 1774, that the journey began. At this juncture in his life Girard could not have been giving much thought, if any, to getting rich. He was just trying to become solvent, hoping to be able to pay off his debts.

Girard left Port-au-Prince for New York in early July of 1774, even while the *Julie* was still somewhere in the Atlantic, en route to Bordeaux. The merchants there did not yet know they had subsidized the purchase of sugar and coffee that Girard was taking to America. They also did not know how long they would have to wait to get their money back.

When Girard arrived in New York in late July of 1774 after a voyage of a little over three weeks, rebellion was in the air. It was in the summer of 1774 that the First Continental Congress was convening at Carpenters' Hall in Philadelphia to discuss counter-measures against British tyranny. The colonies were seething. The gathering maelstrom would soon change Girard's life in ways he could not have predicted, and also in ways his creditors in Bordeaux could not have imagined.

As a Frenchman, Girard had no love for the British. France and Great Britain had been at each other's throats in war after war for centuries. If American colonists decided to rebel in quest of independence, his sentiments almost certainly would be on the side of

America. Nonetheless, revolution or not, Girard had no time for dillydallying during his debut in New York. On foreign soil, thousands of miles from home, he had to face financial reality. He needed income. That meant he had to head out to sea again, fairly quickly and preferably under generous terms that would again allow him to make his nest egg grow. In the circumstances it did not seem feasible to try to send payments in full to some of the creditors, or partial payments to all of the creditors, in far-away Bordeaux.

After selling his sugar and coffee in New York at higher prices than he had paid for them in Port-au-Prince, Girard began to have an appreciation for the American market. He had learned two important truths from this transaction: first, agricultural products grown on islands in the West Indies were in great demand on the North American mainland; and, second, satisfying this demand did not require nearly as long a trip as sailing all the way across the Atlantic Ocean between the West Indies and France. In years ahead Girard would repeat the same money-making procedure many times, buying sugar and coffee in the West Indies to sell in America, while also developing markets in the West Indies for American goods so that trade could be profitable in both directions.

It did not take Girard long to become acquainted with merchants and shipowners on the New York waterfront. There was a demand for the services of a bright and studious seafarer with a captain's license. He soon struck a bargain with Thomas Randall, owner of the *Amiable Louise*, a vessel that was taking on cargo for New Orleans and was in need of a first mate. Girard signed on in that capacity under an arrangement that allowed him to buy a substantial quantity of goods of his own for resale in New Orleans with no charge for transportation.

New Orleans had been founded by the French early in the eighteenth century and, even though nominally under control of Spain in 1774, was still essentially a French city with commerce and culture flavored by France. It was to Randall's advantage to have a ship's officer who was a French citizen familiar with French ways of conducting business and fluent in reading, writing and speaking French as a first language. Randall, in addition to carrying on regular trade between New York and New Orleans, sent cargoes occasionally to the French colony of St-Domingue. Girard, having just come from St-Domingue and having been there a number of times previously, had developed business connections that could be useful to Randall.

Thus Girard and Randall began a business relationship that would last for several years. Randall liked the cut of Girard's jib, recognizing in him a man with valuable talents as a merchant and a mariner. He knew ships and he knew cargoes. He knew how to sail and he knew how to sell. He knew sugar, one of the most important of the maritime commodities, and he knew the Sugar Islands.

Girard, moreover, was a bundle of energy. He had spunk. Newly arrived in a strange land, with a deformed eye and hair that was flaming red, he had stood out in the crowds around New York's busy wharves. If Randall had not pegged the industrious and serious-minded French mariner as a diligent young man who showed promise, some other shipowner certainly would have.

For the remainder of 1774 and most of 1775 Girard sailed on round trips from New York to New Orleans (sometimes with a stop at St-Domingue) as first mate on Randall-owned ships, first the *Amiable Louise* and then the *Catherine*. Sailing distance between New York and New Orleans was a little under two thousand miles and could be covered in less than a month, one way, in good weather. The sailing distance between New Orleans and Port-au-Prince in St-Domingue was about thirteen hundred miles.

On each leg of each voyage Girard had a portion of the cargo space available to him without charge for his own goods—bought at one port and sold for a profit at another. Typical goods from New York were firearms, tools, utensils and other household items. Furs, sent down the Mississippi River by trappers, were popular items for purchase in New Orleans. The furs could be sold in New York for local use. They could also be sold either in St-Domingue or in New York for shipment to Europe. Sugar (sometimes in the form of molasses) was a mainstay out of St-Domingue, and there was a growing market for coffee also.

By late 1775 Girard had accumulated enough capital to acquire two-thirds ownership of a sloop, a small sea-going vessel with one mast, named the *Marie*. Randall owned the other third. Girard sailed the sloop on one of his voyages from New York to New Orleans. Later,

Girard and Randall each owned half of a two-masted schooner, the *Jeune Babe*.[3] A schooner, larger than a sloop, usually had two masts, sometimes three or more, but never less than two.[4] Masts on a schooner were rigged fore-and-aft, often with square topsails on at least one of the masts.

At 8 A.M. on May 14, 1776, Girard began what would turn out to be the most important voyage of his life. At that hour on that day he was in command of the *Jeune Babe* as the schooner sailed out of Cap-Francais in St-Domingue. (The city of Cap-Francais, also known as Le Cap, would be renamed Cap-Haitien early in the nineteenth century.) When he reached the open sea Girard headed in a northerly direction, as he normally would do when sailing from St-Domingue to New York. However, there would be nothing normal about this journey. In the ship's log (written in French) Girard gave the destination as St-Pierre and Miquelon.[5] This was the name of a French colony consisting of a group of small islands in the Atlantic Ocean about ten miles south of Newfoundland.[6]

Some persons who have written about Girard have taken him at his word and have assumed that he really intended to sail to St-Pierre and Miquelon. However, it is extremely unlikely that this was the case. He had never been to those remote and sparsely inhabited islands before. He would never, in his entire life, go there. Moreover, there are compelling reasons to believe he was planning to go to New York. It had been his home port for nearly two years. It was where Randall, his business associate and half-owner of the schooner, lived. It had been Girard's destination on previous voyages north from St-Domingue. Why, then, would Girard write in the log that his destination was St-Pierre and Miquelon?

To fully appreciate Girard's predicament, and to have a clear understanding of why he would not want to list New York as his destination, it has to be realized that relations between Great Britain and the American colonies had deteriorated to a point of open hostility by the spring of 1776. Indeed, a state of war, at least informally, had existed for more than a year, since early in the spring of 1775, when the battles of Lexington and Concord had been fought on April 19.

Giving a false destination made sense, as a precautionary measure, in case he was stopped on the high seas by a British warship. He had heard from the captains of other cargo ships, while he was in Cap-Francais, that the British had blockaded Boston and were in the process of extending the blockade southward along the Atlantic Coast. He knew that the British, if they stopped him at sea, would want to inspect his log. He could claim, citing the log, that he was sailing from one French colony to another French colony and was not trying to penetrate the blockade of Great Britain's colonies. If the British knew his intended destination was New York, his ship and cargo would be subject to confiscation. Everybody on board might be taken captive.

The voyage was plagued by heavy going right from the start. Girard noted in his log for the first day and night out: "The sea very rough. During the night we shipped several great waves which increased the water in the hold."[7] The sea calmed down a bit the next day, May 15, and by the middle of the afternoon Girard sighted one of the islands in the Bahamas.[8] The weather soon worsened, however, and he recorded in the log that the sea was "very rough" at 4 A.M. on May 17. A half-hour later "a great wave of the sea threw off two hogsheads of fresh water which I had stowed."[9] (Water was stored in sixty-three-gallon wooden casks called hogsheads, which were tied down with ropes to the deck.)

Two days later, at 7 A.M. on May 19, according to the log, Girard opened a cask of water and found it was salty, "as were all the others that I examined. I believe that this was caused by the great gale when the waves washed over us. I hope the remainder of the water, which is in very small quantities, may not be the cause of making us all ill."[10] His hope was quickly dashed. Girard reported in the log on May 20 (his twenty-sixth birthday, but he did not mention it): "At 10 o'clock in the morning one of my sailors was seized with a violent fever. I fear that this is caused by the bad water which we are obliged to drink because there is no other."[11]

Then the weather grew nasty again, even more so this time. Girard's log entries told of "several squalls" on the night of May 20 and several more the next morning.[12] On the afternoon of the 21st he reported the winds "blowing a tempest, the sea frightful."[13] At sunset the sea was "frightfully rough."[14] About midnight "several great waves" hit the ship and "carried away one of my hogsheads of water which was stowed to starboard on the quarter deck."[15] The waves also "unwedged my masts" and "cracked" one of them.[16]

The crisis came to a head on May 22. At 3 P.M., as Girard reported in the log, the sea had calmed down a little and the crew approached to speak "to me of the small quantity and bad quality of the water, which was only one cask and would not be sufficient for the remainder of our voyage. After considering this I decided to steer N. $\frac{1}{4}$ N.W. and put into either Philadelphia or New York, believing that on these coasts I would meet with some vessels of the King of England which would supply me with water or grant me protections in entering some port. In short to be under shelter from dangers incident to this country, which they say has rebelled against its Prince."[17]

There may have been a hint of mutiny in the air when the crew confronted their captain about the water situation. Girard, who by now had considerable experience as a ship's officer, knew that sailors at sea could become dangerously unstable when they were on the thin edge of a real or an imagined emergency. A potential shortage of drinking water had to be taken seriously. Changing course was the prudent thing to do. It also was a convenient thing to do. Changing course because of a water shortage, duly recorded in the log, underscored the gravity of the shortage and gave Girard a perfect excuse for trying to take the schooner through the British blockade to New York. If he was stopped by a British warship, its officers could easily see there was not enough water on board for a voyage to St-Pierre and Miquelon. However, from Girard's point of view, there was another problem. He might not have enough water to get to New York either.

The change in course actually was only a minor adjustment. Girard had been heading in the general direction of New York all along. The *Jeune Babe* was several hundred miles off the South Carolina coast when the crew approached him. He changed course from slightly east of north to slightly west of north. He could not turn any farther to the west until he was safely past a bulge in the North Carolina coast that was known as Cape Hatteras. When the course adjustment was made, no land had been sighted since the Bahamas. Girard had kept his ship far removed from the coast of America.

The weather soon worsened again. The log reported "several squalls" during the night of May 22 and the morning of May 23.[18] After that, the weather was fairly good for several days. On May 26 the *Jeune Babe* passed Cape Hatteras and proceeded on a direct line toward New York. On the morning of May 29 at 9:30 while off the Virginia coast, as Girard wrote in his log, "I sighted a ship with three masts, standing to the N.N.W., which I recognized as a frigate [warship]. I then tacked to starboard, steering to the nearest point, the wind to the N.E. At that moment I hoped to get some water from this vessel, which would prevent my putting into harbor, which would be very expensive. It crowded on all sail to run after two vessels which were to leeward of us."[19]

Girard was not able to make contact with the warship that day. It is significant that, according to the log, he was determined to get water from another ship, if possible, and avoid the expense of an emergency stop at an unscheduled port. At this time the *Jeune Babe* was less than one hundred miles from the entrance to Delaware Bay and less than two hundred miles from Philadelphia. The clear implication of Girard's comments in the log, in the context of his ship's location at the time, was that he wanted to keep on sailing approximately north to New York instead of turning west into Delaware Bay to get water. He was trying very hard to avoid going to Philadelphia or anywhere near Philadelphia. This is a noteworthy point considering that, as it turned out, he would spend most of his life in Philadelphia.

Girard knew that, if he were to succeed in obtaining an emergency ration of water from a passing ship, it most likely would be just a small quantity, enough to sustain life temporarily but not enough for a voyage to St-Pierre and Miquelon. He still would have a convenient reason, if stopped by a British warship on blockade patrol, to ask for safe passage to New York to obtain more water and also to get repair work for storm damage. The masts of the *Jeune Babe* remained in a dangerously weakened condition.

On the morning of May 30, as Girard narrated in the log, "At break of day I sighted an English vessel which I signaled to speak. At 5 o'clock in the morning it perceived me and reached me at 6 o'clock. It came along side me and proved to be an English frigate. It was coasting between Philadelphia and the Carolinas to seize any vessel which had on board any powder as freight. I asked for water and the captain said in reply that he was going to send some by his long boat; the which said long boat came along side with a lieutenant, who did not bring any water and made me embark with my papers in his long boat to go on board to his captain, who appeared to me to be a very gallant man. He examined my papers and kept on board an Irish sailor who had gone with me to interpret. In doing this he did me a great injury as he was the best sailor that I had on board any vessel."[20] Girard did not yet have thorough command of the English language, not in sufficient degree to let him feel comfortable conversing on important matters with the captain of a British warship. The presence of the Irish sailor as an interpreter had given the British an opportunity too good to resist. Britain had an autocratic but effective way of recruiting people for the navy: impressment. It was another word for kidnaping. Victims were simply grabbed, wherever they could be found, and forced to serve. The Irish were favorite targets because they usually spoke English. Most British sailors had been "impressed" from the streets of English port cities; impressment was not limited to those taken at sea, or to Americans.

It would be a long time coming, but Girard would get revenge for the impressment of his Irish sailor. Officers of the British warship in May of 1776 could never have imagined in their worst nightmares the vital role that this one-eyed Frenchman, the captain of a storm-battered schooner, would play someday in a war between Great Britain and the United States, a war that would be caused in large measure by British impressment of American citizens.

Girard's encounter with the British warship occurred off the Maryland coast. The *Jeune Babe* at that time was less than fifty miles from the entrance to Delaware Bay. Water was available at Lewes, Delaware, the first town inside the breakwater separating the ocean from the bay. Lewes was the pickup and drop-off point for pilots guiding ships up and down Delaware Bay and the Delaware River to and from Philadelphia.

The pages of Girard's log for the *Jeune Babe* after May 30 were lost for some unexplained reason and have never been found. It is known, in part from stories later told by Girard himself, that he arrived in Delaware Bay off Lewes on May 31 or soon thereafter and took on a supply of water. Lacking sufficient currency or coin, he borrowed money from the captain of another ship to pay a pilot to take the *Jeune Babe* to Philadelphia.[21]

With a fresh supply of water, Girard might have headed back to the Atlantic Ocean from Lewes instead of proceeding to Philadelphia. However, he had two good reasons for postponing a return to the ocean. First, he had received up-to-date information at Lewes on the British blockade in nearby coastal waters, a blockade that seemed to be drawing tighter with each passing day. He faced the prospect of being stopped and searched and harassed again (maybe repeatedly) if he took the *Jeune Babe* north along the New Jersey coast toward New York. More members of his crew might be impressed into the British navy. Second, the sheltered water of the Delaware Bay had given Girard an opportunity to examine closely the cumulative damage to his ship inflicted by the series of severe storms. The damage was worse than he may have realized. Weakened masts and other weather-weary super-structure were being held together on a temporary basis with impro-vised repairs, but he could see that the vessel needed more effective rehabilitation. Skilled work could be done in Philadelphia. To brave the Atlantic again with a schooner of questionable seaworthiness would be risky. Another major storm could have dire consequences.

So the *Jeune Babe*, with a pilot on board, sailed a hundred miles—the first fifty in the Delaware Bay, the second fifty in the Delaware River—to Philadelphia. For most of the trip the scenery was no different than William Penn, the city's Founding Father, had seen on his first journey to Philadelphia ninety-four years earlier. The bay was still flanked by marshes or forests on both shores, Delaware on the port side (to the left) and New Jersey starboard.

Delaware Bay is twelve miles wide at its entrance between Cape Henlopen, Delaware, and Cape May, New Jersey. The bay broadens to thirty miles at its widest point before narrowing to four miles where it meets the Delaware River. Sailing up the middle of the bay in clear weather, with early June's abundant daylight and short nights, Girard could see both shores simultaneously much of the time. After he entered the Delaware River his views of the shorelines were closer and sharper. After stormy weeks at sea, the Delaware was a pleasant change of pace in a slowly unfolding sequence of scenery. Both banks, for mile after mile, were wild with no evidence of civilization. The land was heavily wooded, with trees and undergrowth coming right down to the water's edge. Wildlife was abundant. This was the home of the eagle and the bear.

Mother Nature produces many exquisite works of art, but nothing more exciting, more enticing, more enthralling than a beautiful river. Its flow is timeless, its journey perpetual. There is magic in its continuity. It keeps rolling along, yet it is always there. The current moves, but not the river. No one, though, had to tell Girard about the charm and the majesty of a river. They were well known to him long before he sailed on the Delaware. He had gone up and down the Garonne many times en route to and from Bordeaux. He had walked beside that river since before he could remember. Now, going up the Delaware and enjoying an introduction to its splendors, he could not help noting similarities between Philadelphia and Bordeaux. Both were Atlantic seaports situated a long way from the ocean. Both were accessible by ship only after a long ride on a river.

Girard saw some towns as he sailed up the Delaware: Salem in New Jersey, New Castle and Wilmington in Delaware, Chester in Pennsylvania, among others. They added to, rather than detracted from, the picturesque landscape. They were places of refuge on the edges of fields and forests.

As Girard neared Philadelphia, and the river made a sharp bend to the right, the shores were still heavily wooded. A short distance farther upstream the river began a wide, gentle, sweeping turn to the left. As the *Jeune Babe* completed passage around that bend, Girard got his first look at Philadelphia, about three miles ahead on the left. Cities in those days did not have skylines; they had sky. The tallest edifices were church towers, not office buildings—monuments to God, not to mammon. As Girard proceeded, the highest and most magnificent structure in view was the spire of Christ Church.

The last miles slipped by quickly. Soon Girard was approaching the waterfront of a city he had not planned to visit and had tried hard to avoid. If the captain of that British frigate had just given him some water, Girard might never have seen Philadelphia. Nonetheless, there he was. The date was June 6, 1776. Girard stepped ashore just a little more than half a mile from Independence Hall where, on the very next day, Richard Henry Lee of Virginia would stand before his colleagues of the Second Continental Congress and introduce a resolution declaring that "These united Colonies are and of right ought to be free and independent States." Within a few days, at a rooming house three-quarters of a mile from the berth of the *Jeune Babe*, Thomas Jefferson would start writing the Declaration of Independence.

Girard had landed in the middle of a revolution.

CHAPTER 4

In Philadelphia, Just in Time for a Revolution

1776-1777

In 1776 the most exciting place to be in all the world was Philadelphia. History was in the making.

ON THE DAY in June that Stephen Girard arrived in Philadelphia it was the largest city in America and the second largest in the English-speaking world (London was No. 1). The population of Philadelphia in 1776 was 35,000, including inhabitants of two outlying areas: Northern Liberties (north of Vine Street) and Southwark (south of South Street). Philadelphia would remain America's largest city until 1830 (just one year before Girard's death) when New York advanced to the top of the list.

The Philadelphia that Girard saw for the first time was surprisingly civilized by eighteenth century standards, considering that it was less than a hundred years old. In a striking resemblance to London, Philadelphia had row after row of brick homes, some three stories or more. It had an abundance of skilled craftsmen who built houses and ships and made furniture, clothing, clocks, wagons and other necessities and amenities. It was the busiest port in America, with a waterfront that was often a veritable forest of masts as a hundred ships or more were frequently tied up at wharves or anchored in the river. It was a convivial city, with sailors and landlubbers sharing a mutual enjoyment of sociability and strong drink at 165 inns and taverns.[1]

If there was anything that Philadelphians did more than drinking,

51

it was praying. Girard could see, while still on the deck of his ship, that Philadelphia was a city of churches. Such was the legacy of William Penn, the founder of both Philadelphia and Pennsylvania. He was a staunch Quaker who had been imprisoned in England because of his religious beliefs. Pennsylvania had been settled as a haven for people of all religions—a place where people could enjoy freedom of worship. This had been a radical idea in the seventeenth century, and it was still a radical idea in the eighteenth century. Catholics, Jews and numerous denominations of Protestants were conducting religious services in Philadelphia, the City of Brotherly Love, with no fear of interference or reprisal.

Quakers—also called Friends because the name of their sect is the Society of Friends—had been the dominant political and economic force in Philadelphia since the founding of the city in 1682, although their power was beginning to diminish by the time of Girard's arrival. They tried to maintain solidarity within their ranks by refusing to sanction marriage of a Quaker to a non-Quaker. A Quaker who married outside the faith was "read out of the meeting," a Quaker term meaning expelled. Notwithstanding these lapses into religious intolerance, the Quakers remained scrupulous in defending the rights of persons of all faiths to worship as they pleased and to hold true to their convictions and beliefs.

Girard, when he first stepped ashore in Philadelphia, had already been told by his pilot where he could meet prospective buyers of cargo and make arrangements for repair of his ship. The place to go was the London Coffee House. It was on the southwest corner of Front and Market Streets, two blocks from the waterfront. In operation since 1734 and located in a building erected even before that, the coffee house was a venerable institution where business was transacted by shipowners, sea captains, supercargoes, merchants and others engaged in maritime trade and related activities. It was a gathering place for exchanges of information and making deals pertaining to servicing and supplying ships and to buying, selling and transporting cargoes in international and coastal commerce. It was for eating, drinking and camaraderie, too, and for getting the latest news from officers of ships that had just arrived from the West Indies, Europe and other far-away places. Coffee (also tea) was served, as would be expected of an establishment called a coffee house, but many patrons favored stronger drink. Alcoholic beverages were available. The list of libations included wines, rums, whiskeys and ales, a variety similar to the offerings in the taverns of that time.[2] The coffee house was busiest around midday when people with business to discuss would get together for lunch. As Girard walked west from the Delaware River on Market Street in June of 1776, headed for the London Coffee House, he could see up ahead the city's main market. It was in the middle of Market Street—starting at Front Street and extending three blocks to Fourth Street. Market Street was originally named High Street, and the name was not formally changed until 1853, but it was commonly called Market Street for a hundred years before that.[3]

Black slaves from Africa were sold at auctions outside the London Coffee House. Slavery was legal and widespread in Philadelphia in 1776. More than five hundred slaves lived in the city, serving masters who were city residents. These slaves were in addition to others constantly passing through Philadelphia, arriving in ships, sold at auctions and transported elsewhere by new owners.

Girard would live less than two blocks from the London Coffee House and would see slaves sold at the outdoor auctions there. He would become a slave owner himself but would not transport slaves in his ships. White indentured servants from Europe also were sold at auctions outside the London Coffee House. Hundreds of households in Philadelphia had indentured servants in 1776. Girard would have them for many years. While slavery was an evil institution, with victims captured and enslaved involuntarily, indentured servitude was another matter entirely. Many Europeans, lacking funds to pay for passage across the ocean, went into servitude voluntarily and benefited from the system. They would not have been able to come to America otherwise; it was a sail-now-pay-later plan for those with no credit. Prospective emigrants from England and other countries agreed to work for a specified period, usually four or five years, in exchange for accommodations and meals on ships going to America. Some indentured servants had their fare to America paid in advance by the people they would work for. Indentured servants not already spoken for were sold at the auctions outside the coffee house, with proceeds going to shipowners who had provided passage.⁴

Indentured servants sometimes were treated harshly but many received kind treatment. Some learned a useful trade during their servitude. In any case they were certain of steady employment, with room and board provided, for a specified number of years. Then they were guaranteed their freedom and a chance to pursue their dream of financial security in a land of opportunity. All in all, it was not a bad deal for destitute Europeans who had faced a prospect of life-long impoverishment in their homelands. When a person was bound to a master for a certain number of years, terms of the agreement were written twice: on two sheets of paper or parchment with wide margins on one side. One sheet was then placed on top of the other, and the two sheets were "indented" in an identical manner with one waving cut of a knife through the margins: thus the name, "indentured" servant. The master kept one copy of the agreement; the servant kept the other. If a dispute arose about terms of the agreement, it could be shown that neither copy was a forgery if the curved indentations on the margins matched.

On Second Street north of Market Street stood Philadelphia's pre-eminent house of worship, Christ Church. Its spire, as noted earlier, had been the first Philadelphia landmark to catch Girard's eye when he was coming up the Delaware River. Christ Church was the most prominent Anglican church in America and, by the time Girard arrived in Philadelphia, had become a hotbed of the emerging American Revolution. (Anglican churches in America became Episcopal churches after the American colonies severed their ties with Great Britain.) Fifteen men who would sign the Declaration of Independence worshiped at Christ Church. Seven of them would be buried in the churchyard or in the church's supplementary burial grounds nearby. Regular worshipers at Christ Church, including Benjamin Franklin, Robert Morris, Francis Hopkinson and Betsy Ross, had reserved pews. George Washington, with Martha, sat regularly in a reserved pew when he was President of the United States.

Just around the corner from Christ Church, on Arch Street west of Second Street, Betsy Ross lived in a house that had been built about

1720 (it still stands). She had been a Quaker and had been expelled after marrying an Anglican. They had crossed the Delaware River in a rowboat under cover of darkness and had been married in a tavern in New Jersey by a justice of the peace. It may have been just a few days before Girard's arrival in Philadelphia that General Washington made his famous call on Betsy Ross at her home, accompanied by Robert Morris and Colonel George Ross, an uncle of Betsy's first husband. Written accounts of that meeting by a daughter, a granddaughter and a niece of Betsy, said to be based on her oral accounts, tell the familiar story: Washington showed her a drawing of a proposed American flag and she agreed to make what would be the first flag. She suggested revisions, which he accepted.[5] The thirteen stars were changed from six points to five, and the stars were put in a circle instead of scattered in an irregular pattern.[6] (Some historians doubt that there was a meeting between Betsy Ross and a delegation headed by Washington, although it is well documented that he was in Philadelphia in early June of 1776 and stayed at the City Tavern on the west side of Second Street north of Walnut Street, three and a half blocks from Betsy's house.[7])

Girard and Ross were not far apart in age—she was nineteen months younger—and they lived just a few blocks from each other for more than half a century. He bought flags from her, as did many other shipowners. After losing her first two husbands in the Revolutionary War she married a war veteran, John Claypoole, who was wounded in the Battle of Germantown and endured that memorable winter at Valley Forge. Claypoole was an official in the U.S. Customs House in Philadelphia for many years and, in that capacity, knew Girard and other shipowners and maritime merchants.

Girard could hardly have picked a more turbulent time to arrive in Philadelphia. The city was rocking with calls for revolution and plans for revolution. Meanwhile, the British blockade was growing stronger. Sending cargo ships to sea was increasingly risky. One result of the British blockade was rising demand in Philadelphia for sugar and coffee from St-Domingue, amid fear that supplies might be cut off entirely. Girard had no trouble disposing of his cargo at a profit. Then, with the Second Continental Congress apparently moving toward a complete break with Great Britain, he decided it would not be prudent to sail right back into a British-infested Atlantic Ocean. The best thing to do, he concluded, was to stay put for a while and await developments.

It was in these circumstances that Girard, within three weeks of his arrival in Philadelphia, opened a small store in rented quarters on Water Street in the first block north of Market Street, the block where he would live and do business, with some interruptions, for the rest of his life. Although June of 1776 was hardly an ideal time to open a store, considering all of the imponderables and all of the uncertainties, Girard managed to make a go of it by staying flexible and not being too selective. He bought and sold fruits and vegetables and dry goods and anything else he could get his hands on, including maritime cargoes when available. In the meantime, he kept abreast of the latest reports on activities of the Second Continental Congress and the status of the British blockade. He was in an interlude of uncertainty, not committed to long-term operation of a store and not ruling out an early return to sea if prospects brightened for reasonably safe and reasonably profitable maritime trade.

On the Fourth of July, after the Declaration of Independence had been approved by the Second Continental Congress, a copy was given to John Dunlap. He operated a print shop on Market Street near Second, three blocks from Girard's store. The first public reading of the Declaration was from a printed copy on July 8 outside Independence Hall. In the tower of that building the bell that would be known as the Liberty Bell had summoned people to the reading. The Declaration was read on virtually the same spot where, many years later, Girard would stand as the leader of a protest rally against policies of President Washington.

The rebellion against British tyranny became official and absolute with the Declaration's bold bid for complete and unequivocal independence. There would be no turning back now. The war was sure to intensify and further disrupt maritime trade. Britain would have liked to make quick work of the insolent American rebels, but the realistic prospect was for a long and bitter conflict, and the outcome was in doubt.

Girard had been in Philadelphia less than five weeks on the day of the Declaration's first public reading. With a terrible war in the offing and the Americans appearing to be the underdogs, Girard had options that included getting out of the war zone at the earliest opportunity. He was a citizen of France and could have returned to France or St-Domingue, or he could have gone to some other French colony in the West Indies.

He chose, instead, to stay in America and support the American cause. It was a decision, though, that was not made instantly or impetuously but evolved over time. Events were moving so swiftly in Philadelphia in that historic summer of the Declaration of Independence that Girard, at the age of twenty-six, could not have known for sure what he wanted to do with the rest of his life. Nonetheless, his resolve, however tentative at first, to stay in Philadelphia, tells something about Girard and the kind of man he was. In the crucible of the American Revolution he showed his own Spirit of '76. Perhaps he smelled the sweet scent of adventure. Maybe he saw that world-shaking history was in the making and he wanted to be part of it. There may have been something about the Americans in 1776 that caught his fancy, such as the raw courage and the sheer audacity that they showed in their readiness to take on the British and to do or die.

On a more pragmatic basis, Girard may well have foreseen that Philadelphia could offer enormous opportunities in maritime trade if America won independence from Great Britain. The greatest opportunities would be for those who were in the right place at the right time, for those who got in on the ground floor.

To keep it all in perspective, Girard did not let himself get completely carried away by the excitement of the revolutionary fervor that infected many Philadelphians in 1776, although by no means all of them. There is no indication that he ever considered joining the American army or navy during the Revolutionary War. He wanted America to win, but he had no intention of going into combat. He would be content to contribute in ways that were compatible with his line of work: maritime trade and privateering. He would not participate in the fighting, but he would provide supplies for men who did.

While the Americans were declaring independence in Philadelphia, the British were preparing to take New York. In late June of 1776 a British naval force, warships and transports, began to arrive off the coast of northern New Jersey. By early July the British were getting ready for a landing, not only to capture New York but to drive Washington's troops out of positions they held on Long Island and Manhattan Island. In August an army of thirty thousand British Regulars and hired Hessians went ashore. It was the largest invasion force Great Britain had ever sent across an ocean.

General Washington, in a series of running battles and strategic retreats, pulled his army out of the New York area. He crossed the Hudson River and kept on retreating across New Jersey.

Thomas Randall, co-owner, with Girard, of the *Jeune Babe*, had left New York in early summer when he realized British occupation was imminent. He went to Philadelphia and was reunited with Girard. In the meantime, Girard had become acquainted with Philadelphia merchant and shipowner Isaac Hazlehurst. The three men, Girard, Randall, and Hazlehurst, decided to join forces in mercantile ventures. By early August the British blockade off Delaware Bay had thinned out as Great Britain concentrated on solidifying the occupation of New York and its environs. A voyage to St-Domingue seemed feasible. In war-time America there was a growing demand in both military and civilian markets for not only such staples as sugar and coffee but also for a variety of merchandise from Europe, including French-made products that could be purchased in St-Domingue. Ships sailing from St-Domingue to America often carried sugar or coffee, or both, and also an assortment of other items. A shipload made up of many different things was commonly called a general cargo.

Girard and Randall sold the storm-battered *Jeune Babe* and bought a sloop, the *Sally* (not the same *Sally* that Girard had sailed across the Atlantic years earlier). With Girard as captain, the vessel left Philadelphia in August bound for Cap-Francais in St-Domingue with a general cargo jointly owned by Girard, Randall and Hazlehurst. The latter two remained in Philadelphia. All three men were risking their money, but only Girard was putting himself at risk.

After picking his way, both coming and going, through a well-scattered British blockade, Girard returned to Philadelphia in command of the *Sally* in October with a general cargo. He and Randall sold the

Sally and became co-owners of another sloop, the *Betsy*. It sailed out of Philadelphia late in the fall of 1776, with Girard in command, bound for Port-au-Prince, St-Domingue. A general cargo again was owned jointly by Girard, Randall and Hazlehurst.

By now the British blockade was drawing tighter. Sloops were fast and maneuverable and hard to see at a distance, especially in darkness. Nonetheless, it was becoming more difficult to elude the blockading warships. The danger for Girard was increasing. To the British, the Declaration of Independence was tantamount to a declaration of war. As a French citizen and a blockade-runner moving contraband in and out of an American port in wartime, he could face unpleasant consequences if captured. He might be imprisoned. He might be flogged. He might be hanged. The British were not inclined to be merciful toward foreigners who challenged and defied British authority on the high seas. More specifically, if Girard had been caught sneaking through the blockade with a cargo for Americans in armed rebellion, he could not have qualified for prisoner-of-war status or diplomatic protection. He was a French civilian meddling in a war between Great Britain and British colonists without the knowledge or the consent of the French government. In such circumstances he would not have been entitled to very much in the way of due process. He could have been summarily tried at sea, aboard a British man-of-war, and strung up to the highest yardarm.

Early in 1777 Girard returned to Philadelphia at the helm of the *Betsy* with another general cargo from St-Domingue. Although he did not know it, that voyage would mark virtually the end of his seafaring days. For the remainder of his life, almost fifty-five years, he would go to sea again only once. He was about to meet someone who would give him enticing incentives to stay home.

While Girard was on his last voyage to St-Domingue, significant changes occurred in the military situation in America. In early December of 1776 American troops under command of General Washington, having retreated all the way across New Jersey after withdrawing from New York in August, crossed the Delaware River into Pennsylvania in a flotilla of small boats and encamped in Bucks County, north of Philadelphia. A pursuing force of Hessian mercenaries captured Trenton, on the New Jersey side of the river, thirty-four miles upstream from Philadelphia. British troops occupied nearby Princeton.

Just a few weeks later, on Christmas night in 1776, Washington crossed the icy Delaware in a snowstorm, leading an army of 2,400 men in an armada of rowboats to a victorious early-morning attack on the surprised Hessians at Trenton. In the following week, on January 3, 1777, Washington's troops scored another victory, routing the British at Princeton.

These triumphs allowed Philadelphians to breathe easier for a while, but they knew it would be just a matter of time until the British mounted a major effort to capture Philadelphia, the crown jewel of American cities. In the wake of the American victories at Trenton and Princeton, the bulk of British ground forces concentrated on strengthening positions defensively in and around New York while British generals and admirals tried to determine how to get back on the offensive.

In this situation there was a window of opportunity for some commercial activity in Philadelphia to return to near-normal without fear of British attack. The continuing presence of British warships off Delaware Bay remained a partial deterrent to maritime trade but not to overland economic intercourse. Moreover, as Girard had demonstrated both outbound and inbound, the blockade could be penetrated.

It was in these circumstances that Girard, after returning from St-Domingue on the *Betsy* early in 1777, decided to resume operations in rented space on Water Street, buying and selling whatever kinds of merchandise he could handle profitably, including maritime cargoes when available. There is no reason to believe he was planning to retire from the sea permanently, or even for a long time. He would still have the option to go back to sea whenever prospects were auspicious, just as he had done in 1776 after operating a store for two months, but this time he would not go back.

Thus, after thirteen years at sea, he would plant his feet firmly and lastingly on solid ground, although not deliberately or even consciously at first. He would phase out his business associations with Randall and Hazlehurst, not because of disagreements with either of them but because Girard felt confident about his capabilities and wanted to go it alone. He had captained ships, he had co-owned ships, and he had been in charge of cargoes, but his decisions in these capacities had often been subject to restraints imposed by partners. Now he would be the boss.

There were many ways in which Girard and other merchants could make money in Philadelphia in early 1777 despite the war and the blockade. The city was a trading center by land as well as by sea. Pennsylvania farmers, many of them from as far away as fifty miles or more, would come to Philadelphia regularly in horse-drawn vehicles to sell their products and buy all kinds of goods for the return trip. While in the city they would stay at inns or, to save money, sleep in their wagons parked in the streets or on outlying country roads.

The Great Conestoga Road wound its way nearly seventy miles westward from Philadelphia to Lancaster, a thriving inland city in fertile farm country. Freight wagons pulled by four or six horses carried heavy loads in both directions. Many of the wagons were regularly scheduled common carriers hauling payloads for prescribed fees based on weight and distance. Livestock, mostly cattle and hogs, was herded to Philadelphia on the Great Conestoga Road, sometimes by farmers who owned the animals and sometimes by drovers who charged fees per mile and per head.

Grain, meat, lumber and other items produced in abundance in rural Pennsylvania had ready markets in Philadelphia—and also in the West Indies when ships could get through. Sugar, molasses, rum, tea, coffee and other products from the West Indies were in demand in Philadelphia and the Pennsylvania countryside. So were many kinds of manufactured goods from Europe. When shipping was unfettered by blockades, merchants with warehouse space (owned or rented) on the Philadelphia waterfront could turn a good profit buying and selling incoming and outgoing cargoes on land and sea. Even in difficult times such as that which prevailed in early 1777 there always were some shipowners and sea captains who, if the financial terms were sufficiently attractive, were willing to take the risks involved in blockade-running, just as Girard had been willing to do.

Some merchants owned their own ships but that was not necessary. Arrangements could be made for goods to be transported in ships owned by their captains or by other entrepreneurs in Philadelphia or in other ports in America or abroad. Cargoes could be sold outright to sea captains or shipowners, or cargoes could be transported for fees and sold for commissions at destinations. Merchants with agents in destination ports (which Girard eventually would have, once he got organized) shipped cargoes to those agents who, utilizing their knowledge of local market conditions, disposed of the goods at best available prices.

There were many variations to the process. It was not necessary for a maritime merchant, just getting started, to make a huge capital investment, although substantial operating funds or good credit, or both, were certainly helpful. Merchants low on funds could pool resources and participate in partnerships, as Girard had done. Ships and cargoes could be owned jointly by two, three or four persons, sometimes by many more than that. Percentages of ownerships could vary, with each person owning a share of a ship or a cargo not necessarily equal to shares of others. Moreover, there were often opportunities to make impromptu deals at the London Coffee House or on the wharves. Sometimes ships were ready to sail, but did not yet have full loads, and would take on more cargo at the last minute under terms attractive to shippers.

Some merchants, Girard among them, were able to buy and sell and to wheel and deal because they used their unpaid debts as a source of cash. Girard, in 1777, still had not paid debts he had owed to merchants in Bordeaux since 1774. In three years he had steadily increased the size of his nest egg—especially through skillful buying and selling of cargoes and ships that he had owned in partnerships with Randall or Hazlehurst or both.

In sum, becoming a merchant in maritime trade, with supplemental business in overland trade, was not all that hard to do in Philadelphia, even in the tumultuous year of 1777, and did not require a lot of cash up front. The difficult part was not starting in business but staying in business. The difficult part was making money instead of losing money.

In theory, all that had to be done was to buy low, sell high and choose partners carefully. In practice, it was a steaming cauldron of worry and risk—a highly competitive business in which many things could go wrong and often did. There were innumerable ways to end up with a loss instead of a profit. Entire ships and crews and cargoes could be wiped out at sea by storms or by pirates or by acts of war. There could be a long wait (as Girard's creditors in Bordeaux had found out) between sale of goods and receipt of payments. Sometimes it would be an endless wait. A ship might sail away with a cargo still unpaid for and never return. So, being a merchant in the maritime trade could be a high road to wealth or a low road to ruin. It was not for those who were faint of heart, and it was not for those who failed to pay strict attention to business.

Girard was trying hard to pay strict attention to business in the springtime of 1777 when, suddenly, he made a momentous discovery. He learned that there could be more to a daily routine—a whole lot more—than just work, work, work. That was when he met Mary Lum. That was when he fell head over heels in love. Mary was eighteen years old, a penniless maid of Irish descent working in a boarding house. She was strikingly beautiful—with black hair, a creamy complexion, a lithesome figure and a smile that seemed somehow, subtly, to suggest invitation and promise. Girard was dazzled. She was everything he had always wanted. He soon would lose all desire to go back to sea or to go back to France. She was a light in his life.

CHAPTER 5

Love and War

1777-1778

*A man is like an apple. When he is ripe,
he will fall.*

SOME MEN thirst for wealth. Some men hunger for power. Some men seek neither and are happy to settle for something simpler: the satisfying love of an amiable woman.

Young Stephen Girard did not seek wealth or power, although he would achieve both. An amiable woman is what he wanted, and an amiable woman is what he found when he met Mary Lum. She would give him more pleasure than he had thought was possible. He could not know, nor could she, that ultimately she would give him tragedy.

Stephen was lonely and vulnerable as he approached his twenty-seventh birthday, May 20, 1777. For thirteen years he had spent more nights alone at sea than he would care to count. When he met Mary, out of the blue, on or near his birthday, he never had a chance. She swept him right off his feet.

James Parton, an eminent nineteenth century historian, described the first meeting between Stephen and Mary: "Walking along Water Street one day, near the corner of Vine Street," Girard's attention was "caught by a beautiful servant-girl going to the pump for a pail of water. She was an enchanting brunette ... with luxuriant black locks curling and clustering about her neck. As she tripped along with bare feet and empty pail, in airy and unconscious grace, she captivated the susceptible Frenchman, who saw in her the realization of the songs of the forecastle and the reveries of the quarter-deck. He sought her acquaintance, and made himself at home in her kitchen."[1]

Making Mary's acquaintance was not difficult. She had a tendency to be flirtatious and sometimes teasing. She had an easy laugh to go with her ready smile. Henry Ingram, a nineteenth century biographer of Girard, described Mary's disposition as "exceedingly amiable" and said her "beauty was widely celebrated."[2] Parton called her "a beauty, with the natural vanities of a beauty."[3] Stephen Simpson, a long-time Girard employee, said Mary "was endowed with charms that easily accounted for the conquest she had made."[4]

It was a conquest all right, and a quick one, too, but Mary was smart enough to let Stephen think he was the one doing the conquering.

Mary was more than just young and pretty. She was saucy. She was titillating. Stephen could see that she was someone who would be nice to come home to, that she was someone who could give him anticipation by day and fulfillment by night, that she was someone who could put an end to his loneliness once and for all.

She was a jolly person, and her jovial nature was pleasantly contagious. She had zest. She was good-humored. She was fun. In being nice to him, in a relaxing and folksy way, Mary helped Stephen forget he had that unsightly eye. He felt comfortable when he was with her.

Mary was minimally educated and knew nothing about the intricacies of maritime trade and mercantilism that occupied Stephen in his working hours. Her intellectual capacities had never been challenged in her endeavors as a boarding house maid. She understood quite well, though, that Stephen was not attracted to her by anything that was even remotely associated with intellect. She knew what he wanted, and she would not keep him waiting long.

While Stephen was attracted to Mary by her beauty and good humor, she was attracted to him for an entirely different reason. She had grown weary of poverty and drudgery, doing menial chores in a boarding house. She realized that Stephen was entranced by her beauty and that he provided a golden opportunity for her to achieve a better life. She could not have dreamed how wealthy he would become, but it was evident that he was likely to amount to something. He was industrious and in business for himself, even though still struggling to make a go of it. He was not all that bad looking either, the deformed eye notwithstanding. He was eight and a half years older than Mary but the age difference was not unusual at that time. Thus, all things considered, she could not help but marvel at her good fortune in having a young man who seemed to have such a bright future suddenly and unexpectedly drop into her lap. One thing was certain: She was not going to let him get away.

Stephen, too, could scarcely believe his good luck in meeting Mary. He had grown weary of all work and no fun, and he did not need two eyes to see that she was gorgeous. There may not have been a prettier girl in all of Philadelphia. So, yes, there would be conquest, but it would be mutual conquest. Mary, wanting to be rescued from the hard life of a maid, would find comfort and security in Stephen's arms. Stephen, wanting to be rescued from an empty life of loneliness, would find joy and happiness in Mary's arms. Both of them would get what they were looking for. Each of them would give what the other wanted.

It happened with startling swiftness. When they had known each other only about a week, Mary responded warmly to Stephen's invitation to join him for a tryst in the country. She had tantalized him; now she would satisfy him. Stephen and Mary shared a room at an inn a few miles from Philadelphia for four nights, from May 27 through May 30, 1777, and returned to the city on the 31st.[5] She passed the test with flying colors. The result speaks for itself. Just six days after they returned from the inn, Stephen and Mary were married. It was a whirlwind courtship. From the day they met until the day they wed was less than three weeks. Their wedding day was June 6, 1777, exactly one year after Stephen's arrival in Philadelphia. He hardly could have picked a more enjoyable way to celebrate the anniversary.

Stephen was still nominally a Catholic but he and Mary, an Episcopalian, were married in St. Paul's Episcopal Church, which was built in 1761 and still stands on the east side of Third Street south of Walnut Street. A brief and simple ceremony was performed without fanfare by the Rev. Mr. Shinger.[6] The newlyweds did not go anywhere on their honeymoon, but business records indicate that Stephen took three days off from work.

It would not be an overstatement to say that Mary turned Stephen's life around. It would be difficult to exaggerate the impact that their marriage had on him. From that moment on, as may be seen in his personal and business correspondence, he never seriously considered going back to France to live. From that moment on, for as long as Mary shared his bed and gave him her love, he never seriously considered going back to sea. He had a woman now, a good-natured woman, an affectionate woman, a beautiful woman, and every night, when his work was done, she was there. That made a world of difference in his outlook. He had no desire to leave home. The young salt had become an old salt. He did not have his sea legs any more.

Some writers in the nineteenth century took the view that Stephen made a mistake marrying a lowly maid with little education. They speculated that his personal life might have been more rewarding and might have risen to a loftier level if he had married someone better attuned to social graces. Mary knew a lot about boarding houses. She did not know much about drawing rooms. James Parton called Stephen and Mary "the incongruous two."[7] Henry Ingram said: "It was a very hazardous undertaking to link himself permanently with one who, notwithstanding her rare physical beauty and many admirable qualities, was still incontestably not the person he should prudently have chosen. The difference in their social status alone was enough to have caused him to hesitate long before taking the irrevocable step."[8]

Stephen Simpson wrote in a similar vein: "The temptation of an offer of marriage to a young servant girl, by a captain and merchant, who even then was supposed to be a favored votary of fortune, was certainly too great to permit her to question or scrutinize the emotions of her heart .... He never looked forward to the day when he might blush for his choice, or regret her want of accomplishments to adorn a higher circle."[9]

These critics, putting down Mary for being a maid and putting down Stephen for marrying her, were reflecting a class-conscious outlook that prevailed in early America. It was unfair to portray Mary as unworthy of Stephen because she had done nothing more than menial work in a boarding house. It was equally unfair to criticize Stephen, by implication, for not marrying someone who could have helped him be a social-climber. If, indeed, it can be a mistake to marry a woman who is superbly beautiful and has a sparkling personality, in addition to being amiable and affectionate and accommodating, then it certainly is the kind of mistake that many men would like to make.

Moreover, Mary did not misrepresent herself in any way. Stephen knew she was a boarding house maid, and she never implied she was anything else. He saw nothing wrong in having a wife who had been a servant. It was something he never would have considered being apologetic about.

To put the romance of Stephen and Mary in focus, he had no realistic expectation of becoming a millionaire when he married her. However, even if he had known he was going to be rich, it would have made no difference. He was not a snob. It would have been totally out of character for him to marry a party-goer and a fashion plate who could fit comfortably in high society. That was not Stephen Girard's style. It never had been, and it never would be. All he wanted was a wife who was as down to earth as he was, someone he could relate to and enjoy being with. He got that kind of wife when he married Mary. She gave him, in the beginning, a happy and fun-filled marriage with an abundance of love. Later, their happiness would turn to ashes, but that misfortune would have nothing to do with Mary's background.

While Stephen and Mary were enjoying their first weeks together as husband and wife, the war was starting to close in on them. It became known that the British in New York were assembling troops and ships in large numbers, presumably in preparation for an attack on Philadelphia. The situation was fraught with peril for the newlyweds. When the British came marching in, Stephen's life would be in jeopardy if he remained in the city or was caught trying to get away. He was still a citizen of France and still a civilian ineligible for protection accorded uniformed combatants under rules of war. He had been supplying American military units with foodstuffs and whatever other products he could acquire from inland sources or from merchant ships that were able to get through the blockade. The British would not hesitate to hang a foreigner providing sustenance and comfort to the American rebels. It was not likely the British would treat Mary as a criminal, but they would have no compunctions about making her a widow. So Stephen and Mary, even while their love was still crisp and fresh, had to make contingency plans for a quick exit from Philadelphia in a direction that would avoid capture by the British. Stephen guessed correctly that they would not attack by way of New Jersey.

On July 22, 1777, just a little over six weeks after he had married Mary, Stephen bought a house in Mount Holly, New Jersey, about twenty miles from Philadelphia on roads of that time and also accessible by boat via the Delaware River and Rancocas Creek. He purchased the property from his friend and former business associate, Isaac Hazlehurst. The price for the frame house, two stories plus a basement and an attic, on five acres was 525 pounds in Pennsylvania currency. That was equivalent to $1,407 in currency issued by the Second Continental Congress.[10] (After the former British colonies declared independence, each state could issue its own money.)

Soon after Girard's purchase of the Mount Holly house the British began a circuitous move on Philadelphia. An invasion force of fighting ships and troop transports sailed out of New York harbor and headed south along the coasts of New Jersey, Delaware, Maryland and Virginia to the mouth of Chesapeake Bay, and then all the way up the bay to its northern extremity, where eighteen thousand British soldiers and Hessian mercenaries commanded by General William Howe disembarked near Elkton, Maryland, on August 25. They marched north into Pennsylvania and then turned east toward Philadelphia.

General Washington, with eleven thousand troops, tried unsuccessfully to turn back the invaders on the foggy morning of September 11 at Chadds Ford on Brandywine Creek, twenty-five miles southwest of Philadelphia on the Baltimore Pike. The Battle of Brandywine left thirteen hundred Americans dead, wounded or captured, more than double the British losses. Lafayette was among the wounded. Washington made a strategic retreat, preserving the bulk of his army to keep the Revolution alive. Philadelphia lay unprotected, its capture by the British now inevitable.

There was another, smaller battle on September 20, the Paoli Massacre. An American contingent of fifteen hundred men encamped at Paoli, twenty miles from Philadelphia, was attacked before dawn by a much larger British force. Many of the more than two hundred Americans who died in that encounter were run through with bayonets.[11]

A large exodus from Philadelphia began within days after the Battle of Brandywine, and accelerated after the Paoli Massacre, as inhabitants reluctantly faced up to the reality that British occupation was imminent.[12] The Second Continental Congress fled first to Lancaster, then farther west to York. Revolutionary government records were taken north to Easton. The Liberty Bell and other bells, mostly from churches, were loaded into a caravan of wagons that left the city on September 18. The bells were taken north to Allentown and stored in the basement of Zion Reformed Church for the duration of the British occupation of Philadelphia. If the bells had not been removed, the British most likely would have melted them down for ammunition.[13]

Tories in Philadelphia prepared to celebrate. They polished their silver and spruced up their ballrooms. The ladies got ready to put on their party gowns. When the British marched triumphantly into Philadelphia on September 26, without a shot being fired, except in celebration, many inhabitants of the city came to their open doors and windows or poured into the streets to cheer and to welcome.

General Washington tried to dampen the celebration. He attacked the British on October 4 at Germantown, which is part of Philadelphia now but was five miles outside the city then. Suffering yet another defeat, Washington withdrew from Germantown with losses totaling more than one thousand killed, wounded or captured. British casualties were a little over five hundred.[14] Great Britain's grip on Philadelphia was secure, at least for a while. Redcoats walked boldly in the streets of the city where, scarcely more than a year earlier, rebels had dared to declare their independence. General Washington and his troops went to a place in the country to spend a long, cold winter, a place called Valley Forge.

Stephen and Mary left Philadelphia for Mount Holly about a week after the Battle of Brandywine. They went by sailboat twelve miles upstream from Philadelphia on the Delaware River to the mouth of Rancocas Creek, then up the Rancocas about twelve more miles to Mount Holly, arriving on or about September 20.[15]

For understandable reasons they were cautious about keeping detailed written records during this dangerous time in their lives. Stephen, just a jump or two ahead of the British hangman, did not want to implicate anyone who may have helped him make his getaway from

Philadelphia or might be giving him assistance in obtaining supplies for Washington's rebel army.

The house in Mount Holly that Stephen bought (it still stands and is still occupied as a private residence) is located at what is now 211 Mill Street. It was built in the 1730s and thus was about forty years old when he and Mary lived there. On the first floor there are two rooms across the front of the house and a kitchen to the rear. Two more rooms are on the second floor. The stand-up attic, which has several windows, is all one room. There is a full basement. Stairs are in the center of the house, as are the front door and outside steps leading directly to the sidewalk.

Stephen and Mary did not go to Mount Holly simply to lie low and hide out. They promptly opened a store in the basement of their house, offering for sale sundry items including tea, sugar, molasses, soap, candles and rum.[16] These were goods that had also been stocked, when available, in the Philadelphia store. Girard was resourceful in obtaining new sources of supply in New Jersey. The variety of things for sale was soon broadened to include wine, whiskey, cigars, tobacco and coffee. He began supplying American army units that General Washington sent to southern New Jersey to harass British troops, which frequently came across the Delaware River from Philadelphia on foraging expeditions.

Mary helped out in the store and was good for business. Her friendliness complemented her good looks. When soldiers came to buy provisions she gave them a warm welcome. It would have been easy for a young man, homesick and far from loved ones, to fantasize that Mary was being suggestive when she was just being nice. Some women with great beauty, knowing how attractive they are to men, keep them at a distance by being cool and aloof, but that was not Mary's style. She was just the opposite. Being sociable came naturally to her. She did not seem to mind men looking at her and wanting her. That had been a part of her life, day after day, ever since she had turned from a girl into a woman. She could not walk down a street, or into a room, without drawing admiring glances from men, glances that she could not help noticing. There was something about her, the body, the hair, the face, the smile, the whole package, that made men, especially lonely men, lust for her. This was a reality that she had become accustomed to and had learned not only to accept but to enjoy.

It was not surprising then, that Mary became a popular attraction in Stephen's store as American officers and enlisted men came there to see what supplies were available and to buy whatever might be appropriate for their military units or their personal use. So the stage was set for a notable encounter between Mary Girard, whose beauty was both irresistible and irrepressible, and Colonel Walter Stewart, a dashing young officer in Washington's army and the commander of the 13th Pennsylvania Regiment. It was camped on the outskirts of Mount Holly for five days in the fall of 1777, from November 22 to November 27, while on a roundabout route from one New Jersey town to another (from Burlington to Haddonfield) on a lookout for British foraging parties.[17]

The colonel was twenty-one and handsome. It did not take him long to learn that Mary was one of the local sights. He could have instructed junior officers to visit Girard's store and see what supplies were available that the regiment might use. However, according to a story that has come down through the centuries, the colonel decided to undertake the mission himself, accompanied by a captain.

Mary, in a jolly and friendly frame of mind, as usual, was minding the store. She had observed her nineteenth birthday on November 17 and was prettier than ever. Five months of marriage had put fresh roses in her cheeks and extra sparkle in her eyes. There was pleasant conversation between Mary and the colonel, punctuated by laughter and a bit of high-spirited joking and jesting, and a little teasing. Then he apparently was overcome by a combination of his loneliness and her nearness. He may also have interpreted, or misinterpreted, her conviviality as an invitation. Whatever the precise circumstances, he impulsively did something that he knew was not acceptable conduct for an officer and a gentleman: He took her in his arms and kissed her.

It is not known whether Mary made any serious attempt to resist the colonel's advances or whether, to the contrary, she kissed him back. There was not much time for either resistance or reciprocity because Stephen walked into the store just in time to see what appeared to be an amorous encounter in progress. Not surprisingly, he was outraged. According to Stacy Mills, a Girard employee who worked for him in his store, Mary "was a very pretty woman and Stephen was excessively jealous of her and could not bear any man to speak to her." Mills said that when "an army officer who was sojourning here had the audacity to kiss Mrs. Girard ... her husband became incensed."[18] In another account, much later, it was said that Stephen "demanded satisfaction."[19] That, evidently, was the gist of Girard's message, irrespective of what his exact words may have been, as he gave the colonel a severe tongue-lashing. Under a code of honor that prevailed in New Jersey, as in France, a husband had a right to demand an apology or a duel, or both, when his wife had been insulted or otherwise treated with disrespect. Dueling was legal in New Jersey, although it was not in Pennsylvania. When law-abiding people in Philadelphia wished to duel, it was customary for them to cross the Delaware River to New Jersey to make it legal.[20]

Even though Colonel Stewart was an army man and was in command of a regiment from Pennsylvania, these facts were irrelevant in this situation. Anyone caught in the act of kissing another man's wife in New Jersey was in trouble if the husband chose to make trouble. Stewart may not have been afraid of Girard but the colonel knew that fighting a duel in these circumstances could be a no-win situation for him regardless of the duel's outcome. Getting caught kissing someone else's wife was bad enough; killing or wounding her husband could not make things any better.

Girard was generally a man of peace in personal relationships. It might have seemed uncharacteristic of him even to think about challenging someone to a duel. Nonetheless, he had a temper when provoked, and he was never lacking in courage. In later years he would keep a pair of dueling pistols in his house.[21] Whether Girard was, or was not, thinking about challenging the officer to a duel is uncertain, and it is a question that soon became academic. There was no duel. Colonel Stewart managed to extricate himself from a sticky situation by giving an apology that was acceptable to Stephen and, of course, to Mary—the latter having been, perhaps, not terribly angry to begin with.

While the British occupied Philadelphia and the Girards lived in Mount Holly there were momentous events affecting the outcome of the war. On October 17, 1777, less than two weeks after Washington's defeat at Germantown, American forces won a dramatic encounter with the British at Saratoga in upstate New York. British General John Burgoyne, after his army of more than five thousand men had been surrounded by American forces, surrendered to General Horatio Gates. The American triumph at Saratoga convinced King Louis XVI and his advisers in the French government that it was possible for America to win the war. Benjamin Franklin, who had been sent to Paris as special envoy in late 1776, had instructions from the Second Continental Congress to negotiate a treaty that would bring France into the conflict on the side of the Americans. The victory at Saratoga gave impetus to negotiations. On February 6, 1778, France entered the war. Treaties were signed that formally made France an ally of America in its quest for independence from Great Britain. Now the British, in trying to put down the American rebellion, would have the French army and the French navy to deal with. No one in the whole wide world was happier about this than Stephen Girard, a Frenchman now well on his way to becoming an American.

It was at this point in his life—when the British held Philadelphia, when he and Mary were refugees in New Jersey, and when his native France entered the war on the side of America—that Stephen caught the spirit of the American Revolution to a greater degree than ever before, more so than when American independence had been declared in 1776. As an early biographer of Girard observed, it was while he was in Mount Holly that "he became deeply interested in the tremendous struggle for liberty with which he was surrounded .... Intense admiration for a republican form of government, which comes so naturally to a native of Bordeaux, soon implanted in his bosom a hearty belief in the future of the American nation .... Deliberation led him to determine to cast his lot with the struggling states."[22]

To keep Girard's feelings in perspective, though, his warm embrace of America's bid for liberty reflected more than patriotism or altruism or devotion to democracy. He could see profit-making opportunities on the horizon. As a French sea captain he knew, far more than most Americans, that France had a strong army and an even stronger navy and that France's entry into the war increased immensely the prospect of an American victory and American independence. That, in turn, would open the door to virtually unlimited expansion of maritime commerce in a new country in a New World with uncounted thousands of square miles awaiting settlement and development.

French entry into the war brought revisions in Britain's military strategy. It was decided that trying to hold on to Philadelphia would be too risky. If French troops landed in New Jersey and took control of that state, and if French warships blockaded entrances to Delaware Bay and Chesapeake Bay, the British army in Philadelphia could be cut off from reinforcements based in New York, and British ships in Delaware Bay and Chesapeake Bay could be bottled up.

When British occupation forces pulled out of Philadelphia in June of 1778, three thousand American civilians left with them. They included most of the Tories, men and women, who had welcomed the British troops with open arms, had entertained them in their homes, and had collaborated with them in governing the city for nine months. The British, grateful for the good times they had enjoyed with British sympathizers, took them aboard British ships in the Delaware River and, when Philadelphia was evacuated, transported them to sanctuary in British-controlled New York. Many of the Tories who made their getaway from Philadelphia in this manner would eventually conclude that it would never be safe for them to return. They would request and receive passage to England, where they would spend the remainder of their lives.

Some of the British occupation forces were taken from Philadelphia to New York on ships, but most of them, fifteen thousand men, were ferried across the Delaware River for a march through New Jersey. The last contingent of British soldiers left Philadelphia on June 18, 1778. Before the day was over, American troops were back in the city. Martial law was imposed until the end of the month to allow time for orderly restoration of civilian government. Some of the residents who had given aid and comfort to the British, and had not departed with them, were beaten by mobs before being taken into protective custody by American troops. When civilian government was restored, trials would be held for those who had been accused of collaborating with the enemy. Some would be tried for treason, some for lesser charges. Two would be convicted of treason and would be hanged.[23]

After it had evacuated Philadelphia by crossing the Delaware River to New Jersey, the bulk of the British occupation force, fifteen thousand strong, began marching east. It was a formidable array. Keeping track of the huge army's whereabouts when it was on the march was not difficult. Fifteen thousand soldiers, with equipment, covered twelve miles of road from the first man to the last. The clouds of dust they kicked up could be seen for miles, heralding the approach of the men long before they came into view. It soon became apparent that this powerful British military force was heading toward, of all places, Mount Holly.

CHAPTER 6

A Glorious Victory, A Shattering Tragedy
1778-1785

Love is fragile. Enjoy it while you can.

WHEN STEPHEN AND MARY had learned in early June of 1778 that, as a consequence of France entering the war, British evacuation of Philadelphia was imminent, the young couple were elated. It appeared that, in their second year of marriage, they were out of danger and could soon return to Water Street, where Stephen could go back into business as a merchant and maritime trader. The war was still on, with the outcome undecided, but American morale had received a big boost when France joined the fray. Stephen and Mary, besides having each other, seemed to have life by the tail. They had every reason to believe their happiness was forever.

Then, suddenly, a new crisis loomed as the British withdrawal began and it became apparent that a massive enemy force was going to be in the vicinity of Mount Holly. This was evident several days before the last of the British pulled out of Philadelphia on June 18. As British soldiers came across the Delaware by the thousands in ships and boats, large and small, day after day, and encamped on the New Jersey side of the river, it could be ascertained from the locations of the camps that the troops were preparing to move eastward, away from the river and toward Mount Holly, instead of in a somewhat northerly direction along the river. General Washington had demonstrated, on Christmas night in 1776, that he was good at transporting troops across the Delaware under cover of darkness. By moving away from the river after the withdrawal from Philadelphia, the British army would reduce the chances of a surprise interception by American troops.

Inhabitants of Mount Holly knew by the middle of June that they could expect the arrival of British troops very soon, most likely within four or five days. There was no way of knowing whether the soldiers would stay a while or just pass through. In either case the Girards would need to take precautions, just as they had done nine months earlier when they had fled from Philadelphia. As George DeCou, an authority on the history of Mount Holly, has said: "It would be interesting to know where the Girards stayed when the British occupied Mount Holly."[1] No one knows, today, where the Girards went. They were careful to leave no records that would give a clue to their whereabouts. Records—or, rather, lack of records—indicate the Girards did no business in their store after June 16. They probably left Mount Holly on June 17, perhaps to stay temporarily in some other New Jersey town until enemy troops were out of the area. Another possibility is that Stephen and Mary boarded a sailboat and traveled several miles on the Rancocas to some secluded and safe spot, remaining there until the British had passed.

The British arrived in Mount Holly on June 20. The fifteen thousand troops camped in and near the town for two nights, departing on June 22 en route to New York. General Clinton and other high-ranking officers, including General Charles Cornwallis, commandeered a house owned by Isaac Hazlehurst to serve as headquarters during their stay in Mount Holly. It was the same Hazlehurst who had sold another house to Girard.

There is no indication that the British knew about the Girards having a house and a store in Mount Holly and providing supplies for American troops. If the British did know, they must have been too busy with other matters to look for the Girards and their place of business. The principal target of the British in Mount Holly was an iron works. It was destroyed. There was not much time during the brief occupation to reconnoiter the town in search of other places to sack or loot.

A bridge across Rancocas Creek near Mount Holly had been damaged beyond repair by Americans before the British arrived. While British soldiers were building a new bridge they had to fight off attackers. Five Americans gave their lives in this delaying action. Two were captured. Units from Washington's army dogged the British during their entire flight across New Jersey. Bridges were destroyed on routes the British might take. Trees were cut down to block roads. There were frequent skirmishes between pursuing Americans and British rear guards. By the time Clinton's harried army reached Freehold on June 26, pursuing Americans with Washington in command were hot on the British heels. The Battle of Monmouth was fought near Freehold on June 28. The outcome was indecisive, with neither side able to claim clear victory, but the British had all the fighting they wanted. On the night of the 28th they began a retreat toward Sandy Hook, a sliver of New Jersey jutting into the entrance to New York harbor. British ships ferried the weary troops to safety in New York. Crossing New Jersey had been a nightmarish experience.

On July 11 a large fleet of the French navy arrived off Sandy Hook. If Clinton and his army had reached the Hook twelve days later than they did, they could have been blown out of the water trying to reach New York. The war might have ended then and there.

The Girards were back in Philadelphia soon after the British evacuation. Stephen went alone at first to find a place for them to live. He had given up their rented quarters when they left the city, not knowing how long the British occupation would last. It was safe for Mary to stay in Mount Holly for a while without Stephen now that the British were gone. She had servants and was on good terms with neighbors. Soon Stephen and Mary were together again in Philadelphia, in rented space he had found for them. They occupied a building ideally located to serve as both a residence and a place of business. It was on Water Street in the first block north of Market Street. Cargo space could be rented on nearby wharves as needed. With the worst of the war behind them, as far as they, personally, were concerned, Stephen and Mary were ready to settle down.

The British navy still had a blockade, of sorts, off the Atlantic coast, but the blockade was not nearly as effective with France in the war. French warships were out there too, as far north as New England and as far south as the Caribbean. American cargo ships had some protection now. So, Girard and other merchants could send and receive goods by sea with a fairly good chance of profit despite war-time risks.

There was another development in Stephen's favor. His younger brother, John, had become a maritime merchant at Cap-Francais on the northern coast of St-Domingue, still under control of France, in the West Indies. It was from Cap-Francais that Stephen had sailed on the voyage when he unexpectedly wound up in Philadelphia in 1776. With John Girard in a French port and Stephen Girard in an American port, and with France and America allied in the war, there were opportunities for lively trading. Sugar, molasses, rum and coffee, among other items from St-Domingue, were in heavy demand in America. Goods from America, including beef, flour, furniture, tools and many other agricultural and hand-crafted products, had ready buyers in St-Domingue. Tobacco and cotton could be added to cargoes with stops in Virginia and South Carolina.

Thus in the summer of 1778, as in the summer of 1777, Stephen enjoyed the hectic but stimulating life of a Philadelphia merchant, buying, selling and shipping maritime cargoes shrewdly and profitably. This year he did not have to flee to New Jersey to avoid an occupying British army. He could stay in Philadelphia, a city he had come to regard with affection. As a Frenchman in business in America, with an American wife, he thought of himself increasingly as an American. The conversion of Stephen from Frenchman to American was completed with a swiftness that was remarkable considering that, when he had last sailed from France in 1774, he had no intention of even going to America, much less living there. Meeting and marrying Mary had a lot to do with his rapid Americanization.

On October 27, 1778, he became an American formally and officially. President Judge Edward Shippen of the Philadelphia Court of Common Pleas certified that "Stephen Girard of the City of Philadelphia, merchant ... subscribed the oath of allegiance and fidelity to the State of Pennsylvania."[2] That was as close as anyone could come to being an American at that time. Americans were citizens of their respective states, which were engaged collectively in a war for independence. The Articles of Confederation, which created an interim national government, bridging the gap between the Revolution and the Constitution, would not go into effect until 1781. The Constitution of the United States of America, which would be adopted in 1787 and ratified in 1788, would not become fully operational until Washington was inaugurated as the first president in 1789. So Stephen Girard cast his lot with America, becoming a citizen, several years before it was certain there would be a United States of America and more than a decade before there would be a duly constituted and fully functioning federal government.

Stephen saw America for what it was: a land of opportunity. He also saw Mary for what she was: a part of his American dream. In a poignant letter to his father in France a few months after becoming an American citizen, Stephen was as straightforward as a son could be: "I have taken a wife who is without fortune, it is true, but whom I love and with whom I am living very happily."[3] So Stephen Girard, American, was still a happy man, still a man in love, more than a year and a half after he had married Mary. For a long time he had not been quite sure what he wanted in life, but he knew when he had found it. What Stephen could not know and could not foresee, even with his one good eye fixed firmly on the future, was that tragedy lurked ahead. It would be heart-rending and gut-wrenching tragedy. He could not have imagined, nor could Mary, when he held her in his arms, how short-lived their bliss together would be.

The Pennsylvania Assembly complicated matters for Stephen in December of 1778 by passing a law that cast doubts about the validity of his American citizenship. He had become an American (and a Pennsylvanian) under provisions of a law enacted by the Assembly in April of 1778 that were much to his liking. They offered incentives for subscribing to an oath of allegiance to Pennsylvania, such as a preferential rate when paying property taxes and a right to file suits in civil courts (to collect unpaid debts, for example). The wording of the oath of allegiance was changed in the law passed in December. That law said anyone who had become a citizen of Pennsylvania on or after June 1, 1778, had to subscribe to the new oath to retain rights and privileges of citizenship. Stephen, bowing to this early manifestation of bureaucratic red tape, subscribed to the new oath on August 2, 1779.

Back in Bordeaux there was no joy when merchants there learned that Girard had become an American. He still had not paid debts owed since 1774. The unpaid obligations had preyed on his mind, but not enough to cause him to lose any sleep. "I have not forgotten the debt I contracted at Bordeaux," Stephen said in a letter to his father, "and intend to do all I can, even stint myself if necessary, to make good my engagements as soon as the risks of the sea are a little less dangerous."[4] That was a polite way of putting his creditors in Bordeaux on hold until after the war. The lingering debt was another reason, besides his marriage to Mary, that Stephen had no desire to return to France. As long as he stayed in America he was out of the reach of unpaid merchants in Bordeaux.

Stephen and his father wrote letters to each other on a fairly regular basis although not with great frequency, usually several times a year, and maintained a cordial relationship. Sailing time between Philadelphia and Bordeaux in either direction was normally two months or close to it, and sometimes much longer. It was rare to cross the North Atlantic at any time of year without encountering two or three storms, at the very least. When Stephen and Pierre had questions in their letters, the waiting time for answers was a minimum of four months. Pierre kept other members of the Girard family in France informed about Stephen, so he did not need to write separate letters to all of his brothers and sisters and other relatives when there was significant news to report.

Stephen and his brother John, after the latter established a maritime trade business in St-Domingue, became very close. They wrote to each other often, several times a week on occasion, discussing mostly the details of cargoes sent and received, the prices of items bought and sold, and general market conditions. Stephen and John interlaced their business letters with comments about their personal affairs. They had disagreements and quarrels every now and then, but there was warm brotherly affection that flowed both ways.

Stephen became pleasantly accustomed to conducting maritime trade while keeping his feet comfortably on dry land. He discovered that it was quite enjoyable to leave the sailing to others, as he tallied up his profits in his counting-house. When the sun set, he no longer had to pass the hours on a rolling deck, marveling at the moon and the stars and the infinite universe, as he had done as a younger man. Now he had a warm bed and he had Mary. Meanwhile, in his newly adopted country, there was a war still to be waged. There was independence still to be won. Stephen helped the American cause by sending ships through the British blockade and bringing in supplies for American and allied troops. He took risks and he took profits. He had multiple motivations in advancing the war effort of his newly adopted country. His patriotism was genuine and its roots went deeper every day in the sense that he wanted America to win the war against Great Britain and become an independent country. Simultaneously he wanted to turn a profit on every cargo, and he looked forward to a time when there would be more cargoes and bigger profits in an America that was free of British domination and at peace with the world. America's national interest and Girard's self-interest blended well.

Polish patriots, especially notable among them were Casimir Pulaski and Thaddeus Kosciusko, came across the Atlantic to join General Washington and his army in their fight for freedom. General Pulaski was in Philadelphia in 1778 organizing a corps of cavalry and infantry known as the Pulaski Legion. Girard provided supplies for the legion, as he did for other military units. Two officers on Pulaski's staff, Captain Joseph Baldesqui and Captain Paul Bentalou, became friends of Girard and, later, were associated with him in business.

In 1777 Girard had been part owner of a brig that was seized by the British when they occupied Philadelphia. In 1778 and part of 1779 the cargoes he bought and sold were transported in ships owned by others while he conserved and accumulated capital. In late 1779 he began investing in ships again. He sought to increase his profits by moving some of his goods on vessels owned at least in part by himself. He thereby established a pattern that would continue for the rest of his life. He would make millions in maritime trade by being flexible, resourceful and opportunistic, by constantly buying and selling ships (or fractional interests in ships), building ships, leasing ships and renting cargo space on ships he did not own. He put his eggs in many baskets. He maintained a healthy mix of calculated risk and thoughtful prudence.

There was a greater potential for profit when he owned ships as well as cargoes, but there also was a greater potential for loss if ships he owned encountered a storm, an attack by pirates or an act of war.

Girard suffered many reverses, but he was careful not to over-extend himself financially. With years of sailing experience, he was a good judge of ships and their seaworthiness. He bought used vessels at fair (sometimes bargain) prices and sold them (often after just a voyage or two) while they still had good market value. In his early years, especially, he avoided owning too many ships at one time, frequently selling one before buying another and thus limiting his total investment in ships while keeping cash available for purchase of cargoes.

Girard has been called a Midas, but that is a misleading analogy.[5] Not everything he touched turned to gold. Far from it. He built his solvency, and then his fortune, step by step in a painstaking fashion. When things went sour he rolled with the punches and pushed on. He worked and he struggled, inching forward and overcoming adversity. It was not a smooth haul. He had to use a ratchet on his way to prosperity.

He bought an interest in a schooner in late 1779 that was wrecked on the coast of Virginia in early 1780. He became part owner of another schooner that sailed from Philadelphia in April of 1780 but was captured by privateers in the West Indies two months later. Two vessels that he partly owned in 1781 were sold the same year, each after only about three months of service. In May of 1783 he became sole owner of a schooner and named it *Mary* in honor of his wife; it was wrecked on the coast of Maryland three months later.

A superstitious person might have seen the wreck of the *Mary* as an ominous sign. Mary Girard, figuratively speaking, soon would go aground also: on the shoals of an incurable illness.

During the years 1779 to 1781, with the Revolutionary War in climactic stages, Stephen sent some of his ships on privateering missions along the Atlantic coast. Guns were mounted on decks, turning cargo ships into fighting ships. It was legal in America, as in most countries in the eighteenth century, to be a privateer in war-time. Any merchant ship flying the British flag was fair game for American privateers during the Revolutionary War. So was any ship under any flag if the vessel was carrying supplies for British troops or Hessian mercenaries. Ships and cargoes could be taken as prizes by privateers and, with approval of an admiralty court, sold for whatever they would bring. Officers and crews of privateers shared in the proceeds.[6]

Girard's ships had impressive success in privateering, although one of them was buffeted by an Atlantic storm and severely damaged. Among prizes taken were a schooner, a sloop and a yawl. The schooner, while awaiting a decision by an admiralty court in Baltimore, played an important role in the war, transporting part of Washington's army down the Chesapeake Bay en route to the Battle of Yorktown.

Profitable cargoes captured by Girard's privateers included corn and oats, which would have been provisions for the British army in Yorktown if they had not been intercepted. Privateering missions by Girard's ships included raids on coastal areas of the Chesapeake Bay that resulted in seizure of black slaves owned by Tories. An admiralty court in Baltimore decreed that the slaves had to be returned to their owners, who could not be arbitrarily deprived of their property just because they were British sympathizers.[7]

Meanwhile, assistance of the French proved decisive in America's ultimate triumph over the British. It was a French nobleman serving in the American army, General Lafayette, who persuaded a French king, Louis XVI, to send French troops and French ships to America in sufficient numbers to overwhelm the British. It was a French admiral, Francois De Grass, who made the most crucial decision of the war—to attack the British at Yorktown rather than at New York. And it was the defeat of a British naval force by a French fleet off the coast of Virginia that paved the way for the British surrender at Yorktown on October 19, 1781.

During the first days of September in 1781 two thousand American troops and four thousand French troops under the command of General Washington and French General Jean Rochambeau marched through Philadelphia en route from White Plains, New York, to Yorktown for the last battle of the war. The soldiers and their officers passed in review before members of the Second Continental Congress and other dignitaries assembled at Independence Hall. Thousands of spectators lined the streets for what amounted to a parade as the troops, not yet at the halfway point of their long journey into battle, enjoyed the cheers and the applause of the citizenry. Stephen and Mary, witnessing the American and French troops marching together, comrades in arms, had convincing evidence that the American alliance with

France was not just a piece of paper but had decisive meaning in a crucial time.

On September 5, after the allied army had passed through Philadelphia, a courier arrived in the city with news that a French naval force had reached Chesapeake Bay, sealing off the only escape route for the British troops in Yorktown, where they were now trapped. People poured out of their homes and into the streets of Philadelphia to celebrate. Many of the celebrants shouted repeatedly, "Long live Louis XVI."[8] The Girards, Stephen especially, savored the moment, enjoying more evidence that the alliance between his native France and his adopted America was working. Louis XVI would not, of course, have the long life that grateful Philadelphians wished for him. In the French Revolution he was perceived as a foe, not a friend, of liberty.

It was Lafayette who summed up most succinctly the significance of the British surrender at Yorktown when he said in a message to Paris: "The play is over."[9] Another message, from General Washington, officially notifying the Second Continental Congress of the British surrender at Yorktown, was delivered by one of his aides, Lieutenant Colonel Tench Tilghman. He arrived in Philadelphia a little before three o'clock in the morning on October 24. A night watchman hastily made his rounds, waking the town and telling the people. The Liberty Bell rang out atop Independence Hall. Artillery roared ceremonial salutes to victory. Fireworks blazed in the sky. There was celebration in the streets before dawn and after.[10]

For Stephen and Mary Girard, it was a joyous occasion filled with hope for better times in an era of peace. With the war, and all the uncertainty that went with it, now safely behind them, this was the first day of the rest of their lives. The end of the war brought new opportunities to make money in maritime trade. Peacetime conditions reduced risks and released pent-up demands for all manner of goods that had been in short supply or entirely unavailable during the war. In August of 1783 Girard's brother, John, accompanied a cargo from St-Domingue to Philadelphia and was a guest of Stephen in his home for several months. The visit gave them a chance to talk about current and future business in a leisurely manner, face to face, which was far more satisfactory than communicating with letters. Stephen was thirty-three and John was thirty-two. Prospects seemed bright. They had every reason to be bullish about their chances for prosperous and happy lives.

John was accompanied by his black slave, Hannah, who was in her twenties. She had a daughter, Rosette, who also made the trip to Philadelphia. The child had light skin and could easily have passed for white. Her facial features bore striking resemblance to those of John. He was her father. Hannah was not just an ordinary slave. She had been purchased specifically for bedroom duty, to gratify John sexually. In St-Domingue, and wherever else in the New World that there was slavery, legal status followed the mother; hence a child of a female slave was a slave even if the father was not.

While visiting his brother in Philadelphia during that summer and autumn of 1783 John had more on his mind than maritime business. He wanted a white woman to replace Hannah. A pleasant and rewarding relationship developed with an attractive nineteen-year-old indentured servant from Ireland, Eleanor McMullin. John bought her indenture, setting her free, and took her back to St-Domingue as his mistress. They did not want Hannah tagging along, for understandable reasons, so John gave her to Stephen. Rosette also stayed in Philadelphia, to be with her mother.

Stephen knew, of course, that Hannah had performed in bed for her master. After she became Stephen's slave she was available to him if he wanted her. There is no evidence that he ever did, but there is no evidence to the contrary either. They would have a long relationship as master and slave, lasting for the rest of Stephen's life. She would be a thread of continuity through almost half a century of change. She would be with him, living in the same house with him, in good times and bad. She would see mistresses come and go. She would be at his bedside when he died. She would be the first person mentioned in his will.

Pennsylvania in 1780 ostensibly had become the first state to abolish slavery. However, as Stephen's long ownership of Hannah demonstrated, the abolition law had limited application and was riddled with loopholes. Pennsylvania's slave population was about six thousand in 1780.[11] The number diminished after that, but there were slaves in Pennsylvania well into the nineteenth century. Principal beneficiaries of the 1780 law supposedly were babies born to slaves in Pennsylvania after the law was enacted. They could not be held in slavery more than twenty-eight years, the 1780 law said, but it was not enforceable in other states. A plantation owner in the South who purchased slaves born in Pennsylvania was not legally required, nor morally obligated, to set them free when they reached the age of twenty-eight. They could remain in slavery.

Indeed, the 1780 abolition law did not eradicate pro-slavery senti-ment in Pennsylvania. That sentiment remained strong throughout Stephen Girard's lifetime and long after. This was especially true among Pennsylvanians who lived near the Mason-Dixon Line, the state's southern boundary. Maryland and Delaware, both bordering on Penn-sylvania, were slave states, even though they did not secede from the Union in the Civil War. Philadelphia is only twenty miles from the Delaware state line. In 1847 Pennsylvania would enact a law prohib-iting imprisonment of fugitive slaves, but there would be widespread opposition to the law and it would be repealed.[12] Many residents of Pennsylvania would be outspoken in their support of southern states after they seceded. Confederate sympathizers in Philadelphia, when offering toasts to "The President" at social gatherings during the Civil War, would speak in praise of Jefferson Davis, not Abraham Lincoln.[13]

So Stephen Girard, in his time and in his place, had no reason to feel embarrassed or uncomfortable about being a slaveowner. Quakers, who advocated abolition, were a declining political force in Philadel-phia and throughout Pennsylvania during all of the decades that Stephen lived in that city and in that state. Rosette, however, created big problems for Stephen after John returned to St-Domingue. Mary could not help noticing the Girard family resemblance in Rosette's facial features. She not only looked like her father, John Girard; she also looked like her uncle, Stephen Girard. Visitors to the Girard residence in Philadelphia, noting that Rosette resembled Stephen, could be expected to assume that she was his daughter. That assumption quite naturally would lead to another assumption, namely that there had been, and perhaps still was, a sexual relationship between Stephen and Rosette's mother Hannah.

The situation did not bother Stephen at first—he did not much care what people thought—but Mary grew uneasy, and her uneasiness soon turned to anger. Even if people were too polite to say anything about

Rosette, her resemblance to Stephen was unmistakable. Trying to explain that Rosette's father was not Stephen but Stephen's brother could be both frustrating and futile. Bemused guests might accept the explanation as a matter of courtesy, but they would exchange knowing nods of skepticism.

Mary finally found the situation intolerable and insisted that Stephen send Rosette back to St-Domingue. He complied with his wife's wishes, but John Girard, enjoying the companionship of his mistress, was not happy when he was told he would have to take his daughter back. John suggested that Stephen give Rosette her freedom before she left Philadelphia, which he did. This would make it easier for John to send the girl out on her own as soon as she was old enough to fend for herself. Stephen summed up the matter in a letter to John in the summer of 1784: "Following your wish I have given Rosette her freedom. She is a child of excellent character, and I assure you that I would have kept her here with great pleasure if Madame had not taken the idea that she resembles me. Moreover, the prejudices of this country added to that, convinces me that she will be better nearer you, which forces me to send her back to you on the brig, taking with her the freedom papers, according to the laws and customs of Pennsylvania."[14] There is no record of what Hannah's views were, or whether she was consulted, regarding her daughter's return to St-Domingue as a free person while she (Hannah) remained in Philadelphia as a slave.

It was in the early 1780s, after the end of the Revolutionary War in 1781, that Stephen Girard really started to come into his own as a businessman, emerging as a maritime merchant of extraordinary industry and talent. He was not yet wealthy, nor was success assured, but his vigor and dedication to detail were now coming to the fore more impressively than at any time previously. There was no magic formula in his striving to get ahead. He worked long and he worked hard. He did not waste time in chitchat. He was up early, before many of his competitors, and took delight in getting the jump on them.

His early-to-rise habits were well described by a contemporary Philadelphian, Abraham Ritter: "Girard, true to the proverb, taking daylight at its dawn, would slip from his gate to the wharf's edge, and sweep the Delaware with the besom of his powerful eye. An arrival at hand, or afar off, telegraphed itself to his vision, and fired his impulse to board the object of his search; and forthwith a 'wherry,' or a 'bateau,' laid alongside; and whilst his neighbors were dreaming of bargain and sale, he was making himself master of the market by his *coup de main*."[15]

Stephen Simpson, a long-time employee of Girard, made these observations: "He did not, at first, find it so easy to make money, as people sometimes imagine .... One of the most singular traits in the character of Stephen Girard" was that, "whatever he did, he performed well, and would never slight what he undertook."[16] Girard reached a new plateau as a maritime merchant on April 17, 1784, when a brig of two hundred tons, the *Deux Freres* (Two Brothers), was launched. He had bought and sold many ships, or fractional interests in ships, but this marked the first time he had gone to a shipbuilder and put in an order. Construction started in the summer of 1783 at a shipyard in Kensington, now a part of Philadelphia but more than a mile upstream from the city at that time. The vessel cost four thousand dollars, an amount equal to profits of just two or three routine round trips to the West Indies. So all was going well for Stephen Girard, a shining star on the rise, enjoying the sweet taste of prosperity.

Then....wham!....tragedy struck early in 1785. It struck suddenly and devastatingly. Mary went insane.

Occasionally, at first, and then more frequently, she had spells of irrational behavior such as sudden mood changes followed by tantrums. She would be jolly one minute and sullen the next. Then she would start screaming. She would smash dishes and topple furniture. If she was outdoors when a seizure came on her, she might bang her head repeatedly against a tree. Sometimes she would stay up all night shrieking and thumping on anything that would make noise. Her condition, frightful from the start, swiftly deteriorated. Doctors eventually pronounced her not only insane but incurable.[17] Mary was only twenty-six when the initial signs of insanity surfaced. She and Stephen had been married less than eight years. All their hopes and all their dreams came crashing down.

CHAPTER 7

A Mistress Replaces a Wife
1785-1793

*When circumstances force a man to choose between
being faithful and being satisfied, he may find
that flesh is stronger than fidelity.*

MARY GIRARD'S insanity left Stephen not only devastated but in a quandary. He did not know how to deal with his wife's illness, and he could not get much help from doctors. In the eighteenth century there was widespread ignorance about insanity. For many years in early America it was the prevailing view among physicians, especially among those who supposedly had expertise in troubles of the mind, that having too much sexual intercourse was a major cause of insanity.[1] A common form of "treatment" for the insane was to keep them chained in a cellar or an attic.

Stephen steadfastly refused to subject Mary to such indignity. When her condition deteriorated to the point where it was no longer pleasurable or tolerable to share a bed with her, he gave her a room of her own.

Doctors, for all their ignorance about insanity, definitely knew it when they saw it. Mary's patterns of insane behavior, the mood changes, the tantrums, the shrieking, were unmistakable. Stephen's anguish over the condition of Mary was conveyed vividly in letters to his brother in Cap-Francais in 1785. In February Stephen wrote to John: "I fear that I have lost forever the peace which a certain success should procure for life in this world."[2] In May: "Madame continues in the same state ... but fortunately for me I can accept this uncomfortable life and flatter myself that I shall be philosophical enough to overcome all these difficulties which have made me fear that something more sad might follow."[3] In June: "Madame continues always in the same state. I fear that this malady will never be cured as long as she lives. We can only have patience and realize that no one can live in this world without finding some troubles."[4] In July there was a short-lived turn for the better: "Madame continues to recover. She charged me to make a thousand compliments to you for her."[5] In August optimism was fading: "My wife is better but nevertheless she gives me a great deal of trouble. I wanted to send her by the brig [hoping a change of scenery would help her], but having thought of the care and anxiety which she might give you, and also that it might not be easy to persuade her to go, I have thought it prudent to keep her here. It is only right that I should keep all this trouble to myself alone. Adieu, dear friend, be more fortunate than I."[6]

Also in August Stephen commented on Mary's condition in a letter to another business associate in Cap-Francais: "Some time ago I flattered myself that my wife was getting better, but unfortunately for our mutual peace, the illness of this virtuous woman has so unsettled my life it begins to interfere with my business. I can only hope that Providence may end a life so unhappy."[7] Stephen's worst fears about Mary's condition were confirmed in the fall of 1785. He had her admitted to Pennsylvania Hospital in Philadelphia in September and, after she was diagnosed as insane, brought her home in November. Although crushed by the tragic truth, he stubbornly refused at first to face up to it.

Instead of having Mary committed to the section for the insane at Pennsylvania Hospital on a permanent basis in 1785, as he might reasonably have done, Stephen kept clinging to the hope that she might get better in less restrictive surroundings. He showed great fortitude but, in the circumstances, his optimism was unrealistic. After her two-month stay in the hospital Mary was sent by Stephen to their house in Mount Holly, New Jersey, for a number of extended visits over a period of several years. It was the same house in which they had found refuge, and had operated a store, during the British occupation of Philadelphia in the Revolutionary War. Stephen hoped the restful setting on the five-acre tract, offering open spaces, a change of scenery and respite from the hustle and bustle of a congested city, would make her feel better.

Among those who cared for Mary in Mount Holly, at Stephen's expense, were her mother and a sister. Also providing care, on some occasions, were Stephen's friend and former business associate, Isaac Hazlehurst, and his wife. Isaac still owned a house in Mount Holly, not far from Stephen's house. Mary also stayed for a while at the Cloisters, a community maintained by a German religious society in Ephrata, Pennsylvania. Stephen thought that the peace and quiet at the retreat in Lancaster County might somehow improve her condition.

By early 1787, after Mary had been insane for two years, it had become painfully clear to Stephen that their marriage was over and done with, at least in a personal and intimate sense, even though he and Mary remained husband and wife legally. They occupied separate bedrooms when she was in their home on Water Street, which was not often, with Mary now spending much of her time in Mount Holly. Strong doses of opium had been prescribed by a physician to calm her down when she started screaming and throwing things or became unruly in other ways. The sedation made her much easier to manage. Meanwhile, Stephen was lonely. In almost eight years of marital delight with Mary he had become accustomed to all that a beautiful woman could offer. He had been thirty-four when insanity struck her down, a man in the prime of life. He could not stop desire as one might turn off a spigot. He was, as a scholar of a later time would call him, "a very human human being."[8]

Stephen had two choices. He could practice self-denial and self-control, staying faithful to a wife who had lost her mind, was absent much of the time, and was no longer capable of loving him rationally and tenderly. Or he could find another woman.

He chose the latter.

In April of 1787 he banished nighttime loneliness by hiring eighteen-year-old Sally Bickham, a Quaker and a seamstress, to be his live-in housekeeper and mistress.

Being a mistress in the eighteenth century was an honorable occupation. It was a prestigious one, too, if the man to be served had stature and substance. In a time when educational and employment opportunities for women were severely limited, a job as a mistress, especially on a full-time basis in a man's home—was highly prized. Even though Sally was hired in a dual capacity as housekeeper and mistress, she was first and foremost a mistress. She knew from the outset that she would not do housework. There were servants to do that. She would supervise them. Her principal duties were to entertain and satisfy Stephen in the bed they would share.

Her real name was Sarah Bickham, but everyone who knew her on a first-name basis called her Sally. She was eighteen years younger than Stephen and just half his age when he, at thirty-six, employed her. She was beautiful by any fair standard of beauty, not as beautiful as Mary had been, but extremely attractive nonetheless.

Stephen, justifiably proud of Sally, would eventually engage an artist to paint her portrait, something he had never done for Mary. The portrait, painted by Nicolas Vincent Boudet in 1794 for a fee of forty dollars, has survived through the centuries.[9] It shows Sally when she was twenty-five years old and delightfully mature. Taking into account that there may be some flattery courtesy of the painter, it nonetheless portrays a woman who was undeniably lovely. She has a discreetly inviting expression. The mouth is small and the lips are tight, yet there is an unmistakable hint of a smile. The end of a well-proportioned nose does not quite tip upward but almost does. The brown eyes are direct and piercing. Curly auburn hair crowns the head, covers the ears, plays at the edges of a graceful neck and frames the face, quietly complementing and accenting without intruding.

Stephen and Sally had become acquainted through her work as a seamstress. Eighteenth century seamstresses made and repaired clothes for men as well as for women. Stephen, in a letter to his brother John, called Sally a "tailoress," which was another word for seamstress.[10]

In the beginning, Stephen underestimated Sally. In a letter to John, soon after acquiring Sally, Stephen spoke of her in a condescending and almost insulting manner. He told him that he was keeping her for amusement "at small expense and when I have the leisure for it."[11]

She turned out to be much more than merely amusing. He was captivated by her charms. She made him fall in love with her. After that, her influence over him steadily grew. She told him what she needed for the house and the colors she wanted, such as pink blankets for their bed, and he bought them or gave her the money to buy them.

She kept the servants busy and respectful, which pleased Stephen, and he granted her requests for more of them.

She gently prodded him to dress neatly and saw to it that his clothes were in good repair. She watched over his health and general well-being, making sure he was properly attired when he went out in inclement weather. She did more than love him, she mothered him. She became, for all intents and purposes, a surrogate wife.

Meanwhile, the insanity of Mary was showing no signs of abating, and Stephen's attitude toward her was becoming increasingly sour, even vitriolic. In a letter to his brother John in 1787 Stephen lamented "having been so foolish as to marry this unfortunate vixen .... I treat her properly but at the same time despise her as much as it is possible to despise anyone .... I hate her like the devil and note with pleasure that this feeling increases from day to day."[12] Those were harsh things for a man to say about a woman who had given him so much. One of the horrors of insanity is the way it affects the sane.

While the personal life of Stephen was in upheaval because of Mary's condition, and while he was enjoying consolation in the arms of Sally, other things of consequence were happening. Foremost among them were the formal creation of the United States of America and the subsequent selection of Philadelphia as the capital of the new nation, a role it would play for ten years, from 1790 to 1800. The Constitutional Convention, at Independence Hall, began its work on May 25, 1787, about the time that, a little over half a mile away, Stephen was starting to fall in love with Sally. The convention completed its business in less than four months, on September 17. Ratification by at least nine states was required to make the Constitution operable. New Hampshire was the ninth state to ratify, on June 21, 1788. Washington was inaugurated as the first president of the United States on April 30, 1789, in New York, where the First Congress had already begun its first session.

On December 6, 1790, after Philadelphia had become the nation's capital, Congress convened in Congress Hall, about thirty yards west of Independence Hall. President Washington, with Martha, (and, later, President John Adams, with Abigail) lived in a house one block north of Congress Hall, on Market Street. Stephen and Sally, living on Water

Street, were six blocks from the president's home and seven blocks from Congress Hall. They could not walk very far in the city, when it was the capital of the United States, without encountering people who had powerful roles in the government of the new country.

No one in the federal government, when setting up shop in Philadelphia in 1790—not President Washington, not Vice President Adams, not Secretary of State Thomas Jefferson, not Secretary of the Treasury Alexander Hamilton, not Congressman James Madison— could have guessed that the one-eyed Water Street merchant with a French accent would someday have the fattest wallet in America. If they had known, they surely would have hastened to make his acquaintance and invite him to lunch.

In the years that America was adopting and ratifying a constitution and becoming a country, Girard was taking large strides in maritime trade despite the distractions of Mary's illness and her replacement by Sally as a bedtime companion. In December of 1787, the same month that the first states were ratifying the constitution, Girard began his first venture into the China trade. He and sixteen other Philadelphia investors financed the first voyage to China by a ship built in Philadelphia.[13] This was a straw in the wind, foreshadowing Girard's emergence as a world trader on a grand scale. He had started out trading mostly with the West Indies. From this point on, his perspective was increasingly global.

Also in December of 1787 Girard went to sea again, for the first time in more than a decade, for the first time since shortly before he had married Mary. On December 7, the same day that Delaware became the first state to ratify the constitution, he sailed out of Philadelphia as the captain of a brig he owned, *Deux Amis* (Two Friends).[14] He was bound for Marseilles.

The round-trip voyages to France and then back to America marked the last time Girard captained a ship. The stop in Marseilles would be the last time he set foot in the country of his birth. As America was becoming a nation, Girard was becoming an American more firmly than ever, not just an American citizen but an American in thought and spirit and enthusiasm.

His main purpose in going to sea again was not to get away from

America but to get away from his personal trials and tribulations. Mary was occasionally brought back from Mount Holly so that Stephen could see for himself how she was doing and so that doctors in the city could examine and observe her and perhaps prescribe changes in treatment or medicine. The visits also gave respite to Mary's mother and others who cared for her in New Jersey. Sally and Stephen and their servants provided care for Mary when she was in the house on Water Street. It was not easy. She continued to shriek in the night. She continued to have tantrums and smash dishes. Heavy doses of opium-based medicine would calm her down or put her to sleep temporarily but not continually.

Stephen, in correspondence with his brother John, had talked about going to sea for more than a year before the voyage began. It became feasible when John agreed to come to Philadelphia to oversee Stephen's business while he was away. The two brothers, who had been working cooperatively as maritime merchants for many years, had a partnership arrangement by this time. During Stephen's absence from Philadelphia in late 1787 and most of 1788, more than seven months altogether, Mary stayed in Mount Holly. Sally lived in a house in Philadelphia that Stephen rented for her, and John Girard and his mistress Eleanor McMullin occupied the Girard residence on Water Street.

Accompanying John and Eleanor on their trip to Philadelphia from St-Domingue was Rosette, John's daughter. She also stayed at the Girard residence on Water Street and visited with her mother, Hannah, John's former slave who was now Stephen's slave. It was a rather odd family reunion, to say the least. However, John apparently was not embarrassed to be under the same roof with his current mistress and his former slave who had also been his bed partner. John, by this time, had lived nearly ten years in St-Domingue, where the French community was inclined to be tolerant of unconventional sleeping arrangements.

To make matters more interesting, Eleanor was pregnant. Rosette, born to a black slave, soon would have a half-sibling born to a white mistress.

It would have been more logical for Stephen to go to Bordeaux than to Marseilles. A return to his birthplace would have allowed him to see his father, brothers, sisters and other relatives. There was, however, a lingering embarrassment: Stephen still had not paid all of the debts he had owed to Bordeaux merchants for almost fourteen years, since 1774. If he landed in Bordeaux, his creditors might try to have his ship and cargo impounded and sold, by court order, so that the proceeds could be used to pay his debts. He would be safe in Marseilles, where he had never been. No one there was likely to care, or even to know, about his old debts in Bordeaux, an Atlantic port. Marseilles, a Mediterranean port, was hundreds of miles away.

There was no excuse for the debts owed since early 1774 not being paid in full by late 1787. Girard was, by this time, doing quite well financially, not only in net worth but also in cash flow. He could have made good on his obligations to the Bordeaux merchants with no hardship to himself. Soon after the Revolutionary War had ended officially with the Treaty of Paris in 1783, Girard had paid off some of his old Bordeaux debts and had indicated he would make additional payments within eighteen months. In 1785 he had received a letter from Pierre, his father, itemizing all of the debts still owed to Bordeaux merchants.[15] There were nine creditors. The amounts owed totaled $1,926. Stephen's response had been to pay off one creditor in full, in the amount of $225, leaving the other eight creditors still unpaid, with no explanation for the continuing delay.

Since Stephen's objective in setting sail for Marseilles in December of 1787 was to find some peace and quiet, far removed from his insane wife and her disruptive behavior, he was in no hurry once he left the turmoil of Philadelphia behind. After eleven uneventful days at sea he pulled into Charleston, South Carolina, a week before Christmas. He stayed there until early February.[16] During that sojourn of almost seven weeks he sold beef and other products he had brought from Philadelphia and took on a cargo of tobacco and other items he could sell in Marseilles. In January he became a Mason, joining a lodge in Charleston. Seven weeks ashore were followed by seven weeks at sea. That is how long it took Girard, with a first mate and a crew of eight, an average complement for a cargo-carrying brig, to go across the Atlantic Ocean and into the Mediterranean Sea, from Charleston to Marseilles.

While in the French port, beginning in late March, Girard was the house guest of his agent, Timon Samatan. Neither could have been too surprised when a revolution erupted in France in the following year, but neither could have guessed that, before the revolution was over, Samatan would die on the guillotine. On April 27, 1788, while Stephen was still in Marseilles, his father Pierre died in Bordeaux at the age of seventy-two. Stephen did not learn of the death until months later. Ironically, if Stephen had paid his debts and had gone to Bordeaux instead of Marseilles, he could have been at his father's bedside when death came.

Stephen sailed from Marseilles on May 11 with a cargo of wine, brandy, nuts, lemons, soap and other items, along with wall mirrors and silk stockings as gifts for Sally. He learned of the death of his father after arriving back in Philadelphia on July 18 following a rough return voyage of more than two months marred by several storms.[17] For the remaining forty-three years of Stephen Girard's life, from 1788 to 1831, he never left America again and did not venture more than forty miles from Philadelphia.

During the settlement of Pierre Girard's estate, completed in 1790, much of Stephen's share was used to pay off all of his debts to Bordeaux merchants. His remaining inheritance amounted to less than one hundred dollars in cash. In addition, as a part of his inheritance as the oldest son, he became sole owner of the house where his father had lived and where he (Stephen) had been born. Repayment of all of his outstanding debts to merchants in Bordeaux enabled Stephen to conduct business in the city of his birth. The native son who had gone to America was recognized by this time as an up-and-coming world trader in a new country of great promise. The long delay in payment of past debts was quickly forgiven and forgotten. Now there were new money-making opportunities. Everybody on the Bordeaux waterfront wanted a piece of the action, a piece of Stephen Girard's action. The late Pierre Girard's oldest boy was not only a native son but a favorite son.

Henceforth, Stephen's credit record was excellent. He paid his bills promptly and he expected others to pay theirs promptly. Moreover, as the merchants of Bordeaux could readily see, he knew how to generate profits not only for himself but also for others who hitched their wagons to his star. His network of trade routes soon encompassed the globe, and his old hometown in the southwest of France became a principal port of call.

While Stephen was away on the voyage to Marseilles, Eleanor McMullin gave birth to a boy, an all-white half-brother to half-white Rosette. Then John Girard married Eleanor, making his mistress his wife. After Stephen returned to Philadelphia, John went back to St-Domingue, taking his bride and their infant son with him. John's daughter, Rosette, also went back to St-Domingue with her father. Rosette's mother, Hannah, still Stephen's slave, even though Stephen had given her daughter freedom, remained in Stephen's house in Philadelphia. So, a rather strange situation continued: A mother who was a slave had a daughter who was free, and a daughter who was free had a mother who was a slave, and the same man, Stephen Girard, who had given freedom to the one, also had the power to give freedom to the other but chose, at least for the time being, not to do so.

Sally Bickham, after the visitors had departed for St-Domingue, left her rented house and came back to Stephen's house on Water Street to resume entertaining him as his mistress. There was, at this time, a significant addition to the household: Martin Bickham, Sally's brother. Sally brought him with her, with Stephen's permission. Martin was nine years old and started learning the business of maritime trading as an apprentice in Stephen's counting-house. It soon became evident that Martin was on his way up in the Girard organization. Stephen treated him like a son.

Sally's success in bringing a brother into the Girard firm, and virtually into the Girard family, was indicative of her growing influence with Stephen, influence that was manifested in other ways also. Exercising her powers of persuasion, which were considerable, she convinced Stephen that he ought to upgrade the quantity as well as the quality of his wardrobe. She had chairs upholstered. She spruced up the house with new curtains. In sum, Sally was becoming increasingly assertive in household matters and was having her own way in a broadening range of important decisions about costly furnishings and major purchases. She was much more than a housekeeper and a mistress. She was the lady of the house.

Meanwhile, history was being made on the Delaware River virtually at Girard's doorstep. John Fitch invented the steamboat. Unfortunately, it might be more accurate to say that Fitch *should* have been making history. Many historians have given him little or no notice. Some encyclopedias do not mention him. In July of 1786 (there was no U.S. Patent Office back then) Fitch had successfully tested a boat propelled by twelve steam-driven oars. It had achieved a speed of eight miles an hour. In ensuing years he successfully tested steamboats using paddle wheels instead of oars. In 1790, with a stern-wheeler, he began regularly scheduled freight and passenger service between Philadelphia and Trenton, New Jersey, on a route that was thirty-three miles each way. He soon had more business than one boat could handle, but he went bankrupt trying to build a second one. He died broke in 1798.

Much later, Robert Fulton, with financial backing from prominent and wealthy New Yorker Robert Livingston, a signer of the Declaration of Independence, tested a steamboat at six miles an hour on the Hudson River in 1807. Fulton got a patent and was later hailed far and wide as the inventor of the steamboat. Such are the fortunes and the misfortunes of history.

Invention of the steamboat notwithstanding, all of Girard's ships continued to be sailing ships and all of his ocean-going cargoes continued to be carried under sail throughout his entire lifetime. It would not be until 1838, seven years after Girard's death, that a ship would cross the Atlantic Ocean entirely under steam power for the first time.[18]

However, river-going steamboats would have major impact on economic development and population growth in many states, including Pennsylvania, during Girard's lifetime. In 1811 the first voyage was made by a steamboat from Pittsburgh, where the Ohio River begins, to New Orleans.[19] Dozens of cities and towns on the Ohio River and the Mississippi River would enjoy boom times in the heyday of the steamboats, and they would enhance the value of property that Girard would acquire in Louisiana.

On July 14, 1789, just seventy-five days after the inauguration of George Washington as the first president of the United States, the French Revolution began with the storming of the Bastille in Paris.

Repercussions were felt far beyond the boundaries of France. Girard would be affected in many ways for many years. Pent-up suffering, anger and frustration from centuries of political, social and economic injustice erupted in a torrent of violence, hate and retribution. From relatively mild beginnings—as when a woman in Paris was spanked in public for daring to express views not compatible with the views of revolutionaries[20]—the vengeance and the punishments would grow. Before the revolution had run its bloody course, full-blown terror reigned. The guillotine became the symbol and the engine of revenge. The terror notwithstanding, the French Revolution produced many laudable achievements such as ending the rule of corrupt nobility, transforming oppressed subjects into free citizens, and adopting American-like principles of human rights.

The French Revolution began at an especially awkward time for the United States and for Girard. In the summer of 1789 the U.S. government, under the U.S. Constitution, was just becoming operational. Individual states no longer could operate their own customs offices. Individual states no longer could control navigation in and out of ports engaged in interstate or international trade. Hundreds of state laws pertaining to foreign commerce became null and void when the U.S. Constitution took effect. It put the federal government in charge of trade and commerce, duties and tariffs, customs and navigation. The states got their wings clipped.

These changes were good for Girard and other Americans involved in maritime trade. Instead of a conglomeration of confusing and conflicting state laws to deal with, merchants had federal law. This made it easier to conduct trade between and among American states as well as with foreign countries. Then the French Revolution knocked world trade into a cocked hat.

For Girard, the frustrations that closed in on him in 1789 were highly unsettling. He had come to Philadelphia in 1776 and had been caught up in the American Revolution. It had taken the Americans thirteen years to win the Revolutionary War and create a country and a government. Now there was a revolution in France and Girard knew that maritime trade was not going to be free of tumult and turmoil any time soon. He knew that the troubles in France were likely to last a long time, although he had no idea how long. (He would be sixty-five years old before the French Revolution and its sequel, the Napoleonic Wars, finally came to an end.) He knew that, if he was going to be successful in world commerce, he would have to confront and overcome formidable obstacles. He knew that he could not wait for the luxury of normal times.

Girard had long been appalled by the extravagances and the wanton idleness of French royalty and thus was sympathetic with the democratic ideals of the French Revolution from the outset. He hoped that France, like America, would become a republic. He was outraged, though, when the revolution degenerated into the Reign of Terror. He was horrified when his agent in Marseilles, Timon Samatan, was guillotined in 1794 for no reason—no reason at all—except that he was wealthy. Samatan's real estate and other tangible assets were confiscated by authorities who were in control of the revolution, and therefore in control of France, at the time of his execution. His widow and eight children were left destitute.

In a letter of condolences to Samatan's widow, Girard made an offer: "I have heard that my old friend left a numerous family and if among them there is a boy whom you would be willing to entrust to me, I assure you that I shall take the best possible care of him and that, as I am childless, I should make it my duty to be a father to him."[21] Samatan's widow did not accept Girard's offer. There was another overturn in the high command of the French Revolution. Robespierre, who had directed the Reign of Terror, came to an inglorious end on the guillotine—poetic justice, many said. Samatan's property and other assets were returned to his widow. She was no longer destitute.

Girard's offer to be a father to one of Samatan's boys underscored how much he wanted sons to raise, educate and take into his business. He was essentially doing that with Martin Bickham, Sally's brother, but would have been happy to have an additional boy on board.

The French Revolution intensified Girard's interest in the works of French philosophers and their views on social and political injustice in France. In 1790 he became a member of the Library Company of Philadelphia. Founded by Benjamin Franklin in 1731 (and still going strong), it is the oldest circulating library in America. Stephen, continuing his self-education, immersed himself in the writings of one of his old favorites, Voltaire, who had died in 1778 at the age of eighty-four.

Stephen Simpson, who knew Girard for many years in an employee-employer relationship, said the author that Girard liked best was Voltaire, "whose sentiments found a congenial abode in his bosom."[22] Simpson cited Girard's arduous examination of the works of Voltaire as an example of how thoroughly Girard "was self-taught. The hours and the moments he could steal from business, he gave to the improvement of his mind; and whatever he undertook to learn, there is ample reason to believe, he was not long in mastering."[23]

In 1790, though, Stephen Girard had more on his mind than Voltaire, more on his mind than the French Revolution, even more on his mind than Sally. He had on his mind, most of all, what to do about Mary. A decision was made after consulting with doctors to determine what, in their view, would be best for her. It was a difficult and agonizing time for Stephen. As one scholar would say, many years later, "Girard had loved Mary. He had fallen in love and married her, and had lived and cohabited with her for eight years, as long as she would have him without making a fool of him."[24] Now, though, Stephen knew that the good times with Mary could never come back. She was not the same woman he had loved and married. On August 31, 1790, more than five and a half years after Mary had gone insane, she was committed to quarters for insane patients at Pennsylvania Hospital.

Samuel Coates, manager of the hospital, approved Mary's admission after she had been certified as an "incurable lunatic" by two prominent Philadelphia physicians, John Jones and John Foulke.[25] All three men—Coates, Jones and Foulke—were pioneering medical professionals with impeccable reputations and illustrious careers. Coates was manager of America's first hospital for forty-three years, from 1785 to 1828.[26] Jones, in 1775, had written the first American textbook on surgery.[27] Foulke taught anatomy at America's first medical school (University of Pennsylvania) and was a disciple of Dr. Benjamin Rush, who was a signer of the Declaration of Independence and widely recognized as the father of American psychiatry. Foulke and Rush were among the doctors making the first diagnosis of yellow fever in 1793 when Philadelphia was struck by a devastating epidemic.[28]

Thus Stephen Girard allowed his wife to be committed to a hospital only after such action had been recommended and approved by a medical team that ranked among the most prestigious in America, if not in the world. The doctors made their recommendation after Mary's condition had declined dangerously. In 1789 and 1790 she had become increasingly unpredictable and uncontrollable. Caring for her in a safe and sound manner at Mount Holly had become extremely difficult, and when she was at home on Water Street she had a habit of wandering off and refusing to return. She would stay for varying lengths of time in boarding houses, with Stephen paying the bills. Sometimes she would wander aimlessly on the waterfront, frequenting taverns that were hangouts for sailors. Stephen continued to refuse to make her a prisoner, to lock her in a room or chain her to a bed or a wall, as was commonly done with the insane in that time.

So it was only after years of delay and with the greatest reluctance that Stephen let Mary be placed under institutional care. It was only after numerous other options had been explored and exhausted, including long visits to the restful countryside in New Jersey and Lancaster County, Pennsylvania. Putting her in a hospital was not a hasty act by an insensitive husband. It was a carefully considered and compassionate response to a terrible tragedy. By the time Mary went to the hospital, as a commentator would say in the late nineteenth century, "the faint glimmer of light in her mind" had "deepened into the lasting night of permanent insanity."[29] She was, mentally, "in total blindness."[30]

Stephen was able to provide hospital care for Mary by a stroke of good fortune. When she went insane there was only one hospital in the entire thirteen newly independent states of America.[31] That one hospital, it just so happened, was located about a mile from the Girard residence. (America's second hospital, New York Hospital, was being organized and planned in the 1770s and 1780s but did not begin receiving patients until the 1790s.[32]) Pennsylvania Hospital had been organized in 1751, with Benjamin Franklin and Dr. Thomas Bond as the principal founders, and had begun receiving patients at a temporary location on Market Street in 1752. The first building had opened in 1756 on the permanent site at Eighth and Spruce Streets, where the hospital (greatly expanded) is still located. The first building was the only building in 1790 when Mary was admitted. It remains in use today and is known as the East Wing of the Pine Building.

Stephen made special efforts and spared no expense to keep Mary comfortable in the hospital. She had private quarters, paid for entirely by Stephen. Henry Ingram, an early biographer of Stephen Girard, interviewed a number of people who had visited Mary in the hospital. Based on their accounts, Ingram described Mary's accommodations: "She was pleasantly situated on the first floor of the main building in a spacious and comfortable apartment, with parlor attached, and was permitted the freedom of the large grounds of the hospital, being also allowed to receive visitors with the fewest restrictions possible."[33] Stephen insisted that Mary be given maximum freedom consistent with the safety of herself and others.

During the late 1700s those insane who were the most disruptive or the most violent, or both, were the ones most likely to be admitted to the hospital.[34] Those who were not disruptive or violent were cared for at home. Treatments in the insanity wards included bleeding, purging and blistering.[35] Unruly patients inclined to damage furnishings, or to inflict injury on themselves or others, were restrained with various devices including leg chains, manacles and straitjackets.[36] Despite these early and quite primitive methods of treatment and restraint, Pennsylvania Hospital became a world leader in advocating and practicing humane care for the insane. Dr. Rush, who was an attending physician at the hospital for thirty years (from 1783 until his death in 1813), earned international renown for his pioneering work in liberating the insane from chains and other physical restraints whenever feasible and providing care that was appropriate for patients, not for criminals.[37]

Hospital authorities and attendants gave Mary total care. They supervised, made decisions, ministered to her needs. This left Stephen free to lead a more-or-less normal life, not just with Sally but in tending to business without distractions and in entertaining guests in his home without fear of a sudden, jarring intrusion by Mary. Yet she was only a mile away. The proximity was a convenience. It was a short walk for Stephen or anyone he designated, including Sally, to visit Mary, to inquire about her condition, to pay bills, and to make sure she was being cared for properly and humanely.

It might be conjectured, although there is no evidence to support such speculation, that Stephen may have decided to have Mary institutionalized to get rid of her and be relieved of caring for her, and also because he had fallen in love with Sally. No one can read Stephen's mind more than two centuries after the fact. Nonetheless, in the absence of any evidence to the contrary, it must be assumed that Stephen's primary motivation in confining Mary to a hospital was to provide the best available care for her in accord with the recommendations of two distinguished doctors.

There is another, more sinister, speculation that needs to be dealt with, namely, that Mary was not insane and Stephen had her declared insane falsely so he could have her committed to the hospital, thus allowing him free rein in the enjoyment of his mistress. Rumors to that effect, totally unfounded, were heard in Philadelphia during Stephen's lifetime. More recently, in the 1970s and 1980s, a stage play—*The Insanity of Mary Girard*, by Lanie Robertson—was performed in Philadelphia implying that Mary Girard was not insane and was institutionalized unjustly.[38] It is quite possible, of course, that someone could have been certified as insane in the eighteenth century who was not actually insane. However, in the case of Mary Girard, there is overwhelming evidence that she was insane. Her insanity was plainly apparent to those who saw her in that wretched condition (as already documented in this chapter).

Stephen Simpson, in his biography of Stephen Girard, ridiculed the rumors that Mary Girard was not insane. "It has been alleged by some, but the suspicion is utterly groundless, that his wife was not deranged, and that a motive, the very reverse of humanity, had prompted Girard to place her in confinement," Simpson wrote. "But the character of those who presided over the management of the Pennsylvania Hospital appears to be a sufficient refutation of this unworthy surmise. Had she been oppressed, her family would not have been slow to redress her wrongs, even if society had neglected to interfere in her behalf."[39]

Simpson's points are well made. It is hard to believe that Dr. John Jones, Dr. John Foulke and Samuel Coates would enter into a conspiracy to declare a sane woman insane. Even if they did, it is even harder to believe that their deception would go undetected and unchallenged, even by Mary's mother and other close relatives, during

all the years that Mary was in the hospital. Moreover, Mary was cared for by her mother and one of her sisters for long periods of time in Mount Holly after she had gone insane. It would be preposterous to suggest that Mary's mother and sister were part of a conspiracy to pretend that Mary was insane when she was sane.

There is nothing in the records of Pennsylvania Hospital (examined by the author) to indicate anything other than that Mary Girard was precisely what the doctors said she was: an incurable lunatic.

Early in 1791 the real-life soap opera of Stephen, Sally and Mary took a bizarre turn. Officials at Pennsylvania Hospital discovered, five months after Mary had been admitted, that she was pregnant. A delegation from the hospital called on Girard to tell him the news and to request that he take Mary home to have her baby. He refused, contending that he could not possibly be the prospective father because he had not slept with Mary, due to her illness, for a long time. She had been insane for six years, and Stephen had been sleeping with Sally nearly four years. Stephen had his way. Mary stayed in the hospital to have her baby. However, he paid an advance on his account with the hospital to be sure that any additional expenses resulting from pregnancy and birth would be fully covered at no cost, even temporarily, to the hospital.

On March 3, 1791, six months and three days after Mary entered the hospital, she gave birth to a girl, who also was named Mary Girard. Four days later the baby was taken from the hospital to be cared for by a wet nurse in her home, with all expenses paid by Stephen. The infant died on August 26, 1791, at the age of five months and twenty-three days.[40] There is no record that Stephen ever saw the baby, but the absence of a record is inconclusive. He could have walked to the hospital or to the wet nurse's home and seen the infant without leaving a written account of the visit. It is highly probable that he did so, out of curiosity, at least, and perhaps in search of a clue regarding the identity of the father.

Who was the father of Mary's child? It is a question that, to this day, has no answer. Mary, in her condition, may not have known. If she did know, there is no indication that she ever told anyone. The possibility of rape cannot be ruled out. It is probable that she was pregnant before her admission to the hospital. In the eighteenth century there were considerable odds against a baby being viable at birth if carried by her mother only six months.

Early generations of Girard College students and graduates were encouraged to believe that their benefactor and his wife were beyond reproach and that neither would have committed adultery. In 1912 the Girard College alumni presented to their alma mater a tablet (it was put on display in an auditorium) headed "Stephen Girard, Founder" and listing important events associated with his life. The list included, for the year 1791: "Birth and death only child, Mary Girard."[41]

It is highly improbable, to say the least, that Stephen was the father of Mary's baby. Considering that Stephen and Mary lived together for eight years without having children, before she went insane, it is likely that Stephen was physically incapable of fathering a child. It is quite possible that Mary became pregnant while frequenting waterfront taverns that were hangouts for sailors, which, as previously noted, she had been doing in months preceding her admission to the hospital. However, that is only speculation, with no supporting evidence.

CHAPTER 8

Catastrophe in the Capital of the United States
1793

The defining moment in a human life often comes suddenly and unexpectedly—as when a person is caught in a crisis situation and faces a simple and straightforward test of courage and character.

ON AUGUST 23, 1791, three days before Mary Girard's baby died, there was a revolution in St-Domingue. Black slaves from Africa, taking a cue from the peasants in France, rebelled against their masters and slaughtered them in large numbers. The slaves in this French colony in the West Indies did not have guillotines but they had machetes, and they knew how to use them to cut down people as well as sugar cane. The reign of terror in St-Domingue, unlike the terror in France, was informal and impromptu. There were no trials and no official death sentences in St-Domingue. French plantation owners and their families were summarily hacked to death on the spot, wherever they could be found, and their homes were burned. Given the extreme cruelty slaves had borne for many years, such a violent reaction was not surprising.

John Girard, in Cap-Francais, had seen trouble brewing for years. "We are in the midst of a terrible crisis, contre-coup of the European revolution," he had said in a letter to his brother Stephen in 1789. "[We] are constantly armed to protect ourselves against the Africans, who have already revolted in various places. Several of these were executed yesterday evening."[1] After the rebellion erupted in 1791 Stephen Girard received a letter from Aubert, Rouch & Co., business

113

associates in St-Domingue. A member of the firm reported: "These maniacs have set fire to all the plantations and massacred all the whites they could find. Words fail me in trying to describe all the horrors they have committed .... They have set fire to all homes in their path .... Our safety lies in this city [Cap-Francais], which is well fortified and well garrisoned. When the trouble began we found that our own servants, who are very numerous, would join forces with the brigands and set fire to our houses; but, by the most watchful vigilance both by day and by night, we have escaped their plots. Nevertheless a number of servants were arrested and put to death."[2]

The rebellion in 1791 was quelled in less than two months, but not before more than two thousand whites had been killed. There was an uneasy quiet for about a year and a half. In the spring of 1793 large numbers of slaves rebelled again. More homes were burned. More whites were massacred. Many French families fled St-Domingue and came to the United States, arriving in the summer of 1793. Stephen Girard gave financial assistance to refugees who landed in Philadelphia and were destitute. Some had run from their homes at the last minute with little more than the clothing they wore. They were lucky to be alive.

In Philadelphia, late in that summer of 1793, another kind of disaster was about to strike—a plague brought to the city by some of the refugees from St-Domingue. In a time of tragedy Stephen Girard would emerge as a hero. The scourge was yellow fever, a dreaded disease also known as the black vomit. It was an ugly, agonizing killer that would leave more than five thousand people dead in Philadelphia and adjacent neighborhoods.[3] The capital of the United States, which was also the largest city in the United States, would be dealt a devastating blow. Thousands fled. Almost everybody in the federal government, including President Washington, with Martha, sought sanctuary outside the city. Newspapers suspended publication, and editors ran for their lives. Even some churches closed, as ministers locked the doors and abruptly departed.

In the first U.S. census in 1790 Philadelphia and contiguous communities such as Northern Liberties and Southwark had a population of forty-two thousand. (Within the city limits, between Vine

Street and South Street, there were twenty-eight thousand inhabitants.) By 1793 the population had risen from forty-two thousand to about forty-eight thousand. Of that number, seventeen thousand left for distant points during the yellow fever epidemic.[4] To put it another way, more than one-third of the forty-eight thousand people of Philadelphia and vicinity withdrew during the epidemic, most of them in late August or September. The five thousand who died of yellow fever constituted about sixteen percent of the thirty-one thousand who did not flee. Deaths from the fever, calculated in proportion to the pre-epidemic population of forty-eight thousand, amounted to more than ten percent. Philadelphia was decimated.

J. H. Powell, author of a book about the epidemic published in 1949, called it "one of the great tragic episodes in the human history of this land. It was the most appalling collective disaster that has ever overtaken an American city."[5] That was no exaggeration. Nor did Powell overstate the case when he advised people not to read his book before eating, "for it is a revolting book, filled with disgusting details of a loathsome disease."[6]

Girard did not flee, although, as a prosperous merchant, he could easily have gone to some distant haven and stayed there until the danger had passed. He chose to remain in Philadelphia and devote all of his energies to caring for the sick, risking his own life to save the lives of others and to give whatever comfort he could to the dying in their final days and hours. In an infant nation that had produced an abundance of heroism in rebellion and war, Girard would become, at the age of forty-three, one of America's earliest peacetime heroes. Sally also stayed. The mistress did not leave her man.

From the very beginning of the epidemic Stephen and Sally were in the thick of it. The outbreak of yellow fever began on Water Street north of Market Street, on the street and in the neighborhood where they lived and where he conducted his business. The address of his store and office was 43 North Front Street. His home address was 31 North Water Street, even though his residence and his place of business shared the same building. It extended a full block east and west, from the east side of Front Street to the west side of Water Street. At 77 North Water Street, a block north of the building where Girard lived and worked, three doctors diagnosed yellow fever in a patient on August 19, 1793. It was the first official case and marked the beginning of the epidemic. Before then, for about two weeks, a number of people had died with high fever, accompanied by vomiting, but physicians had not realized they were treating yellow fever victims.

The patient diagnosed on August 19, who died, was Catherine LeMaigre, thirty-three, a merchant's wife. The three diagnosing doctors were Benjamin Rush, John Foulke and Hugh Hodge. Dr. Foulke, as previously noted, was one of the physicians who had committed Mary Girard to facilities for the insane at Pennsylvania Hospital three years earlier. Dr. Hodge, who lived on Water Street near Girard, was the father of a little girl who had died with a high fever, probably yellow fever, in early August.[7]

Panic came quickly. Frantic flight from the city began within a week of the first diagnosis. Mathew Carey, notable Philadelphia author and publisher who lived through the epidemic and wrote a book about it, described the scene: "The removals from Philadelphia began about the 25th or 26th of this month [August], and so great was the general terror that for some weeks carts, wagons, coaches and chairs were constantly transporting families and furniture to the country in every direction. Many people shut up their houses wholly; others left servants to take care of them."[8] The stampede from the city began, Carey said, just about the time that the College of Physicians published on August 26 "an address to the citizens, signed by the president and secretary, recommending to avoid all unnecessary intercourse with the infected; to place marks on the doors or windows where they were; to pay great attention to cleanliness and airing the rooms of the sick; to provide a large and airy hospital in the neighborhood of the city for their reception; to put a stop to the tolling of the bells [churches traditionally rang their bells to announce a death]; to bury those who died of the disorder in carriages [i.e., transport the dead to burial grounds in closed vehicles] and as privately as possible; to keep the streets and wharves clean; to avoid all fatigue of body and mind, and standing or sitting in the sun, or in the open air; to accommodate the dress to the weather, and to exceed rather in warm than in cool clothing; and to avoid intemperance, but to use fermented liquors, such as wine, beer and cider, with moderation. They likewise declared their opinion that fires in the streets were a very dangerous, if not ineffectual, means of stopping the progress of the fever, and that they placed more dependence on the burning of gunpowder. The benefits of vinegar and camphor, they added, were confined chiefly to infected rooms; and they could not be too often used on handkerchiefs or in smelling bottles by persons who attended the sick."[9] (A smelling bottle, usually filled with smelling salts, was normally used to revive a person who was feeling faint or to provide relief from a headache.)

Very little was known about yellow fever in the eighteenth century except that it was a fairly common and frequently fatal disease in the West Indies. Doctors in Philadelphia in 1793 guessed, correctly, that yellow fever had been brought to the city in the summer of that year by some of the refugees who had fled from St-Domingue after the slaves had revolted.[10] However, it was not known how the disease was transmitted. Many years would pass before, late in the nineteenth century, a theory was advanced about yellow fever being carried from infected people to other people by mosquitoes, more specifically, by mosquito bites. The truth of that theory would not be proved beyond question until early in the twentieth century.

Yellow fever, it is known now, is an infectious disease caused by a virus. Most of the fatalities in the 1793 epidemic occurred within four to eight days after appearance of the initial symptoms, which included high fever, headache and backache. Typically, these symptoms soon would be accompanied by long periods of vomiting, which sapped the patient's strength. The vomit, predominantly black, usually contained blood, an indication of internal hemorrhaging. A doctor who treated yellow fever patients in Philadelphia in 1793 said the vomit was "commonly called the black vomit" because it resembled "coffee grounds in color and consistence."[11] Even when not vomiting, a victim often was bleeding from nose and mouth. The liver, kidneys and heart deteriorated. The skin turned yellow, hence the name, yellow fever. If a patient somehow managed to stay alive for nine days, chances for recovery gradually improved. By the tenth or eleventh day the fever most likely would subside. Vomiting would diminish. The illness would run its course and fade away.

Sometimes it was hard to tell whether victims had been killed by the disease or by their doctors. Treatment for yellow fever patients could be harsh and counter-productive. They commonly were subjected to bleeding and purging, which, in addition to amputation, were the staples of medical practice for physicians at that time. A person suffering from yellow fever, already weakened by internal bleeding caused by the disease, would be further weakened when a doctor removed blood from a vein. The debilitating effects of repeated vomiting would be exacerbated by repeated bowel movements as the doctor administered cathartics, which usually consisted of calomel and jalap. Carey, in his account of the epidemic as an eyewitness, made this observation regarding cathartics: "I am credibly informed that the demand for purges of calomel and jalap was so great that some of the apothecaries could not mix up every dose in detail, but mixed a large quantity of each, in the ordered proportions, and afterwards divided it into doses; by which means, it often happened that one patient had a much larger portion of calomel, and another of jalap, than was intended by the doctors. The fatal consequences of this may be easily conceived."[12]

From the outset of the epidemic large fires were kept burning in the streets at many intersections in the city by citizens who thought the flames and smoke could help to purify the air and halt the spread of yellow fever. The College of Physicians, as previously noted, said fires in the streets were dangerous and ineffectual; people were advised to use gunpowder instead. Whereupon large numbers of citizenry began walking around firing guns in the air. The almost constant sound of gunfire added to the panic. City ordinances were passed outlawing both fires and gunfire in the streets, but enforcement was difficult. Nothing could stop people from hoping that fire and smoke and the smell of gunpowder might ward off the fever.

There was great reliance on tobacco and other products too. As Carey described the pitiful, yet almost comical, situation: "The smoke of tobacco being regarded as a preventative, many persons, even women and small boys, had cigars almost constantly in their mouths. Others, placing full confidence in garlic, chewed it almost the whole day; some kept it in their pockets and shoes."[13] Carey, recording in detail what he saw first hand, described the general scene in Philadelphia as the epidemic tightened its grip:

Some of the churches were almost deserted, and others wholly closed. The coffee house was shut up, as was the city library, and most of the public offices—three out of the four daily papers were discontinued. [The one daily newspaper that continued, never missing an issue, was the Federal Gazette, published and edited by Andrew Brown.] .... Those who ventured abroad had handkerchiefs or sponges impregnated with vinegar or camphor at their noses .... Others carried pieces of tarred rope in their hands or pockets, or camphor bags tied round their necks. The corpses of the most respectable citizens, even of those who did not die of the epidemic, were carried to the grave on the shafts of a chair [a two-wheeled carriage], the horse driven by a negro, unattended by a friend or relation, and without any sort of ceremony. People hastily shifted their course at the sight of a hearse [any vehicle carrying a corpse] coming towards them. Many never walked on the foot path, but went into the middle of the street, to avoid being infected in passing by houses wherein people had died. Acquaintances and friends avoided each other in the streets and only signified their regard by a cold nod. The old custom of shaking hands fell into such general disuse that many shrunk back with affright at even the offer of the hand. A person with a crape, or any appearance of mourning, was shunned like a viper.[14]

Stricken by panic, people behaved in amazing ways. Carey said there was "a total dissolution of the bonds of society in the nearest and dearest connections. Who, without horror, can reflect on a husband, married perhaps for twenty years, deserting his wife in the last agony—a wife unfeelingly abandoning her husband on his death bed—parents forsaking their only children—children ungratefully flying from their parents and resigning them to chance, often without an inquiry after their health or safety ... who, I say, can think of these things without horror? Yet they were daily exhibited in every quarter of our city."[15]

As the most authentic primary source for day-to-day happenings during the 1793 epidemic, Carey described numerous death scenes. Some examples:

A man and his wife, once in affluent circumstances, were found lying dead in bed, and between them was their child, a little infant, who was sucking its mother's breasts ....

A woman, whose husband had just died of the fever, was seized with the pains of labor, and had nobody to assist her, as the women in the neighborhood were afraid to go into the house. She lay for a considerable time in a degree of anguish that will not bear description. At length, she struggled to reach the

window, and cried out for assistance. Two men, passing by, went upstairs, but
they came at too late a stage. She was striving with death—and actually in a
few minutes expired in their arms.
Another woman, whose husband and two children lay dead in the room with
her, was in the same situation as the former, without a midwife, or any other
person to aid her. Her cries at the window brought up one of the carters
employed by the Committee for the Relief of the Sick. With his assistance,
she was delivered of a child, which died in a few minutes, as did the mother,
who was utterly exhausted by her labor, by the disorder, and by the dreadful
spectacle before her. And thus lay in one room, no less than five dead bodies,
an entire family.[16]

Beginning in early September, Philadelphia was gradually isolated
from most of the country despite being the nation's capital. States and
cities, one after another, passed laws or issued emergency proclamations
prohibiting or restricting entry by anyone who was a resident of
Philadelphia or had visited it recently. In some jurisdictions there was
a quarantine period, commonly thirty days or more. People from
Philadelphia would not be given permission to enter until they had
gone through the stipulated period of time without showing symptoms
of yellow fever. Port cities such as Boston, New York, Baltimore and
Charleston forbid entry into their harbors by any ship that had been
in Philadelphia in recent weeks. Some cities set up road blocks two
miles or more from the city limits so that travelers from Philadelphia
could be stopped before they got too close for comfort. A few
communities, though, were more charitable. Wilmington, Delaware,
(thirty miles from Philadelphia) welcomed people who had fled from
the yellow fever epidemic. Some Wilmingtonians graciously and
bravely opened the doors of their homes and accepted refugees from
Philadelphia as guests. Similar hospitality was offered in a number of
towns in New Jersey.

President Washington and his wife left Philadelphia on September
10 and arrived at Mount Vernon four days later. He explained that
Martha was unwilling to leave Philadelphia without him, and he did
not want her to stay and run a risk of contracting yellow fever.[17] By
the time the President departed, the federal government had virtually
vanished anyway. Most federal employees, from clerks to department
heads, had already evacuated. Even the Post Office Department had
ceased operations. One member of the President's Cabinet, Treasury

Secretary Alexander Hamilton, had been stricken by yellow fever, and so had his wife. The illness was not fatal in either case. They had left the city after recovering.

On September 10, the same day that President and Mrs. Washington left the city, Mayor Matthew Clarkson could no longer avoid facing up to a grim reality: Government was disintegrating at every level. Philadelphia was the capital of Pennsylvania as well as the capital of the United States. State employees and officials, along with their federal counterparts, had been leaving in droves. Even the governor, Thomas Mifflin, had left town, taking sanctuary in his country retreat a safe distance from Philadelphia. City employees and officials had evacuated in large numbers too. Clarkson was sixty years old and was getting a lonely feeling as his constituents poured out of Philadelphia by the thousands, but he was determined to stay no matter what. With the President and the governor gone, the mayor constituted the last thin line of governmental leadership. He put a notice in the city's one remaining daily newspaper on September 10, asking the citizenry to attend a meeting at City Hall on September 12 to indicate a willingness to help their severely stricken community in a time of dire need.

Only ten people volunteered their services on September 12 in response to the mayor's appeal. One of them was Stephen Girard.[18] Two of the ten would die of yellow fever before the epidemic was over.[19] The original ten, with their courage providing inspiration for others, were soon joined by twelve additional volunteers who also played active roles in pulling the city and its inhabitants through the crisis. Two of those twelve also died of yellow fever.[20]

To volunteer for public service in a time of such a deadly epidemic was, as each volunteer most certainly knew, a high-risk enterprise. Indeed, the fainthearted said it was foolhardy. The volunteers formed an ad hoc Committee for the Relief of the Sick, which met daily to assess the situation and improvise courses of action. At the meeting of September 15 Girard dropped a bombshell. He offered "voluntarily and unexpectedly," in Carey's words[21], to take charge of Bush Hill, a makeshift hospital that had been set up hurriedly in a private home as a place for yellow fever victims to go and, for many, to die. Girard's colleagues on the committee were stunned. They could scarcely believe what they had heard. A prosperous merchant, who had so much to live for, was volunteering for what seemed to be a suicide mission.

There was nothing in Girard's early years that could have served as a harbinger of such selfless and courageous action. Stepping forward as he did, to flirt with death in arduous and extremely unpleasant civic service, was the defining moment in the life of Stephen Girard. It brought to the surface an extraordinarily noble aspect of his character that had been dormant while waiting for some perilous urgency. Girard was not reckless, ordinarily, and certainly not suicidal, but he threw caution to the wind when he perceived, quite correctly, that his city—his adopted city in his adopted country—needed him and his leadership in a time of crisis. His gallantry in taking charge of Bush Hill was akin to the heroism of a soldier in battle who rises to an occasion and performs an act of incredible bravery far above and beyond the call of duty. This was the real Stephen Girard, showing what he was really made of, who came to the fore in the yellow fever epidemic when he could easily have followed the thousands of others who fled in fear and panic.

The College of Physicians, as previously noted, had recommended on August 26 that "a large and airy hospital in the neighborhood of the city" be provided for yellow fever patients. Sending them to Pennsylvania Hospital, it was believed, would jeopardize unfairly the patients who were in that institution for other kinds of illness. In response to the recommendation of the College of Physicians it had been decided initially to take yellow fever patients to an open-air amphitheater on the southwest corner of Twelfth and Market Streets, where a circus had performed earlier in the year before moving on to New York. The location, however, was within the city limits and near a residential neighborhood. Seven patients were taken there, but the city was unable to get anyone to tend to them. As Powell described the scene: "Two of them died; the rest lay retching and vomiting day and night, cared for by no one. Somebody came and removed one of the corpses, but the other lay there among the sick more than forty-eight hours because no one would touch it."[22]

There was more to the story, as told by Carey: "On this occasion occurred an instance of courage in a servant girl, of which at that time few men were capable. The carter who finally undertook to remove the corpse, having no assistant, and being unable alone to put it into the coffin, was on the point of relinquishing his design and quitting the place. The girl perceived him, and understanding the difficulty he labored under, offered her services, provided he would not inform the family with whom she lived. She accordingly helped him to put the body into the coffin ... [The body] was by that time crawling with maggots and in the most loathsome state of putrefaction."[23] Carey, to protect her, did not reveal the identity of the brave servant who helped put the body in the coffin, nor did he identify the family with whom she lived. "Had they known of the circumstances," Carey emphasized, "an immediate dismissal would have been the consequence." He did report, though, that the girl survived the yellow fever epidemic "notwithstanding her very hazardous exploit."[24]

As for "the inhabitants of the neighborhood of the circus," Carey reported that they "threatened to burn or destroy it, unless the sick were removed, and it is believed they would have actually carried their threats into execution, had compliance been delayed a day longer."[25] It was after these harrowing threats about the amphitheater at Twelfth and Market Streets that Bush Hill was selected as a more appropriate site for a temporary hospital. Bush Hill was a three-story mansion on an estate outside the city limits. The location was on high ground (accounting in part for the name Bush Hill) near the present-day intersection of Sixteenth and Spring Garden Streets. It was a little over two miles from Girard's home.

Bush Hill had been built about 1740 by Andrew Hamilton, a distinguished Philadelphia lawyer and architect who designed Independence Hall. He was the victorious defense attorney in the landmark trial of John Peter Zenger, whose acquittal helped to establish freedom of the press. After Philadelphia became the capital of the United States in 1790, Bush Hill served for two years as the home of Vice President John Adams and his wife, Abigail. They moved to a more convenient location in 1792 after she complained that Bush Hill was too isolated during winter months, when snow and ice sometimes made travel to and from the city difficult.[26]

In 1793 Bush Hill was owned by William Hamilton, a grandson of Andrew. When the yellow fever epidemic struck, William was in

England and the mansion was unoccupied. A caretaker and his family inhabited another house on the estate. Temporary confiscation of Bush Hill by the city was accomplished without due process. There was no time for legal niceties. Mayor Clarkson had to have a place for patients right away. Trying to contact an absentee owner across an ocean was out of the question. The city just moved in and took over as an emergency act in an emergency situation, ignoring property rights and other constitutional considerations. Yellow fever victims who were still alive in the amphitheater were transferred to Bush Hill. Others followed from all over the city and environs.

Many of the carters who transported the sick to Bush Hill, and the dead to burial grounds, were black. In late August and early September black residents of the city had been among the first to accept extremely hazardous employment as carters when yellow fever was emerging as an epidemic of crisis proportions. Providing leadership and inspiration in the recruiting of carters were two black clergymen, Richard Allen and Absalom Jones. They had founded the Free African Society in 1787 and were pioneers in civil rights activism with emphasis on equal opportunity in education and employment regardless of race. There were approximately twenty-five hundred blacks in Philadelphia and vicinity in 1793. About five hundred of them were slaves.

Peter Helm, a member of the Committee for the Relief of the Sick and a cooper who had made barrels for President Washington, followed Girard's lead by volunteering to assist him at Bush Hill.[27] What Girard and Helm found there was a terrible scene. The dead and the dying were intermingled, lying in their vomit, with almost no staff to provide even minimal care or basic housekeeping. Carey described the conditions: "The ordure [excrement] and other evacuations of the sick were allowed to remain in the most offensive state imaginable. Not the smallest appearance of order or regularity existed. It was, in fact, a great human slaughter house .... A general dread of the place prevailed through the city, and ... a removal to it was considered the seal of death."[28]

Powell called Bush Hill (as it was before Girard arrived) "the Augean stables," so permeated by "filth" and "stench" that sufferers from yellow fever "would rather lie in the city streets than be dragged to certain death at the pesthouse."[29] Bush Hill contained fourteen rooms and three large hallways. When Girard arrived, the floors were littered with about 140 patients—including those who were dead. He took charge of the mansion, assuming responsibilities for care of the patients, along with cleaning and housekeeping, while also handling administrative duties.

Helm supervised the grounds, the outbuildings and the carts. His jurisdiction included receiving patients and removing and burying the dead. He repaired things that could not be replaced, and he built things that could not be procured. He renovated buildings on the estate for various purposes such as meal preparation for patients and living quarters for staff. Although the principal work of a cooper normally was to make and repair barrels and casks, Helm had valuable skills in general carpentry also. He was good at improvising. He was, in the finest sense of the word, a handyman, a very handy man to have around.

With Girard working inside and Helm working outside, Bush Hill went through an astounding transformation in just a few days. The dead were carried away and buried. The patients were bathed and given beds so they did not have to lie on the floor. (Many of the beds were donated by Philadelphia residents in response to a public appeal.) The rooms and hallways were cleaned. Girard did much of the work himself. His example, as an unpaid volunteer willing to do the most disagreeable chores, inspired others to sign on as paid staff. He was remarkably successful, considering the risks involved, in recruiting nurses and attendants, cooks and waiters, carters and laborers, a matron, a steward and a barber.

One of Girard's first official acts as administrator was to dismiss summarily all four doctors who had been billing the city for treating patients at Bush Hill. The doctors had been working sporadically and on a part-time basis, mostly by bleeding and purging, and could not be counted on to be there when needed. In the first fifteen days of September they had made, collectively, only twelve visits to Bush Hill. One doctor had made five visits; another had made three; the other two doctors had made two visits each. Thus there had been days when no doctor put in an appearance.[30] Girard replaced the four unreliable doctors with two who could be depended on, John Deveze and Benjamin Duffield. They were willing to visit the patients twice a day, without pay at first, although compensation subsequently was provided by the city. Like Girard, Deveze and Duffield were opposed to harsh treatments such as repeated bleedings and purgings that weakened the patients. Apothecaries were hired to prepare and administer medicines prescribed by the doctors, mild medicines that would relax the patients and help them rest and get their strength back. Deveze was a Frenchman who had practiced medicine in St-Domingue and was experienced in treating yellow fever patients. He had arrived in Philadelphia with other refugees from St-Domingue in early August.

The four doctors dismissed by Girard did not go quietly. As established Philadelphians they resented the appointment of a newly arrived refugee from St. Domingue as a replacement. They also were indignant about the introduction of benign methods of treatment, remaining convinced that bleedings and purgings were the way to go. Girard's authority to dismiss doctors was challenged by the four who had been sacked. They appeared before the Committee for the Relief of the Sick and tried to get reinstated. The committee waffled on the issue for six days, trying to appease the doctors and also Girard. There were attempts at some form of compromise whereby the four dismissed doctors would be reinstated and the two doctors selected by Girard would be allowed to remain also. Girard would have nothing to do with any scheme that smacked of surrender or even partial surrender. As director of the hospital he insisted on the right to hire and fire, absolutely and unequivocally.

He won the battle. In the end, after nearly a week of acrimonious dispute, the committee gave its backing to Girard unconditionally. The four doctors who had been dismissed stayed dismissed. Girard won the committee's confidence not just by the power of his persuasion and the soundness of his position but also by his relentless energy and his ability to get things done. He turned chaos into order. Male and female patients were put in separate rooms. Patients hovering near death were separated from those with better chances for recovery. Hot, nourishing meals were served on a regular schedule to patients who were able to eat. Moreover, and perhaps most importantly, cleanliness was given top priority. There was no way to stop the vomit, but the patients no longer had to lie in it.

No doctor, no apothecary, no nurse, no attendant was asked by Girard to work any harder than he worked. He went from patient to patient, cleaning, feeding, serving, encouraging. He demonstrated, by his own incessant industry and by his own upbeat attitude, that caring for the sick, even in the most menial ways, was noble enterprise.

Dr. Deveze, who on numerous occasions saw Girard making his rounds among the yellow fever patients, wrote an account of a typical day:

"The unfortunate persons in the greatest danger were those who first attracted his attention. He approached them with that philanthropy that proceeds from the heart alone, and which must give the greater lustre to his generous conduct: He encouraged, took them by the hand, and himself administered the medicine I prescribed. I even saw one of the diseased who, having nauseated his medicine, discharged the contents of his stomach upon his benefactor. What did Girard then do? Entirely devoted to the public welfare, firm and immovable, and forgetting himself to think only of the sufferings of his fellow-creatures, whom he wished to succour; he wiped the patient's clothes, comforted, and by the force of persuasion and patience, induced him to swallow the remedy. He did not stop here. Before he quitted him to show the same attention to another, he felt his feet and head, in order to judge the degree of heat, that he might take from or add to his coverings, according to the nature of the case; he arranged the bed, inspired him with courage, by renewing in him the hope that he should recover.

"From him he went to another, that vomited offensive matter that would have disheartened any other than this wonderful man. Then seeing one at a distance at the point of death, with the eyes and skin yellow, covered with black blood that ran from both mouth and nostrils, and feeling about with a bloody and tremulous hand for a vessel which he could not obtain; Girard ran to his assistance, gave him the vase, replaced him in his bed, which he set to rights, and only quitted him to show the same attention to another.

"The hour of repast arrives—he is hungry, yet complains of the necessity he was under of recruiting his strength; [he] ran, ate a morsel in haste, and reappeared immediately, still more earnest, and full of zeal to pay over again the same attention; and never quitted but when forced by the calls of nature to take some few hours of rest."[31]

Although Girard did most of his work during the epidemic inside the temporary hospital, he also performed other services. They included removing yellow fever victims from their homes and transporting them to Bush Hill. Another Philadelphia merchant, who knew Girard, saw him making one of his house calls to pick up a patient and gave this account:

"A carriage, rapidly driven by a black servant, broke the silence of the deserted and grass-grown street. It stopped before a frame house in Farmers Row, the very hotbed of the pestilence, and the driver, first having bound a handkerchief over his mouth, opened the door of the carriage and quickly remounted to the box. A short, thick-set man [Girard] stepped from the coach and entered the house. In a minute or two the observer, who stood at a safe distance watching the proceedings, hears a shuffling noise in the entry, and soon saw the visitor emerge, supporting with extreme difficulty a tall, gaunt, yellow-visaged victim of the pestilence. His arm was around the waist of the sick man, whose yellow face rested against his own, his long, damp tangled hair mingling with his benefactor's, his feet dragging helpless upon the pavement. Thus, partly dragging, partly lifted, he was drawn to the carriage door, the driver averting his face from the spectacle, far from offering to assist. After a long and severe exertion the well man succeeded in getting the fever-stricken patient into the vehicle, and then entering it himself, the door was closed and the carriage drove away to the hospital."[32]

Even though he was unafraid of yellow fever, and unafraid of death, Girard was tolerant of those who were afraid and who behaved in a cowardly manner. Thus he did not berate drivers who were fearful and would not come into contact with a yellow fever patient.

Girard was as modest as he was fearless, downplaying his role at Bush Hill. When he took over the direction of the makeshift hospital there, he wrote letters to business associates explaining that he would be too busy to communicate on a regular basis for a while. He was matter-of-fact about the dangerous mission he was undertaking.

In a letter to a firm in Baltimore Girard wrote: "The deplorable situation to which fright and sickness have reduced the inhabitants of our city demands succor from those who do not fear death, or who, at least, do not see any risk in the epidemic which prevails here. This will occupy me for some time, and if I have the misfortune to succumb,

I will at least have the satisfaction of having performed a duty which we all owe to each other."[33]

In another letter to an address in Baltimore—this one written to his agent in that city, Paul Bentalou, a long-time friend going back to the Revolutionary War—Girard said: "It is half past four in the morning. The sleepless night I have just passed, my constant fatigue, and the fact that my health is not of the best, combine to forbid my writing to you at great length .... I have devoted all my time and my person, as well as my little fortune, to the relief of my fellow citizens."[34]

Writing to a New York business associate, Girard was extremely low key about his remarkable accomplishments during the epidemic: "I only regret that my strength and ability have not fully seconded my good will."[35]

Throughout the epidemic Girard was a bona fide hero by any standard, but he would never admit it. Despite all that he was doing, he kept wishing that he could do more.

On October 2, 1793, while the epidemic was raging, there was an addition to the Girard household. Peter Seguin arrived in Philadelphia at the age of eighteen on a ship from Bordeaux and became a guest in Girard's home while serving as a temporary employee in his counting-house. Seguin was en route to Baltimore, where he was to serve as an indentured apprentice for five years with a shipping firm that did business with Girard, but the lad never got to that city. He came down with yellow fever on October 10 and died on October 16 in Girard's home.

Notwithstanding his long labors at Bush Hill, Girard joined Sally in night-time vigils at Seguin's bedside before his death. Dr. Deveze took time out from his busy schedule at Bush Hill to come to Girard's home in a futile effort to save Seguin's life. The deceased was buried in the graveyard of Holy Trinity Catholic Church at Sixth and Spruce Streets. Funeral expenses were more than fourteen dollars, a substantial sum reflecting inflated costs of burial during the epidemic. The standard rate for a funeral "with a rough coffin" had been four dollars.[36]

Seguin's brief stay with Girard was of greater importance than would otherwise have been the case because the young man kept a diary. From his arrival on October 2 to the beginning of his terminal illness on

October 10, his daily entries provide insight into the way of life in Girard's home, even though the times were far from normal because of the yellow fever epidemic. The diary was found after Seguin died, and Girard took good care of it along with his personal papers. It is preserved at Girard College in Philadelphia, a boarding school for orphans founded and funded by Stephen Girard.

On his first day in Girard's home Seguin quickly grasped the relationship between Stephen and his mistress. In his diary entry for October 2 he referred to Sally Bickham as the "housekeeper which, as I could see, was wife and all."[37] Seguin also could see right away that Sally was completely in charge of the house and not to be trifled with. According to the October 2 diary entry, "She seems to be very much obeyed, for everything she said was a law." Also on October 2 the diary gave this description of Sally: "She is ... tall and slender and walks as if she had a withe [a twig or stick] between her legs and she has a round face, black eyes and eyebrows, a long nose and a small mouth and a round chin with a dimple in it and she is pale." Sally has brown eyes and reddish brown eyebrows in the portrait of her that was described in a previous chapter. Seguin may have seen her wearing black mascara on her eyelashes and eyebrows. (Women have been using mascara for thousands of years and it was often worn by mistresses in early America, especially by those with a fair complexion.)

The diary tells of seating arrangements and menus for meals at a table in the living room on the second floor. Girard, when he was there, sat at the head of the table. Sally Bickham sat on one side and Peter Seguin on the other. Martin Bickham, Sally's brother, sat at the foot of the table. (Martin, now age fourteen, had been by this time a part of the Girard household for five years, and Girard was raising the lad as he would have raised a son, giving him a good education and teaching him the business.) Sitting next to Martin was Ernest Baethgen, a young clerk.

Peter, Martin and Ernest slept in the same room, in the garret. They arose at 5 A.M. and did considerable work before breakfast was served at 8. The morning meal consisted of bread and butter and coffee, sometimes supplemented with cheese or fish. (Most households had a more substantial breakfast, which might include bacon or sausage and eggs or pancakes, but Girard believed that people who had a light breakfast did more work.)

Dinner, the biggest meal of the day by far, was at 3 P.M. and typically included boiled beef and roast chicken or duck, white or sweet potatoes (or both), one or two vegetables such as beets and/or celery or cucumbers, sometimes fruit such as pears, bread and butter, and a dessert, pie, cake or pudding. Wine always accompanied dinner. There were variations in the main course: for example, beef steaks or crabs. (In normal times, without an epidemic raging, there would be a greater variety of food, especially in the categories of meat, fish, fruits and vegetables.) Supper, which was actually a bedtime snack, consisted of tea and bread and butter, sometimes accompanied by eggs.

The daily death toll from yellow fever in Philadelphia and environs reached 119 on October 11, one day after Seguin was stricken. That was the high water mark. For the remainder of October and into November and December the epidemic gradually diminished as the weather turned colder. In the first week in November the deaths per day ranged from eleven to twenty-one. By the first of December the epidemic was in its last gasps insofar as new cases of yellow fever were concerned, although there were still seventy patients at Bush Hill. That was a big drop from the two hundred or more who had been there on a number of days in October, after a temporary building had been erected to handle the overflow from the mansion.

Meanwhile, President Washington had left Mount Vernon on October 28, without Martha. On November 1 he had arrived in Germantown, which was still not a part of Philadelphia and was several miles outside the city. On November 10, against the advice of his aides, the President went into Philadelphia alone on horseback and rode leisurely through the almost deserted streets, exchanging greetings and having brief conversations with some of the startled pedestrians he encountered. On the basis of what he saw and heard during that impromptu and unannounced visit, he decided it was too early for him to re-establish residence in the nation's capital.[38] Washington did not come back to Philadelphia to stay until December. It was in that month also that most of the members of Congress returned, along with other federal officials and employees. By the end of the year the United States had a government again.[39]

Of the more than five thousand men, women and children who died of yellow fever in the Philadelphia area, fewer than ten percent (about five hundred) died at Bush Hill after Girard took charge. During his tenure at the improvised hospital approximately one thousand patients were admitted, so their chances of death or survival were about even.[40] It was January before the hospital at Bush Hill ceased operations. Girard kept it going until all of the surviving patients were well on the way to recovery.

In the aftermath of the epidemic a public meeting was held in City Hall to honor Girard, Helm and fifteen other citizens deemed worthy of special tribute for their heroism during the crisis, and to honor the memory of four additional citizens who had also given heroic service and had died of yellow fever. Resolutions of gratitude adopted in behalf of the people of Philadelphia and the adjacent communities of Northern Liberties and Southwark cited the honorees for "totally disregarding their own personal preservation" and for "magnanimity and patriotism worthy of the highest eulogium." They were given "most cordial, grateful and fraternal thanks for their benevolent and patriotic exertions." The net result, for Girard, was his emergence as a prominent Philadelphian, widely known and highly esteemed. Heretofore he had attained a degree of prominence in mercantile and port circles but not among the citizenry at large. Now everybody knew his name.

In the first biography of Girard, published a few months after his death, Stephen Simpson summed up in appropriate perspective Girard's extraordinary actions and risks and sacrifices during the yellow fever epidemic:

"When Girard made a proffer of his services, in the fever of 1793, it was not merely to aid by his counsel, or cooperate by his money, in alleviating the calamity of his fellow-citizens; but it was to undertake in person the performance of the most laborious and loathsome duties of a nurse in the public hospital, for those who were then laboring under, and hourly dying of malignant fever! It was not the mere influence of a name that Girard proffered for the benefit of his suffering fellow-creatures, but the free use of his hands and his head, on all occasions, and for all purposes. We have already seen that he never attached ideas of degradaton to any occupation that was useful, and his offer of acting as nurse on this occasion tested that feeling deeply. The act spoke the man. It was not the practice of Girard to talk, or to boast, without acting. He was made for great deeds in extreme emergencies; to act with the most calm fortitude in the most appalling times; and rolling up his sleeves to his elbows, he entered on his duty, prepared to discharge it at the peril of his life. We here behold the accumulator of wealth in a new character. Suddenly all his ideas of profit and gain are abandoned. He comes forth the champion of humanity and serves her cause with unshrinking fidelity and devotion, instead of flying on the wings of his wealth to a place of safety, to enjoy ease, affluence, and luxury!"[41]

After 1793 no one could have any doubts about Girard's courage. Defiantly and audaciously, unselfishly serving others, he had looked death in the eye.

CHAPTER 9

Trouble on the High Seas
1793-1795

Oceans are the last frontier, unowned and untamed. Control, even by the mightiest navies, is piecemeal and intermittent—exercised by whoever can muster the most power in one place at one time.

STEPHEN GIRARD, in the wake of the yellow fever epidemic of 1793, focused his attention anew on fighting for freedom of the seas. Maritime trade in Philadelphia had virtually dried up for three months as the fever mowed down its victims by the thousands. As the year drew to a close, the waterfront came alive again. World commerce in and out of America's No. 1 port was resumed, but there were troubled waters. Outbound ships, after they left the sanctuary of Delaware Bay and entered the Atlantic Ocean, were sitting ducks for whatever superior force with hostile intentions they might encounter. Inbound ships also had to run a gauntlet. Figuratively speaking, it was a jungle out there: The strong devoured the weak. Pirates and privateers were running amuck. The brave new nation called America got no respect. It no longer had a navy. Its cargo and passenger ships were easy pickings.

American independence had been won on the strength of French naval forces. They had played a crucial role in the victory at Yorktown, but in the 1790s they could not be counted on to defend and protect American interests. France and Great Britain were at war again but, this time, it was not just another of their frequent wars against each other; rather, England was part of a European alliance determined to squash the French Revolution. President Washington, wanting to avoid involvement in European hostilities, proclaimed American neutrality. This left American shipping on the high seas at the mercy of all belligerents. French privateers as well as British privateers were plundering U.S. merchant vessels with impunity. Moreover, France in 1793 and 1794 was in the bloodiest and most chaotic stages of its revolution. Mobs ruled and terror reigned. Guillotines worked overtime. The squishy, sickening sounds of heads being severed could be heard all over the country. France was careening out of control.

The British, still licking their wounds from the humiliation at Yorktown, were enjoying a measure of revenge by having a field day against ships flying the flag of the United States, which were routinely stopped and boarded and searched in international waters by British privateers or by warships of the British navy. American ships and cargoes were confiscated and taken to British ports, along with crew members and passengers. The most able-bodied among the American crews and passengers often were impressed into service in the British navy.

Great Britain unilaterally claimed a right to do these things in war-time conditions. It was asserted, for example, that Britain could lawfully seize any ship or cargo that the British believed to be going to or coming from France or a French colony. The same powers of seizure were claimed, regardless of where a ship was sailing from or to, if any part of the cargo consisted of products that the British had reason to believe had been made or grown in France or a French colony. In practice, regardless of specific provisions in various decrees, the British could claim the right to confiscate almost any ship or cargo on one pretext or another. France claimed similar rights of confiscation. They were applicable, for instance, to ships and cargoes going to or coming from British-controlled ports, and to products made or grown in Great Britain or in a British colony.

Girard, to put it mildly, was justified in being concerned about the situation. In the early months of 1794 he owned five ships. All of them had been seized by Britain or France (two by the British, three by the French) and the cargoes of all five ships had been confiscated. The ships were being detained in widely scattered British or French ports. One ship was in Bermuda and another was in Jamaica, both British colonies. One was in Guadeloupe, a French colony. Two were in France, at Bordeaux and Marseilles.

It was bad enough that American shipping was being preyed upon by British and French privateers and warships, with official sanction of the governments of Great Britain and France, but that was only part of the problem. Another part was piracy. American ships and cargoes were being plundered by pirates from the New World and the Old. The New World pirates were of many nationalities, but mostly they were English, French and Spanish. They operated out of secluded bases in Florida and the Florida Keys and on remote islands in the Bahamas and the West Indies. Their forays covered a wide range in the Atlantic Ocean, the Caribbean Sea and the Gulf of Mexico. Far from being gallant, dashing and chivalrous, as they are often portrayed in movies and novels, the New World pirates were typically ill-mannered, unwashed and uncouth. They were thieves who not only robbed but also raped and murdered. Many of them were, quite literally, cutthroats.

Compared to their New World counterparts, the Old World pirates were better financed and better organized. They were the Barbary pirates, so called because they were based on the Barbary Coast of North Africa. Operating in both the Mediterranean Sea and the Atlantic Ocean, they not only seized ships and cargoes but also imprisoned crew members and passengers, holding them for ransom. The Barbary Coast was the name given to the coastal area of North Africa between the Atlantic Ocean and the western border of Egypt, thus including most of the southern shore of the Mediterranean Sea. In the late twentieth century the area encompasses parts of four countries: Morocco, Algeria, Tunisia and Libya. In the eighteenth century the territory was divided among autocracies called, collectively, the Barbary States, principal among them Morocco, Algiers, Tunis and Tripoli.

Barbary is a name derived from *Berber*, but the Barbary States were not controlled by Berbers. The Berbers, nomads, originally, as some of them still are, were the earliest known inhabitants of the Barbary Coast, going back to at least 3000 B.C. In ancient times, over the course of many centuries, there were numerous waves of conquest: the Greeks, the Romans and the Vandals, among others. Arabs from the Middle

East invaded the Barbary Coast in the seventh century and controlled most of the territory until the middle of the nineteenth century, although there were some incursions by Turks during those twelve hundred years. Piracy, starting on a large scale in the sixteenth century, was a mainstay of the economy in the Barbary States for two hundred years prior to American independence. Moslem pirates from North Africa systematically prowled in quest of ships of European Christian nations for many generations. It was a form of state-sponsored terrorism. Rulers of the Barbary States outfitted and funded the pirate fleets and became so brazen about their piracy that they sold "protection." European countries routinely paid extortion to the Barbary States, ostensibly to obtain immunity from acts of piracy for a specified time, usually one year. Blanket protection was expensive because each state required its own payments. Even then, protection was not reliable. Some Barbary rulers had no scruples about committing acts of piracy against clients after receiving their payments for protection.

Captives of Barbary pirates could be rescued from imprisonment, and a possibility of being sold into slavery, upon payment of a specified amount of money as ransom. The fee varied according to an individual's importance. It cost more, for example, to buy the freedom of a ship's captain than an ordinary sailor. When America won independence from Great Britain, the Barbary pirates assumed that they could play the piracy game with Americans just as they had been doing with Europeans for two hundred years. As early as 1785, when fledgling America was limping along under the Articles of Confederation, the Dey of Algiers started capturing U.S. merchant ships and imprisoning their crews and passengers. He set a schedule of ransoms. Freedom for the captain of a ship could be bought for six thousand dollars. The rates were four thousand dollars for a passenger and fourteen hundred dollars for a sailor. The Dey, not in a bargaining mood, rejected a U.S. offer to pay a flat-rate ransom of two hundred dollars per person.[1] The Bey of Tripoli, meanwhile, had tried unsuccessfully to extort protection money from America. He had attempted to negotiate an arrangement whereby the U.S. government would pay an annual fee to Tripoli. In return, the pirates of Tripoli would promise to refrain from plundering American ships and taking Americans into captivity.[2]

Americans were alarmed, and justifiably so. Despots who ruled the

Barbary States were barbarians in the ugliest sense of the word. The Dey of Algiers was perhaps the most barbaric. A Philadelphia newspaper in 1788 published this dispatch from a correspondent:

> Some idea may be formed of the Algerines, even at this enlightened period of time, by the following account of their punishments, as regulated by the present Dey ....
> All those who are convicted of a conspiracy or treason are impaled; that is, a sharp spit is run up their body, on which they are left to writhe in torment till they die. Others are bound hand and foot, and cast from a high wall or tower, upon an iron hook, whereon they are sometimes staked by the belly, head, or other parts of the body, where they sometimes languish many days, till death puts an end to their tortures. Many are tied with a rope about the middle and, with four sharp spikes, fastened to a cross against the city wall; they are torn alive piecemeal; others are brayed to pieces in a mortar.
> They have another mode of punishment ....
> Two hooks are fixed to a gallows, the one fastened to a short, the other to a large chain: The malefactor is forced up the ladder with the executioner, who, thrusting the hook through his left hand, hangs him by it on the shortest chain; then to the hook on the longest he fastens him by the foal of his right foot, where he hangs some days in the most insufferable torment till he dies. Such are the ferocious manners of those inveterate barbarians.[3]

The United States submitted to extortion, but the payments made, no matter what the amounts, were never enough. Over a span of ten years, beginning in the administration of President George Washington and continuing under his successor, President John Adams, the U.S. government paid nearly two million dollars to the Barbary States in ransoms to obtain freedom for imprisoned Americans and in protection payments that were supposed to buy occasional relief from further attacks on American shipping by Barbary pirates.[4]

Huge payoffs notwithstanding, the attacks and the imprisonments continued. At the dawn of 1794 more than one hundred Americans were held by the Barbary States, and the number was increasing almost every week. Most of the captives were in Algiers.

Thus it was a combination of interrelated factors—the French Revolution, the war between France and Great Britain, America's proclamation of neutrality in that war, attacks on American shipping by French and British privateers and warships and by New World pirates and Barbary pirates—that brought the issue of freedom of the seas to a head in America in 1794 and ensuing years. Girard was becoming disenchanted with the Washington administration because of a U.S. foreign policy that, in Girard's view, was seriously flawed. Others, most notably Thomas Jefferson and James Madison, were feeling the same way.

First and foremost, Girard believed that President Washington made a fundamental error when he declared U.S. neutrality in the war between Britain and France. This was, from the perspective of Girard and other critics, a slap in the face of France by America, an appalling display of ingratitude considering how much the French had done to make it possible for Americans to win their revolution against the British and become a free people. Girard wondered how some Americans could forget, so soon, what France had done for them. It had been during the darkest days of the American Revolution, when all seemed lost, that France had become an ally of the American rebels in a treaty of friendship and commerce, in the middle of a terrible winter when General Washington and his troops were at Valley Forge and the British occupied Philadelphia and New York. It was in the spirit of that treaty that France sent troops and warships to America's rescue in sufficient numbers to enable the Americans to defeat the British. Now, in 1794, with France and Great Britain at war with each other again, it seemed to Girard that the U.S. government, instead of embracing neutrality, should be siding with America's old friends and liberators, the French, against America's old enemies and oppressors, the British.

However, part of the debate over U.S. foreign policy in the early 1790s concerned the French Revolution itself. Treasury Secretary Alexander Hamilton was opposed; Secretary of State Thomas Jefferson, who had spent considerable time in France, was sympathetic. Hamilton persuaded President Washington to issue the neutrality proclamation soon after the war between France and Britain broke out early in 1793. Hamilton was strongly in favor of maintaining good relations with Great Britain. To do so, he argued, would be good for the economy of the United States. In the early 1790s ninety percent of U.S. foreign trade was with Britain, a rather remarkable statistic considering not only that Americans had fought a long and bitter war to win independence from the British but also that animosity between American and British governments had continued in the postwar period. Formal diplomatic relations between the United States and Great Britain were not established until late in 1791, more than two years after President Washington had taken office.

Most Americans were of British descent and, despite the unpleasantness of the war, continued to look upon Great Britain as the mother country. Maternal ties were not easily broken. Americans who had long been accustomed to an English way of life remained a major market for goods produced in England.

It was not surprising that Washington took Hamilton's advice on maintaining neutrality in the war between Britain and France. Hamilton had become a close adviser of the President on a wide range of matters. Jefferson resigned as secretary of state in December of 1793 in part because he had become fed up with Hamilton's incessant butting into foreign affairs. Jefferson's resignation also was intended to dramatize his view that U.S. foreign policy should be more pro-French and not so much pro-British and that America's closest political and commercial ties should be with France, not with Great Britain.

Girard, besides being upset about President Washington's efforts to develop a cozy relationship with the British, was outraged at the failure of the President and Congress to build warships that could give merchant vessels protection from pirates. This failure was made worse, Girard believed, by the federal government's inability or unwillingness to pay sufficient ransoms to the Barbary States to obtain prompt release of Americans held captive. Thus crew members and passengers on U.S. merchant ships were forsaken by their government twice: once when it failed to protect them from pirates, and again when it declined to secure an early release from captivity in North Africa. In a letter to French business associates in Bordeaux in January of 1794 Girard vented his frustration: "The war now being carried on by the European pirates [the Barbary pirates] is very disturbing to our commerce .... Our ships are not only stopped and plundered daily, but even run the risk of being taken to the ports of these despots."[5] Girard was incensed that the U.S. government not only failed to protect American shipping but also seemed to be unconcerned about the problem. In February of 1794 he wrote a letter to Treasury Secretary Hamilton explaining that a ship owned by Girard was being detained in a French port and asking that steps be taken by the federal government as "justice and the interests of a citizen of the United States may require."[6]

Hamilton replied perfunctorily that he had forwarded a copy of Girard's letter to the State Department. Even as early as the 1790s U.S. government officials in high places had learned how to pass the buck and give people the run-around. Hamilton had no compunctions about meddling in foreign policy and usurping powers of the State Department when it suited his purposes to do so, but he discreetly deferred to the State Department when he wanted to escape accountability.

Beginning in January of 1794 and continuing into March, Girard conferred informally and privately with other maritime merchants and shipowners in Philadelphia on numerous occasions, quietly building a consensus on specifics of a public protest against U.S. foreign policy. Encouraged by the support he received during the two months of conversations, he was ready to make his move in early March. On March 8, and again on March 11, Girard chaired meetings of merchants and shipowners at the Harp and Crown, a tavern on Third Street between Market and Arch Streets. Three resolutions were approved. They urged the Washington administration and Congress:

1. To give higher priority to protecting American ships engaged in international trade.

2. To provide compensation for losses suffered when American ships and/or cargoes were confiscated by foreign entities.

3. To impose higher tariffs on goods exported to the United States from countries that failed to respect the rights of American shipping— with proceeds from the increased tariffs to be used to compensate owners of confiscated ships and cargoes.

A week later, on March 18, 1794, Girard chaired an outdoor rally called to mobilize opposition to U.S. foreign policy on a broader scale. Six thousand people gathered on the grounds of the U.S. Capitol in Philadelphia to participate in the protest at the site later known as Independence Square, the open area in back of Independence Hall and the Capitol. (Also known as Congress Hall, the old Capitol of the United States is now a part of Independence National Historical Park.) The large crowd attending the rally reflected more than widespread opposition to President Washington's foreign policy. Girard's enormous personal popularity also was a drawing card. He was riding the crest of a great wave of public acclaim. Just three days earlier, on March 15, Girard and others had been honored in ceremonies at City Hall for their heroism during the yellow fever epidemic. Consequently there was a high level of freshly kindled public appreciation for Girard's courageous service at Bush Hill.

In that context, and in that circumstance, the cheering throng on the Capitol grounds appeared to be ready and waiting to roar approval of whatever Girard might propose. He was held in high esteem, and he had their confidence and trust. If he, their hero, said there was something wrong with America's foreign policy, then it must be so. Girard was well prepared for the occasion and the opportunity. He and others had written a lengthy report that was read to the crowd and was reminiscent of the Declaration of Independence, which also had been read to a crowd assembled in the same place in 1776. The report, like the Declaration, gave a long list of grievances against Great Britain. Encroachments by the British in violation of American rights on the high seas were enumerated. Demands were addressed to President Washington and to Congress. They were exhorted to redress the grievances of the people.

In summary, the report read at the March 18 rally accused Great Britain of:

1. "Violently" seizing American ships.

2. "Arrogantly" attempting to impose limits on American maritime commerce.

3. "Insultingly" imprisoning American citizens and impressing some of them into service in the British navy.

4. "Insidiously" encouraging the Barbary States, especially Algiers, to prey on American shipping.

5. "Arbitrarily" refusing to abandon British outposts on America's western frontier.

6. "Clandestinely" fomenting war by Indians against Americans on the frontier.

7. "Contemptuously" ignoring American complaints about all of these matters.

After the report was read at the rally, those who were assembled approved two resolutions. One called upon the U.S. government to take whatever action was necessary to stop violations of American rights

by Great Britain and the Barbary States, particularly Algiers. The other
called for the creation of a committee of five citizens to supervise a
public fund-raising campaign, with the money to be used to pay the
ransoms and win the release of Americans imprisoned in the Barbary
States. Girard volunteered to serve on the committee and also as one
of thirteen trustees to manage and disburse the funds.

So the heat was on. Girard and the thousands who rallied on the
Capitol grounds put heavy pressure on President Washington and
Congress to take action. They responded in a number of ways. On
April 16 President Washington nominated John Jay, who was serving
on the Supreme Court as its Chief Justice, to undertake a special
mission to London as an envoy extraordinary to try to resolve U.S.
differences with Great Britain and to put an end to British attacks on
American shipping and the impressment of Americans into the British
navy. The nomination of Jay was quickly confirmed by the Senate and
he sailed immediately for England, arriving in June. He retained his
position as Chief Justice and thus served in the executive and judicial
branches of government simultaneously.

Meanwhile, foreign trade was suspended for sixty days at all U.S.
ports. This was accomplished by congressional enactment of two
thirty-day embargoes, back to back. The objectives were to hurt the
economy of Great Britain, which had the most to lose from a
suspension of trade with the United States, and to generate in Britain
and other countries more respect for the rights of American merchant
ships in international waters and in foreign ports. Congress also
appropriated funds to build warships and strengthen coastal defenses,
especially at the entrances to bays, rivers and harbors. Since the United
States had no navy in the early 1790s, the Revolutionary War navy
having been phased out after independence was won, a new navy had
to be built from scratch, an effort that would take years. America,
having relied so heavily on French naval forces, had very little
experience in design and construction of large, ocean-going combat
vessels. There was an abundance of shipbuilders in the United States,
including many in Philadelphia, but their expertise was in cargo and
passenger ships.

Building warships was just part of the challenge. Recruiting and
training sufficient manpower for a substantial naval force was a

formidable task. Life in the new navy would be rigorous, with stern discipline. Young American men, citizens of a newly independent country, were enjoying their hard-won freedom. There would be no rush to join the navy.

Shoring up coastal defenses was a difficult challenge also. Forts at strategic points were either nonexistent or badly neglected in the early 1790s. Many of the forts in use during the Revolutionary War had fallen into disrepair and had little or no manpower or firepower.

As it turned out, actions taken in 1794 in response to criticisms by Girard and others were positive contributions to the security of America early in the nineteenth century. In 1801 and ensuing years President Thomas Jefferson made good use of the navy to defeat the Barbary pirates, making them no longer a menace to American shipping. In the War of 1812 Fort McHenry, built in 1794, held off an English armada on the approaches to the harbor at Baltimore, withstanding a ferocious bombardment that was immortalized by Francis Scott Key. "The rockets' red glare, the bombs bursting in air, gave proof through the night that our flag was still there." If Fort McHenry had not been there, Americans would not have had much to sing about.

Besides voting to build a navy and strengthen coastal defenses, Congress considered taking a number of additional actions in 1794 in accord with proposals of Girard and other critics, most notably, Representative James Madison. However, President Washington was able to keep the measures from being passed. Even though his political power was diminishing in his second term, the President still had many staunch supporters in both the Senate and the House of Representatives. Madison, from President Washington's home state of Virginia, was a leader of the opposition to the President's foreign policy. He believed, agreeing with Jefferson and Girard, that the United States ought to cultivate close ties with France while avoiding too cozy a relationship with Great Britain.

In 1794 Madison was still fifteen years away from becoming president of the United States, but he already was a national leader. He was revered as the Father of the Constitution, having taken a leadership role at the Constitutional Convention in Philadelphia in 1787 and then having worked hard to win ratification by the states. Madison, with Alexander Hamilton and John Jay, had co-authored the

Federalist Papers, which were instrumental in building popular support for ratification of the Constitution. Moreover, Madison had been a central figure in writing and enacting the Bill of Rights as the first ten amendments to the Constitution.

In the early months of 1794 Madison had more on his mind than foreign policy. He was courting recently widowed Dolley Todd, who lived with her young son in a large house that still stands on the northeast corner of Fourth and Walnut Streets. Her husband, a lawyer, had died of yellow fever during the 1793 epidemic. A whirlwind romance between Madison and Todd early in 1794 led to a wedding in the summer of that year. He was forty-three (just ten months younger than Girard). She was twenty-six (the same age as Sally, Girard's mistress). The seventeen-year age difference did not bother the congressman or his bride. Their marriage was quite seemly for both. He was wealthy and famous. She was vivacious, with a sparkling personality and a radiant smile. Contemporaries described her as plump and pretty. To call a woman plump in the 1790s was highly complimentary. It was not fashionable, back then, for women to be thin. A woman who wanted to be attractive in the eyes of men did not go on a diet. She did not count calories. A hearty appetite was an asset. Women who were well-rounded and full-bodied were much sought after.

Madison was a most conscientious man. Even while he was falling head over heels in love with Dolley Todd early in 1794, he did not let this distraction deter him from trying to alter the direction of U.S. foreign policy. He introduced a bill in the House of Representatives that called for precisely the kind of change that Girard had been seeking. Madison's bill would have increased duties levied at American ports on the cargoes of merchant ships from countries having no treaty of commerce with the United States, while duties would have been reduced for cargoes of ships from countries with such a treaty. The effect of this proposal would have been higher U.S. duties on the cargoes of British ships and lower U.S. duties on the cargoes of French ships. The bill was passed in the House but could not get through the Senate.

Several other bills introduced by Madison could not even get House approval. They would have mandated U.S. retaliation against foreign countries that discriminated against America in trade matters. For example, if a nation banned products made or grown in the United States, Madison wanted the products of that nation banned in America. President Washington and his allies in Congress were opposed to that kind of retaliation for a number of reasons, mainly because they thought America would have more to lose than to gain from an all-out trade war, especially against Great Britain, and also because they feared that a trade war could lead to a military war, for which the United States was pitifully unprepared.

Some trade bills sponsored by congressmen other than Madison had tough sledding too. One bill would have sequestered all debts owed to British citizens by American citizens. The money would have been used to compensate owners of American ships and cargoes seized by Great Britain. Another bill, which was almost passed but fell short by the narrowest of margins, would have suspended indefinitely all maritime trade between the United States and Great Britain. The measure was approved in the House and received a tie vote in the Senate. Vice President John Adams broke the tie by voting against the bill.

Congress was concerned about British depredations on the western frontier as well as on the high seas. Girard got action, but not enough to satisfy him, on his demands that the U.S. government do something about the continuing British military presence in the American West, where Indians were being incited by the British to attack American settlements. President Washington sent troops under command of General Anthony Wayne to the frontier, which, in 1794, was not very far west. The vanguard of American settlers had reached areas that would later be in western Ohio and southern Michigan. On August 20, 1794, Indians allied with the British were defeated by U.S. forces under General Wayne in the Battle of Fallen Timbers, not far from the present site of Toledo, Ohio.[7] However, President Washington failed to follow up General Wayne's victory with further military ventures, or with diplomatic initiatives, to force a complete withdrawal of British troops from the Ohio-Michigan area. To the contrary, the President's envoy in England, John Jay, was being conciliatory in negotiations with the British instead of exerting pressure on them to put an end to their aggressions on the western frontier and on the high seas.

A treaty negotiated by Jay and the British was signed in London on November 19, 1794. Provisions of the pact, which came to be known in America as the Jay Treaty, were not made public until the summer of 1795. President Washington received a copy early in that year but did not disclose its contents to the American people. He submitted it to the Senate for its advice and consent on June 8. After deliberating behind closed doors for two weeks, the Senate rejected one article of the treaty and consented to the remainder, but just barely. The vote was 20 to 10, exactly the two-thirds majority that was required for approval. Even after ratifying the treaty, the Senate did not make it public. President Washington was advised by the Senate to inform the American people about the contents of the treaty at his discretion, whenever he thought it was appropriate to do so.

Governmental secrecy of this kind was not unusual in early America. (The Constitutional Convention had conducted all of its business behind closed doors in Philadelphia for four months in 1787.) However, during the presidency of George Washington a method was devised to circumvent secrecy, a method that would become common-place in the United States and many other countries. Secret information was made public simply by leaking it to the press.[8] A few days after Senate ratification of the Jay Treaty a Philadelphia newspaper, the *Aurora*, published a substantially accurate account of the treaty's main provisions. Shortly thereafter, the same newspaper obtained a copy of the treaty and printed it in full. In the ensuing weeks it was reprinted in newspapers all over the country.

Publication of the treaty produced widespread revulsion against many of the provisions. Jay, a large number of Americans concluded, had given away the store. He seemed to have bent over backwards in granting trade concessions to the British while getting very little in return. The citizenry expressed outrage over the treaty in ways that were highly emotional and sometimes violent. Burning Jay in effigy became a popular pastime. An angry crowd threw stones at Alexander Hamilton when he tried to speak in favor of the treaty and in defense of Jay.

The Jay Treaty established the most-favored-nation principle in international trade.[9] Great Britain was guaranteed access to American markets for ten years on terms at least as favorable as terms granted to any other nation. Yet the British gave almost nothing in return. Despite General Wayne's victory on the battlefield at Fallen Timbers, Great

Britain was allowed to be equivocal and tentative in making vague promises to withdraw from frontier outposts. Boundaries of Canada were left unsettled. Britain retained navigation rights on the Great Lakes and the Mississippi River. The upshot of it all was that the British remained a powerful force in North America and a potential stumbling block to U.S. territorial expansion, particularly in the vast area between the Great Lakes and the Pacific Ocean. Moreover, there were no assurances in the Jay Treaty that the United States, as a neutral, could trade with France without harassment of American ships by the British navy or British privateers, or Barbary pirates subsidized by the British. There were no guarantees that American merchants and shipowners would be compensated for losses resulting from past seizures of cargoes and ships by the British, although the treaty authorized creation of arbitration panels to try to resolve these and other matters in dispute.

Article XII of the treaty, the Article that the U.S. Senate refused to accept, would have forbidden American ships of more than seventy tons to trade with the British West Indies. Ships of seventy tons or under, while suitable for coastal and Caribbean trade, were too small to participate profitably in trans-Atlantic trade. Britain thus was trying to keep American merchant ships on trans-Atlantic routes from stopping at British ports in the West Indies. Additionally, Article XII prohibited U.S. export of certain products—including molasses, sugar, coffee, cocoa and cotton. These were items produced by British colonies in the West Indies. Britain did not want competition from the United States. This provision was particularly significant because cotton was on the threshold of becoming a major U.S. export. In terms of mercantilism, the generally accepted economic theory of the day, there was nothing unusual in Britain endeavoring to prevent trade competition from outside its colonial empire. Indeed, one could argue that Americans wanted both worlds: the autonomy of independence and the economic privilege of a colony.

When the treaty's contents were made public, Girard could see it was a victory for Great Britain. He was appalled. So were other Philadelphia merchants and shipowners. The Washington administration's foreign policy seemed now, more than ever, to be designed to favor Britain at the expense of France. Democratic Republicans called for a public rally in the nation's capital on the afternoon of July 23,

1795, to protest the Jay Treaty at the site behind Independence Hall and the Capitol, the same place where Girard had held his rally the year before.

At this point in the very early history of the American Republic, midway through the 1790s and midway through President Washington's second term, "factions" were just emerging into political parties. The Democratic Republican Party, the party of Jefferson, Madison and Girard, was the opposition party to the administration in power, President Washington, Vice-President Adams and Treasury Secretary Hamilton, who were Federalists. (The Democratic Republican Party, which was sometimes referred to simply as the Republican Party, was the forerunner of the Democratic Party and should not be confused with the Republican Party of a later time, the party of Abraham Lincoln.)

The French Revolution, but not the Reign of Terror, was seen by the Democratic Republicans as a laudable development with long-range implications and opportunities for democracy in Europe. In essence, the Democratic Republicans wanted American foreign policy to focus on cultivating close relations with an old friend, France, instead of kowtowing to an old enemy, Great Britain. How the Democratic Republicans viewed France and Great Britain was made clear in a handbill announcing the July 23 rally. "France is our avowed friend and in the hour of adversity was our vigorous and undaunted advocate," the handbill said. "Great Britain is the universal foe of liberty."

The rally on July 23, a Thursday, was a preliminary event. A resolution was adopted denouncing the Jay Treaty in general terms. A committee of fifteen persons was appointed to draw up a bill of particulars to be presented at another rally at the same location two days later. Girard was a member of the committee, along with other maritime merchants and shipowners and several leaders of the Democratic Republican Party. Two days later, on Saturday, July 25, 1795, an estimated six thousand people assembled on the Capitol grounds, about the same size crowd as the one that had attended Girard's rally against President Washington's foreign policy in 1794. The fifteen-member committee had worked under extreme pressure in a span of forty-eight hours to prepare a detailed and perceptive critique of the Jay Treaty. The statement was addressed to President Washington from "the citizens of Philadelphia, the Northern Liberties and the District of Southwark, in the state of Pennsylvania."[10]

As each section of the statement was read at the July 25 rally, there was a vote by a show of hands. Every section was approved unanimously or nearly so.

"The treaty is objected to," the statement said:

> Because it does not provide for a fair and effectual settlement of the differences ... between the United States and Great Britain—inasmuch as it cedes, without any equivalent, an indefinite extent of territory to the settlers under British titles within the precincts and jurisdiction of these posts .... and inasmuch as it refers all the hopes of indemnity, for the recent spoilations committed on the commerce of the United States, to an equivocal, expensive, tedious and uncertain process.
>
> Because by the treaty the federal government accedes to restraints upon the American commerce and navigation, internal as well as external, that embrace no principle of real reciprocity, and are inconsistent with the rights, and destructive to the interests, of an independent nation—inasmuch as it fetters the intercourse with the West Indies, with India, and with the American lakes, by means of the navigable rivers belonging to the British—inasmuch as in many instances it circumscribes the navigation of the United States to a particular voyage—and inasmuch as some of our staple commodities ... it makes liable to confiscation as contraband; and others ... it makes liable to seizure ... as articles useful to the enemies of Great Britain.
>
> Because the treaty is destructive to the domestic independence and prosperity of the United States .... inasmuch as it enables Great Britain to draw an invidious and dangerous line of circumvallation round the territory of the Union, by her fleets on the Atlantic, and by her settlements from Nova Scotia to the mouth of the Mississippi.
>
> Because the treaty surrenders certain inherent powers of an independent government, which are essential, in the circumstances of the United States, to their safety and defense ... inasmuch as the right of sequestration; the right of regulating commerce, in favor of a friendly, and against a rival, power; and the right of suspending a commercial intercourse, with an inimical nation, are voluntarily abandoned.
>
> Because the treaty is an infraction of the rights of friendship, gratitude and alliance, which the Republic of France may justly claim from the United States; and deprives the United States of the most powerful means to secure the good will and good offices of other nations—inasmuch as it alters, during a war, the relative situation of the different nations, advantageously to Great Britain, and prejudicially to the French Republic—inasmuch as it is in manifest collision with several articles of the American treaty with France—and

inasmuch as it grants to Great Britain certain high, dangerous and exclusive privileges.[11]

This analysis by Girard and others on the committee has stood up under the tests of time and history. A resounding ring of truth and accuracy still comes through clearly. It is even more apparent today than it was in 1795 that the Jay Treaty was a low point in the early history of the United States, a step backwards in the young country's search for recognition and esteem on the world stage. The stinging criticism was justified.

Ironically, no one knew that better than President Washington himself. He did not like the treaty either. He knew as well as Girard that it was a victory for the British and a defeat for America. Washington believed, however, that America's best interests were served by accepting a temporary diplomatic setback rather than risking a military disaster. He also believed, as he would later warn in his Farewell Address, that America should "steer clear of permanent alliances with any portion of the foreign world," although he had no objections to "temporary alliances for extraordinary emergencies."

As a pragmatic president, Washington saw the Jay Treaty as a way of buying time. He felt that America needed time to build a respectable navy before it could realistically even think about challenging British domination on the high seas. He knew, and he knew the British also knew, that the American victory over the British at Yorktown in 1781 could not have been achieved without help from France, especially from the French navy. He believed it would be foolhardy, perhaps even suicidal, for America in the mid-1790s, a struggling nation barely out of infancy, to blunder into another war with Great Britain while France was in the throes of revolution and anarchy and in no condition to help America again. To put President Washington's views in perspective, it needs to be kept in mind that, in 1795, Napoleon had not yet emerged as the leader of France, and it was unclear what the outcome of the French Revolution would be.

In a letter to Gouverneur Morris, who had been U.S. minister to France during the Reign of Terror, President Washington gave what was perhaps his most cogent and concise explanation of why he was willing to accept the Jay Treaty. "Peace has been the order of the day with me since the disturbances in Europe first commenced," Washington wrote. "My policy has been, and will continue to be, while I have the honor to remain in the administration of the government, to be upon friendly terms with, but independent of, all the nations of the earth; to share in the broils of none; to fulfil our own engagements; to supply the wants and be carrier for them all; being thoroughly convinced that it is our best policy and interest so to do. Nothing short of self-respect, and that justice which is essential to a national character, ought to involve us in war; for sure I am, if this country is preserved in tranquillity twenty years longer, it may bid defiance in a just cause to any power whatever; such in that time will be its population, wealth and resources."[12]

So, President Washington swallowed hard and accepted the Jay Treaty even while knowing it was an embarrassment to himself and to America. Appeasement, although it was not a word that Washington used, was the kernel of his foreign policy in 1795. Having led America in one war against the British, he knew more than anyone how unprepared America was to fight another. As the Father of His Country and its first president, he knew more than anyone how fragile American independence was. Discretion was the better part of valor. The new country needed time to grow up and develop some muscles.

Trade concessions to the British would be politically unpopular, Washington had known all along, but he believed they were something the country could live with. Therefore, while the Democratic Republicans railed at the Jay Treaty, the President stood his ground. Perhaps John Jay had not been as assertive as he ought to have been in negotiating terms of the treaty, and maybe he had made more concessions than were really necessary, but Washington, as president, was willing to bear the responsibility and the consequences. He took the scoldings stoically, as would be expected of an old soldier, but they hurt.

Implementation of the Jay Treaty was delayed, but not prevented, by the U.S. Senate's rejection of Article XII. The British, knowing the treaty was a good deal for them even without Article XII, accepted the deletion.

Political repercussions in the aftermath of the bitter battle over the Jay Treaty were far reaching and long lasting. In the presidential election of 1796 John Adams just barely won over Thomas Jefferson. The electoral vote was seventy-one to sixty-eight in the last presidential election won by the Federalist Party. Adams was a one-term President. Jefferson was elected the next time around, and the Federalists faded away.

A second war between the Americans and the British was postponed, but not averted, by the Jay Treaty. War did come, but not until 1812. It would be President Madison's war but, financially speaking, it also would be Stephen Girard's war.

CHAPTER 10

At Middle Age: The Kind of a Man He Was

1795

*There is no one recipe for happiness. It requires
different ingredients for different people.*

IN THE SUMMER OF 1795 Stephen Girard was in the summer of his
life. He was forty-five years old and over halfway through his journey
on earth, well past the midway mark in his pursuit of happiness.
Important events in his personal and business affairs were about to
happen. He was on the threshold of significant change. This is a good
time to pause and take a long look at Girard, to consider what kind
of a man he had become at mid-life.

Contemporaries of Girard who knew him in his middle years, or
talked to people who did, described him in various modes: heroic,
eccentric, industrious (a workaholic in the terminology of a later time),
brusque but kind-hearted, generous for the most part but sometimes
tightfisted. He was a man of many parts. He knew how to say *yes* and
he knew how to say *no*. Underneath a gruff exterior there was a gentle
and tender man. He was, in the views of some, neither lovable nor
likable, while others thought he was misunderstood and unappreciated.
He was hard to get to know, some said, but others got to know him
well and admired him with great devotion and deep affection.

In a nineteenth century biography of Girard, based in part on
conversations with people who had known him, Henry Atlee Ingram
gave this description:

Girard was heavily built, broad and square-shouldered, of middle stature, with strongly marked, rather handsome features, and gray eyes, of which the right, as has been said, was blind .... In matters of dress he was as particular as his favorite people, the Quakers, whom, indeed, he much resembled. Like theirs, his clothing, while not in the prevailing fashion, was made of the best broadcloth, after his own directions, plain, large, and comfortable, and never changing the cut.[1]

Ingram also described Girard's personality and temperament, portraying him as a multi-dimensional man:

He was grave, but not at all morose. Fear was utterly unknown to him, and under threats or abuse he was inflexible. He was not easily aroused, but when angered was very passionate, though in later years his temper was completely under his control; and a salient feature of his character was his great love for children, for strong horses, good dogs, and singing-birds. In his private office several canaries swung in brass cages, and these he taught to sing with a bird-organ specially imported for that purpose from France, while his love for animals was further manifested in the shape of a large watch-dog which he always kept in the yard of his city house. Each of his ships was similarly provided, and he was in the habit of saying that the faithfulness of these trusty animals not only economized the employment of men, but protected his property much more efficiently than services merely rendered for wages.[2]

Abraham Ritter, who wrote a book in the nineteenth century recording, from his own experiences and recollections, what Philadelphia was like in the early decades of American independence, told about Girard when he was young and also when he was middle-aged. Ritter called him

a meteor of the mercantile community .... He was celebrated for his perseverance, indefatigable industry, economy, and almost unparalleled success in all his undertakings .... He did not begin his [large financial] increase until he was forty years of age—encouraging to early unsuccessful strife, and a beacon of perseverance, and the changes and chances of life. In 1791, Mr. Girard kept a greengrocery and provision store at No. 43 North Front Street, occupying through to and on Water Street, at No. 31, where he lived and moved carefully and economically in all his domestic arrangements.[3]

Ritter could remember when Stephen and Mary Girard were a happily married couple, before insanity struck her down. They had to live frugally because money was scarce and Stephen's limited resources were tied up in his business, invested mostly in ships and cargoes. A seamstress who did work for Girard's "wife at this early period of his life," Ritter said, "has often told me that neither he, she, nor they, were ever allowed to indulge in more edibles than were absolutely necessary."[4]

As Girard became increasingly prosperous, he also became increasingly generous in sharing what he had with others. "I knew him as good to the poor, and kindly indulgent to the sick," Ritter said. "He was a liberal contributor to the building of churches."[5]

Ritter told a story that, he said, illustrates Girard's "ready wit." It also illustrates other traits of Girard, including his shrewdness as a businessman and his willingness to help others get started in business.

"He had a cargo of salt at his wharf," Ritter recalled, but the principal salt dealer in Philadelphia, trying to hold his costs down, refused to buy at the price sought by Girard. Whereupon Girard went to Tom, his porter (a janitor and handyman), and asked, "'Why can't you buy that cargo?'

"Tom laughed, and replied, 'Why, sir, how can I buy? I have no money.'

"'Never mind,' said Girard, 'you can buy it all. Take it and sell it by the load, and pay me as you sell it.' The porter took the hint. The salt was out of the market—his opponents were foiled—and Tom, from this hint, became a prominent salt merchant, and as such flourished for many years after."[6]

Girard's devotion to hard work was legendary. Ingram put it this way:

So fully was he impressed with the idea that active employment is one of the greatest duties of life, that it was one of his favorite maxims that no man should leave off business because he considered himself rich enough. He used to say that he attached importance only to labor, valuing his wealth no more than he did his old shoes, and an amusing anecdote illustrative of this creed is told of an Irishman who had applied to him for work. This being a form of appeal that touched Girard's theories very dearly, he was quite willing to assist the applicant, but having no work that needed to be done, he considered it an excellent opportunity to illustrate his theory that the pleasure of labor lay in the simple gratification of finding oneself employed. Accordingly, engaging the man for a whole day, he directed the removal from one side of his yard to the other of a pile of bricks which had been stored there awaiting some building operations; and this task, which consumed several hours, being completed, he was accosted by the Irishman to know what should be done next. "Why, have you finished that already?" said Girard. "I thought it would take all day to do that. Well, just move them all back again where you took them from; that will use up the rest of the day," and upon the astonished Irishman's flat refusal to perform such fruitless labor, he was promptly paid and discharged, Girard saying at the same time, in rather an aggrieved manner, "I certainly understood you to say when you came that you wanted *any* kind of work."[7]

Girard once expressed his thoughts about work thus: "When I rise in the morning, my only effort is to labor so hard during the day, that when the night comes, I may be enabled to sleep soundly."[8] On another occasion, writing to a friend, Girard said: "As for my fortune, I do not seek for it. The love of work is my greatest ambition."[9]

Ingram described Girard's relationship with his employees:

He never scolded his apprentices, his opinion of an employee being expressed by cutting down a salary, or, if matters had gone so far that this was not sufficient, by the offender's summary dismissal. He had no patience with incompetence .... Each man felt he was watched, and so long as he did his best, and his best suited, he was confident of the most impartial justice. Honesty, soberness, and punctuality were exacted .... The secrecy of his operations was secured by the habit of entrusting a matter of business to the smallest number of persons that could properly perform it.[10]

Girard was remarkably kind to employees even when they made a mistake or did wrong. Ingram told two stories that make the point.

An apprentice, in making up an account, credited a tanner with three hundred dollars more than he was entitled to. Having drawn a check for that amount, he forwarded it with the account to the creditor, who, at once discovering the mistake, returned the letter and enclosures to Girard. The latter said nothing to the apprentice, but contented himself with silently laying the letter and check upon the former's desk, where it was discovered by him the morning after the occurrence, this being the only reproof the act of carelessness ever received. On another occasion, small sums of money having been missed from the counting house, the errand boy was suspected of the thefts, and being watched, was at last caught in the act. Instead of the severe punishment which might naturally have been expected to follow, however, Girard merely directed that a new and more intricate lock should be obtained for the money-drawer, and this being accordingly done, the matter was passed by without further comment. Girard probably felt that the remorse shown by the lad was a sufficient token of his repentance, but it was such acts of judicious forbearance toward his employees, at times when they were undoubtedly derelict, that implanted in the bosoms of the better of them such personal admiration and regard as grew in time almost to veneration.[11]

Stephen Simpson, a son of a Girard employee and a Girard employee himself, wrote a biography of Girard published four months after his death. Simpson capsulized the essence of his employer in just nine words: "Perhaps no man *enjoyed life* more than Stephen Girard."[12]

Some people do not equate hard work with happiness, but Girard did. He enjoyed working, and he liked the company of others who enjoyed working, all the more so if they were working for him.

He also enjoyed his mistresses (Sally being the first, but not the last). They ate with him. They slept with him. They gave him companionship. They gave him affection. They gave him love.

As he grew increasingly prosperous, then enormously wealthy, Girard continued to relish a simple life filled with simple pleasures. He still believed that the basics for enjoyment of nonworking hours were a satisfying meal, a fine wine, a stimulating book and an amiable woman.

Although he remained a man of moderation, he did not skimp at the dinner table after he had achieved prosperity. He could enjoy and appreciate hearty eating as much as anyone. "He fed well," in Simpson's words. "He ate what pleased his palate, and drank what he was most fond of, good claret. But temperance marked him."[13]

Much of Girard's time at home was devoted to reading. For forty-one years, from 1790 to his death in 1831, he was a member of the Library Company of Philadelphia, and he made good use of his membership to borrow an abundance of reading material with emphasis on serious nonfiction. Girard's personal papers, including memos to remind when books were due, and records of fines paid for books overdue, indicate he was borrowing many books from the library in the 1790s, especially works by Voltaire and other French philosophers of the eighteenth century.[14] By 1797, Girard had the complete works of Voltaire, in seventy volumes, in his personal library.[15]

Simpson, noting that some people are born to wealth and power while others have to work to achieve them, concluded quite appropriately that "it is easier to be a King, than a Girard."[16] Simpson also spoke of "sobriety, prudence, economy and industry" as qualities that carried Girard to the heights.[17] In terms of influence in financial affairs

he would become "the Napoleon of the monied world"[18], as Simpson
put it, but Girard would never aspire to the grandeur of Napoleon.

"Some men are frugal in respect to others, and yet extravagant to
themselves," Simpson said. "This, however, was not the case with
Stephen Girard. A sense of justice was always paramount in his actions,
and he never laid down a rule for others, which he was not willing to
observe himself .... He allowed himself no extravagance that he denied
to others. In his personal apparel, he was a strict economist; wearing
one coat for five, six, or ten years .... He was in the habit of boasting
of one of his threadbare greatcoats—that he had worn it fourteen years.
His hats and boots were, in general, of the same antiquity."[19]

Stories about Girard's frugality are legion, not only in his personal
affairs but in his commercial transactions as well. He insisted on
collecting every last penny due him, but he had a sense of humor in
the process. He was not a dour businessman. He loved the give and
take of mercantile activity. He thoroughly enjoyed the affairs of the
counting-house, especially when dealing with someone who enjoyed
them too. Simpson told this story:

> A gentleman from Europe who visited this country a few years since, had
> purchased in London a bill of exchange on Mr. Girard, to defray the expenses
> of his projected tour. The bill was, of course, duly honored upon presentation;
> but in the course of their transactions it so happened that one cent remained
> to be refunded on the part of the European; and on the eve of his departure
> from this country he was reminded by Girard that he was indebted to him in
> that amount. The gentleman apologized for the inadvertent omission, and
> tendering a six and a quarter cent piece, requested the difference. [What the
> gentleman actually tendered was a six-cent English coin, which was worth six
> and a quarter cents in American money.] Mr. Girard returned him the change
> of five cents, which the gentleman declined to accept, contending that
> according to the specific value of the current money of the United States, that
> coin was in the value of six and a quarter cents; and that consequently he was
> entitled to an additional quarter of a cent! In reply, Girard admitted the fact,
> but informed the European that it was not in his power to comply, alleging
> that the government had neglected to provide the fractional coin in question;
> upon which he returned the gentleman the six cent piece, reminding him at
> the same time, that as he could not accommodate him with the precise change,
> he must still consider him his debtor for the balance! This tender, retender,
> and peculiar manner of surmounting the difficulty, had a pleasing and
> compromising effect; the gentleman could not refrain from indulging a laugh,

and the good nature of Girard getting the better of his disappointment for not receiving so large a balance, he joined in the laugh, and after a cordial shake of hands, they separated, well pleased with each other.[20]

Another story, also told by Simpson:

He [Girard] at one period of his changeful life, sold salt by the bushel, and conceiving that his measure for half bushel was too large, he determined to regulate or re-adjust it himself; for this purpose he took a half gallon liquid measure, and repairing to the wharf, which was at the time constructed with steps, for the convenience of supplying the citizens with water from the river, he deposited the requisite number of half gallons into his half bushel; and then drawing a chalk line around the water mark, he found it was too large by an inch, or more; then he went to a neighboring cooper's shop, and borrowing a saw for the purpose, reduced the measure of his half bushel accordingly, to what he conceived it ought to be. This fact gave rise to the saying, 'that Mr. Girard was a just man, but it was according to his own measure of justice.'[21]

Girard enjoyed every aspect of doing business: hard work for himself, providing employment for others, the satisfaction of solving problems and making a profit, the challenge of investing profits to generate more jobs and more profits. As Simpson perceived Girard: "The great object of his life was to *produce*. He detested an idle man, and never kept a dollar from circulation that he could find employment for. If he could not invest it in one branch of trade, he gave it a new direction; and thus by keeping it in circulation, made it profitable; for he held to the maxim that small gains are better than none."[22]

Girard enjoyed giving money away almost as much as he enjoyed making it, but one thing he could not stand was any haggling or lack of appreciation when he made a contribution for a charitable purpose. An anecdote is illustrative:

A delegation of Episcopalians went to Girard's office to solicit a contribution for a building fund. He gave them a check for five hundred dollars. This was the same amount he had previously given to the Methodists—a fact that the Episcopalians knew. They were expecting a much bigger donation because, in Philadelphia at that time, the Episcopalians were a substantially larger and more influential denomination than the Methodists, and also because the Methodists had built a small, plain church whereas the Episcopalians were seeking funds for a grand edifice. The delegation of Episcopalians looked at the check for five hundred dollars, conferred among themselves briefly, and handed it back to Girard—suggesting as politely as they could that there must be some mistake, for surely he intended to give the Episcopalians more than he had given the Methodists. It was further suggested that he may have intended to write a check for five thousand dollars but had inadvertently omitted a zero. As the check was handed back to him and he looked at it, Girard said: "Ah, gentlemen, what you say? I have made a mistake? Let me see—I believe not—but if you say so, I must correct it." He then tore up the check and declared: "I will not contribute one cent. Your society is wealthy—the Methodists are poor—but I make no distinction; yet I cannot please you."[23]

Sometimes Girard tore up a check in a way that was profitable for a beneficiary. Samuel Coates, the manager of Pennsylvania Hospital, called on Girard early one morning to solicit a donation. He was having breakfast and invited Coates to join him, which he did. They were old friends. Girard was a frequent and generous contributor to the hospital, in addition to payments to cover costs of Mary's apartment, meals, medical treatment, custodial care and other expenses. After breakfast Girard wrote a check for two hundred dollars and handed it to Coates. He thanked Girard and put the check in his pocket without looking to see how much it was for, knowing that Girard did not want anyone, even a friend, to be critical of, or show disappointment in, the amount of a contribution. Girard, amused by his friend's behavior, chided him for not seeming to be interested enough in the donation to care what the amount was and demanded good naturedly that the check be returned to him. Coates, just as good naturedly, refused to give up the check, assuring Girard that his gift, whatever the amount, was badly needed and much appreciated. Whereupon Girard wrote another check, this time for five hundred dollars, and handed it to Coates.

"Will you now look at it?" Girard asked, referring to the second check.

"Well, to please thee, Stephen, I will." And he did.

"Now give me back the first check."

Coates complied and, in handing it back, had an opportunity to see the amount. Both men were greatly pleased with the transaction and parted in good humor.

Simpson, who told this story, not only had known Girard for many years but also had known Coates since he (Simpson) was a boy. "This little incident is characteristic of both individuals," Simpson said, "and may be relied on as authentic."[24]

When being asked for a charitable donation, Girard wanted the solicitor to be brief and to the point. On one occasion, according to another story told by Simpson, an elderly woman who was inclined to be talkative called on Girard to ask for funds for a needy family in her neighborhood. She talked and talked and talked, describing the family's plight in great detail. She went on and on and on. Girard, who had listened patiently through all of this, finally interrupted her:

"If you will promise never to trouble me again, I will give you something. Will you promise me never to come again?"

"Why, Mr. Girard, I will, if you say so."

"Well, then, never come again, and I will give you thirty dollars."

Whereupon he gave her a check for that amount, and she never came again.[25]

Beginning in the 1790s, when Girard was in his forties, philanthropy on a substantial scale played an important and ever-growing role in his life. The more money he made, the more he gave away, and the more he enjoyed giving it away. Yet he was unchanging in his philosophical approach to philanthropy as reflected not only in the sizes of his gifts to a great variety of beneficiaries during his lifetime but also in the amounts of bequests in his will and in the curriculum he specified in the school for orphans he founded and funded in his will. While conceding there are exceptions to every rule, Girard believed that individuals were generally destined for a certain station in life, as determined largely by economic and social circumstances at birth, unless they took strenuous and persistent initiatives, as he did, to rise to a significantly higher financial level through hard work, frugal living and shrewd investment. Girard's view was realistic in the America that he knew, in approximately the last quarter of the eighteenth century and the first third of the nineteenth century. The land of opportunity was also a land of limitations. A son of an unskilled laborer was unlikely to attend a university and become a physician or a professor, but he might become an apprentice to a skilled craftsman, a clockmaker or a cabinet-maker, for example, and eventually achieve prosperity by turning out products of high quality that commanded high prices.

Girard, with much personal satisfaction, helped the most talented and the most dependable of the apprentices in his own counting-house become prosperous, or even wealthy, as his supercargoes or port agents or as independent entrepreneurs in maritime trade, and he loaned money at affordable interest rates to many hundreds of responsible and industrious young men to help them go into business for themselves and/or to acquire homes of their own. In philanthropy, though, he adhered to his fundamental philosophy, tailoring his generosity to financial need and helping recipients get through difficult times while being careful never to give anyone so much that it might reduce incentive for honest labor and frugality. Girard was absolutely determined that no man would ever be a gentleman (i.e., rich and idle) with his money, and he never wavered from that resolve.

One statistic of Philadelphia in the 1790s tells a great deal about the kind of a man Girard was in the middle of his life, and the kind of a man he would be for the rest of his life. Midway through the 1790s there were more than three hundred four-wheel carriages in Philadelphia.[26] Not one of them was owned by Girard. He never, in his entire life, would own a four-wheel carriage, not even when he was the richest person in America. A carriage—with opulent interior, distinctive craftsmanship inside and out, drawn by at least two horses, more often by four and sometimes by six, manned by a coachman and footmen, all liveried—was a standard symbol of wealth and power and prestige in Girard's time, but he wanted no part of such display. Wherever he went in the city, irrespective of the weather, he walked.

When Girard acquired a farm a few miles from the city he went there in a two-wheel, one-horse gig, driving it himself. It was "the plainest, least comfortable gig in Philadelphia, drawn by an ancient and ill-formed horse," according to James Parton, the nineteenth century historian who profiled many famous persons in early America.[27] Even after buying the two-wheel gig to get to his farm, Girard continued to walk to destinations in the city. Parton described Girard's appearance when he was a familiar figure walking the streets of Philadelphia. He was "short, stout, brisk" and walked "in his swift, awkward way." He was "quite unprepossessing. His dress was old-fashioned and shabby .... Though his bushy eyebrows gave some character to his countenance, it was curiously devoid of expression. He had the absent look of a man who either had no thoughts or was absorbed in thought; and he shuffled along on his enormous feet, looking neither to the right nor to the left."[28]

Parton also captured the essence of Girard as an entrepreneur:

"His neighbors, the merchants of Philadelphia, deemed him a lucky man. Many of them thought they could do as well as he, if they only had his luck. But the great volumes of his letters and papers, preserved in a room of the Girard College, show that his success in business was not due, in any degree whatever, to good fortune. Let a money-making generation take note, that Girard principles inevitably produce Girard results. The grand, the fundamental secret of his success, as of all success, was that *he understood his business.* He had a personal, familiar knowledge of the ports with which he traded, the commodities in which he dealt, the vehicles in which they were carried, the dangers to which they were liable, and the various kinds of men through whom he acted. He observed everything, and forgot nothing. He had done everything himself which he had occasion to require others to do. His directions to his captains and supercargoes, full, minute, exact, peremptory, show the hand of a master. Every possible contingency was foreseen and provided for; and he demanded the most literal obedience ....

"Add to this perfect knowledge of his craft, that he had a self-control which never permitted him to anticipate his gains or spread too wide his sails; that his industry knew no pause; that he was a close, hard bargainer, keeping his word to the letter, but exacting his rights to the letter; that he had no vices and no vanities; that he had no toleration for those calamities which result from vices and vanities; that his charities, though frequent, were bestowed only upon unquestionably legitimate objects, and were never profuse; that he was as wise in investing as skilful in gaining money .... that he held in utter aversion and contempt the costly and burdensome ostentation of a great establishment, fine equipages, and a retinue of servants."[29]

Girard had servants, mostly maids who did household chores under supervision of his mistress or, earlier in his life, under supervision of his wife, but he had no band of flunkies and lackeys bowing and groveling. Even when he became the richest person in America he would have no entourage. Walking alone, or riding alone in his gig, was the plain and simple style of life he preferred. When he was well up in years, and not quite as steady as he once had been, he was sometimes accompanied by a driver in his gig. They would sit side by side on the one and only bench the gig had.

For Girard, unlike others of his time with far less wealth, there were no grand entrances, no grand appearances, no grand processions. He did not wear his prosperity on his sleeve. He did not proclaim his riches throughout all the land unto all the inhabitants thereof. He did not sally forth with the sound of trumpets. He was a humble man. Humility was not just a trait but a definitive characteristic. It was his strongest suit, and he led with it. He was called *peculiar* precisely because he steadfastly refused to live as other rich men lived, to act as other rich men acted, to dress as other rich men dressed, to mobilize the pomp and the ceremony and all of the other trappings of wealth as other rich men did, even when he had become the richest of them all.

Nonetheless, as unpretentious as he was, he had outbursts of temper now and then, and he was good at sarcasm if an occasion called for it. When engaged in a heated argument, he was not one to back off. Confronted with a put-down, he could recover with a fast rejoinder. Thomas P. Cope, a Philadelphia merchant who was a contemporary of Girard and a friendly competitor, recounted in his diary an incident involving Girard and Jacob Ridgway, a rich Philadelphian: "They had some personal altercation about property. When Ridgway exclaimed petulantly, 'I could buy and sell you,' Stephen cooly replied, 'I could buy you, Mr. Ridgway, but I do not think that I could sell you again.'"[30]

Henry W. Arey, an early biographer, portrayed Girard as "possessing elements of greatness," in part because of his "penetrating sagacity and massive intellect." Recalling Girard's heroism during the yellow fever epidemic, Arey concluded that "no danger was too great, and no service too severe, for this misunderstood but really kind-hearted man."[31] In sum, Girard at forty-five was prosperous and influential, well on his way to becoming wealthy and powerful. He was a success in business but not nearly as successful as he would be in another decade or two. He was generous but not profligate in charitable enterprise. Despite all the complexities of his commercial ventures, he was a person of simple tastes and wants in his domestic affairs. He could be cold and cantankerous, yet he could also be warm and compassionate. Although he had not yet gotten there, he had what it would take to reach the top. Quoting Arey again, "He was a most remarkable man."[32]

Albeit, there was a cloud that cast a shadow overall. There was Mary. Out of sight and, quite literally, out of mind, she was at this point in the story of Stephen Girard almost as invisible as the persistent ache she had left in his heart. She was, as one writer put it many years later, "a wife who sat staring emptily out of a hospital window."[33]

It continued to be a hospital of outstanding quality and reputation. Carl and Jessica Bridenbaugh, twentieth century historians who did extensive research on Pennsylvania Hospital as it was in the eighteenth century, described the character of that institution: "Nowhere in the western world were such comfortable accommodations and enlightened care provided for the mentally ill."[34]

Knowing that Mary was well cared for gave her husband great comfort. Yet there must have been occasions, even while he was in the arms of a mistress, when he could not help remembering how Mary used to be, the way she was at eighteen when their love was new.

Those memories are an uncharted dimension of Stephen Girard's life. They cannot be measured, for there is no way to fathom his unrecorded thoughts, but they must have been a bittersweet blend of vinegar and honey. Thinking about old times, the good times, with Mary: That must have been nice. Thinking about what might have been, but never would be: That must have hurt.

CHAPTER 11

A New House, A New Mistress: So Long Sally, Hello Polly
1795-1799

You can build a house with bricks and mortar,
but it takes love to make a home.

STEPHEN GIRARD had the best of both worlds. He built a solid brick house and he found a solid gold woman to fill it with her love. She was young and beautiful, and the pleasure she gave was twenty-four carats.

Girard acquired a site for a new house in 1794. Construction began in 1795 and was completed early in 1796. When he and Sally Bickham moved into their new home, he had no inkling that she would be leaving him soon to marry another man. He had no idea that, within just a few months, he would have a new mistress.

The new home included a counting-house, and making a move was primarily a business decision. Girard needed more office space more than he needed more living space. Despite piracy and privateering on the high seas and war in Europe, Girard's business was booming. In 1794 the first private turnpike company in America had completed a toll road of sixty-two miles between Philadelphia and Lancaster, opening up large areas of eastern Pennsylvania to increased commerce with the nation's biggest city and busiest port.[1] Freight-carrying Conestoga wagons, each pulled by six horses, moved farm products to

Philadelphia, for consumption in the city or for export, and took back goods manufactured in Philadelphia or imported through Philadelphia.

Prospering rapidly with cargoes coming and going by land and sea, Girard in 1795 built the first of his four "philosopher" ships, that is, ships named in honor of French philosophers. The *Voltaire*, at 305 tons with three masts, was launched on December 5 in Kensington (now a part of Philadelphia) and sailed for many years on numerous voyages to China, India, Russia and South America in addition to major ports of western Europe.

The move to a new house by Stephen and Sally was a short one, across the street and a few yards south. The rear entrance of the old house was at 31 North Water Street. The front entrance of the new house was at 23 North Water Street. Both houses were in the first block north of Market Street, a block that extended to Arch Street. The old house was on the west side of Water Street. The new house was on the east side. (That block of Water Street no longer exists. An expressway, Interstate 95, passes through the area where the street and the houses used to be.) Although the move was not very far, it put Girard conveniently closer to the Delaware River. The new house backed up almost to the river.

What it actually backed up to was a narrow alley, muddy in wet weather, dusty in dry weather, that ran adjacent to docks and wharves.[2] Girard built a small dock in back of his house and across the alley. To the south of the dock he built a large wharf, extending more than a hundred feet into the river.[3] (In the 1830s the alley separating his house and offices from his dock and wharf became part of Delaware Avenue, which was built with funds bequeathed in Girard's will; the name was changed to Columbus Boulevard in 1992.[4] In the middle of the nineteenth century Girard's house and offices were torn down and replaced by warehouses.[5])

Girard's new house was not sumptuous, nor was it gaudy, and it certainly was not pretentious, but it was adequate for his needs. It provided residential accommodations and office space in ample but not excessive amounts. It was well designed, well built and conveniently located. It was a house that Girard could be proud of without being embarrassed by. He had come a long way in twenty years in Philadelphia, and he erected a symbol of success that was quiet and dignified but impressive. A twentieth century authority on early American architecture described the building as "an utterly conventional late-eighteenth-century five-story brick structure with a parapet linking two end chimneys."[6] Girard would have liked the "utterly conventional" label. In architecture he was anything but avant-garde. He relished the traditional and the classic. Abraham Ritter, who described Girard's house from personal observation, said it was built of "pressed brick of the first-class."[7] The combination home and place of business had thirty-seven feet of frontage on Water Street. Part of the building, on the north side, was five stories, for residential purposes. The remainder, on the south side, was two stories, for business purposes. There were two front entrances. The one on the left (if you were facing the building from the street) was for the living quarters. The one on the right was for the place of business, which was called the public counting-house or counting-room. There was a hallway, with a door, connecting the living quarters with the place of business, so that Girard could go to and from work without going outside.

In addition to the public counting-house, Girard had a private counting-house in the residential part of the building. It was on the first floor, as were the dining room and kitchen. The dining room was paved with marble; so was the vestibule inside the front entrance to the living quarters. The kitchen was paved with tile. Other rooms had hardwood floors. For warmth, in cold-weather months, heavy Turkish carpets were put over the marble floor in the dining room and over the hardwood floors in some of the other rooms.

A parlor and drawing rooms were on the second floor of the residence. Furnishings included a table that could be used for meals and snacks, as an alternative to eating in the dining room.

Bedrooms, including accommodations for servants and apprentices and Hannah, the slave, were on upper floors. The bedroom where Girard slept was on the third floor at the rear of the house, with windows providing a spectacular view of the Delaware River. His bedroom connected directly with an adjoining bedroom, so that he and his mistress could go from one bedroom to the other without going into the hallway. This provided privacy and flexibility in sleeping arrangements.

Henry Atlee Ingram, the nineteenth century biographer, talked to many people who knew the house and offices intimately, including relatives of Girard who had lived there and employees of Girard who had worked there. Ingram said the structure:

> united in a happy combination both comfort and a very considerable degree of elegance .... The furniture of [Girard's] office was of the simplest character .... Two canary birds swung in cages .... [Girard] sat and wrote at a mahogany desk, by the side of which stood a small fire-proof safe, about four and one-half feet high, with two doors and a marble top; and this last was piled high with French editions of Voltaire, Montesquieu, and Rousseau .... An even greater simplicity marked the public counting-room. One single and one double pine desk [used by apprentices] ... a good desk of walnut [used by a clerk] ... three or four chairs ... constituted the whole outfit of the office, where [eventually] more business was done than in any other in the city of Philadelphia.
>
> The windows of his house were casemented, and vaults in the cellar provided storage for the wines he imported for his private use. The sanitary arrangements were especially considered, among others a marble bath-room being provided, and this was justly regarded a very unusual luxury, owing to the scarcity of water, street mains being a convenience not yet understood in the city.
>
> Another great innovation was the introduction of open coal fires throughout the house and in the counting-rooms; and Girard designed ingenious sheet-iron shutters, sliding up and down in iron grooves let into the front masonry of the brick hearths, completely doing away with risk of fire from sparks thrown off into the room at night. He brought a cargo of coal from England, which lasted him more than a year, storing it upon his wharf, and this novel form of fuel burning in the counting-house fire-place attracted considerable attention, its use being then practically unknown in Philadelphia.[8]

This, then, would be Girard's home for the rest of his life. It would be his home when he was the richest person in America. It was a substantial residence-business combination, but there was no ballroom, nor were there other trappings of wealth and high society. Girard would continue to shun parties, dances and receptions featuring small talk. However, he would enjoy hosting dinners, especially on Sunday afternoons, with a small number of guests, perhaps six or eight, leisurely partaking of food and wine while engaging in conversation on subjects that might include local and national politics, general business conditions and world affairs. French refugees from the revolutions in France and St-Domingue were often among the guests. Much later, after the Battle of Waterloo, a standard fixture at Girard's house for Sunday dinner would be Joseph Bonaparte, a brother of Napoleon and a former king of Spain.

So, even though Girard would never be plugged into Philadelphia's social circuit, and would always manage to avoid spending long evenings kissing delicate hands and powdered cheeks, he was by no means a recluse. Marvin W. McFarland, a 1936 Girard College graduate who became curator of the Girard Papers and an authority on Girard, summed up the essence of his role as dinner host: "No one set a more bounteous table, no one served more sumptuous wines, or offered better coffee and cigars, brandies and cordials, and conversation, than Girard."[9]

Sally Bickham helped Stephen get settled in the new house in the early months of 1796 before leaving in the spring to get married. The parting was amicable. Stephen paid for her trousseau and "loaned" her some chairs and other furnishings to help the newlyweds get started in housekeeping.[10] The loans were actually gifts; he would never ask for their return. Sally's portrait remained on display in Stephen's new house and still may be seen in Founder's Hall at Girard College.[11] Martin Bickham, Sally's younger brother, who had lived in the Girard home during many of the years that Stephen and Sally were together and had learned the fundamentals of maritime trade under Stephen's tutelage, prospered in a life-time career as a Girard employee, agent and business associate.

Stephen loved Sally and was sorry to see her go. He had lived with her for nine years, longer than he had lived with Mary before she went insane. Sally almost certainly would have married Stephen if she could have, but that was impossible. Mary was still very much alive physically, if not mentally, at Pennsylvania Hospital and was showing no signs of dying. Sally knew about Mary's condition from personal observation. The mistress visited the wife regularly, at Stephen's behest, to see how she was doing and to make sure she was being cared for properly with funds provided by Stephen.

Although hurt by Sally's departure, Stephen could understand why she left him. She did not want to go on being a mistress indefinitely when she had an opportunity to be a wife.

So, out went Sally, parting from Stephen on friendly terms. He knew he would miss her, but he had no intention of sitting around and moping about losing her. Almost as soon as she was out the door, he had a replacement in his bed. There was virtually no interruption in his pleasure. And...oh!...what a replacement she would turn out to be!

Her name was Polly Kenton, and she was twenty years old when she came into Stephen's life. She was twenty-six years younger than Stephen, young enough to be his daughter. She gave him the best years of her life and all the joys of an enduring and satisfying relationship with a beautiful woman. She made his new house a home.

Polly was a laundress who had done washing for the Girard household and therefore was known to Stephen when he invited her to be Sally's replacement. Polly quickly accepted. Serving as mistress for a man of Girard's financial stature was an opportunity too good to pass up. His net worth at the end of 1795, according to his own calculations, had surpassed the $250,000 mark.[12]

His profits kept accumulating and were reinvested mostly in more ships (built, bought or chartered) and more cargoes. Girard's nest egg kept on growing, and the rate of growth kept on accelerating. He was still nowhere near becoming a millionaire, but he was on his way. In that comfortable and promising situation he could have had his pick of dozens of pretty young women. His decision to invite Polly was a high compliment to her. It also was an indication of how much he was impressed by her and attracted to her.

It is noteworthy that Girard consistently preferred women who were far removed from high society. His wife had been a boarding house maid. His first mistress had been a seamstress. His second mistress had been a laundress. It might be inferred from this pattern that Girard always wanted a woman who could be counted on to "know her place" in a domestic relationship and to be deferential to him in every situation. His choice of women from the "lower class" could even be construed as a sign of immaturity or insecurity, possibly the result of continuing self-consciousness over the appearance of the blind and deformed eye although it was gradually closing and becoming less frightful. It might well be more on the mark, however, to consider that Girard himself valued devotion to hard work and frugality while disdaining idleness and extravagance, so it was only natural for him to seek the companionship of women with similar values. Indeed, perhaps he was demonstrating an exceptional degree of maturity and security, not to mention independence and self-confidence, when he chose a laundress instead of a powder-cheeked, white-gloved dilettante to be his mistress even when he was already worth a quarter of a million dollars and still counting.

Polly Kenton's first name actually was Mary, but everybody had called her Polly long before Stephen met her. That was fortunate. Having a Mary for a wife and a Mary for a mistress could have been cause for confusion. No portrait was ever made of Polly, so far as is known. From what has been written about her, she had dark hair and was a little shorter than Stephen. She was pretty in face and body, both being well rounded. She was solidly built, projecting the kind of figure that was considered most desirable by men in America before the advent of the dieting mania. She has been described as "robust"[13] and "buxom"[14]— also as "happy" and "competent."[15]

Her competence was not only as a mistress but also as a housekeeper. Furnishing and decorating the new house was largely Polly's work, with Stephen being regularly consulted. Polly had good taste. She also was industrious. She had grown up in a large family on a farm in Whitemarsh, which was at that time a rural area north of Philadelphia. (It is now a Philadelphia suburb in Montgomery County.) As a farm girl she was accustomed to hard work and expected hard work from others. In this respect, especially, she was Girard's kind of woman. She was a no-nonsense keeper of the house. Servants under her jurisdiction acquired good work habits and learned to be efficient and respectful. She ran a tight ship.

As Stephen's surrogate wife, Polly soon became the female equivalent of a major-domo, ruling the house absolutely while showing deference to Stephen at all times. He relied on her judgment in household matters and let her have her way. She gradually brought some of her relatives into the house to live and, in some cases, to help with the work, eventually having four sisters and two nieces on the premises. One of the sisters, after marrying the captain of one of Girard's ships, continued to live in Girard's house, her husband being away most of the time. Thus the new house became a Kenton homestead as well as a Girard homestead. For quite a few years more Kentons than Girards were under Stephen's roof, although, later, a goodly number of his relatives also moved in. Stephen did not mind at all having a house full of people. The more the merrier seems to have been his reaction to Polly's open-door policy.

It was during Polly's tenure as mistress that Girard bought handsome ebony chairs with velvet plush seats for the parlor. She helped him acquire good china and silverware, and encouraged him to entertain in style, with memorable menus and libations.

As a former farm girl, Polly was enthusiastically supportive of Stephen when he made decisions to buy a farm and to expand its acreage. She was also in favor of buying a gig to make travel to and from the farm faster and easier. Polly was assertive but not brash. She could be gentle and prodding at the same time. Despite being a generation younger than Stephen, she gave him a little mothering when he needed it. For all his independence, Stephen did not mind being told to button up his overcoat.

Marvin W. McFarland, the aforementioned authority on Stephen Girard, discussed the quick replacement of Sally by Polly in forthright terms in an address at a Girard College banquet in 1977. "Until extreme old age," McFarland said, Girard "could not live without a woman in his life."[16]

That was the crux of it.

That was a fundamental truth about Stephen Girard.

That was why Mary, when she went insane, was replaced by Sally.

That was why Sally, when she left Stephen, was replaced by Polly.

That was why Polly was still giving her love to Stephen when he was in his seventies.

Stephen Simpson, Girard's first biographer, was less delicate and more direct than McFarland on the subject of Girard's love life. Simpson, who knew Girard during most of the years that Polly was his mistress, wrote at considerable length about Girard's immense and frequent enjoyment of her sexual favors. He enjoyed them in the afternoon, after the main meal of the day, as well as at night. Regarding Girard's "susceptibility of solace from female intercourse," to use Simpson's words, "he [Girard] never professed to be fastidiously chaste; and there is good reason to believe that he was disposed, both by constitution and habits, to the free indulgence of lubricity. It is believed that, in this particular, the force of his passions overcame his love of frugality, and led him into what he, in other matters, would have deemed extravagance."[17]

In commenting on Girard's departure from his usual frugality, and his embrace of uncharacteristic extravagance, Simpson was referring to what would become a long-time practice of Girard to buy expensive jewelry for Polly. Officers on Girard's ships, or his agents in foreign ports, were frequently instructed by Girard to purchase a necklace or a brooch or some other jewel-laden accessory, costing an equivalent of fifty dollars or thereabouts in American currency, that would make a suitable gift for Polly. Fifty dollars was a lot of money in the late eighteenth and early nineteenth centuries. Typically, a man working on a farm was paid one hundred and ten dollars a year plus room and board.[18] A woman living and working on a farm was paid less than half that much: fifty-two dollars a year.[19] The cost to be a hospital patient was forty-three cents a day, a sum that included "board, lodging, nursing and medical attendance."[20]

The extreme generosity of Stephen in his gift-giving to Polly was powerful evidence of how intensely he was captivated by her and by the pleasures she lavished upon him. He showered her with expensive jewelry and she, in response, must have been tireless in expressing her appreciation. The gifts from Stephen to Polly also demonstrated how prosperous he had become. He did not have to count his pennies when buying finery for his mistress, although he continued to count every penny in business transactions.

As Simpson shrewdly observed: "Though remarkable for a serious-ness approaching to austerity, Girard resembled neither a monk, nor an ascetic, in his habits of life."[21] Stephen routinely took a long dinner break in the afternoon, allowing ample time for the biggest meal of the day to be followed by a nap. If he wanted recreation as well as rest, Polly was available. He reportedly had strong recuperative powers after lovemaking and did not let a matinee interfere with his work. Simpson put it this way: "Physical passions ....he [Girard] was wise enough to bow to, and no doubt took delight in their transient gratification, careful never to sacrifice duty to pleasure, or to neglect business for enjoyment .... Physical nature, for who can resist, often found him a prostrate votary at its smoking altar; but its reign was fleeting, and soon left him undivided empire over his favorite domain of enterprise and intellect."[22]

To his credit, Girard was not promiscuous. He did not have brief, casual affairs, according to all available evidence, but chose instead to be faithful to each of his mistresses as, earlier, he apparently had been faithful to his wife while she was sane.

In 1797, the year after Girard moved into his new house, he bought a farm. It was in Passyunk Township southwest of Philadelphia, about three miles from his home. It was not a gentleman's farm and never would be. Nor was it a country estate such as many rich men maintained. It was a working farm, and it would stay that way, with Girard doing much of the work. He initially purchased a little over seventy acres at $170 an acre (totaling about $12,000) on December 26, 1797.[23] As part of the deal and at no additional cost he also acquired, on the premises, a brick farmhouse built about 1770. (It still stands, near the intersection of Twenty-First and Shunk Streets, in what is now Girard Park in Philadelphia.) Girard purchased tracts of adjoining acreage in 1798 and subsequent years until, early in the nineteenth century, the farm encompassed 567 acres and extended all the way to the Schuylkill, bordering on that river at what is still called Girard Point (where a bridge now carries Interstate 95 traffic across the Schuylkill).

The farm added an important dimension to the remainder of Girard's life. As noted earlier, his ancestors had been farmers in the interior of France before they had become seafarers in Bordeaux. Stephen, harking back to deep roots, made farm work a part of his daily routine. There were always others on the farm, employed to do whatever needed to be done, and there was usually a foreman living in the farmhouse with his family, but Girard was a hands-on manager. He did not live on the farm, but he was there almost daily. His work schedule varied. Sometimes he arrived at the farm late in the afternoon or early evening and stayed for an hour or two, or more. On some days he was there in the morning, occasionally arriving so early that the foreman and the workers were still in bed. Girard kept them on their toes. They could never be sure when he was going to arrive or how long he was going to stay.

Girard found farm work a pleasant diversion from tedious hours in the counting-house writing letters to captains and agents, going over account books, analyzing commodity markets and prices worldwide, and devising strategies for the timely buying and selling of cargoes. Farm work was harder physically, but it was dramatically different from office work. Girard liked to toil in the soil. He liked to get dirty. He liked to plow and harrow. He liked to prune and weed. He liked to have a good workout and generate a good sweat. He made farming fun. He also made it profitable. He was innovative, always striving for improvements in farm products and in farming methods.

Ingram, in his nineteenth century biography, gave this perspective on farmer Girard:

> His chief relaxation was the management of his farm .... He took the keen interest of a man who finds in a favorite pursuit at once the most effective means of preserving his physical health and a relief from the multiplicity of cares overburdening a restless mind. When he found himself unable to make his daily visit, an apprentice, charged with the minutist directions for the labors of the day, was sent in his stead, for in this, as in all other matters, he left nothing to hazard or to the unguided discretion of subordinates. As soon as he stepped from his chaise the work he had planned to do was at once commenced, and he superintended in person all the farm operations, in which task he took the greatest pleasure. Few of his vessels ever sailed for distant places without taking out orders for choice plants, seeds, or fruit-trees, which new varieties of fruits and flowers were gradually extended throughout the neighborhood, much of the celebrity which the markets of Philadelphia have enjoyed being thus due to his enterprise and love of such pursuits.
> He had two stalls in the South Second Street Market where the produce of his farm was sent to be sold, and this was of such remarkably excellent quality that its immediate sale at prices above the ruling rates was always assured. In addition, he reared, fattened, and killed, every December, from one hundred and fifty to two hundred oxen for the provisioning of his ships, and this period was one of the greatest tribulation to such of the apprentices as were obliged to attend to the little-relished duty of selling the fat and hides. Every part of the animals thus killed was utilized after the most approved methods of experimental farming, and Girard demonstrated practically the great value to a farmer of economical administration, for his products, although of a most superior quality, as has been said above, were nevertheless put upon the market at so much less cost than his neighbors', that they could have been sold profitably at the same rates had not the demand justified a considerable advance.[24]

When Girard was on the farm he did not like to be distracted from his work. Simpson told a story that makes the point: For many years Girard was represented in London by Baring Brothers & Co. One of the Barings happened to be in Philadelphia on business when the *Voltaire* returned from a long voyage to India. Girard was down on the farm when the ship arrived, and Baring rode there on horseback to tell him the news.

"'Where is Mr. Girard?' exclaimed Mr. Baring [to a farm worker].

"'In the hay loft, Sir.'

"'Tell him Mr. Baring wishes to see him immediately, on particular business.'

"In an instant Girard stood before him, covered with sweat and hay, with his sleeves rolled up to his shoulders. 'Well, Mr. Baring, what is the matter?'

"'I have come to tell you good news, Mr. Girard. Your ship, the *Voltaire*, has arrived safe at Philadelphia.'

"'Oh! Mr. Baring, is that all; my ships always come safe. I knew the *Voltaire* would arrive safe. I am very busy with my hay, Mr. Baring,' and up he mounted again to his darling hay loft."[25]

Besides being abrupt and almost rude, Girard was inaccurate. Oftentimes his ships did not return safely. Some fell prey to hostile forces, captured at sea or seized in foreign ports. Some were wrecked in storms. Ironically, the *Voltaire* eventually did come to a stormy end. It ran aground and broke up off the coast of The Netherlands.

Although farming would never be Girard's main line of work, he did attain considerable success and recognition as a farmer. He won exceedingly high praise from the Horticultural Society of Pennsylvania for his achievements in the cultivation of trees, flowers and vegetables.[26] He imported many varieties of fruit trees from Europe and was especially noted for his quince trees and for significant improvements in the taste and texture of pears grown in America.

As the end of the eighteenth century approached, Girard was having a wonderful time. His enjoyment of life was greatly enhanced with a new house, a new mistress and a farm. He was well established and successful in maritime trade. He was rich and getting richer. Yet his most spectacular achievements were still ahead of him. There was no way he could have foreseen or imagined the magnitude of challenges and opportunities that would come his way.

He greeted the dawn of the nineteenth century in a spirit of joie de vivre. He was under full sail, with a favorable wind at his back.

CHAPTER 12

At the Turn of a Century: The World Was His Oyster

1799-1805

*When you think you have too many fish to fry,
don't back off. Put more coals on the fire.*

STEPHEN GIRARD, working harder than ever to keep up with an ever-expanding empire of maritime trade, came roaring into the nineteenth century like he owned it. Before it was much older he almost did. The old sailor had a tiger by the tail. The more money he made from buying and selling cargoes, the more money he had available to invest in still more cargoes. The more cargoes he acquired, the more ships he needed to carry them. The more ships he built or bought or chartered, the more letters he had to write to captains and supercargoes and port agents, giving detailed instructions on where to sail and when to buy or sell, and at what price. He was having a merry ride and he could not let go. His plate was never empty. No matter how hard and how long he worked, there was always another transaction to conclude. There was always another letter to write. There was always another instruction to give. There was always another detail to take care of.

Why did he work so hard? Why did he keep on working so hard when he no longer had to work at all? Why did he continue interminably to expand his enterprises, his profits, his responsibilities? Why did he do these things when he despised the trappings of wealth and steadfastly refused to live like a rich man? Ultimately it was so he could have money to give away for charitable purposes, in his lifetime and also after his death. However, there is another answer that is not so complicated. Simply put, he worked hard, and he kept on working hard, because he was loving every minute of it. He liked to work and he liked what he was doing. He enjoyed the challenge of trying to make money from a kind of business in which it was very easy to lose money. He found great pleasure in working as a maritime merchant even though he had diversions—his farm, his mistress—that also gave him great pleasure.

The thousands of letters he wrote at various stages in his life shed light on the real Stephen Girard. It becomes clear, not in any single sentence or paragraph but in the broad sweep of his writing, that he genuinely enjoyed the give and take and the ups and downs of the maritime business. Notwithstanding occasional complaints about working too hard, it becomes apparent that he relished the challenges. In the hundreds of painstaking instructions he gave to captains and supercargoes and port agents, Girard's enthusiasm for his work comes through again. He gave explicit directions for acquisition and disposal of cargoes with a thoroughness and an intensity that could only have come from someone who was not only dedicated and devoted to planning, to preparation, and to profit, but who was also enjoying himself immensely.

Read a random but representative selection of other material in the Girard Papers and a man who loved to triumph over uncertainty comes to life. The hit-or-miss nature of long-distance trading in sailing ships tickled his fancy. There was a strong streak of the gambler in Girard, but he was a very careful and very shrewd gambler. He sent cargoes to destinations thousands of miles away, through perilous waters and hostile forces, and hoped those ships, somehow and sometime, would come back with money and/or goods of greater worth than what had been dispatched.

Every time Girard watched one of his ships sail down the Delaware River he knew there was a risk, if not a probability, of partial or complete loss. The thrill of working as a maritime trader was in rolling the dice and beating the odds. The excitement was in preparing for contingencies and overcoming the unexpected. Girard was successful on an enormous scale because he worked, worked, worked and planned, planned, planned—and because he gave attention to details, details, details. Thus there was the combination of liking his work and being good at it that had a lot to do with Girard's phenomenal profits in world trade. He knew how to cut through the flotsam and jetsam and focus on the bottom line.

Remarkably, considering his seafaring background, Girard had never been to most of the places he sent his ships—a fact that made his extraordinary success in maritime commerce all the more impressive. He had never been to China. He had never been to India. He had never been to Russia. He had never been to South America. He had never been to any of the countries of western Europe except France. He would never, in his entire life, go to any of those places. Indeed, he would never see very much of America. He would never even see very much of Pennsylvania. From the time he met Mary, and then Sally, and then Polly, he was for the most part a sit-at-home and stay-at-home maritime trader.

All of the years he was at sea his travels were on narrowly defined routes. He knew the ports in the French colonies of St-Domingue and Martinique in the West Indies. He knew Bordeaux and Marseilles in France. He knew some ports in North America: New York, Charleston, New Orleans and, of course, Philadelphia. That was about it. During the years he was becoming prosperous, then wealthy, he did not go gallivanting around as rival merchants did. When decisions needed to be made, he was there to make them. When instructions needed to be given, he was there to give them. He minded the store.

Others who were prosperous went on great excursions. They took grand tours of Europe. They ventured into the scenic hinterlands of America. They retreated to country estates to chase foxes or sit on porches sipping drinks while admiring the view. When not on a trip, they took days off to go for rides in the countryside in their carriages accompanied by liveried servants and, sometimes, the makings of a four-course picnic.

Not Girard. He did not take vacations, even after becoming the richest person in America. As near as can be determined from his correspondence and his business records, he almost never took a day off. (The days he took off during his first few weeks with Mary were exceptional.) He worked on Sundays and hired people who were willing to work on Sundays. When he entertained at dinner on a Sunday afternoon, it was only after rising early and getting lots of work done in the morning. While others were singing the praises of the Lord in their churches, Girard was laboring hard in his counting-house. He did not just keep up with his competitors. He did not just beat his competitors. He trounced them.

Although Girard was not a church-goer he was nominally a Roman Catholic from cradle to grave, from his baptism in a Catholic church in Bordeaux on the day after he was born to his burial in a Catholic churchyard in Philadelphia. Attending religious services regularly was a ritual for most Americans of all faiths in Girard's time, but he was never one to follow the pack. He contributed to building funds of Catholic churches, and churches of other demominations, and showed no signs of hostility toward religion in general or any particular religion. There is no indication in any of his correspondence or other papers that he was an atheist; he apparently felt he could make better, and more profitable, use of his time in his counting-house than in a church. However, he was familiar with the works of Voltaire and Rousseau and perhaps other Age of Enlightenment writers who were raising questions about what they construed to be excessive power and authority of both secular and sectarian leaders. In provisions of his will regarding establishment of a school for orphans, Girard stirred up a storm of litigation by forbidding members of the clergy of any faith to set foot in the school or its grounds even as visitors, although he emphasized that he meant no offense against the clergy of any sect and just wanted to spare the students from distracting entreaties in behalf of competing religions. Girard did not bar religious instruction or services from the school (Girard College) as students quickly discovered when they were required to attend two religious services each weekday and four on Sunday, all conducted by laypersons.

Girard was the first, or among the first, to develop and maintain American trade on a large scale to many parts of the world, including China, India, Russia and South America. Although he had never been to any of these places, he was intimately knowledgeable about their ports, their economies and their governments because of a rigorous regimen of study and correspondence and conversation. He read books and newspaper dispatches about foreign countries, and he pored over maps and charts of ports and harbors. He asked his agents abroad endless questions, and he took the time to read and reflect on their replies. He talked to his captains and supercargoes when they returned from long voyages, learning and benefiting from their observations and experiences. Putting his knowledge to practical use, he demonstrated the feasibility of cultivating markets for American products in very-far-off places, beyond the mainstream trade routes to the West Indies and western Europe. He proved it could be profitable for American cargo ships to travel on a regular basis to destinations ranging from five thousand to ten thousand miles from home port.

Trade between America and China had been forbidden by Great Britain when the American colonies were under British control. American colonists wanting Chinese products, principally tea, had been required to buy from the British. Ships flying the flag of Great Britain had sailed from England to China, around the southern tip of Africa and across the Indian Ocean, and returned to England by the same route. Large quantities of tea then had been transported in British ships to America. In the last half of the eighteenth century most Americans were drinking tea at least twice a day.[1] That is one reason a British tax on tea resulted in the Boston Tea Party and was a major cause of the American Revolution.

Soon after Americans won the Revolutionary War they initiated direct trade with the Chinese even though formal diplomatic relations between the United States and China were not established until 1846. The first American ship to China left New York in 1784 and returned fifteen months later in 1785. The route was around the southern tip of South America and across the Pacific Ocean and back. The cargo to China consisted principally of ginseng, furs and woolen cloth. The return cargo included tea, cinnamon, porcelain, silk fabrics, cotton fabrics, silk gloves, hand-painted wallpaper, window blinds made of silk and bamboo, and other home furnishings. Four American investors who had put up a total of $120,000 to finance the first voyage received $150,000 collectively after all accounts had been settled. The $30,000 profit, a twenty-five percent return on investment, made American trade with China financially attractive.[2]

Ginseng, which grew wild and in abundance in the Appalachian Mountains from New England to Georgia, had significant value in China because the herb's root was believed by the Chinese to be an aphrodisiac and also to have medicinal powers in the treatment of many ailments. One pound of ginseng could be traded for two pounds of tea.[3]

There were many products from China besides tea that found a ready market in the young United States. Almost anything made of silk, and to a lesser extent bamboo, was popular. It became fashionable for Americans to display Chinese paintings, vases and other works of art in their homes. Dishes from China made of porcelain became enormously popular in America and soon were called "china."

Girard, who had not been an investor in the first American voyage to China, subsequently entered the China trade on a very large scale. One of his strengths was follow-through. He was good at capitalizing on discoveries made by others. He eventually derived more profits from the China trade than any of those who were in on the ground floor by investing in the first American voyage to China.

Robert Morris, the wealthy Philadelphian who had gained fame as the financier of the American Revolution, was one of those investors who shared in the large profits of America's first ship to China. Later, he fell on hard times, largely because of rash speculations in land, and eventually spent three years in the Walnut Street Prison. People who could not pay their debts in early America went to jail. Borrowing money and not paying it back was looked upon as precisely what it was: a form of stealing. Unlike Morris, Girard avoided risky land speculations and other get-rich-quick schemes designed to ensnare the greedy. He knew how to respond to such temptations: No.

By the end of the eighteenth century Girard was well on his way to becoming the most successful American in the China trade, if, indeed, he had not already achieved that distinction. He had tested the waters in 1787, joining sixteen other Philadelphia maritime merchants in a consortium to send the first Philadelphia-built ship to China. The vessel carried a large quantity of brandy in addition to ginseng. During the last decade of the eighteenth century and the first decade of the nineteenth century he invested heavily in trade with China. He built a number of three-masted ships designed specifically for the China trade and other exceptionally long voyages. The first four were the "philosopher" ships named in honor of French philosophers. The previously mentioned *Voltaire* was followed by the *Rousseau*, 300 tons,

1801, the *Helvetius*, 330 tons, 1804, and the *Montesquieu*, 372 tons, 1806. William Rush, noted Philadelphia sculptor and one of the founders of the Pennsylvania Academy of the Fine Arts in 1805, was commissioned by Girard to carve wooden figureheads of the philosophers to adorn the bows of the ships.

Girard's ships went from Philadelphia to China by two routes—around South America and across the Pacific Ocean, or around Africa and across the Indian Ocean—but there were countless variations on each route. A ship sailing to China might stop at several ports on the way and at several more on the way back, buying and selling cargoes or parts of cargoes when markets were favorable. A ship might sail from Philadelphia with a cargo of flour and stop at Norfolk, Virginia, where the flour could be sold and a cargo of tobacco purchased—or a ship might go to Charleston, South Carolina, with the flour and take on cotton there. A ship loaded with tobacco or cotton, or both, could sail to a port in Europe, to Bordeaux or Antwerp or Copenhagen or maybe all the way to St. Petersburg in Russia, where tobacco and cotton could be exchanged for gold coins or some other specie acceptable as money in China. Part of the specie might then be spent in Europe for additional merchandise—brandy, wine, gin, soap, candles, umbrellas—that could be sold not only in China but in places along the way such as India and the East Indies (principally Sumatra and Java). A ship might stop at two or three ports in Europe, and perhaps at a port or two in Arabia or elsewhere in the Middle East, before going on to India, the East Indies and China. No two itineraries were exactly alike.

The name of the game was parlaying profits. There was one basic strategy: Sell at a profit, then buy something else to be sold later for still another profit—and so on, and so on. It was not as easy as it sounds. The trick was in knowing what ports to go to, what goods to buy, what prices to pay, and then knowing where and when those goods could be sold profitably.

There were standard purchases in some places, for instance tea and porcelain in China, and spices and coffee in the East Indies, but for the most part, a maritime merchant or his port agents (or in some cases his captains or supercargoes) had to make decisions based on knowledge of the markets and analysis of economic and political trends. It was helpful, too, if informed and accurate predictions of future events were part of the plan. Intuition and guesswork might also be useful, sometimes, but a world trader who tried to muddle through without doing his homework could lose his shirt.

Doing his homework was a strong point for Girard. He was a master of the game. He spent hours and hours, day after day, week by week, month upon month, year in and year out, doing the tedious things that needed to be done: writing letters, reading replies, poring over price lists, studying newspaper dispatches from home and abroad, giving detailed instructions to port agents and to captains and super-cargoes. Nobody outworked Girard. Nobody.

When Girard's ships sailed to and from China by way of South America, the same general procedures applied as on sailings via Europe. Among the South American ports frequented by Girard's ships were Rio de Janeiro, Montevideo, Buenos Aires, Valparaiso and Guayaquil— in what later would become, respectively, Brazil, Uruguay, Argentina, Chile and Ecuador. All of these cities were under Portuguese or Spanish control in the first decade of the nineteenth century and were good markets for a wide variety of agricultural and manufactured products including tobacco, clothing and cotton cloth. Cargoes purchased in South American ports included cowhides, wool, tallow, copper and tin.[4] Since Spanish America was a closed mercantilist empire, it was technically illegal for Girard's ships to stop at ports under Spanish control, but such illegalities were commonplace. So were bribes. Laws could be circumvented if the right price was paid to the right official, or to his authorized intermediary.

When Girard's ships left Philadelphia for China, whether going around Africa or around South America, the captains and supercargoes had written instructions from Girard. He specified ports to be visited and cargoes to be bought and sold. There usually was some flexibility. He might want general cargo to be bought at some ports without saying precisely what the cargo should consist of. He might specify a price, or a range of prices, for purchase or sale of certain items at certain ports, or he might leave it up to the supercargo to make decisions on prices. A trip to China and back, with many intermediate stops coming and going, might take two or three years, sometimes even more than three years. It was hard to forecast market conditions and prevailing prices years in advance, although Girard was able to do so with remarkable accuracy on a number of occasions. He had agents in most ports visited by his ships. When a Girard ship put into a port, the first thing the captain and the supercargo did was to contact Girard's local agent, if there was one. He might have received letters from Girard modifying the instructions he had given to the ship's officers when they sailed from Philadelphia. In any case the officers would get the latest information from the agent on local market conditions and prices. The agent also had the latest available information on markets and prices at other ports.

Girard's agents communicated regularly among themselves as well as with Girard. He was a firm believer in the value of networking as a basic business tool. Agents and ships' officers conveyed information about political conditions and economic trends as well as about markets and prices. Girard's world trade organization was tantamount to a global intelligence apparatus. The U.S. State Department and American embassies were ill-equipped for extensive gathering of information in Girard's time. There may well have been occasions when he was as well informed, if not more so, than the U.S. secretary of state and the President of the United States on some elements of foreign affairs and international relations, particularly on matters with a direct bearing on maritime trade.

Within the framework of Girard's instructions, the captains and the supercargoes of his ships were expected to follow fundamental principles of maritime commerce that they had been taught by him. Supercargoes on Girard's ships usually were former apprentices in his counting-house. Many of them had lived in his home during their apprenticeships. They had, literally, learned the business at the master's knee. They had been the very best of his apprentices, the cream of the crop, young men deemed by Girard to be exceptionally competent, extremely industrious and completely trustworthy. Most of them lived up to his expectations. He was a good judge of character and ability and dedication.

The last-mentioned trait—dedication—was especially important. Performance at ninety-nine percent of capacity was not good enough. Girard wanted and demanded one hundred percent. He looked for people who would go the extra mile, who would not just get the job done but would get it done right and on time. Apprentices who were unable or unwilling to meet his high standards fell by the wayside. He was a tough taskmaster. He had no qualms about winnowing the lads who would not give him full measure. Thus Girard employees who rose to positions of responsibility and authority were truly extraordinary people. They were quality people. They were loyal people.

One such employee was William Wagner, who served his apprenticeship in Girard's counting-house in the first decade of the nineteenth century and was a supercargo on Girard's ships for many voyages, including four to China. Wagner eventually went into business for himself as a maritime merchant and became wealthy. In 1855 he founded the Wagner Free Institute of Science at Thirteenth and Spring Garden Streets in Philadelphia. In 1865 the institute was relocated at Seventeenth Street and Montgomery Avenue, where it has remained in operation. For many years it had a major role in educating young people in the sciences, most notably in mineralogy, geology, anatomy, physiology, chemistry, botany and civil engineering.

In 1879, when he was eighty-eight, Wagner granted an interview to a correspondent for the Philadelphia *Times*, resulting in a long newspaper article that provides authoritative insight on how Girard functioned as a maritime merchant. It "was a great honor to become bound to Stephen Girard [as an apprentice] in those days," according to Wagner as reported in the *Times*. It "was for young men as great a lift in life as it is now for a young man to receive an appointment to West Point or Annapolis." Girard "watched every penny and demanded an account of every farthing. He exacted attention to detail .... He was not a tyrant, however. To his clerks in whom he had confidence he was all kindness and goodness."[5]

Events of an unforgettable day were recalled by Wagner and described in the *Times*. It was the day that—as a bolt out of the blue, without any prior hint—he was chosen at the age of eighteen to go on his first voyage. "Stephen Girard, passing through the counting-house, scanning all the young men, laid his hand upon the young clerk's shoulder and said: 'William, you will go to the sea with two ships. You will go next week if you please, sir' .... The young clerk, slipping down from his high stool and blushing in the agony of pleasure and delight, said, 'Yes, sir,' and stood trembling lest he should be asleep and would presently awake to find his joy only a dream ....

"Sent on a voyage half way around the world ... entrusted with the possession and investment of a quarter of a million dollars," Wagner was given sealed orders to be opened only when he had sailed down the Delaware River, through the Delaware Bay and into the Atlantic Ocean far enough that "from the masthead of his ship he could no longer discern the green fringe that the pine trees make on the sandy shore of southern New Jersey."[6]

The orders—which were sealed to prevent the leaking of information to competitors—are an example of Girard's remarkable combination of precision and conciseness in giving instructions. Wagner was told to take the two ships to Charleston, South Carolina, and load them with cotton, and then: "Sell the cotton at market price at Antwerp; buy gin in London; sell it in the Brazils [entailing another trip across the Atlantic Ocean, from Europe to South America]; bring coffee from Rio de Janeiro to Liverpool, and take fabrics up the Straits [through the Straits of Gibraltar to the Mediterranean coast of France]. Buy olives, wine and raisins at Marseilles and sell them at London. Load with general cargo for East Indies and [after selling the general cargo in the East Indies] buy mocha coffee up the Red Sea for nineteen cents a pound. Arrive at The Hague ... with both ships and sell for thirty cents a pound. Return to the East Indies [to sell general cargo bought in The Hague, and then go on to China] and bring two cargoes of tea, making a forced passage from China to Amsterdam. [After selling the tea in Amsterdam] make another voyage for mocha coffee and bring it with dispatch to New York [and then return to Philadelphia]."[7]

Whew! What a maiden voyage for a clerk who, at eighteen, had suddenly been promoted to supercargo! The journey took more than three years. It included four crossings of the Atlantic Ocean (two in each direction), six crossings of the Indian Ocean (three in each direction) and six trips around the southern tip of Africa (three in each direction). There was no Suez Canal back then. During the long voyage the original captains of both ships died, as did a number of crew members. Both ships ran aground at least once but were floated again without major damage.

Girard's calculations on coffee prices, nearly two years in advance, turned out to be amazingly accurate. When the ships arrived at The Hague with cargoes of mocha coffee (which had been bought for nineteen cents a pound, as instructed) the best available price was twenty-three cents a pound. Wagner waited patiently, but he did not have to wait very long. In the next three weeks the price went up to thirty cents a pound! Wagner deviated from Girard's instructions just once. While en route to the Red Sea for the second time to buy mocha coffee, which could be obtained at the city of Mocha, an Arabian port, Wagner learned during stops for food and water that large numbers of pirates were active off the Arabian coast. To proceed as scheduled might result in seizure of the ships and capture or death for all on board. So Wagner diverted the ships to Java, in the East Indies, to buy coffee.

Java coffee, although not considered as good as mocha coffee, was of very high quality nonetheless. Indeed, coffee from Java would become so popular in the United States that the word "java" became virtually synonymous with coffee. It still is not unusual for Americans to call a cup of coffee a cup of java. Thus Wagner seemed to have shown sound judgment in deciding to substitute java coffee for mocha coffee when he learned that pirates were infesting waters around Arabia. Girard, however, did not see it that way. When he received word from New York that his two ships had arrived there with coffee from Java instead of Mocha, he was not happy about the substitution. Wagner recalled the conversation with Girard when the two ships arrived back in Philadelphia and he walked into Girard's private counting-room after an absence of more than three years:

"Why you not go for mocha? Why you not obey orders?"

"I was afraid to trust your ships and money with the pirates [Wagner answered]. It would have been at the cost of your property and our lives to have gone there. I have trebeled your money in the voyage."

"That is good [Girard said], but you ought to have gone for mocha."[8]

Even though Girard had been an American since 1778, he was still speaking English in less than perfect fashion (as illustrated by the foregoing quotation), and he never lost his French accent. Moreover, he never forgot his French roots. He opened up his heart and his wallet, time and time again, when French refugees from the revolutions in France and St-Domingue arrived in Philadelphia in desperate need of assistance. He gave financial support to Azilum, a community of French refugees on the banks of the Susquehanna River in northern Pennsylvania in the 1790s, where there were dozens of houses, several places of business, a school, a church and even a theater. The venture was short-lived, with most of the inhabitants moving on after just a few years. Many returned to France because after the rise of Napoleon to power in 1799 it was safe for French exiles to go back to their homeland.[9]

It was also in 1799 that Girard became completely fed up with the failure of President John Adams to take effective action to protect American ships from privateers, pirates and hostile governments. Taking matters into his own hands, after one of his brigs, *Sally*, had been seized by the British and detained for three months, Girard had guns mounted on the decks of his cargo vessels. He also sent his ships in convoys so they could protect one another. In the first such arrangement, in November of 1799, Girard sent a three-ship convoy from Philadelphia to Havana, Cuba. Two of the ships carried a total of forty guns. Girard described the convoy in a letter to one of his agents:

Ship *Good Friends*, Caleb Earl, Master, armed with 20 guns, small arms and upwards of 50 men and boys, well fitted and sails fast. Brig *Liberty*, William Henderson, Master, armed with 20 guns (18 of which are mounted), completely manned and equipped, having on board about 45 persons, sails fast. Ship *Voltaire*, Ezra Bowen, Master, without arms, sails fast.[10]

Captain Earl was put in command of the convoy. Detailed instructions to Earl from Girard provide some insight on how he believed an armed convoy should function:

My ship *Good Friends* under your command, being loaded and ready and armed with 20 carriage guns, well manned and in all respects equipped in a complete manner, you are to proceed with her as soon as possible, in company with my brig *Liberty*, Captain Henderson, also armed with 20 guns, to the port of Havana, taking under the protection of your ship and brig *Liberty*, my ship *Voltaire*, commanded by Ezra Bowen, which you will convoy all the way to the said port of Havana. Before leaving our river you are requested to plan and agree with Captain Henderson and Captain Bowen on the signals which in your opinion will be easily executed, clearly seen and understood night and day so no separation of any one of my vessels can take place under pretense of ignorance, neglect or a bad lookout.

My intention in arming the ship *Good Friends* is to protect and defend my property from being captured by pirates or enemies of our country. This circumstance will point out to you the necessity of keeping yourself, as well as the brig *Liberty*, on the defensive and avoiding as much as possible to meet with or speak to any vessels. This may be effected by keeping a constant lookout up your mast, and more particularly by not trusting to colors, as often an enemy will disguise himself by hoisting the flag of a friendly nation.[11]

As 1799 drew to a close it was becoming increasingly likely that John Adams, in the third year of his administration, was going to be a one-term president. He had been elected to a first term by a razor-thin margin, defeating Thomas Jefferson (who became vice president) seventy-one to sixty-eight in electoral votes. Adams had begun his presidency with grim forebodings. Just before his inauguration he had visited outgoing President Washington and had written later in a diary: "I believe that I envied him more than he did me, and with reason."[12] Adams, the last president from the Federalist Party, became extremely unpopular as American cargo ships were seized with impunity by pirates and privateers. His unpopularity increased when he tried to silence critics. The Sedition Act, passed by Congress in 1798 and enthusiastically enforced by the Adams administration, prohibited "any libellous attack by writing, printing, publishing or speaking" when the target of the criticism was the president of the United States or a member of Congress and there was an "intent to defame" or to hold up to "contempt or disrepute."

Punishment for violating the Sedition Act could be a fine up to two thousand dollars or a prison term up to two years. If a violator was fined instead of sentenced to prison, he would go to prison anyway if he could not pay the fine. A number of newspaper editors who were critical of the policies of the Adams administration were tried, convicted and imprisoned. Girard came to the rescue of one editor convicted in 1800 by paying his fine of four hundred dollars.[13] James Madison, who was second only to Jefferson in championing freedom of speech and press, called the Sedition Act "a monster that must forever disgrace its parents."[14]

Girard, who had twice run unsuccessfully for Philadelphia Select Council (now City Council) in the late 1790s, ran a third time in 1800 and was elected. All three runs were as a Democratic Republican. He used his candidacy in 1800 to advance the cause of Jefferson, who was running again for President as a Democratic Republican in that year. Electoral votes for the election of 1800, cast by electors of the sixteen states (Vermont, Kentucky and Tennessee had been added to the original thirteen) were officially counted before a joint session of Congress on February 11, 1801, in Washington, which had replaced Philadelphia as the nation's capital in 1800. There was a tie in the electoral vote: seventy-three votes for Jefferson and seventy-three also for Aaron Burr, who was Jefferson's running mate on the Democratic Republican ticket. Adams, seeking a second term, had sixty-five electoral votes. His running mate on the Federalist ticket, Charles Pinckney, had sixty-four.

At that time, before the system was changed in 1804 by ratification of the Twelfth Amendment to the Constitution, each elector had two votes but could not designate one for president and the other for vice president. The candidate with the highest number of electoral votes was president and the candidate with the second highest was vice president. The tie between Jefferson and his own running mate resulted from administrative failure of Democratic Republican Party leaders, who should have instructed one Democratic Republican elector to withhold his vote from Burr. The tie vote in the Electoral College threw the election into the House of Representatives. Adams was automatically eliminated because he had come in third. The Constitution required the House to choose for president one of the candidates in the tie, with the other becoming vice president.

Balloting in the House was by states. Each state had one vote. If representatives of any state were equally divided, and thus deadlocked, that state had no vote. To elect a president required votes of a majority of the states. Since there were sixteen states, it took at least nine votes to constitute a majority. A lame-duck House of Representatives would make the decision, before members of Congress newly elected in 1800 were seated. The outgoing House consisted of fifty-eight Federalists and forty-eight Democratic Republicans.

Jefferson was considered a dangerous radical by many Federalists. Burr was not liked much by Federalists either, but many considered him the lesser of two evils. However, some Federalists thought it would be a disastrous mistake to elect Burr. Alexander Hamilton called Burr "the most unfit man in the United States for the office of President."[15] (It was three years later, when Burr was vice president, that he killed Hamilton in a duel.)

On the first ballot in the House no one got a majority. Eight states voted for Jefferson and six for Burr. Two states were evenly divided. The stalemate, with no change in votes, continued through thirty-five ballots over six days. Then James A. Bayard of Delaware announced he was going to change his vote from Burr to Jefferson, which put Delaware in Jefferson's column and gave him the required nine states. "You cannot well imagine the clamor and vehement invective to which I was subjected," Bayard commented later in a great understatement.[16] Bayard's switch inspired other Burr supporters to climb on the Jefferson bandwagon now that the die was cast. On the thirty-sixth ballot, on February 17, Jefferson was elected with the votes of ten states, one more than he needed.

It was a landmark election. The Jeffersonian Republicans were a new political wave. Perhaps Girard summed up as concisely as anyone what they stood for (at least in principle, but not always in practice) when he said in a letter to a friend: "They make a strong appeal to the people by their doctrine of humanity, and of being the friends of the common people."[17]

Paul Bentalou, former aide to General Casimir Pulaski and a friend of Girard since the early years of the American Revolution, was Girard's agent in Baltimore. During the balloting in the House, Bentalou sent messages to Girard from Washington and Baltimore to inform him of developments. After Jefferson was elected, Bentalou hailed him as "the best and most virtuous of men."[18] Bentalou also said to Girard: "Let us hope that the great efforts made by the Republicans will be rewarded by national prosperity."[19] (Democratic Republicans often were referred to simply as Republicans.)

On March 4, 1801, Jefferson became the first president to be inaugurated in Washington. Girard, as soon as he received word of Jefferson's election, took action to assure that on Inauguration Day there would be a festive celebration in Philadelphia that all people could enjoy. Girard volunteered to donate gunpowder for a grand display of fireworks. The Committee of Arrangements accepted the offer and formally expressed its gratitude on February 20 when it was "Resolved unanimously that the thanks of the Committee of Arrangements be presented to our Republican fellow-citizen, Stephen Girard, for his patriotic offer of the necessary supply of gunpowder for the celebration of the 4th of March next, an offer which the committee accepts with the more pleasure as coming from a citizen whose zeal is always manifest and distinguished on every humane and patriotic occasion."[20]

President Jefferson made dramatic changes in American foreign policy in two ways that Girard had advocated: U.S. relations with France were improved, and U.S. cargo ships received meaningful protection from pirates and privateers. Capitalizing on his friendly relations with France, President Jefferson was able to make one of the greatest real estate buys of all time: The Louisiana Purchase. For a bargain-basement price of fifteen million dollars the United States acquired a vast territory stretching from New Orleans to what later became Montana, more than eight hundred thousand square miles in the heartland of America. The area of the United States was virtually doubled at the stroke of a pen.

President Jefferson also took on the Barbary pirates, something that neither President Washington nor President Adams had been willing to do. The pirate strongholds on the Barbary Coast of North Africa were thousands of miles from America's East Coast, but Jefferson was undaunted by the distance. Within a few weeks after his inauguration he sent a U.S. naval squadron of four ships to the Mediterranean. The pasha of Tripoli, when he learned that the ships were on their way, sent a contingent of troops to the American consulate in Tripoli, where they proceeded to chop down the flagpole. That was the pasha's way of declaring war. During the next four years, from 1801 to 1805, a series of steadily escalating U.S. skirmishes against Tripoli came to be known collectively as the Tripolitan War, although war was not declared by Congress. Jefferson sent the United States Marines to the shores of Tripoli, to join the United States Navy in fighting battles on land and sea.

When an American frigate, the *Philadelphia*, ran aground, it was seized by Tripoli. More than three hundred Americans on board were taken prisoner. Whereupon a young navy lieutenant, Stephen Decatur, became an international hero when he led a small band of Americans on a dangerous mission to scuttle the frigate. They set it afire, and it was consumed by the flames in the harbor of Tripoli. Even Horatio

Nelson, the indomitable British admiral, was impressed. He called Decatur's feat "the most bold and daring act of the age."[21]

By 1805 the pasha of Tripoli had finally had enough. He agreed to peace on America's terms. This was after Jefferson had amassed fourteen American warships off the shores of Tripoli and sent an American army, allied with Arabs and Greeks, across the Sahara Desert from Egypt to invade Tripoli from the east. If the pasha had known how determined and persistent President Jefferson would turn out to be, that flagpole would never have been chopped down.

Thomas Jefferson was to be the kind of president that Girard thought he would be: a man of action. Jefferson was decisive. He was courageous. He was relentless. He got things done. He was also a scholar and a gentleman, a scientist, an architect, a philosopher, a man of culture. He was Girard's kind of president.

Stephen Girard... A portrait by Bass Otis, 1832. There were no portraits of Girard during his lifetime. He steadfastly refused to sit for any artist. Otis did several portraits of Girard shortly after his death. One of the originals is in the Stephen Girard Collection at Girard College in Philadelphia.

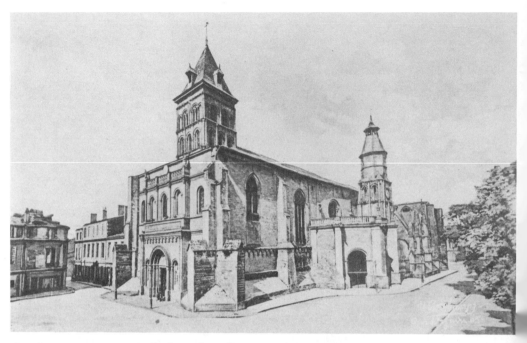

St. Seurin Roman Catholic Church in Bordeaux... Stephen Girard was one day old on May 21, 1750, when he was baptized in this church—shown as it appeared in the nineteenth century.

ABOVE : *Stephen Girard's House in Mount Holly, New Jersey...* An early twentieth century photograph. Girard bought this house in 1777 and lived in it for nine months (from September 1777 to June 1778) while British troops were occupying Philadelphia. The house still stands, at 211 Mill Street, and is a private residence.

LEFT BOTTOM : *The Street Where Stephen Girard Was Born...* This photograph of the Rue Ramonet in Bordeaux was taken in 1905. The view is toward the street's archway entrance. Beyond the archway are the Quay des Chartrons and the Garonne River. When Stephen Girard was growing up on the Rue Ramonet it was only eight feet wide. Girard's birthplace and other houses were torn down in the nineteenth century when the street was widened. An old woman interviewed in 1905 could remember vividly how narrow the street used to be. She said she could stick a broom out of a window in her house and touch the house across the street.

ABOVE : *Stephen Girard on the Philadelphia Waterfront...* A portrait by Frede
James, 1885. The original is in the Masonic Temple in Philadelphia. Girar
standing on one of his wharves on the Delaware River, to the rear of his h
and counting-house on Water Street.

RIGHT TOP : *Stephen Girard's Residence and Counting-House...* A painting
William L. Johnston, early nineteenth century. The original is in the Step
Girard Collection at Girard College. Girard lived and worked in this build
in Philadelphia for thirty-five years, from the time of its completion in 1
until his death in 1831. The five-story section on the left (23 North Water Str
was his home. The two-story section on the right (21 North Water Street)
his counting-house. The entire structure was torn down in 1845. Since the 19
northbound lanes of Interstate 95 have passed through this site.

RIGHT BOTTOM : *Another View of Girard's Home and Counting-House...* A pain
by Simon Greco, 1950. The original is on the first floor of Founder's Ha
Girard College. This imaginative art work shows quite accurately how c
Girard lived to his wharves on the Delaware River.

ᴏᴠᴇ : *Sally Bickham...* A portrait by Nicolas Vincent Boudet, 1794. The iginal is in the Stephen Girard Collection. Sally Bickham was the first of e women who served as housekeeper and mistress for Stephen Girard after wife went insane.

ᴛ ᴛᴏᴘ : *Stephen Girard's Gig...* This twentieth century photograph was taken the second floor of Founder's Hall at Girard College, where the gig is a t of the Stephen Girard Collection. Girard used the two-wheel vehicle, wn by one horse, to go to and from his farm. He never owned a four-wheel riage, even when he was the richest person in America.

ᴛ ʙᴏᴛᴛᴏᴍ : *The House on Stephen Girard's Farm...* An early twentieth century tograph. This house, which still stands, was in Passyunk Township when ard bought it in 1797. It now is in Girard Park in Philadelphia, serving in t as a neighborhood community center and in part as the residence of the k's caretaker.

The Helvetius... A nineteenth century painting of Stephen Girard's ship—330 tons, launched in 1804—that he named in honor of the renowned French philosopher. Captain Alexander Taylor was the master of this vessel for many years. His widow, Jane Taylor, was Girard's last housekeeper.

The Good Friends... A nineteenth century painting of a 246-ton ship that was acquired by Stephen Girard in 1792. It became the focal point of an amazing sequence of strange events that began at Amelia Island off the coast of Florida in 1812.

Larger-than-life Statue of Stephen Girard... Dedicated in 1897 on the West Plaza of Philadelphia's City Hall, this bronze statue by John Massey Rhind is nine feet, three inches tall and stands on a pedestal that is more than nine feet high. This photograph was taken in 1900. The statue was later moved to the West Plaza of the Philadelphia Museum of Art.

Stephen Girard's Bank... An early nineteenth century engraving by William Birch. A copy is in the Stephen Girard Collection. When this building was completed in 1797 it housed the First Bank of the United States. In 1812, after Congress had refused to renew the bank's charter, Girard bought the building and started his own bank. The building still stands, on Third Street south of Chestnut Street in Philadelphia, and is now across the street from the Visitor Center of Independence National Historical Park.

The Chapel at Girard College... This magnificent structure—completed in 1933 and shown in an old undated photograph—symbolizes the importance of religious services in the lives of Girard College students. It has been that way from the beginning. In the college's earliest years the students were required to attend fifteen religious services every week—two each day from Monday through Friday, one on Saturday and four on Sunday.

Girard College... A photograph taken in 1850, two years after the college opened. The large building is Founders Hall. All of the buildings in this photo are still in use.

Thomas U. Walter... This distinguished Philadelphian was the architect for Founder's Hall at Girard College. He later designed the dome of the Capitol of the United States.

Founder's Hall... A twentieth century photograph. This architectural treasure is the centerpiece of Girard College both physically and spiritually. The Tomb of Stephen Girard is in this building. So are the Papers of Stephen Girard, the Personal Library of Stephen Girard, and the Stephen Girard Collection.

ABOVE : *President Harry Truman at Girard College...* In 1948 Girard College celebrated its one-hundreth anniversary. The most festive day of the year-long centennial observation was May 20—Stephen Girard's birthday. On that occasion the President of the United States was foremost among many distinguished guests of honor. A long-time tradition at Girard College—in the dining hall, in the dormitories, in gatherings of students anywhere on campus—is enjoyment of delicious ginger cookies. President Truman found the custom to be a most pleasant one.

LEFT TOP : *Interior of the Chapel, Looking Toward the Rear...* The chapel at Girard College has one of the largest pipe organs in the United States. The pipes are in the ceiling. This is a 1946 photograph.

LEFT BOTTOM : *Girard College as It Appeared from an Airplane in 1927...* Founder's Hall is in the upper part of the photograph. The tract of forty-five acres that became the Girard College campus was farm land when Girard bought it in 1831. The area became a part of Philadelphia in 1854. In the ensuing decades the campus was hemmed in by row-house residential neighborhoods, effectively ruling out any significant expansion of acreage.

The Tomb of Stephen Girard... On the first floor of Founder's Hall at Girard College. Girard's remains were moved to this building in 1851 from the graveyard of Holy Trinity Roman Catholic Church in Philadelphia, where he had been buried in 1831. The life-size marble statue by Nicolas Gevelot was completed in 1845.

CHAPTER 13

Arms for Simón Bolívar: A Good Neighbor in South America

1805-1811

*Freedom cannot be won with proclamations and
platitudes. It takes blood and guts.*

WARS FOR INDEPENDENCE were brewing in South America early in
the nineteenth century. They were led by Simón Bolívar, who became
known as the Great Liberator, and they were successful because there
were brave men willing to fight to be free. Most importantly, victory
was achieved because these men had arms and ammunition to fight
with. Wars are not won by bravery alone.

Stephen Girard's role in supplying weapons and munitions to Bolívar
and his freedom-fighters is a noteworthy sidelight in the history of
South America. Girard gave Bolívar the lift he needed when he needed
it the most—when he was a nobody, when he was unknown, when he
was unsung, when he was unheard of. Later, there were many who
climbed on Bolívar's bandwagon, but it was Girard who led the parade.

When Bolívar, with few guns, little money and hardly any followers,
first dared to dream of challenging and defeating the mighty European
powers that were entrenched in South America, there were many who
thought he was a fool. Nonetheless, Girard could see the potential for
triumph against seemingly impossible odds. U.S. foreign aid had not
been invented yet. Covert operations abroad were a nonexistent
concept in Washington. A fledgling America was still shying from

international entanglements. The laws of the United States frowned on unauthorized acts of war by private citizens against sovereign governments. In spite of these deterrents, Girard financed the shipment of guns and ammunition to subjugated peoples in South America in the name of liberty and justice. He put weaponry in the hands of rebels desperately and urgently in want, rebels who were asking only for a chance to fight and perhaps to die for their objectives. Girard was not the kind to let legalisms stand in the way of a good cause.

There are many dimensions to this improbable story. It seems odd that a maritime merchant sitting in his counting-house in Philadelphia would become involved in the activities of an obscure would-be revolutionary thousands of miles away. Yet, that is what happened. It happened, in part and indirectly, because the slave revolt that had begun in St-Domingue in the early 1790s culminated in a fiery and bloody climax in the early 1800s when French plantation owners and their families were slaughtered in huge numbers. Napoleon sent tens of thousands of French troops across the Atlantic in a futile effort to quell the uprising. Toussaint L'Ouverture, the leader of the rebellious slaves, was captured by the French and removed to France, where he died in prison in 1803. Nonetheless, former slaves continued to rebel and were successful in winning both individual and national freedom. The former French colony of St-Domingue became the independent country of Haiti, formally founded in 1804.

Stephen Girard's brother, John, and his family fled from St-Domingue during the last stages of the revolution. The wife, Eleanor, and the three daughters found refuge in Philadelphia. The only son was sent to a school in France. There is no record of what happened to Rosette, the daughter of John Girard and his former slave, Hannah. Rosette would have been a young woman when her father fled with his wife and their children. If she was left behind, Rosette may have spent the rest of her life in Haiti.

John Girard made a brief and ill-fated attempt to earn a living in trans-Atlantic trade. He bought a brig and hired a captain to sail it. John served as supercargo. However, with Britain and France at war, French cargo vessels were fair game for the British navy. The brig was captured by a British warship and taken to the island of St-Vincent in the West Indies where, on November 4, 1803, John died of a tropical fever at the age of fifty-two.[1]

Eleanor Girard was in Charleston, South Carolina, at the time of her husband's death. She had left her three daughters in the care of a woman in Philadelphia. According to a book written many years later by one of Eleanor's great-grandchildren, she had gone to Charleston "on account of her impaired health"[2]—but Stephen Girard did not see it that way. After he received word of his brother's death, Stephen said in a letter to one of his agents that Eleanor was "a mother who does not deserve the name. She left here about two months ago to go to Charleston on the pretense of regaining health. Her residence seems to be a secret. She intends to return next spring."[3] In the same letter Stephen said he had been "supplying the needs" of his brother's family. "As far as I can see he has no means here. He is even my debtor for about 2,600 dollars, a sum daily increased by the maintenance of the children, house, rent, etc."

On January 29, 1807, just a little over three years after her husband's death, Eleanor died in Philadelphia. The three daughters of John and Eleanor (Antoinette, Caroline and Henriette) had already moved into the house of their Uncle Stephen in the summer of 1805 when they were, respectively, nine, six and four years old. Stephen raised his three nieces as though they were his daughters. Polly served as their mother. William, the boy who had been sent to France to be educated, died in his teens while still in school.

In these circumstances, with St-Domingue in turmoil and no longer a French colony, and with his brother dead, Stephen Girard began to put less emphasis on trade with the West Indies and to give more attention to other shipping routes he had developed over longer distances, particularly to China. This meant more trade with South American ports en route to and from China, and this resulted in a growing interest on the part of Girard in economic and political conditions in South America.

As the war between Britain and France intensified, and as Napoleon gained control of vast amounts of territory in Europe, it became increasingly difficult for Girard and other American maritime merchants to trade with European countries and increasingly dangerous for American ships to sail in waters off the European coast. Both Britain and France imposed a series of embargoes and trade restrictions designed to disrupt and discourage maritime commerce to and from enemy ports. The troubles in Europe caused Girard to utilize, increasingly, the route around South America when trading with China. This led, in turn, to a steady growth in Girard's trade with South American ports. It reached unprecedented heights in the years 1809 through 1811, precisely at the time Simón Bolívar was launching his career as a revolutionary. As one historian has put it, Girard was among "the first of the more responsible American merchants to engage in large-scale trade with continental Spanish America at the beginning of the wars of independence."[4]

Meanwhile, Simón Bolívar was feeling the impact of history from different directions. The most important events leading to Bolívar's revolutionary activities in South America, from his perspective, were the conquest of Spain by Napoleon in 1808 and the installation of Napoleon's brother, Joseph Bonaparte, as king of Spain. For the next five years, from 1808 to 1813, Spain was torn by civil war. One faction, backed by British troops, was seeking to overthrow Joseph Bonaparte, whom they considered to be an alien king and a usurper of power. Another faction, backed by French troops, was trying to keep Bonaparte on the throne.

During these internal hostilities in Spain there was a significant decline in the authority and power of Spanish colonial governments in South America. Bolívar, even though he recognized formidable obstacles, perceived correctly that the time was ripe for revolution. That view was shared by Girard and also by other Americans familiar with political developments in South America and Europe. Thomas P. Cope, a Philadelphia merchant who was a friendly competitor of Girard, wrote in a diary in June of 1810: "It seems probable that Spanish America will become independent of the Mother Country. Some of the provinces on the Main have taken the reins of government into their own hands."[5]

It was later in the year 1810 that Vincent Bolívar, a brother of Simón Bolívar, arrived in Philadelphia on a secret mission. Vincent called on Stephen Girard without prior contact or appointment. Girard received the stranger courteously and consented to talk with him in private. The essence of Vincent Bolívar's message was that he had come as an emissary of Simón Bolívar, who was seeking support for a revolution against Spanish rule in Venezuela. Guns and ammunition were needed. Would Girard be willing to help? That was the crucial question, at this critical juncture in the history of South America, that Vincent Bolívar asked on behalf of Simón Bolívar. Girard's answer, in a word, was yes—even though Simón Bolívar was only twenty-seven years old and his name was not yet familiar in the United States.

Helping people fight European colonialism in the Western Hemisphere was something that appealed to Girard. The Bolívars, Simón and Vincent, had surmised that. Girard was well known in South America, not personally, since he had never been there, but by reputation, because of his activities in maritime trade. It was common knowledge that he was wealthy. The Bolívars may have known also that he had provided supplies to the rebels during the American Revolution and that he had been in sympathy with the objectives, although not some of the tactics, of the French Revolution.

Moreover, Simón Bolívar had been favorably impressed and encouraged by the fact that Girard had named one of his ships in honor of Rousseau. Like Girard, Bolívar was deeply influenced by, and in hearty agreement with, the French philosopher's writings in support of civil liberties and in opposition to tyranny practiced by autocratic despots in governmental and religious hierarchies. Simón Bolívar in 1810 was an obscure protege of Francisco de Miranda, a brave but frustrated Venezuelan revolutionary who was later captured by Spanish royalists and died in prison. Bolívar, setting out on his own as a revolutionary leader, had much more success than Miranda, not only in Venezuela but also in other South American countries, but there was no way of knowing this in 1810. Girard was backing a long shot when he agreed to help Bolívar.

The arms deal between the Bolívars and Girard was a complicated one. Enough records have survived to piece together what happened, although it is possible that some details of the transaction were not put in writing for security reasons. Girard knew as well as the Bolívars that he was playing an extremely dangerous game. Secrecy was imperative. Supplying arms from the United States to overthrow the government of a Spanish colony in South America would be considered an act of war by the exiled government of Spain and perhaps also by the British, who were still trying to oust the French from Spain and restore the Spanish monarchy. France might consider it an act of war too, considering that Napoleon, having conquered Spain, had eyes on the Spanish empire overseas.

Meanwhile, the Government of the United States was striving hard to avoid entanglement in European wars. Federal officials could lawfully prosecute an American caught exporting arms to overthrow a foreign government. President Madison, who wanted South American countries to be free of European domination, was making no great effort to prevent smuggling of arms from the United States to revolutionaries in South America, but he could not openly condone illegal arms trafficking and he would not obstruct justice by giving an arms supplier immunity from federal prosecution, as Girard would soon find out.

The Bolívars had chartered a schooner and sent it to America with a cargo of indigo, coffee and cowhides. The plan was to sell the cargo and apply the proceeds toward the purchase price of guns and ammunition. Assistance from Girard was needed to cover expenses and close a deal for a substantial acquisition of arms. Vincent Bolívar, a stranger in a strange country, was operating on a shoestring.

Contact had been made with a potential arms supplier in New York. However, the schooner's owner, upon arrival in that city, refused to release the cargo until transportation expenses and other fees had been paid. Vincent Bolívar said the charges were excessive. He had no money to pay them in any case. Girard, at Vincent Bolívar's request, intervened and ended the impasse. In a letter to the shipowner, Girard assumed all obligations: "In regard to the expenses of these goods and such other claims as you may have against Mr. Bolívar, have the kindness to send me your account, which I will at once present to Mr. Bolívar and will pay you cash for every item that shall be approved by him. Should he reject same, they shall be put in the hands of two or four referees, chosen by you and me together, on the understanding that I will submit to their judgment."[6]

Thus the matter was resolved, with some assistance from referees required. The cargo was sent to Philadelphia and Girard put it in storage. Without waiting until the goods could be sold, he paid cash to a New York supplier for an order that Vincent Bolívar had placed for 425 muskets.[7] Early in the spring of 1811 the weapons, with ammunition, were shipped to Venezuela. In an accounting submitted to Vincent Bolívar, Girard calculated that his out-of-pocket costs, including cash advances he had given to Vincent, totaled $17,801.22. Girard, without complaint, added a comment: "I do not expect to be able to sell your goods except at a sacrifice."[8] It was in this way that Girard made possible, with substantial expenditures of his own money, a shipment of weapons and ammunition to Simón Bolívar at the onset of his revolutionary adventures. Requests from Vincent Bolívar for additional cash advances, to cover personal expenses before he left the United States to return to Venezuela in the summer of 1811, were turned down by Girard. However, he soon was asked to arrange a much larger arms deal.

On November 30, 1811, two representatives from revolutionary juntas in the southern part of South America (forerunners of the republics of Argentina and Chile) called on Girard in Philadelphia with a letter of introduction from Telesforo Orea, an agent of Simón Bolívar in Washington. The gist of the message from the junta representatives, presented to Girard both orally and in writing, was that a consortium of revolutionaries in South America, including Simón Bolívar and his rebels in Venezuela, had "an urgent need" for "20,000 muskets and a million flints for the same, or as many of those two articles as can be procured." Additionally, there was a need for "a much larger number of muskets, pistols, swords, sabres ... contracted for and delivered as fast as they are manufactured .... If, as it is hoped, it should suit Mr. Girard to undertake this transaction, which offers the opportunity of large profits to a merchant of his knowledge and resources, it would be left to his integrity and discretion, which are well known, to fix a compensation commensurate with the advances he will have to make and the trouble he will have in the matter. It will also be left to his knowledge and experience to suggest the most proper and suitable manner of carrying out the operation."[9]

This was a crass and presumptuous proposition. Girard was being told, in effect, that he could write his own ticket relative to prices he would charge for weaponry and fees he would receive for his services, and he was being enticed with a purported opportunity for large profits. Where, though, would the profits come from? Girard was being asked not only to arrange, but to pay for, the purchase and shipment of weapons. The rebels, with no money to buy and ship, were not likely to have money to pay fees and profits. Girard, under the rebels' proposal, would face a long wait merely to be reimbursed. The prospects for collecting fees and profits would be slim, indeed.

Aside from the financial commitments and risks that would be entailed, there also were impracticalities to be considered. Girard was being asked to underwrite revolutions to win freedom from European domination for most of South America, if not all of it. This could entail the subsidization of prolonged warfare against major European powers such as Spain and Portugal and perhaps also Great Britain and France. If Joseph Bonaparte could be maintained on the throne of Spain, Girard might wind up supplying arms in a war against Napoleon. It was easy for Girard to understand what had happened. His generosity in providing weapons and advancing money for Simón Bolívar's revolution in Venezuela had become known to other would-be revolutionaries in South America. All of them were figuring, or at least hoping, that Girard was a "soft touch" who might bankroll all of their revolutions.

Girard knew that, in addition to the enormity of the financial commitments being asked of him by the consortium of South American revolutionaries, there would be other risks. If he were to become a gun-runner for every revolution on an entire continent, it would not take long for his role to become known in Washington, and in every capital in Europe as well. As a practical matter, it would be impossible for him to procure and export weapons in such huge quantities over a long period of time without the knowledge and consent of the Government of the United States. There was something else to consider also. Girard knew, as President Madison knew, that the United States was edging closer and closer to war with Great Britain. (The two countries were at war in less than seven months.) How could large and frequent arms shipments to South America be justified when the United States was in need of arms for its own defense?

All of these grim realities notwithstanding, Girard was sympathetic to the needs and aspirations of the South American consortium. He was willing to send more weapons to Simón Bolívar and his revolutionary allies if the federal government would give its consent. On December 2, 1811, two days after his meeting with the emissaries from South America, Girard wrote a letter to Telesforo Orea, Bolívar's agent in Washington. "These gentlemen have communicated to me the object of their mission," Girard said, choosing his words carefully, for security reasons, and avoiding any mention of weapons. "Although several difficulties appear to be in the way of the project which they have in view, yet I will endeavor to be as serviceable to them as circumstances will admit."[10]

On the same day, December 2, Girard also wrote a letter to James Monroe, the secretary of state.

> "Envoys from the juntas of Buenos Ayres and Chili have applied to me," Girard said, "to purchase and to ship on account of their respective governments twenty thousand muskets with their bayonettes. Although I am disposed to be serviceable to those gentlemen, yet I do not wish to contract with them unless I am assured that the shipment alluded to will not be considered as unlawful or disagreeable to the President &c, &c of the United States, and that the Government will facilitate me the means of obtaining said muskets &c, either by selling or lending them to me under such terms and conditions as will be judged reasonable."[11]

This was a strong and straightforward appeal from Girard to the President of the United States, through the secretary of state, to provide arms for peoples of South America to help them win freedom from European colonial rule. Madison was not being asked for money. He was not being asked to donate arms. He was merely being asked to make arms available under reasonable terms. If he would do that, Girard was promising to take it from there. He would see to it that the weapons were paid for and were delivered to revolutionary armies in South America, an extremely generous offer. In addition, and prudently, Girard was seeking assurances in advance and in writing from the highest level of the federal government, specifically, from the President of the United States or from the secretary of state on behalf of the President, that he (Girard) would have the President's support and would not be prosecuted as a lawbreaker for supplying arms to South American revolutionaries. With understandable caution, Girard judiciously refrained from mentioning that he had already sent a shipment of guns and ammunition to Simón Bolívar.

Girard's proposals were tactfully ignored rather than explicitly rejected by the Madison administration. The letter from Girard to Secretary of State Monroe was simply not answered, not officially and not formally and, as far as is known, not in writing. There may have been an unofficial and off-the-record reply, conveyed orally or in an informal note that was subsequently destroyed. There was no way, in the circumstances, that Girard could comply with the request for massive and ongoing arms shipments starting with twenty thousand muskets and a million flints. The Government of the United States, under President Madison, was not yet ready to indulge in either foreign aid or covert action on so grand a scale.

From the perspective of President Madison, he had good reason to steer clear of the imbroglio in South America even though his sympathies were with the revolutionaries. From the beginning of his first term in 1809 he had been under a shadow of impending war with Great Britain, and he knew it would be a tough war to win. He did not want to complicate matters by inviting war with any other country. In 1807, during President Jefferson's second term, the British had committed a flagrant act of war when a frigate of the U.S. navy, the *Chesapeake*, was intercepted by a British warship, the *Leopard*, off the coast of Virginia. The British wanted to put a boarding party on the *Chesapeake* to search for deserters from the British navy. When permission was denied, the *Leopard* opened fire, leaving three Americans dead and eighteen wounded. The British then boarded the U.S. frigate and forcibly removed four members of the crew who were alleged to be deserters from the British navy. Three were U.S. citizens who had been impressed into the British navy and had escaped. They were impressed again. The fourth was an Englishman who had, indeed, deserted from the British navy. He was hanged.[12]

U.S. relations with Great Britain deteriorated rapidly after that. Continuing impressment of American citizens for involuntary service in the British navy was a major cause of the War of 1812. As that year approached, and President Madison could see a growing probability of war with Britain, the last thing he wanted to do was let the United

States get entangled in revolutions in South America. Secretary of State Monroe, in the aftermath of Girard's letter of December 2, 1811, was increasingly alert to the importance of South America to the United States. Exactly twelve years later, on December 2, 1823, as the President of the United States addressing a joint session of Congress, Monroe issued his famous doctrine putting the Western Hemisphere off limits to territorial expansion and further colonization by European powers.

It may be readily seen, in retrospect, that Girard was a dozen years ahead of his time in 1811—or, at least, a dozen years ahead of James Monroe—when he (Girard) gave personal assistance to Simón Bolívar and sought U.S. support for him and other South American revolutionaries.

There were several miscellaneous happenings, totally unrelated to South America, that may be mentioned appropriately at this point in the story of Stephen Girard. Among them was his acquisition of real estate in Philadelphia on a large scale for purposes of investment and development. His purchases included houses, and lots, on which he built houses, to produce rental income. Many of them were on Front, Second and Spruce Streets. He also bought a full square block of vacant land, from Market Street to Chestnut Street between Eleventh Street and Twelfth Street. In a fenced-in portion of that block he maintained for many years a large supply of firewood, including scraps of lumber left over from construction work and renovation work on his rental houses. In cold-weather months a gate on Eleventh Street was opened daily so that the city's poor could come and take wood, free of charge, to heat their homes.[13]

Another of Girard's ongoing charitable enterprises was a standing request to physicians in Philadelphia to keep him informed of patients who were in financial need. He would respond with gifts of money, food, clothing or other appropriate assistance. Girard was generally on good terms with doctors in the early nineteenth century even though in the 1790s he had been critical of them because, in his judgment, the treatments they had prescribed for yellow fever patients frequently did more harm than good. On at least one occasion Girard had referred to doctors as "poor imbeciles."[14]

Girard's philanthropies, while usually systematic and well organized, could also be extemporaneous. On one occasion, while walking in Philadelphia, he came upon a man whose horse, which had been pulling a cart loaded with goods, had dropped dead in the street. A crowd had gathered. Onlookers were expressing sympathy but doing nothing to help. Girard went up to the man and handed him a five-dollar bill, at the same time addressing the throng: "I am sorry five dollars' worth. How sorry are you?"[15]

Girard was constantly seeking ways to be innovative. On his farm he introduced the artichoke and several varieties of European grapes to America. In his home he continued to burn coal in his fireplaces even though it still had failed to gain public acceptance. Anthracite coal, which had been discovered in northeastern Pennsylvania late in the eighteenth century, was called "stone coal" for a number of years because it was so hard to ignite. To convert fireplaces and stoves from wood to coal required installation of grates. People did not want to go to the trouble and expense. Wood ignited quickly and produced a roaring fire in just a few minutes. Coal was generally considered too slow to be practical. It took too long to generate enough heat to cook a meal or warm a room, skeptics said. Girard's successful use of coal for heating was dismissed as peculiar behavior of an eccentric.

Coal first gained popularity in Philadelphia as an industrial fuel, rather than for home heating, after two owners of a wire mill in the city decided in 1812 to experiment with anthracite in their furnace. They tried to get a fire started but at first could not; at least they believed they could not. They were impatient and had given up too soon. They had closed the heavy iron doors of the furnace and walked away in disgust. Some time later, one of their employees made a momentous discovery. The furnace doors were so hot they had turned bright red. The coal, albeit slowly, had finally ignited and produced heat with greater intensity than anyone at the mill had thought possible.[16]

Quickly, after that, the use of coal became widespread in Philadelphia mills and factories and, later, in homes. Girard, with characteristic foresight, had sensed an extraordinary investment opportunity. He was a major buyer of coal lands in the anthracite region of northeastern Pennsylvania, most notably in an area of Schuylkill County around a town that still bears his name: Girardville.

Even though Girard continued to live a relatively simple life in a relatively modest home, it was widely known that he had accumulated great wealth. In 1811 there was, allegedly, a bizarre plot to kidnap him and hold him for ransom. Two or three men supposedly were involved in a scheme to lure him to a rented house in Philadelphia on a pretext of having some goods for sale. Then, it was alleged, he was to be taken to a ship in the Delaware River and held captive until a ransom was paid. One plan for collecting the ransom was said to have entailed persuading him to write checks payable to his kidnappers, which they would take to a bank and convert into cash. The plot was revealed by a man who said he had been recruited to help carry it out. No charges were filed against him. Two other men were arrested and brought to trial on charges of conspiracy. Both were acquitted. For one of them, the man who was accused of being the ringleader, the acquittal was on grounds of insanity.[17] Girard was not unduly disturbed by the would-be kidnapping that never materialized. He felt there was nothing to fear from bunglers and incompetents who were too lazy to toil and sweat in productive labor and earn an honest living.

Girard's wealth escalated rapidly in the first decade of the nineteenth century and there were unfounded rumors during his lifetime (some of them persist) that he made large amounts of money unscrupulously in conjunction with the slave rebellion in St-Domingue. It was said that Toussaint L'Ouverture, the leader of the revolt, gave two million dollars to Girard for safekeeping (or to buy arms, according to another version of the story) before leaving St-Domingue for France and eventual death in prison, but Girard (so the story goes) just kept the money for himself. It was also said that Girard kept for himself money and valuables that French residents of St-Domingue gave him for safekeeping during the rebellion. No such sums appear in Girard's financial records, and it is inconceivable that millions of dollars, or any substantial amount, could have been kept hidden from view indefinitely, even in the settling of his estate. In the 1820s, two decades after St-Domingue became the independent nation of Haiti, with former slaves in control, the Haitian government conducted an investigation. During the course of the inquiry an emissary was dispatched to Philadelphia to talk with Girard and his key employees and examine his books. Girard was fully cooperative. The Haitian government concluded there was no substance to the rumors. In the 1880s, more than half a century after Girard's death, a woman living in Paris who said she was a descendant of Toussaint L'Ouverture filed a civil suit in Philadelphia against trustees of the Girard estate seeking restitution of the two million dollars allegedly given to Girard. The case was heard in the Court of Common Pleas, which concluded there was no evidence to support the claim.[18]

CHAPTER 14

Bringing the Money Home:
A Bizarre Incident at
Amelia Island
1811-1812

*Being wealthy is nice—and it is even nicer when
it is the kind of wealth you can get your hands on,
the kind of wealth you can spend.*

STEPHEN GIRARD faced a serious and potentially disastrous financial problem in 1811. He was very rich, at least on paper, but his wealth was scattered all over the world. He had accounts receivable in far-flung places, oceans away from the United States. He had cash balances in dozens of ports in Europe and Asia and elsewhere. He had ships and cargoes thousands of miles from home. As the likelihood of war between America and Great Britain intensified, he had to give first priority to bringing his vast accumulations of profits to Philadelphia for safekeeping. To fail in that mission could result in heavy losses.

A declaration of war on Britain by the United States would have immediate and wide-ranging repercussions. U.S. citizens with assets abroad, especially if those assets were in Great Britain or in British colonies, would be vulnerable. American-owned money and property on foreign soil could be impounded or confiscated. American-owned ships and cargoes in foreign ports or on the high seas would be subject to seizure. There were no neat and tidy international financial arrangements in the early nineteenth century. Money transfers across oceans could not always be accomplished simply by writing a check or a draft or a bill of exchange. Currency or equivalents of currency did not flow freely, without restrictions, across national boundaries. Specie was in short supply and unavailable for export in many countries.

Drawing down accounts abroad would entail for Girard a massive purchasing of cargoes in foreign ports for shipment to America. Upon arrival, the cargoes could be sold promptly for a profit, if market conditions were favorable, or held for sale later when prices rose. In either case, bringing his assets home would make Girard's wealth readily accessible and usable as an instrument of financial power.

The colossal size of Girard's wealth, as the War of 1812 approached, was mind-boggling by standards of that time. Steadily, quietly, unobtrusively, he had become the richest person in America. His net worth had reached half a million dollars around the turn of the century.[1] By 1807 he had become a millionaire,[2] possibly the first in the United States and certainly one of the first. Elias Derby, a maritime merchant in Salem, Massachusetts, is sometimes credited with being the nation's first millionaire.[3]

In 1811, at the age of sixty-one, Girard reached another major milestone: the two-million-dollar mark in net worth.[4] He was America's first multi-millionaire. He remained the richest person in the United States for twenty years, i.e., the rest of his life. During the War of 1812 he was recognized as the richest American by no less an authority than the U.S. Treasury secretary, Albert Gallatin.

It is significant, and characteristic of Girard, that he became a millionaire, and then a multi-millionaire, in times of extraordinary economic difficulty for persons engaged in maritime trade. Some people get rich by being in the right place at the right time. Girard got rich despite, quite often, being in the wrong place at the wrong time. He had become an American through a series of unplanned events, unforeseen results and unlikely circumstances. He had doggedly pursued a career in maritime trade under the flag of a new nation that, in its first decades, for a variety of reasons, had been unable or unwilling to prevent its merchant vessels from being subjected repeatedly to attack, capture and confiscation by hostile forces. He had made his first million dollars, and then his second million, by thriving on adversity, by embracing it and, ultimately, by overcoming it.

His success was a triumph of the spirit as much as the consequence of industry and acumen. Just as he had risen above the physical affliction of blindness in a deformed eye, just as he had persevered through crushing personal tragedy as a beautiful young wife plunged helplessly into insanity, so had he achieved unprecedented prosperity in a hazardous enterprise by going full sail in stormy seas. Especially significant, in Girard's accumulation of wealth in world trade, was his attention to fundamentals such as good captains, good crews and good ships. The ships, particularly, were without equal in performance and reliability. Marion Brewington, a renowned twentieth century authority on maritime history, called Girard's ships "the finest merchant sailing vessels ever constructed in the United States at any time. The materials that went into them were the very best the forest, mines and looms could produce .... Thought and skill [were] lavished on their design and building."[5]

Becoming the richest American and his country's first multi-millionaire had taken Girard thirty-five years from the moment he set foot in Philadelphia in 1776, virtually on the eve of the Declaration of Independence. From 1776 to 1811 the American people had come full circle. They were about to go to war with Great Britain again. Girard, in a way, had come full circle too. He would, again, supply American troops in a war with the British. This time, though, he would not be doling out skimpy provisions from a basement store in Mount Holly, New Jersey. As the wealthiest American, he would be providing large subsidies of cash to an impoverished U.S. Treasury.

Girard, as detailed in previous chapters, had been active in efforts to confront and overcome obstacles to international trade in the last decade of the eighteenth century during the administrations of the two Federalist Presidents, George Washington and John Adams. In the first dozen years of the nineteenth century, leading up to the War of 1812, Girard continued his activist role in behalf of American rights on the high seas during the administrations of the first two Democratic Republican presidents, Thomas Jefferson and James Madison. Twice during Jefferson's presidency, and again in the first term of President Madison, Girard served on committees of maritime merchants and shipowners in Philadelphia that submitted formal protests to the White

House and to Congress regarding seizures of American ships and cargoes by Great Britain, France and other countries.

On one such occasion, in January of 1806, a lengthy and sharply worded protest had been sent by Girard and mercantile colleagues to President Jefferson and Congress denouncing the "regular and systematic plunder" of American cargo ships by foreign governments. The written statement deplored "the unavailing nature of any efforts" by the U.S. government to put an end to this "ruin" and "destruction" and "degradation." The merchants went on to say that "a most deep and deadly wound" had been inflicted on their trade. Then they focused their attention on the British: "Many American vessels, with cargoes unquestionably American, have been carried into the ports of Great Britain .... Some have, indeed, been liberated after a long delay, and with great expense; but many are still detained without a clear understanding of the precise grounds of detention." To surrender to such behavior, the merchants said, "would derogate from the national character and independence of the United States."[6]

Girard and his fellow merchants, in the same protest, also decried depredations by "pirates and plunderers in the West Indies .... The defenceless and unprotected state of our shipping exposes it to the most outrageous ravages of the daring and unprincipled. That our seamen should be exposed to the meanest insults and most wanton cruelties, and the fruits of our industry and enterprise fall a prey to the profligate, cannot but excite both feeling and indignation, and call loudly for the aid and protection of government."

In the same protest Girard and others on the committee made it clear that, while they favored a peaceful solution, they were not afraid of war. "To preserve peace with all nations," they said, "is admitted, without reserve, to be both the interest and the policy of the United States .... Every measure, not inconsistent with the honour of the nation, by which the great objects of redress and security may be attained, should first be used." The merchants also said, however, that "if such measures prove ineffectual," the government should take "whatever measures" are necessary "to preserve private property and mercantile credit from violation." It may be readily seen from the foregoing that Girard, even though he was a Democratic Republican and a staunch supporter of Jefferson on most matters, was not averse to employing strong language in criticism of some of his policies. Girard, who was in his fifties and sixties when Jefferson and Madison were president, was simultaneously a nationalist and an internationalist who wanted the federal government to take an assertive role in defending the rights of American business wherever American products were transported and stored and sold. Far more than most of his countrymen, his focus was global. The price of a pound of coffee on Market Street, around the corner from his home, was of interest to him, but of much greater interest was the price in Arabia. Girard wanted the United States to have a foreign policy that was commercially oriented and encouraged American investment and intercourse beyond America's boundaries. Girard's frontier was not the forest and the prairie; it was the oceans and beyond.

President Jefferson, having devoted his first term to warfare against the Barbary pirates, was in no mood to get into another war in his second term, so it was left to his successor, President Madison, to take on the British, which he would do in the War of 1812. Nonetheless, Jefferson and Congress took quick action, short of war, after receiving the complaint from Girard and his maritime colleagues in Philadelphia, as well as protests from maritime merchants in other cities. In April of 1806 Congress passed the Non-Importation Act and the President signed it, thereby prohibiting entry of a long list of British manufactured goods and agricultural commodities into the United States. The objective was to inflict economic hardship and widespread unemployment on Great Britain unless it agreed to stop seizing American ships and cargoes and impressing U.S. citizens into the British navy. The act was not to go into effect until November of 1806 (subsequently postponed to December of 1807) to allow time for the British to change their policies on ship seizures and impressment, in which case the ban on imports would not take effect.

James Monroe, who was U.S. minister to Great Britain at the time, was instructed to start negotiating with the British. Jefferson sent a special envoy, William Pinkney, to London to assist in the negotiations. It was an all-out effort by the United States to give diplomacy a chance, but the effort failed miserably. Instead of making concessions, the British became more belligerent, issuing new edicts that virtually banned all neutral ships from Europe unless licenses were obtained, for a fee, from the British government. Moreover, the British government refused to give any ground on impressment, which was, in the words of one historian, "the most corrosive issue ever existing between Great Britain and the United States .... Submission to impressment marked the nadir of national disgrace in the history of American diplomacy."[7]

Meanwhile, Napoleon was issuing a series of decrees that were aimed initially at the British but had negative effects on American maritime trading. First he barred from French ports any ship that had stopped in Great Britain. Then he banned British goods from the entire continent of Europe. Soon after that, he declared a blockade of the British Isles and tried to keep ships from getting in or out, although he lacked sufficient naval forces to achieve such a difficult objective. Later he proclaimed all of Europe off limits to American ships, but he had difficulty enforcing this decree also. The English navy was dominant in European coastal waters.

Thus, as seen from an American point of view in the early nineteenth century, the United States was abused by both Britain and France. From a broader historical perspective, however, there was nothing unusual in belligerents prohibiting neutrals from trading with the enemy. (The United States did much the same in World War II.)

During the administrations of both President Jefferson and President Madison, the United States carried on a vigorous trade war of its own in retaliation against the shipping restrictions imposed by Britain and France. The Non-Importation Act was followed by several Embargo Acts, and they were followed by the Non-Intercourse Act. The main thrust of these various measures was to restrict or suspend U.S. trade with Britain or France, or both, in an effort to win repeal of British and French trade restrictions detrimental to U.S. interests.

Without going into specifics of all of the aforementioned steps and counter-steps in trade wars waged on both sides of the Atlantic, and without recounting all of the adventures and misadventures of Napoleon's armies as they ran amuck in Europe, it may be said in summary that Girard could plainly see by 1811 an inescapable truth: His assets in Great Britain and on the European continent were too much in jeopardy to let them remain at risk any longer. Moreover, there was a window of opportunity in that year, 1811, to bring those assets home. Napoleon was in no position to interfere. He had reached the high-water mark of his European conquests in 1808, when he controlled almost the entire continent outside of Russia, but he was losing his grip in many areas of northern Europe by 1811, especially in ports on the Baltic Sea.

Girard owned large quantities of maritime cargo in storage in Baltic ports. Some was in St. Petersburg, in Russia, and some in Baltic ports west of Russia, particularly in Riga, Stralsund and Copenhagen. He also had cargoes in storage in non-Baltic ports in northern Europe, in Hamburg, for example, which was accessible from the North Sea via the Elbe River. Agents in ports of continental Europe were instructed by Girard to sell as much of his cargoes as they could and to send the proceeds as soon as possible on any available ship to any available destination. This meant, usually, sending the proceeds to England, where all specie and many kinds of currency were welcome, and where they could be used to buy English goods for export.

Some cargoes stored in Baltic ports that could not be sold at acceptable prices were brought home safely to Philadelphia. Girard sent four of his ships to the Baltic Sea in 1811. They all returned, fully loaded, without incident, evading interception by British warships patrolling the Baltic Sea, the North Sea and the Atlantic Ocean. This phase of Girard's Baltic operation, moving cargo after cargo from Baltic ports to Philadelphia under the noses of British captains and admirals, had significant consequences for the United States. These cargoes, having arrived safely in America for sale in America, gave Girard a fresh supply of cash to help America in a desperate time.

Girard sent Charles N. Bancker, a Philadelphian with expertise in maritime shipping matters, to London to assist in drawing down accounts there, large accounts that had grown even larger with the influx of specie and currency from Girard's agents in continental Europe. Instructions from Girard to Bancker and to Girard's agents in London, Baring Brothers, were to buy English goods and ship them across the Atlantic for storage in safe places outside the United States, places where they could be held until the latest U.S. ban on imports from Great Britain was lifted. Bancker's mission was to utilize his knowledge of American markets and select items in England that most likely could be sold in the United States at some future time for, in the words of Girard, "a reasonable profit."[8] In a letter to Baring Brothers, Girard said he had "decided to limit my maritime operations and to retain here [in Philadelphia] the remainder of my funds" until "our commerce to Europe opens a more favorable prospect."[9] Thus the stage was set for one of Girard's ships to accidentally become involved in a strange occurrence off the coast of Florida, at a place called Amelia Island.

On December 25, 1811, the *Good Friends*, a ship of three hundred tons that had been owned by Girard for nineteen years, sailed from London bound for Amelia Island with a miscellaneous cargo of dry goods selected by Bancker. No one on board on that Christmas Day could have imagined the odd sequence of events that lay ahead.

Captain Robert Thompson was in command. A thoroughly seasoned old salt, he had been master of the *Good Friends* since 1804. William Adgate was the supercargo. Bancker also was on board. His work in England was finished and, with war in the offing, he was anxious to get out. This was not a good time for an American to be in London.

President Madison, although he was absolutely fearless about another war against the British, still had hopes of avoiding it. He had indicated a willingness to lift the ban on U.S. importation of British goods if Great Britain would ease or abolish restrictions on American trade with continental Europe. There were some in Washington, in the Madison administration and also in Congress, who thought that the British, as they prepared for a military showdown with Napoleon, might want to improve relations with the United States.

Girard initially had ordered Captain Thompson to take the *Good Friends* to Rio de Janeiro, where the cargo could have been sold or put in relatively safe storage either briefly or for a long term. Brazil was still a colony of Portugal, under control of a Portuguese government-in-exile, even though Napoleon had conquered Portugal in 1807 and it remained in his possession. The Portuguese royal family, which had fled from Lisbon and was living in Rio de Janeiro, was in favor of free trade and actively promoted it.

The destination of the *Good Friends* was changed from Brazil to Amelia Island by Girard because he thought that an end to the U.S.

ban on British imports might be imminent. Amelia Island, situated off the northern tip of the east coast of Florida, was virtually on the border of the United States, less than three miles from the mainland of Georgia and less than a mile from the nearest coastal island belonging to Georgia. Florida, including Amelia Island, remained under control of a Spanish colonial government despite the conquest of Spain by Napoleon and the continuing presence of his brother, Joseph, on the Spanish throne.

Girard became so optimistic about chances for an early end to the U.S. ban on imports of British goods that he thought it might be lifted by the time the *Good Friends* crossed the Atlantic Ocean. He sent instructions to Captain Thompson requiring him, when sailing from London to Amelia Island, to pass by the entrance to Delaware Bay close enough to be sighted and contacted by pilot boats based at Lewes, Delaware, just inside the breakwater at Cape Henlopen. This would give Girard an opportunity to modify his orders. If the U.S. ban on British imports was lifted while the Good *Friends* was crossing the Atlantic, Girard could instruct Captain Thompson to bring the ship to Philadelphia instead of proceeding to Amelia Island. If the ban was still on, but seemed likely to be lifted very shortly, Thompson could be ordered to anchor off the Delaware coast and await further instructions. As it turned out, though, the ban was not lifted while the *Good Friends* was crossing the ocean, and prospects for an early end to the ban were fading rapidly. With 1811 drawing to a close, Great Britain stubbornly refused to make any trade concessions to the United States. Accordingly, while the *Good Friends* was on the high seas en route to Delaware Bay, Girard wrote a letter to Captain Thompson directing him to keep on sailing and to stay out of American ports. To make sure that the captain got the letter, Girard made six copies and gave them to six pilots, offering a bonus of fifty dollars to the one who could produce a receipt showing that he had been the first to deliver the letter.

Captain Thompson was ordered, in Girard's letter, to "proceed to Amelia Island" and, upon arriving there, to "wait for further instructions."[10] A letter to Adgate, the supercargo, was enclosed. Girard told him: "My principal object in ordering the ship *Good Friends* to Amelia Island is to put that ship and cargo in a place of safety."[11]

The *Good Friends* arrived in Spanish waters off Amelia Island in early February of 1812. Officers and crew were anticipating a pleasant interlude of relaxation and recreation, but it was not to be. Adgate, in a letter to Girard, described the island as "one of the most miserable spots on the globe."[12] Sparsely inhabited Amelia Island, twelve miles long and less than four miles wide at its widest point, offered living conditions that were primitive even by early nineteenth century standards. Moreover, Adgate soon found that storage facilities on the island for maritime cargo were inadequate and expensive.

A Spanish customs officer boarded the *Good Friends* off Amelia Island and set duties on the cargo at a level that Adgate considered excessive. Partly to avoid a hassle over customs collection, and partly for security reasons, Captain Thompson kept the *Good Friends* anchored offshore. The cost of the cargo had been more than two hundred thousand dollars, and there did not seem to be much police protection on the island. The location of the anchorage was, in Adgate's words, "in the Spanish waters, but near the United States line," about nine miles "by water" from St. Mary's, a town in Georgia. Adgate recorded, additionally, that "boats are permitted freely to go to and fro with passengers only."[13] Bancker, not relishing the prospect of a long wait riding at anchor, and seeing no need to stay with the ship, got a ride to the U.S. shore on a passing boat. He then made his way from Georgia back to Philadelphia.

In mid-March, when the *Good Friends* had been in Spanish waters off Amelia Island more than a month, the situation unraveled with startling swiftness. There was an insurrection on the island. A group of self-proclaimed "patriots" took control in a coup that was bloodless, or nearly so. After hauling down the Spanish flag and raising their own flag, they announced that they wanted Amelia Island to be a part of the United States. An obliging American general, George Matthews, who was in command of U.S. troops in coastal Georgia, responded quickly, taking control of Amelia Island within forty-eight hours.

Officers and crew on the deck of the *Good Friends* had ringside seats. They could see clearly what happened, and what they saw was an early exercise in U.S. "gunboat diplomacy." It was an amphibious operation, and they were right in the middle of the action, but there was no cause for alarm. Not a shot was fired, except in celebration, as American forces occupied the island. They were welcomed with open arms by the islanders. Adgate, in a letter to Girard, summed up what happened:

"The flag of the United States is now flying in Amelia, the garrison and town having capitulated to people styling themselves patriots, and by them has been delivered over to the United States troops."[14]

Captain Thompson, in a letter to Girard, gave details:

"At present we are in the American waters and under protection of our own government as our flag is flying here and the place garrisoned by United States troops with the gunboats around us. The first we heard of this change was on Sunday last when it was understood that there was a revolution in the province and that they had hoisted a white flag with a man in it with some writing on it the substance of which was: the voice of the people, the law of the land. On Monday we could see it from this place. At the same time seven gunboats came down and lay off the point of the island. On Tuesday five gunboats went abreast of the town .... About 2 o'clock we could see seven gunboats a coming with troops .... Fifty of the United States troops came over .... After some forms were gone through, the white flag came down and the American flag hoisted."[15]

In a subsequent letter to Girard, Adgate said he had met with Matthews, after the American general had taken command on Amelia Island, and had been told: "I might consider myself in the United States .... He is perfectly convinced that the property is not safe here and will give us his sanction to proceed to Philadelphia .... I have given him my own security that we will not violate any of the revenue laws of the United States .... We shall proceed to sea at first fair wind."[16]

General Matthews believed that he did not have enough troops and gunboats to give the *Good Friends* adequate protection. He was concerned that the ship, whether at anchor or at a wharf, could be a sitting duck for pirates believed to be prowling in the area. Moreover, Spanish troops on the Florida mainland might try to recapture the island. The *Good Friends*, if it stayed put, could suddenly be in the middle of a war zone.

On April 10, just a little over three weeks after the day (March 18) that the American flag had been raised on Amelia Island, the *Good Friends* weighed anchor and sailed for Philadelphia. Adgate had been given a letter from General Matthews addressed to the Collector of the

Port of Philadelphia stating "full conviction that neither the ship or cargo will be subject to the penalties of the non-importation and non-intercourse laws, in consequence of her entering a port or ports of the United States. I have ... thought proper to grant permission for her to proceed to the Port of Philadelphia—I consider her now to be under the protection of the flag of the United States and within the waters of a port of an integral part of our common country."[17]

Matthews also emphasized, in the same letter, that the valuable cargo aboard the *Good Friends* would "invite the attack of piratical marauders" if the ship remained at Amelia Island. With that kind of endorsement, in writing, from an American army officer in command of Amelia Island, Captain Thompson and his supercargo thought they had nothing to worry about in taking the *Good Friends* to Philadelphia. They had sailed the ship to a Spanish port that, through no fault of theirs, had become an American port. They had the permission of the highest-ranking American authority accessible to them to take the ship and its cargo to Philadelphia. They were going from one American port to another American port in an American-owned ship flying the American flag, and they were doing it with the full blessing, in writing, of an American general. How could anyone in America possibly object to that? Little did they know!

Thompson and Adgate, in their euphoria over getting permission to sail to Philadelphia, did not stop to think that General Matthews, although he meant well in wanting to get the ship and cargo to a safe place, did not have the authority to grant an exemption from penalties under the non-importation and non-intercourse laws. This became apparent in ensuing litigation.

On April 20, 1812, Girard was at work in his counting-house in Philadelphia when Adgate rushed in, justifiably excited, with alarming news. The *Good Friends* had been sailing up the Delaware River, bound for Philadelphia, when the ship was intercepted and taken into custody by the Collector of Customs in Wilmington, Delaware, thirty miles downstream. He alleged that trying to bring a cargo of British goods into an American port was in violation of American law, the Amelia Island episode notwithstanding.

Girard was flabbergasted. He had gone to a great deal of trouble and expense to comply with the U.S. ban on British imports. It was in that spirit, as a law-abiding citizen, that he had sent the *Good Friends* to Amelia Island. It was beyond his understanding how the U.S. government, after suddenly turning a Spanish island into an American island and giving his ship clearance to sail to Philadelphia, could then seize the ship when it tried to reach Philadelphia.

The turn of events was especially galling to Girard because he had gone out of his way to keep high-ranking officials in the U.S. government, in both the executive and the legislative branches, including Secretary of State James Monroe and Secretary of the Treasury Albert Gallatin, fully informed of all plans and decisions regarding the *Good Friends.* Taking every precaution, Girard had wanted to be sure it was clearly understood in high places that he was sending a cargo of English goods to Amelia Island because he was obeying the law, not evading it. Making his plans known no doubt was intended to eliminate any suspicion that he might be sending English goods to Amelia Island with the idea of smuggling them into the United States later through Georgia.

After being told by Adgate what had happened in Wilmington, Girard sent a letter to Allen McLane, the Collector of Customs in that port. The message was remarkably restrained in the circumstances: "I have long ago informed Congress, the Secretary of State, and the Secretary of the Treasury, of the arrival of that ship at her last port of departure, also of the articles composing her cargo and the amount thereof," Girard wrote. "Consequently there could be no intention on my part to evade the laws of our country."[18] Court action ensued. Girard hired a distinguished Delaware lawyer, Caesar Rodney (a nephew of a Delawarean by the same name who had cast a crucial vote for independence in 1776) to represent him in this case. In the first round of litigation in a courtroom in Wilmington, in May of 1812, a judge ordered release of the *Good Friends* and its cargo upon payment of normal duties. Girard promptly paid the duties, and the ship proceeded to Philadelphia.

However, this was not the end of the matter. Even though the ship and cargo were in Girard's possession, without qualification, and he was free to store or sell the goods as he chose, the federal government still had the option to initiate a civil suit to try to collect penalties from Girard. Penalties might be assessed if the government could argue persuasively in court that, despite the happenings at Amelia Island and the actions of General Matthews, Girard had brought British goods into the United States in violation of the law. It did not take the Government of the United States, specifically, the Treasury Department, long to decide to exercise its right to try to collect penalties. On June 11, 1812, Girard was notified that his country was suing him. Federal law allowed penalties to be assessed, with court approval, in sizable amounts, such as, typically, two or three times the value of the cargo, when it could be proved the cargo was imported illegally. The Treasury Department was alleging that the entire cargo aboard the *Good Friends*, cargo with a value in excess of two hundred thousand dollars, had been brought into the United States by Stephen Girard in violation of federal law.

The timing of the suit could not have been worse, from the government's point of view. Just one week later, on June 18, 1812, the United States declared war on Great Britain. The case of the *Good Friends* and its cargo, and the U.S. Treasury's attempt to extract penalties from Girard, would not be settled quickly or easily. The dispute dragged on during a war in which, by a fascinating twist of irony, the U.S. Treasury became desperately dependent on Girard for financial support.

Meanwhile, just as the United States was about to plunge into war with Great Britain, Girard was plunging boldly into a new career at the age of sixty-two. He would rise, swiftly and dramatically, to a new plateau of national stature and power as a banker.

CHAPTER 15

Flying Solo in Banking: A Daring Venture
1812

*Life does not really begin at forty, or at fifty, or at
sixty, or at any other particular age. Life begins
every day, when you wake up in the morning.*

IN 1812 Stephen Girard had been making a living on the high seas,
literally or figuratively, for almost half a century, for forty-eight years,
to be exact. The first thirteen of those years, from 1764 to 1777, had
been spent, for the most part, serving on ships. The next thirty-five
years (except for final voyages to and from France) were concentrated
on buying, selling and transporting cargoes as a land-based maritime
merchant with a fleet of ships and a network of agents. Additionally,
for the fifteen years since 1797, Girard had been a part-time farmer.
After all that, and having become in the process the richest person in
America, and having reached an age at which it might be expected
Girard would want to start slowing down, he was still vigorous and
still looking for new challenges and new opportunities. He would find
them in banking.

The mariner, the merchant, the farmer became a banker. Already a
man of many parts, he put yet another feather in his cap. In a very
broad sense, Girard knew a whole lot more about banking at the age
of sixty-two than he had known about sailing when he first went to
sea at thirteen. As a fabulously successful world trader he had a
thorough understanding of the intricacies and the complexities of
business and finance, especially at the international level. Nonetheless,

he had never worked in a bank for even one day in his entire life. He knew virtually nothing about the routine operations. Plunging head-first into banking was an audacious act, to say the least, but one trait that Girard never lacked was audacity.

Banking goes back a long way—into ancient times. The Babylonians had banks four thousand years ago. However, the English colonies in America managed to develop through their entire colonial period without banks. There were, during colonial times, a few financial firms in America that were called banks, but they had narrowly limited functions and were essentially mortgage companies or loan companies. The institution generally recognized as America's first bank was the Bank of North America. Located in Philadelphia, it was chartered in December of 1781, two months after the Revolutionary War ended with the surrender of Cornwallis at Yorktown. The bank first opened for business in January of 1782.

On December 13, 1790, just one week after the First Congress convened in Philadelphia for the first time, Treasury Secretary Alexander Hamilton submitted a report proposing creation of a national bank. Accordingly, the First Bank of the United States was authorized by Congress on February 25, 1791, and began operations later that year in temporary quarters at Carpenters' Hall, where the First Continental Congress had met in 1774. A permanent home for the bank, in the architectural style of ancient Greece, was erected on the west side of Third Street south of Chestnut Street. That edifice, built solidly of brick and granite and marble, has been described quite accurately as "elegant and commodious."[1] It was completed in 1797, opening for business in July of that year, and still stands as the oldest surviving bank building in the United States. (It is now across the street from the Visitors Center of Independence National Historical Park.)

The First Bank of the United States was controversial from the outset. Some said there was no need for it. Some questioned the authority of the federal government to go into the banking business. Among the opponents in 1791 were Secretary of State Thomas Jefferson and Congressman James Madison. The bank was given a charter for twenty years and, of course, no one could know that

Madison would be president of the United States twenty years later, when the charter would come up for renewal.

Although the First Bank of the United States was headquartered in Philadelphia for its entire existence, branches were established in other cities. The bank became, in effect, a national banking system. Within the first year of operations, branches were opened in Boston, New York, Baltimore and Charleston.[2] By 1805, additional branches were operating in Washington, Norfolk, Savannah and New Orleans.[3] Conceived by the secretary of the Treasury and created by Congress, the First Bank of the United States was an entity of the federal government, owned principally by the federal government. However, shares were available for purchase by the general public, and they would turn out to be an excellent investment. Annual dividends per share averaged more than eight percent. Girard, as he prospered, became a major investor and, by 1811, was the bank's largest individual shareholder.

Shares of the bank could be purchased in London. Some of Girard's shares were bought there as part of his activity to reduce holdings abroad and bring his wealth to America for safekeeping. When the twenty-year charter was about to expire in 1811, it was up to Congress to vote for renewal or to get the federal government out of the banking business. Opinion was divided in Congress, as it was in the country at large. Alexander Hamilton had argued, twenty years earlier, that banking was a public service. A government that operated lighthouses as a public service, he had reasoned, could quite appropriately operate banks as well. However, having been killed in a duel with Vice President Aaron Burr in 1804, Hamilton was not around in 1811 to fight for renewal of the charter.

Girard was strongly in favor of charter renewal. He served on a committee that campaigned vigorously to muster support for renewal in Congress. In doing so, he was not motivated by financial considerations of a personal nature, despite being the bank's largest shareholder. He knew that, if the charter was not renewed, and if the bank's assets were liquidated, there would be an attractive return to shareholders in addition to dividends already paid.[4] Thus he was in a position to profit if Congress rejected renewal. The public good and the national interest were Girard's main motivations in advocating charter renewal. He believed, as did many of his mercantile colleagues and others, that the First Bank of the United States deserved to be kept alive on merit, because it was efficiently run, provided good service and was a stabilizing force in the nation's financial and economic affairs.

There was powerful opposition, though. Much of it came from officers and stockholders of other banks who did not like competition from a government bank.

Girard's advocacy of charter renewal exemplified his political independence. Even though he was a staunch supporter of the Democratic Republican Party and was generally in agreement with the views of Jefferson, the party's founding father, Girard did not hesitate to take contrary positions when so inclined. Just as he had been a vociferous critic of Jefferson's foreign policy in 1806 relative to maritime trade and freedom of the seas, so did Girard come to a philosophical parting of the ways with Jefferson in 1811 on the question of continuing the First Bank of the United States. Girard did not see anything wrong, in theory or practice, with the government operating a bank. On this issue he was more Hamiltonian than Jeffersonian, more Federalist than Democratic Republican.

Congress defeated renewal of the bank charter early in 1811 by the narrowest possible margin in each chamber. Renewal lost by one vote in the House of Representatives and by one vote in the Senate. In the House the tally was sixty-five to sixty-four. In the Senate a tie vote of seventeen-seventeen was broken by Vice President George Clinton, who opposed renewal. Both rejections came on procedural or preliminary motions, an indefinite postponement in the House, a crippling amendment in the Senate, but the results were conclusive and final. The charter was dead. After it had expired without renewal, and after depositors had been given an opportunity to withdraw or transfer their funds, the bank closed on March 3, 1811.

The bank's shareholders appointed trustees to manage the assets of the bank and to settle affairs equitably with creditors and debtors. The trustees were instructed also to try to obtain a state charter that would allow the bank to reopen. Buildings and other property were to be sold if efforts to obtain a state charter failed. Officers and shareholders of existing banks with state charters wanted to reduce competition, not preserve it, so there was heavy pressure on state legislators to refrain from taking any action that would resurrect the First Bank of the

United States. Early in 1812 the Pennsylvania legislature refused to grant a charter. A subsequent attempt to obtain a state charter from the legislature in New York also failed. Under that proposal, the branch office in New York City would have become the bank's headquarters.

The trustees then proceeded to put the bank's property up for sale. Girard, sensing a once-in-a-lifetime opportunity, moved quickly. He had an abundance of wealth that was immediately spendable—currency, specie and negotiable securities that had accumulated during a year of drawing down accounts abroad and bringing assets to sanctuary in America. He had, in a phrase of a later time, deep pockets, the deepest in the country. He did not have to worry about getting a mortgage or some other kind of loan, or putting together a syndicate of investors, or arranging to make payments on an installment plan. He had the wherewithal to pay cash on the barrel-head for what was at that time (and still is, some believe) one of the handsomest buildings in America.

A deal was consummated on May 9, 1812. Girard bought the bank's real estate and furnishings in Philadelphia for $115,000. The transaction included the bank building and a house next door. The house was occupied by George Simpson, cashier of the First Bank of the United States for many years. Also included in the sale were the furniture in the bank and, essentially, everything else in the building used in banking operations, vaults, scales, etc. Except for a few odds and ends, Girard had a complete bank, ready to go. He was a turnkey buyer. All he had to do was hire some people, put some money in the cash drawers, unlock the door and open for business.

He did precisely that on May 18, just nine days after he bought the building and exactly one month before the start of the War of 1812. He began operations with eight employees: a cashier, two tellers, two bookkeepers, a clerk, a messenger and a janitor. George Simpson, the cashier, was in charge of day-to-day operations and supervised the other employees. He was, in modern business terminology, the manager of the bank, second in command to Girard himself. Simpson, in seventeen years as cashier of the First Bank of the United States, had carried out duties and responsibilities similar to those he had under Girard. It was Simpson's experience, and it was Simpson's expertise, that allowed

Girard to gear up and open up so quickly after he had acquired the building and furnishings. Simpson, to say it simply, ran Girard's bank.

There was never any doubt, though, about who was in top command, especially when Girard was on the premises, as he was for at least a part of every business day. Girard established the policies. Girard set the tone. Girard made the decisions on major loans and investments. Many people knew, in general terms, that Girard was rich, despite his plain and simple life style. However, almost no one had any idea how rich he was until he opened his bank. He launched the business with $1,200,000 of his own money. Philadelphia was astounded. So were the nation and the world as the word spread.

On opening day Girard had $71,000 in cash on hand, in the drawers at the tellers' windows and in the vaults.[5] This money was ready for immediate disposal, especially to meet the requirements of borrowers with urgent financial needs. The remainder of the $1,200,000, which was available from opening day if needed, was transferred formally into the bank in several steps over a period of six weeks. On one day Girard deposited $556,000 in negotiable securities to the accounts of the bank.[6] On another day he deposited $450,000 in cash and checks. This sum included, in part, payments he had received from the sale of a miscellaneous assortment of English manufactured goods that comprised the cargo of the *Good Friends*.[7] The ship had just recently been released from custody of the Collector of Customs in Wilmington, Delaware, by court order (as detailed in the previous chapter). On still another day Girard added $125,000 to the coffers of his bank simply by writing a personal check for that amount, drawn on an account at another bank.[8] Girard thus demonstrated convincingly that he had plenty of money, and then some, to start a bank entirely on his own. The $115,000 purchase price for real estate and furnishings seemed almost inconsequential after he had put more than ten times that amount into the till for start-up funds.

His cash position was even further enhanced at the commencement of banking operations because the trustees, as part of the deal, gave him more than six months, until December 1, 1812, to pay the purchase price of $115,000 with no interest charge. He made the payment at that time. Under terms of the purchase agreement he could have waited even longer by paying interest.[9]

Girard and his employees did not have the bank building entirely to themselves. Trustees of the First Bank of the United States retained use of some offices and furniture, and space in the vaults, while winding down their affairs. Girard reserved the right to request and collect annual rent in the amount of one peppercorn. This was a fairly common provision in rental agreements in early America when a property owner did not want to collect significant rent from some special tenant (such as a relative or a charitable enterprise) but nonetheless wanted to safeguard ownership rights by establishing a legally binding landlord-tenant relationship. An annual rent of one peppercorn meant, literally, a dried berry from a black pepper plant. In customary usage it meant any object of inconsequential value (maybe a cookie or a piece of candy). Girard, in essence, was letting the trustees use parts of his building gratis, while affirming his sole ownership.

To add another remarkable dimension to an already remarkable business venture, Girard bought the building and furnishings and started a new bank without really knowing, for sure, that what he was doing was legal, although he thought it was. In 1810 the Pennsylvania legislature had enacted a law that was intended to make it illegal to operate an unincorporated bank. The same law also was intended to make it illegal to be a customer of an unincorporated bank or to circulate and spend (as money) the notes of a bank that was unincorporated. However, the law was worded in such a way that it might not apply to the kind of banking operation that Girard had begun.

He hired two prominent Philadelphia lawyers, Jared Ingersoll and Alexander Dallas, to scrutinize the law and give him an opinion. (Dallas later became U.S. secretary of the Treasury.) By the time the lawyers finished their work and submitted a report, Girard had already opened his bank. Ingersoll and Dallas advised Girard that his bank was legal and that he could lawfully do everything that an incorporated bank with a state charter could do, which included lending money, charging interest and issuing in a variety of denominations bank notes that were payable on demand and could be lawfully circulated and spent as currency by the general public.

The state law enacted in 1810, as the two lawyers emphasized, prohibited "any unincorporated association of persons" from establishing a bank and performing the functions of an incorporated bank.[10]

Girard was unincorporated, but he was not an association of persons. He was an individual citizen. The lawyers concluded that "any individual citizen of Pennsylvania may ... engage in the business of banking."[11] State legislators, when they had passed the law in 1810, could not imagine in their wildest fantasies that any individual ever would be so rich that he could start a bank all by himself, using his own money entirely. Wealth of such magnitude was beyond their comprehension. They assumed that a bank would have to be founded by an association of persons. They did not foresee a man of the financial dimensions of Stephen Girard.

What Girard had done, commercially speaking, was to open a bank in much the same manner that someone might open a store. He was the sole proprietor. The bank had no charter and, because it had no corporate identity, it had no board of directors and no stockholders. It paid no dividends. All of these factors, cumulatively, gave Girard a competitive advantage over other banks, which were beholden to stockholders and thus were under constant pressure to make impressive profits and pay attractive dividends.

Girard, independently wealthy and accustomed to a frugal way of living, was under no compulsion to make any profit at all from his bank although, as matters of principle and pride, he liked to show a profit in every business enterprise he undertook. His bank was profitable right from the start but, for the first several years, he refrained from taking the profits out. He kept them in the bank, increasing its capital, strengthening its operations, expanding its services.

Moreover, he could operate more efficiently than competing corporate banking bureaucracies. Having no directors and no stockholders to report to, and to mollify, was a big advantage. He could make decisions promptly on loans and other bank business without having to worry about justifying his actions to anyone else. He could even make mistakes without fear of testy second-guessing or reprimand. Being a sole proprietor meant never having to explain his intentions. He was his own boss, beholden to no one, accountable to no one, and he loved every minute of it. He had the authority and the discretion and the options that heads of other banks could only dream of.

Almost instantly, virtually overnight, Girard became the most powerful banker in America, and the most envied banker in America. He gave a name to his bank that was as straightforward as it was appropriate: Stephen Girard's Bank. That is exactly what it was. Uniquely and totally, it was his bank. There had never been anything like it before, and there would never be anything like it again. There was one problem, however. Suppose Girard suddenly died! What would become of the bank? Who would protect the depositors? Girard recognized, early on, that he had to address this matter in a way that would inspire public confidence. He did so, swiftly and impressively. Just a few days after his bank opened, he had in place an arrangement to take effect upon his death. In a nutshell, it was the appointment of five Philadelphians of impeccable reputation to serve as trustees of his bank, and vested in them clear legal authority to take command of the assets of the bank at the time of his death and to discharge all obligations to the bank's depositors and creditors during the settlement of his estate. Four of the trustees were prominent merchants: David Lenox, Robert Smith, Robert Wain and Joseph Ball. The fifth trustee was the bank's cashier, George Simpson.

In a detailed indenture, duly notarized and recorded, Girard gave explicit instructions to the trustees. They were told to take a number of carefully stipulated actions when he died because, as Girard put it, "He is desirous in case of his death to prevent any delay or inconvenience arising therefrom."[12] Trustees were directed to fulfill the bank's responsibilities with "promptitude and punctuality."[13]

Thus Girard was both farsighted and fearless as he embarked, quite suddenly and quite unexpectedly, on a new career at a rather advanced age. Once again he took a momentous step more by accident than by design.

He had favored renewal of the charter of the First Bank of the United States and had been active in the fight for renewal. That fight had been lost by the narrowest of margins. If there had been a switch of one vote in the House and one vote in the Senate, Girard would not have become a banker. After that, if the attempts to win a state charter had been successful in either Pennsylvania or New York, as Girard had hoped, he would not have become a banker. Even with charter battles lost in Congress and in the legislatures of two states, Girard would not have been able to buy the bank and operate it as the sole proprietor except for an unrelated set of circumstances. America's drift toward war with Great Britain had prompted him to draw down accounts abroad and bring his wealth home. Were it not for this coincidental timing, Girard would not have had in excess of a million dollars sitting at his fingertips, enabling him to become a banker.

All things considered, it may be said that Stephen Girard, by 1812, had become America's first tycoon. He had become the first American to combine, simultaneously, unprecedented wealth in mercantile affairs with unprecedented power in the financial arena. He had become not only the richest person in America and the most powerful banker in America but also the first extremely wealthy American to have a substantial part of his wealth in cash or in equivalents of cash.

Other rich Americans in the country's early years typically had the bulk of their wealth tied up in assets not easily liquidated, including land and other real estate. Many family fortunes in the South were based on ownership of slaves and operation of plantations dependent on slave labor. Girard, being not just rich but cash rich, had a new kind of wealth. He would demonstrate that money is power. Ready cash would enable him to be a positive force not only in large ways, such as coming to the rescue of the government of the United States in the War of 1812, but also in small ways, such as making loans to persons of modest means to help them get started in business or in farming or to acquire a home. Financial assistance primarily to ordinary people and small business, and only secondarily to rich people and big business, was the hallmark of Stephen Girard's Bank. Thus he used the power of money in an enlightened fashion to advance social change and economic opportunity.

Later, as the mercantile society in America began to give way to the Industrial Age (an age that generated tycoons by the dozens), Girard became a pioneer in the development of coal and railroads. He would show how wealth, instead of being selfishly conserved and zealously protected, as it traditionally had been in many wealthy families, can be used more constructively on the cutting edge of innovation. Ultimately, he would raise charitable giving to levels unprecedented in America, breaking new ground in the commitment of wealth beyond the grave to benefit the poor and the disadvantaged of future generations.

So, in sum, America's first tycoon was progressive and benevolent and humble, with no castles on the heights, no mansions by the sea, no estates in the country, no carriages at his command. He was very much unlike many of the tycoons who would follow.

Having a bank meant that Girard was busier than ever. He now had three jobs, each occupying a part of his work day. He was a merchant, he was a banker, and he was a farmer. He usually began each day and ended each day in his counting-house, attending to business related to maritime trade. That was the most convenient schedule because, with his counting-house and his residence in the same building, he did not have far to go to get to work in the morning or to get home at night. He spent much of each business day at the bank, in his office on the second floor or keeping a watchful eye on operations on the first floor.

Almost every day in spring, summer and autumn, and with surprising frequency in winter, he continued to go to his farm. He would perform, and thoroughly enjoy, hard labor for an hour or two, and sometimes for several hours. He might go in the morning, or in the afternoon. In spring and summer he might go in the daylight of early evening. The times and durations of his visits continued to be erratic and unpredictable, as they always had been, keeping the farm manager and the farm hands busy and alert. They would never know from day to day when their boss would arrive or when he would leave.

Girard's new career in banking did not affect his relationship with Polly Kenton. She continued to be an important part of his day. From Girard's bank on Third Street, half a block south of Chestnut Street, to Girard's home on Water Street, half a block north of Market Street, was an easy walk of about half a mile. Girard had his mid-day meal at home during a long break from work that routinely lasted two hours or more. Many merchants and bankers gathered in taverns and coffee houses at mid-day to eat and drink, socialize and talk business, but Girard would have none of that. The richest person in America came out of his bank, turned north, and walked up Third Street, down Market Street and up Water Street to his home, where Polly (she was thirty-six years old in 1812) was waiting.

They would eat together in the parlor on the second floor, having what could more accurately be called dinner rather than lunch, for it was the biggest meal of the day and, in the French tradition, included wine. Almost always, there would be at least two or three others, often many more, at the table. There usually were apprentices, and maybe also a clerk or two, who worked in the counting-house and had sleeping quarters in Girard's house. Three nieces of Stephen, in age from eleven to sixteen (the daughters of his deceased brother, John) joined in the mid-day meal if they were not in school, and Polly had relatives on the premises much of the time, typically sisters or nieces, who might have places at the table. The Girard household was a lively place, and Stephen liked it that way. He enjoyed having people around. In the absence of a family of his own, he made do with whatever family could be improvised from whoever was at hand.

After a leisurely repast, Polly would accompany Stephen up the stairs to their bedroom on the third floor, where windows offered a sweeping view of the Delaware River, including Girard's wharves directly behind his house. If he had ships being loaded or unloaded, he could observe the work in progress. Polly would soon know if Stephen wanted her before he took a nap. He might prefer to wait.[14] Whatever his wishes, she was available. That was her job. She had been his mistress since 1796. By now, in 1812, each of them knew all of the little quirks and mannerisms of the other. They had the kind of relationship that can be attained only over a long period of time. Even though she was not his wife, they had in fact become virtually a married couple.

He had become rich and famous and powerful during their years together, and his name was known around the world, but nobody knew Stephen like Polly knew Stephen. She was the one he went to when he wanted to be wanted. She was his respite from work, work, work. She was not counted in his net worth, but she was a precious and tangible asset.

Sixteen years had passed since, at the age of twenty, she had come to Stephen's house to live with him and to give herself to him with youthful enthusiasm. Now she was experienced and self-assured, with the depth of beauty and femininity that comes when age has advanced a little, but not too much. The pretty girl had become a pretty woman, a mature woman, but still a young woman. Polly, in 1812, had lived with Stephen longer than he had lived with Mary before she went insane, and longer than he had lived with Sally before she left him to marry another man.

Mary, in her fifties now, was still in the facilities for the insane at Pennsylvania Hospital. Polly visited her regularly (and so did Stephen occasionally) to be sure she was being cared for properly. She was declining physically. It was becoming increasingly likely, as Polly could plainly see, that Stephen was going to be a widower someday, free to marry again if he wished.

No one can say for certain what Polly was thinking in 1812 but, surely, after sleeping with Stephen for sixteen years, she must have been giving some thought to her own future. When she was waiting for him to come home for his mid-day meal, she must have wondered, every now and then, if she might someday be Mrs. Stephen Girard. It must have crossed her mind, at least occasionally, when she was holding the richest man in America in her arms, that she might someday be the richest woman in America.

CHAPTER 16

A Crisis in the War of 1812: The Treasury Runs Out of Money

1812-1813

The only thing more difficult than winning freedom is keeping it.

THE AMERICAN REVOLUTION ended on October 19, 1781, when Cornwallis surrendered at Yorktown. It resumed thirty years and eight months later—on June 18, 1812—when the United States declared war on Great Britain. The Americans, bold and brash, were trying to score two wins in a row against the most powerful nation on earth. This time they would not have the French to bail them out.

King Louis XVI, who had sent his army and navy to America's rescue in the Revolutionary War, making the victory at Yorktown possible, could not do it again in 1812. He had lost his head on the guillotine in the French Revolution. Napoleon was in charge of France in 1812, but he was in no position to come to anybody's rescue. It was in 1812 that he made the calamitous mistake of invading Russia.

During the three decades between the Revolutionary War and the War of 1812 the Americans and the British had been almost constantly at each other's throats, as discussed in detail in previous chapters. Great Britain had repeatedly imposed trade restrictions on American shipping and had made a habit of seizing American ships and cargoes in international waters, including some ships and cargoes belonging to Stephen Girard. The British had routinely removed American citizens from American ships for involuntary service in the British navy. Meanwhile, the British had taken numerous hostile actions, sometimes in concert with Indians, against American settlers and U.S. military outposts on the western frontier, particularly in the Great Lakes region. One of Britain's objectives, Americans could plainly see, was to establish the border of Canada far enough south to provide access to the Ohio River and the Mississippi River, either directly or through tributaries.

Britain had, in sum, committed numerous acts of war against the United States while rebuffing American efforts to achieve peaceful solutions through negotiations. American reprisals short of war, such as trade restrictions and embargoes, had failed to evoke a conciliatory response from the British. So, finally, America declared war, knowing full well that the outcome was in doubt. Great Britain had far superior armed forces on land and sea.

Despite the many provocations by the British, declaring war was clearly a high-risk gamble for the Americans. However, to keep on postponing effective action in face of continuing British aggressions and humiliations would also have been a high-risk gamble. If the United States continued to convey an impression of being so weak that it was afraid to defend its rights as a sovereign nation, Great Britain might have been tempted to become even more aggressive. After the defeat of Napoleon, war in Europe no longer occupied a substantial part of the British army and navy. They would be free to turn their attention to America.

Girard had been warning about the dangers of appeasing the British for many years. He had criticized the first three presidents of the United States—Washington, Adams, Jefferson—for failing to take adequate steps to uphold and defend American rights (as detailed in earlier chapters). President Madison was determined to take a strong stand in defense of America's sovereign rights on the high seas and on the western frontier. Yet he had tried hard to avoid war, devoting the early years of his presidency to diplomatic efforts to improve relations with Great Britain. Failing in that, he had utilized measures short of war, such as trade restrictions, to try to persuade Britain to show respect for American shipping, American citizens and American territory, all to no avail.

On June 1, 1812, his patience exhausted, President Madison sent a special message to Congress. He listed America's grievances against Great Britain, just as Thomas Jefferson had done in the Declaration of Independence thirty-six years earlier. Madison cited numerous British acts, formally called Orders in Council, that were designed to restrict American maritime trade and subject American ships and cargoes to seizure on the high seas. He condemned British impressment of American citizens, forcing them into service in the British navy. He deplored continuing British hostilities against Americans on the western frontier. The President stopped short of asking Congress specifically for a declaration of war against Great Britain, but the tenor of his message dispelled all doubt about his readiness to sign a declaration of war if Congress was willing to take that course. Madison told Congress that Great Britain was already in "a state of war against the United States" while the United States was in "a state of peace towards Britain."[1]

A declaration of war was approved seventy-nine to forty-nine in the House of Representatives and nineteen to thirteen in the Senate, with congressional action completed on June 17. President Madison signed the bill on June 18, making that the day the war officially began. The votes were along party lines. Although the Federalist Party was never able to elect another president after Washington and Adams, there were still thirty-nine Federalists in the two houses of Congress in 1812, most of them from New England states. All thirty-nine voted against the declaration of war. There were 121 Democratic Republicans (President Madison's party) in Congress. They were overwhelmingly, but by no means unanimously, in favor of war. Ninety-eight Democratic Republicans voted for the declaration. Twenty-three Democratic Republicans voted against it.[2] Ironically, on June 16, 1812, just one day before the U.S. Senate approved the declaration of war by a margin of just six votes, the British government announced in London a suspension of the Orders in Council. If this had been known in Washington, it is almost certain there would not have been a declaration of war. Suspending the Orders in Council was a significant concession by Great Britain, even though it did not affect some major American grievances such as impressment of U.S. citizens into the British navy and British hostilities on the western frontier. The suspension removed trade restrictions that had been used by the British as justification for seizure of American ships and cargoes in international waters.

Congress adjourned on July 6. Members left Washington, returning to their home states, long before news reached America about the suspension of the Orders in Council. It was a lot harder to stop a war than to start one. War had been declared, so the war was fought. Although it would come to be known, simply and unimaginatively, as the War of 1812, many Democratic Republicans called it the Second War of Independence. There was a touch of hyperbole in that label at first, but it was closer to the mark than many people may have realized initially. It could be argued, and, indeed, it had been argued by some members of Congress, that the war was neither advisable nor necessary. Nevertheless, once war had been declared, there were harsh realities that had to be faced. The situation was fraught with danger for America. Loss of American independence was a distinct possibility.

The British did not have to worry about an invasion of England by America, which did not have the ships or the men to mount such an offensive. The British, however, were quite capable of invading the United States and perhaps reclaiming portions of the country, if not all of it, as British territory. It is impossible to know for sure how events that did not happen could have changed the course of history. However, there is strong evidence that a clear and decisive victory for Great Britain in the War of 1812 would have drastically altered the history of the United States. In a worst-case scenario, from America's point of view, the United States could have ceased to exist as an independent nation. It could have become a part of the British Empire, as a separate colony or as a part of Canada. In a more likely scenario, a part of the United States could have retained independence but substantial territory could have been lost to the British. Opportunities for future expansion of the United States could have been significantly reduced.

Specifically, the northern boundary of the United States was not firmly established or clearly defined in 1812, and the future states of Maine, Michigan, Wisconsin, Minnesota, North Dakota, Montana, Idaho and Washington were mostly wilderness. If Great Britain had won the war, it is probable that portions of at least some of those states, and maybe portions of all of them, would have become part of Canada. Also in jeopardy would have been portions of other states bordering on the Great Lakes: New York, Pennsylvania, Ohio, Indiana and Illinois. A major objective of the British was full control of navigation on the Great Lakes. This might have been achieved, if Britain had won the war, by making the shorelines of all the lakes a part of Canada. Some indication of how strongly Great Britain felt about expanding the territory of Canada was evident when the War of 1812 finally ended. Even without winning the war, the British made a concerted effort to push the Canadian boundary southward, especially in the Great Lakes region and also in Maine, when terms of the peace treaty were being negotiated.

Loss of New Orleans and the mouth of the Mississippi River to Great Britain would have been another probable consequence, if the British had won the war. Indeed, the largest offensive of the British was aimed at New Orleans. If they had gained control of that city, there would have been no U.S. access to trade routes of the world for ports upstream on the Mississippi, Ohio and Missouri Rivers and their tributaries, except on terms set by Great Britain.

Thus there was much at stake in the War of 1812. In the perspective of history it is often viewed as a minor war, but that is only because Great Britain was unable to win it. If the British had won, there would have been nothing minor about the consequences for America. In this context, from an American viewpoint, it is startling to contemplate how close the British came to winning.

It was plainly evident in 1812 that, if the United States was to have a realistic chance of winning the war, the army would have to be strengthened rapidly. Congress provided generous incentives to stimulate enlistments. Pay for privates was raised from five dollars to eight dollars a month.[3] Recruits were given enlistment bonuses of thirty-one dollars in cash and 160 acres of land, later increased to $124 and 320 acres. These were huge incentives at a time when $2.50 a week was a good wage for unskilled labor, and a farmer could make a comfortable living on 160 acres. One historian has called the bonuses "a princely sum—probably the highest bounty ever paid by any army in the world."[4]

Congress did not enact any increases in taxes to pay for building up the army, or financing the war generally, before adjourning in July of 1812. The government did not seem to require an immediate infusion of additional cash at that time. However, Treasury Secretary Albert Gallatin initiated negotiations in an attempt to borrow $500,000 from Girard in the summer of 1812. Both men knew there was no fiscal emergency yet. Gallatin was engaging Girard in a probing exercise, feeling out the richest American to see if he might be willing to help finance the war and, if so, on what terms. The secretary of the Treasury moved cautiously. He did not want a confrontation with Girard. Instead of approaching him directly, Gallatin used George Simpson, the cashier of Stephen Girard's Bank, as an intermediary. Gallatin came to Philadelphia twice during the negotiations and talked with Simpson. However, their meetings were not held in the bank.

Gallatin's caution was well justified. After all, it had been just prior to the start of the war that the U.S. Treasury Department, with Gallatin in charge, had filed suit against Girard in an effort to collect heavy penalties for bringing British goods into the United States aboard the *Good Friends*, allegedly in violation of federal law prohibiting imports from England. In the summer of 1812 the legal action was still pending in U.S. District Court in Wilmington, Delaware. The Treasury Department had calculated the value of the cargo of the *Good Friends* at $298,482 and was seeking from Girard a penalty of three times that amount: $895,446.[5] In a related civil action the Treasury Department was trying to get court approval for an additional penalty against Girard in the amount of $15,000.[6] So, in total, the Treasury Department wanted to collect $910,446 from Girard in the aftermath of the Amelia Island affair, arguing that the *Good Friends* had no lawful right to sail up the Delaware River with English goods aboard, even though a general in the United States army had said in writing it was all right to do so.

In the circumstances it was hardly surprising that Gallatin did not want to meet with Girard face-to-face to ask for a $500,000 loan. Girard was furious over the Treasury Department's hostile moves to penalize him. This was not an auspicious time for Gallatin to be asking for a loan from Girard. There is nothing in writing to indicate, and there is no evidence to suggest, that Gallatin was planning to use the civil action against Girard as a bargaining chip. It would have been injudicious, if not unethical, for the Treasury secretary to offer, as a quid pro quo, to drop the civil case against Girard in the amount of

$910,446 if he would lend the Treasury $500,000 under favorable terms. An offer of that kind, if it had been made, most likely would have been discussed orally, not in writing.

As it turned out, and perhaps to Gallatin's surprise, Girard was willing to lend money to the Treasury Department, under certain conditions, despite the department's lawsuit against him. Simpson, in a memo to Girard in July of 1812, relayed Gallatin's request for a loan and recommended that it be granted. Girard, in a memo to Simpson, replied that he was willing to lend money to the Treasury Department if it would put his bank "on an equal footing" with other banks in Philadelphia regarding "deposits, receiving duties, paying drafts, etc., etc."[7]

Girard had good reasons for seeking full and unequivocal recognition of his bank by the federal government. State-chartered banks in Philadelphia would not honor notes issued by Stephen Girard's Bank and were trying hard to put it out of business. The competing banks were pushing for enactment of a bill in the Pennsylvania legislature that would outlaw all unchartered banks, without loopholes or qualifications, and force Girard's bank to close. If the U.S. Treasury would give Girard's bank equal status with all other banks in the city, giving his bank a fair share of federal deposits, and using his bank in a fair share of transactions by federal departments when banking services were required, it would be more difficult for his bank to be ostracized by the rest of Philadelphia's banking community. It also would be more difficult for a bill outlawing his bank to get support from a majority of state legislators. Gallatin, though, had good working relationships with state-chartered banks in Philadelphia. He did not want to get embroiled in a local banking dispute by appearing to put the federal government on the side of Stephen Girard's Bank. Thus, in these circumstances, Gallatin declined to make a firm commitment to full equality for Girard's bank. Consequently, a loan was not consummated in the summer of 1812.

Declaring war is one thing. Finding somebody to shoot at is something else. For the United States, in 1812, locating the enemy was the first challenge. There were no British troops on American soil, except in remote frontier areas that were hard to get to. When the

Revolutionary War began—informally with skirmishes at Lexington and Concord in 1775, and formally with the Declaration of Independence in 1776—the British had many troops stationed in populated portions of the American colonies. Engaging the enemy in battle had been no trouble at all. In 1812, however, the most accessible place for an American soldier to find a British soldier was Canada. Consequently, it was in Canada, or near the Canadian border, that the War of 1812 was fought in its early stages.

The British, for their part, were not shy about attacking Americans. As soon as the British learned that war had been declared, they captured Fort Detroit. Two other American military posts in the future state of Michigan fell to the British in the first few months of the war, as did Fort Dearborn (the future site of Chicago). Several American incursions into Canada ended in defeat or in frustration and retreat. All in all, the land war went badly for the United States from the very beginning.

Surprisingly, the United States scored some impressive victories early in the war in naval engagements, supposedly Great Britain's strong suit. Nevertheless, successes at sea were far outweighed by setbacks on land, so much so that the American people did not have much faith in their country's chances of finally emerging victorious over Great Britain. This became apparent early in 1813 when the first serious attempt was made by the U.S. government to raise money on a large scale to carry on the war.

On February 8, 1813, Congress authorized the U.S. Treasury to borrow sixteen million dollars—the largest loan ever sought by the federal government up to that time.[8] On February 20 the Treasury announced details of the loan, offering attractive terms designed to appeal not only to large investors but also to persons of relatively modest means. The aim was to achieve the widest possible financial participation of the general public in the war effort.

Interest would be paid quarterly at an annual rate of six percent for more than twelve years, until December 31, 1825, when the principal would be repaid. Loan certificates would be available in denominations of as little as one hundred dollars and in any multiple of one hundred dollars. A down payment of just $12.50 was required for each one hundred dollars loaned. The balance could be paid in seven monthly installments of $12.50 each. Gallatin was hoping that his loan package would gain acceptance from many thousands of small investors, but he knew it would be a hard sell. The war continued to go badly for the United States. Moreover, Napoleon had made his disastrous retreat from Russia in the final months of 1812, losing men and equipment in vast numbers and quantities. Great Britain, with Napoleon's power diminished, was able to send more fighting forces to America and its coastal waters. British warships patrolled the Atlantic, sometimes within sight of the U.S. shore and sometimes even at the entrances to bays and rivers, seizing American merchant vessels.

In these circumstances many Americans did not see any prospect of the United States winning the war. To lend the government money to carry on the war, in the view of many potential investors, would be not only an exercise in futility but also an extremely risky investment. It was hard to imagine how the United States could repay the loan if it lost the war. The Treasury secretary decided it might be better to persuade some wealthy Americans to invest heavily in the loan at the outset, instead of going first to the general public. He approached David Parish, a Philadelphia financier, and asked him to serve as an emissary. Gallatin wanted Parish to call on wealthy Americans, including Girard and John Jacob Astor of New York, who was the second richest person in the United States, and encourage them to subscribe to the loan in large amounts.

Parish, a smooth talker who kept up an appearance of being wealthier than he actually was, had made a fortune wheeling and dealing in Mexican silver but was in the process of losing a fortune in high living and imprudent speculations, mostly in land and sheep.[9] He declined, at first, to help Gallatin. It was obvious to Parish that trying to promote a loan to finance a war would be immensely difficult when, from all indications, the country that wanted to borrow the money was going to lose the war and default on financial obligations. With Parish seeing no realistic prospect of obtaining funds in impressive amounts from the wealthy, Gallatin proceeded with a public offering of the loan aimed mainly at small investors, people who could afford to put up $12.50 a month for eight months.

Subscriptions were scheduled to close on March 13. However, the sale could be re-opened for another round if the full loan was not completed by the first target date. To protect investors, the loan would not be implemented unless the entire amount, sixteen million dollars, was subscribed. That was considered the minimum sum required to finance a successful war effort and give lenders a reasonable prospect of receiving interest payments on schedule and, eventually, getting their principal back. Meanwhile, the financial condition of the federal government was moving rapidly from desperate to critical. On March 5, Gallatin informed President Madison of the harsh reality: "We have hardly money enough to last till the end of the month."[10] Subscriptions to the loan were accepted in eleven major cities in the United States, at banks, including Stephen Girard's Bank, that were selected to serve as agents for the U.S. Treasury. Girard subscribed to $100,000. His bank received additional subscriptions totaling more than $22,000.

The nationwide effort to attract loan commitments was a dismal failure. Less than four million dollars had been subscribed in the whole country at the close of business on March 13, more than twelve million dollars short of the goal.[11]

With the federal government now running almost on empty, Gallatin made a last-ditch effort to stave off insolvency. He reopened the loan to public subscription one more time, with the books to be closed on March 31. As his ace in the hole, Gallatin set aside five more days, until April 5, to reach the goal of sixteen million dollars. If the public subscription fell short a second time, the last five days would be used to make a final appeal to potentially large investors to subscribe to the remaining balance. The entire loan would be cancelled, and the Government of the United States of America would be without funds, if the sixteen million dollars was not subscribed in its entirety by the close of business on April 5.

With financial disaster now a very real and a very imminent threat, Parish reconsidered and agreed to help Gallatin line up support from wealthy individuals. Girard, reiterating the position he had taken the previous summer, informed Gallatin that an additional subscription, over and above the $100,000 already subscribed, would be considered if the U.S. Treasury would put Stephen Girard's Bank on equal footing with state-chartered banks in Philadelphia. They were still refusing to honor notes issued by Stephen Girard's Bank.[12]

At this juncture, while the suspense was rising and the federal government was edging closer and closer to becoming financially inoperative, an incident occurred that drove home to Girard how firmly the British were in control of American coastal waters and how badly the war was going for the United States. One of his ships, the *Montesquieu*, which had sailed from Philadelphia in December of 1810 on a voyage to South America and China, was approaching the entrance to Delaware Bay on the return trip twenty-seven months later, in March of 1813, with a cargo of tea and other items. The ship was captured by vessels of the British navy. No one aboard the *Montesquieu* had known that the United States and Great Britain were at war. The ship had twenty-one men aboard and six guns mounted on the deck, but Captain Robert Wilson surrendered without firing a shot. The capitulation greatly angered Girard when he heard about it.

On March 30 Girard received a letter from Wilson, sent to Philadelphia on another ship, telling of the capture. The next day, March 31, Wilson and his supercargo, Arthur Grelaud, arrived at Girard's counting-house. They had been set free by their captors and had been instructed to tell Girard that the British were willing to release the *Montesquieu* and its cargo and all remaining personnel on payment of a ransom of $180,000. On the following day, April 1, Grelaud left Philadelphia en route to Washington, about 140 miles away on the roads of that time, with a letter from Girard requesting President Madison's permission to pay the ransom, which Girard had calculated to be substantially less than the value of the ship and the cargo.

Grelaud arrived in Washington on April 4 at about nine o'clock in the evening and went immediately to the home of Navy Secretary William Jones. That same night Jones and Grelaud went to the home of Secretary of State James Monroe, who said he would submit the letter to the President in the morning, which he did. On April 5, on the very day that the final act of America's financial crisis would unfold in Girard's office in Philadelphia, Secretary Monroe wrote to Girard from Washington stating that his letter "has been laid before the President and I have the pleasure to inform you that he has readily assented to the measure proposed by you."[13]

Specie in the amount of $180,000, provided by Girard, was loaded on a ship in Philadelphia and, with the blessing of the President of the United States, was transported down the Delaware River and the Delaware Bay and delivered to a British warship near the mouth of the bay. On April 11 the British released the *Montesquieu* and it resumed its journey to Philadelphia.

Unknown to Girard, while all of this was going on, another of his ships was also in trouble, having also fallen prey to the British. The *Good Friends*, the same vessel that had been involved in the Amelia Island affair, had sailed from Philadelphia in January of 1813 with Captain Robert Thompson again in command and William Adgate serving again as supercargo. They had been instructed to pick up a cargo of cotton in Charleston, South Carolina, and take it to whatever port in France could be reached safely, preferably Nantes.

Guns were mounted on the deck of the *Good Friends*, and Girard had obtained a Letter of Marque from the U.S. government authorizing the ship to attack and capture any British merchant vessel that might be encountered on the high seas. However, Captain Thompson had been instructed by Girard to use the guns only for self-defense on this voyage. Thus instructed, Captain Thompson had taken the *Good Friends* from Philadelphia to Charleston, where he had purchased a cargo of cotton and had sailed from that port on March 5 bound for France. On April 2, within a hundred miles of the coast of France, the *Good Friends* was chased, caught and attacked by three British warships. After a half-hour gun battle Captain Thompson surrendered to superior force. The *Good Friends*, its crew and its cargo were captured and taken to England. They arrived at Plymouth on April 5, on the very day that time was running out on the U.S. government in its attempt to raise sixteen million dollars needed to continue the war.

Thus, on the day that Girard was making a crucial decision about financing America's second war against Great Britain, on April 5, 1813, two of his ships, with cargoes and crews, were captives of the British. Girard knew, on that day, that the *Montesquieu* was being held for $180,000 ransom at the entrance to Delaware Bay, but he did not yet know that President Madison had given permission to pay the ransom. Girard did not know, on that day, that the *Good Friends* had been chased, attacked and captured by the British off the coast of France and had been taken to England.

Irrespective of what was happening to his ships, there were two things that Girard knew for sure in late March and early April of 1813: He knew that America was in grave danger of losing the war. He also knew that a large subsidy of fresh cash in the U.S. Treasury, although desperately needed, could not assure that America would win the war.

When the books were closed on March 31, 1813, after the second round of the public offering for the loan of sixteen million dollars, less than six million dollars had been subscribed.[14] It took several days to get final figures because of the slowness of transportation and communication. However, Gallatin knew on the evening of March 31, on the basis of preliminary and incomplete tallies, that the subscription had fallen pitifully short and that an additional sum of approximatly ten million dollars would have to be raised—somehow, in some way, by some miracle—in the five remaining days before the deadline on April 5. He had already warned President Madison of the necessity "of cutting by the root militia expenses, and of reducing the western expenditure to what is necessary for defensive operations."[15] Now Gallatin knew that even those drastic steps would not be enough unless ten million dollars was forthcoming quickly. Without money to maintain and supply an army and a navy of substantial strength, there would be no realistic prospect of carrying on the war in a meaningful way. Madison would have no viable choice but to try to sustain a holding action in the war zones as best he could while petitioning Great Britain for peace on the best terms he could get. Those terms, in the circumstances, certainly would not be favorable for the United States. Even worse, Britain might refuse to negotiate peace on any terms. Sensing America's weakness and vulnerability, the British might decide it would be to their advantage to keep the war going. They might decide to move in for the kill.

On April 1, 1813, just one day after public subscriptions to the loan had fallen far short for a second time, an already chaotic situation turned from dismal to devastating. The federal government ran out of money. The U.S. Treasury was empty. The United States of America was flat broke. Just as Gallatin had predicted in his warning to Madison a few weeks earlier, there had been scarcely enough funds to get through the month of March. Now the government, besides having no money to carry on the war, did not even have money to perform routine functions.

Bank accounts of the federal government, although not quite depleted, were so close to zero that governmental departments and agencies were effectively without funding. As Gallatin later told Madison, describing the situation at the beginning of April, "The Treasury was so far exhausted on the first day of this month that the small unexpended balance, dispersed in more than thirty banks, could not have afforded any further resources."[16] The problem would have been serious even in peacetime. It was potentially catastrophic in the midst of a war.

Gallatin knew there was only one way out of this mess. He would have to go to the richest person in America. It would not be easy. Gallatin would have to go hat in hand, figuratively if not literally. He would have to face the man he was suing for $910,000, the man who had asked twice, and had been ignored twice, regarding equal treatment for his bank. Gallatin was in trouble, really big trouble, and he had treated shabbily the only person who could help him. The Treasury had no money and Girard had millions, millions that the government desperately and urgently needed.

As he waited for his tormentor to come calling, Girard held all the cards. The old sea captain was sitting in the catbird seat.

CHAPTER 17

Betting It All on America
1813-1815

*Many are willing to risk their lives for their
country, but few are willing to risk their fortunes.*

THE FIRST DAY of April in 1813 was the darkest day for the United States of America up to that time. Never before in the history of the republic had so many things gone wrong. There was gloom in the hierarchy of the Madison administration. The Treasury was empty. The American people had twice refused to subscribe to a loan in sufficient amount to carry on the war and keep the government going, in effect casting votes of no confidence in the ability of the United States to win the war and pay its debts. The British navy was in massive force off America's shore and at harbor entrances. The British army had won battle after battle on the western frontier and along the Canadian border. Napoleon was on the wane in Europe, freeing more units of the English army and navy to come to America and try to avenge, at last, the surrender at Yorktown in 1781. Now it all came down to Stephen Girard. He would be asked to bail out America.

An appeal would be made to his generosity and, equally important, to his patriotism. He would be asked to put his fortune on the line and, no less significantly, to put his prestige on the line. He had a well-earned reputation, nationwide and worldwide, as a man of prudence and perspicacity. His judgment was held in high regard. If he indicated by word or deed that an investment was sound, there could be no doubt that it was sound. If he put a huge amount of his own money into the war loan, his example almost certainly would

271

inspire many others to participate in the loan to a degree commensurate with their financial ability.

Girard was more than just the richest American. He was in a class all by himself. He had millions in a time when most rich people calculated their wealth in thousands. George Washington, who had ranked among the richest Americans of the eighteenth century, had a net worth of $530,000 when he died in 1799.[1] Most of his wealth was in land and slaves. John Jacob Astor, even though he was the second richest American in 1813, did not have a great abundance of cash. He had made a fortune in the fur trade and had invested most of his money in land. It later would be developed as part of New York City and would escalate tremendously in value. He would outlive Girard by seventeen years and would be the richest person in America when he died at the age of eighty-five in 1848.[2] Some historians have estimated there were only a few millionaires in the United States as late as 1861, just before the start of the Civil War.[3] Most of the great fortunes in America in the nineteenth century were made in the last third of that century.[4] Indeed, as late as 1845, long after Girard's death, a net worth of fifty thousand dollars was sufficient for a person in Philadelphia to be considered quite wealthy and a bona fide member of the city's social elite.[5]

So Secretary of the Treasury Albert Gallatin headed for Philadelphia in early April of 1813 because Girard was unique. He was singularly qualified to deal with the financial crisis that confronted the nation. He was America's first tycoon more than half a century before the golden age of tycoons in America at the end of the nineteenth century. He was a big businessman generations before the era of big business. He had, in an agrarian and mercantile society, the kind of financial clout that would come to be associated with the heyday of an industrial society still decades in the future.

Quite simply, in going to Girard, Gallatin was doing what he had to do. He had nowhere else to turn. It was not a matter of going to Girard or going to somebody else. There wasn't anybody else. A viable solution to Gallatin's problem, and to the country's problem, required millions of dollars that were available and spendable. Girard was the only person in America in 1813 who had millions of available and spendable dollars.

Gallatin and Girard had a number of things in common. Both were born in Europe (Gallatin was a native of Switzerland) and spoke French as their first language and English as a second language. Both came to America as young men (Gallatin arriving in 1780 at the age of nineteen). Both had confidence in democracy and in the republican form of government. Both had abiding faith in the future of their adopted country. Gallatin had served in the Pennsylvania legislature and in Congress before his appointment as secretary of the Treasury in 1801 when Jefferson became president. Madison, when he became president in 1809, retained Gallatin in the same position. He was Treasury secretary thirteen years (a longevity record for that position that still stands). He has been called, quite accurately, a "master of finance."[6] However, even though Gallatin was unquestionably a financial wizard, it was hard to practice wizardry without money. It was Girard who had the money on the fifth day of April in 1813.

On that day, with the clock ticking down to the deadline, Gallatin sat down with Girard in his office on the second floor of his bank to try to work something out. The government was still in need of more than ten million dollars, according to the latest figures available to Gallatin, to complete the loan of sixteen million dollars before time ran out at the close of business. The Treasury secretary, fifty-two, was ten years younger than Girard. A contemporary who knew Gallatin during this period described him as "a man of sallow complexion, thin visage, aquiline nose, black hair and eyes."[7] Girard, although robust, was beginning to show his age. Within the past year or so he had become noticeably hard of hearing, and his vision had begun to diminish in his one good eye.[8]

David Parish was also at the meeting. He had obtained a commitment from Astor and a number of his wealthy friends to subscribe to $2,056,000 of the loan if Girard would subscribe to all of the remainder. That was asking an awfully lot of Girard. The precise figures were as follows: Public subscriptions, those that had been tallied by April 5, but not counting the $2,056,000 conditionally subscribed by Astor and his friends, totaled $5,838,200, which was $10,161,800 short of sixteen million dollars. Even with the tentative subscription of $2,056,000 by the Astor group taken into account, the unsubscribed balance was $8,105,800. Girard was being asked to pick up the check for more than half of the loan of sixteen million dollars. He was being asked to subscribe to more than all the rest of the American people put together.

Considering the strength of his bargaining position, Girard could have demanded major concessions from the government in exchange for financial help of this magnitude. He could have pressured Gallatin into cutting a deal that would have strained the limits of propriety, by insisting that the lawsuit filed in the aftermath of the Amelia Island affair be dropped. At the very least, Girard could have called for a substantial reduction in the penalties being sought in that lawsuit. He also could have made Gallatin squirm and plead and beg. Girard did not do any of these things. He chose to be magnanimous when he could have been vindictive.

He was not fazed by the enormity of the obligation he was being asked to assume. The country was in a crisis and needed money, and that was all that mattered. It was no time for quibbling. He was ready to stand up and be counted. That is precisely what he did. Without fanfare, without being argumentative or difficult, without making a big deal out of what really was a big deal, Stephen Girard bit the bullet. He subscribed in writing "to the residue of the said loan."[9] With those deceptively simple words he bailed out the United States of America.

The residue on April 5 was officially $10,161,800 at the time Girard formally made his commitment. That was the amount he was lawfully obligated to produce. However, since he knew when he made the commitment that, if he did so, Astor and his friends would subscribe to $2,056,000, the effective pledge by Girard was for $8,105,800. That was more money than he had. It was a sum larger than his entire net worth.

He knew that, at this critical juncture in American history, he had a better credit rating than the government of the United States. He was confident that, if he had to, he could borrow money in whatever amount was required to provide the entire residue of the loan as the installments came due over a span of eight months. He was putting at risk everything he had, and then some. He was laying on the table his entire fortune plus future earnings. He was betting it all on America. He was wagering that his country would win the war and pay its debts, and he was doing so at a time when many of his countrymen, perhaps most of them, believed that the war could not be won and the debts could not be paid. Girard was hoping that his example, in subscribing to the residue of the loan, would inspire others to relieve him of part of his obligation by purchasing some of his loan certificates. However, there was no certainty this would happen. Even if it did happen, there was no way of knowing how many other investors would step forward and how much they would subscribe.

So the crux of it was this: On April 5, 1813, when the government of the United States was down and out, Girard came to the rescue. He did so knowing that, if America lost the war and did not pay its debts, he could be wiped out. He knew also that a military defeat for America and the financial collapse of America were distinct possibilities. With the British navy, at that very moment, controlling the entrance to Delaware Bay and brazenly holding one of his ships for ransom, he knew how hard it was to be optimistic about the outcome of the war and the future of a young and struggling country with no money in its Treasury.

Girard's bold and courageous act, in subscribing to the residue of the loan, was exemplary patriotism and good citizenship far above and beyond the normal call of duty. However, he was acting in his self-interest as well as in the national interest. It would have been a severe blow to Girard personally if Great Britain had regained complete or even partial control of America. He had tied his own future to a free and independent United States. Preserving America's freedom and independence would also preserve his freedom and independence.

Gallatin may have been expecting tough demands from Girard when he subscribed to the residue of the loan, but Girard simply asked that the Treasury deposit the residue in his bank. Gallatin readily agreed. It was a reasonable request. It seemed only fair that the owner of a bank who was lending the government huge sums should not be required to deposit the money in competing banks. Stephen Girard's Bank would become the major depository of federal funds with the residue of the loan in the bank's vaults. Federal departments and agencies would establish accounts at his bank to facilitate drawing on those funds. This would give Girard's bank added prestige. Nonetheless, state-chartered banks in Philadelphia would continue to refuse to honor notes issued by Stephen Girard's Bank and would keep on trying with all their might to drive Girard out of the banking business.

The 1813 loan of sixteen million dollars was called a six-percent loan, because lenders were to receive quarterly interest payments at an annual rate of six percent. However, the effective annual yield was closer to seven percent. Subscribers, if they wished, could elect to take a discount up front, in effect, collecting part of their interest in advance, by paying only eleven dollars instead of $12.50 in each of the eight monthly installments for each one hundred dollars loaned. If they preferred, subscribers could elect instead to pay the full $12.50 each month and thereby qualify for an annuity of $1.50 for each one hundred dollars loaned. The annuity would be paid thirteen times over the life of the loan, which was almost thirteen years.[10] Irrespective of which option might be chosen by Girard for each loan certificate, the U.S. Treasury would pay to him a commission of one quarter of one percent of the amount subscribed, under provisions agreed to by Gallatin and Girard. The commission was compensation to offset the costs, at least in part, if not entirely, that Girard would entail in trying to persuade other investors to participate in the loan, plus the costs of related paper work when a prospective investor consented to participate, plus the costs of officially transferring and recording ownership for each loan certificate.

With these arrangements, new ground was being broken in the world of high finance. Girard was not only making a loan. He was also making history. As one historian has put it: "This was how investment banking had its origins in America."[11] Another historian has called the transaction "the first real underwriters' syndicate for the purpose of marketing government stock."[12] Girard's effective annual yield over the life of the loan has been calculated at 6.8 percent.[13] This was similar to the effective annual yield of the smallest investor subscribing to just one loan certificate of one hundred dollars. Girard neither sought nor received special consideration. Discounts and commissions notwithstanding, the U.S. Treasury received the full sixteen million dollars that was the minimum deemed necessary to operate the government and carry on the war. The loan was structured to bring in that amount, net.

David Parish was allowed to sign Girard's subscription letter on April 5, as a matter of courtesy. This was in recognition of the helpful role by Parish in drumming up support for the loan from Astor and others, and for the continuing role he was expected to play in trying to persuade people to purchase loan certificates from Girard now that he had subscribed to the residue. Parish had no cash of his own to invest. Living far beyond his means, he had already begun a long and tragic slide into insolvency.

In the final accounting, taking into consideration the investments by Astor and his friends and all of the earlier subscriptions by other investors, including subscriptions not yet tallied on April 5, the amount subscribed by Girard (nominally in partnership with Parish) was $7,055,800.[14] As Girard had hoped, his example would help to restore public confidence in the government and inspire other investors to participate in the loan. Within ten days, by April 15, he and Parish had sold $4,672,800 of their joint subscription to other subscribers.

That left $2,383,000, which was the amount Girard provided with his own cash, in eight monthly installments of $297,875 beginning on April 15, 1813, to fulfill his commitment on April 5 to take the residue of the loan. Subscribers were allowed ten days after the subscription date to pay the first installment. On April 15 the list of subscribers for the residue of the loan showed Girard subscribing to $1,191,500, which is half of $2,383,000. Parish, having co-signed Girard's letter of commitment, was listed also for $1,191,500, which was the other half of $2,383,000.[15] However, Parish did not contribute one penny, despite his ostentatious life style. He borrowed the entire amount, $1,191,500, from Girard in the spring, summer and fall of 1813 to pay the eight monthly installments of $148,937.50 for the portion of the loan listed formally in the name of Parish.[16]

In a spirit of extraordinary generosity, far beyond what might have been expected, Girard loaned the money to Parish interest free until July 15 and, after that, charged him interest at an annual rate of only four percent.[17] Thus Parish, without putting up any money of his own, was making a profit from the outset—collecting for himself the interest, at an annual rate of six percent, paid quarterly by the Treasury. It was in these circumstances that Girard contributed $2,383,000 of his own money in 1813 for the residue of the government loan even though he appeared on the books for only half that much. Counting the $100,000 he had subscribed earlier, Girard's total cash contribution to the loan of sixteen million dollars in 1813 was $2,483,000.[18]

In the fall of 1813, after the loan of sixteen million dollars had enabled American forces to take the offensive, prospects for the United States winning the war were much better than they had been earlier in the year. In October and thereafter there was no shortage of buyers when owners of government loan certificates put them on the market for re-sale. Parish was able to get the cash necessary to repay all that he owed to Girard, with interest, before the end of 1813.[19] In the ensuing years Parish moved inexorably toward financial ruin because of ongoing wild speculations and a continuing stubborn refusal to cut back on his living expenses. In 1816 he left America for Europe and eventually took a position with a bank in Vienna. He spent the remainder of his life in that city. By 1826 the party was over, and he was destitute when he commited suicide, by drowning, in the Danube River.[20]

The entire sixteen million dollars derived from the government loan, and even more than that, went directly into the war effort in 1813. On April 17, just two days after the first installments came pouring in from Girard and others, Gallatin sent letters to President Madison and to the War Department and the Navy Department giving a detailed spending plan for the remainder of 1813. Taking into account some anticipated revenues from Customs collections and land sales, and calculating that $1,500,000 would be sufficient to run the entire government except for the military, Gallatin figured there would be $17,820,000 available for the War and Navy departments. He allocated that sum as follows: $13,320,000 to War and $4,500,000 to Navy.[21]

Results were swift and dramatic. Orders to take the offensive were rushed to American commanders all along the Canadian border and on the western frontier. Before the end of May U.S. troops were victorious time and time again. The British were routed at York (now Toronto). They were defeated again when they countered with an attack on Sackets Harbor, New York. Other British defeats were at Fort Meigs on the Maumee River in Ohio and at Fort Stephenson on the Sandusky

River, also in Ohio. When American troops moved into Canada near Niagara Falls and attacked Fort George on Lake Ontario, the British withdrew and also abandoned three other forts in the area. All of these American victories were within the first six weeks after Gallatin allocated the war loan revenue on April 17.

American forces commanded by General William Henry Harrison subsequently recaptured Fort Detroit, advanced fifty miles into Canada and defeated the British in the Battle of the Thames. (Harrison, twenty-seven years later, would be elected president of the United States.)

Meanwhile, Commodore Oliver H. Perry was sent to Lake Erie in the spring of 1813 with orders to defeat British naval forces, which he proceeded to do in heroic fashion. In the climactic battle, on September 10, Perry was unperturbed when his flagship was disabled. He got into a lifeboat and was rowed to another ship, where he resumed command. The entire British fleet on Lake Erie was sunk or captured. Perry sent a memorable message to Harrison: "We have met the enemy and they are ours."[22]

Girard, knowing that the loan of sixteen million dollars had made this string of American victories on land and sea possible, was quite pleased, not only because America's chances of winning the war had improved, but also because his basic theory about money and war was being substantiated. As a contemporary who knew Girard well would comment later, Girard believed "there could be no victory, no war, without money. Soldiers and generals he considered of secondary importance, observing that they could be created by money, and by money only."[23]

The loan of sixteen million dollars had significant consequences on the peace front as well as on the war front. In March of 1813, when the United States was on the verge of going broke and the American people were showing no interest in subscribing to a war loan, Russia offered to mediate. Great Britain and the United States were invited by the Russians to send peace negotiators to St. Petersburg. President Madison accepted. He sent a three-man delegation to the Russian capital. However, Great Britain rejected the offer, declining to send a delegation to St. Petersburg or anywhere else. The prevailing view in

London was that the Americans were extremely weak, both militarily and financially, and should not be let off the hook by talking peace. The British, sensing victory, wanted to do more than just bloody some American noses. It was time to give the Americans a really good whipping they would not soon forget.

That, though, was in March of 1813, when the war was going badly for the United States and it appeared that the U.S. government would fail in its quest to borrow sixteen million dollars from the American people. What a difference eight months would make!

In November of 1813, after their army had been roughed up in Canada and on the western frontier, and after their fleet had been wiped out on Lake Erie, the British were quite amenable to peace. They were, in fact, anxious for it. The British proposed that the United States join them in direct negotiations for the purpose of restoring peace. President Madison promptly accepted.

Gothenburg, Sweden, was selected at first as a neutral site for the peace conference but, early in 1814, there was an agreement to meet instead in Ghent, Belgium. Napoleon's troops had recently been driven out of Belgium by British and allied forces. Slowness of trans-Atlantic communication, coupled with lost time arising from the site change, resulted in long delays in getting the peace talks under way. Meanwhile, the war dragged on and heated up.

Problems with the *Good Friends* continued to plague Girard in 1813. He was chagrined when he received word that the ship had been captured by the British off the coast of France and had arrived in England on the very day that he had bailed out the U.S. Treasury at Secretary Gallatin's request. Despite the bailout, Girard remained under the shadow of the still unresolved court suit brought against him by the Treasury Department, headed by Gallatin, in the aftermath of the episode involving the *Good Friends* at Amelia Island. Now the ship was in the hands of the British in a time of war, yet Gallatin continued to seek huge penalties from Girard in a case arising from a peacetime voyage.

Girard was not amused by the irony of the situation and the apparent ingratitude of the United States government. He had loaned large sums to his country and, by his example, had inspired other Americans to grant loans also, but the government wanted to coerce more money from him in the form of penalties. He felt that he was being unfairly treated and that he was an innocent victim of circumstances beyond his control. In Girard's view, he had not violated the law by bringing English goods to the United States on the *Good Friends*. To the contrary, he had gone out of his way to avoid breaking the law by sending his ship to Amelia Island.

Girard's case was not an isolated one. Two other American ships with British goods had also been at Amelia Island when the United States took control. Those two ships also had subsequently departed for Philadelphia and had been intercepted by the Collector of Customs in Wilmington, Delaware. The owners of those ships also were defendants in federal lawsuits seeking penalties. In the spring of 1813 Girard joined owners of the other two ships in seeking relief from Congress, where there was majority sentiment favorable to Girard's contention that he and the other shipowners had been treated unfairly. Remedial legislation was passed and signed by President Madison in July. The new law said in essence that American ships which happened to be at Amelia Island with cargoes of British goods, when the island changed from Spanish control to American control, would be exempted from penalties if double duties, plus interest, were paid on their cargoes. The law was not self-activating or self-implementing, however. A shipowner seeking relief had to file a petition in federal court, where a determination would be made pertaining to eligibility for relief and the amount of duties and interest to be paid.

Girard, while glad to be able to avoid penalties, felt that double duties also were unfair. Nevertheless, he filed a petition in federal court in August and soon found out that dealing with the government was never simple, not even when Congress had passed a law. Numerous snags were encountered, including disputes over the amount of duties owed and the amount of interest accrued. Litigation dragged on intermittently for six years and finally was concluded in 1819 with Girard paying duties and interest totaling $53,245.[24]

By that time Girard would no longer own the *Good Friends*. The government of Great Britain sold the ship in 1813. It was acquired by Baring Brothers, agents for Girard in London, for the equivalent of $8,500 in American money. After the war the Barings gave Girard an opportunity to buy the ship back, but he declined to do so.[25] Members of the crew of the *Good Friends*, to their great misfortunes, would not be released from British prisons until after the war.[26]

In the spring of 1814 France was in a state of collapse. Girard's native city, Bordeaux, fell to the British in March. Shortly thereafter, Paris capitulated to British and allied forces. Napoleon abdicated in April and went into exile on the island of Elba. It was these events that prompted the British to move the site of peace talks with the Americans from Gothenburg to Ghent. With Napoleon thought (mistakenly) to be no longer a threat, Ghent was considered a safe city for negotiations. It was relatively close to London, allowing fairly swift communication between British government leaders and their peace negotiators. With the war in Europe seeming to be over (even though it really was not, because Napoleon would return), the British felt they were free to send troops and warships to America in almost unlimited numbers. By midsummer of 1814, a British invasion force was moving up Chesapeake Bay en route to an attack on Washington.

Thus, when negotiations at Ghent finally began on August 8, 1814, the situation had changed radically since the preceding November when Great Britain had proposed peace talks. During the intervening nine months, while enjoying victories in Europe, the British had grown more inclined to impose tough terms on America or perhaps even to carry on the war to an unconditional triumph. Admiral Alexander Cochrane, in command of British naval forces in the Chesapeake in the summer of 1814, favored giving the Americans "a complete drubbing before peace is made."[27] However, the Americans, after going on the offensive in 1813, following completion of the loan of sixteen million dollars, were able to retain the upper hand, for the most part, in 1814. An exception was the grim night of August 24. On that date the British captured Washington and, while holding the city less than twenty-four hours, burned the White House, the Capitol and other buildings, including those housing the State Department, the Treasury Department and the War Department.

After withdrawing from Washington, the British amphibious force continued up the Chesapeake Bay. When word of the British advance reached Philadelphia, Girard began taking precautionary measures. He still had vivid memories of 1777 when British troops had debarked from ships at the northern end of Chesapeake Bay, had marched into Pennsylvania, and had captured Philadelphia. He still had vivid memories of fleeing to Mount Holly, New Jersey, with Mary when she was eighteen and they had been married three months. Now, in late August of 1814, the British might soon be heading his way again. Girard was taking no chances.

He sent an employee to Reading, sixty-five miles northwest of Philadelphia, to make secret arrangements for storage of specie from his bank and other valuable possessions, including maritime cargoes. In the first three weeks of September three convoys, each consisting of about nine wagons, moved from Philadelphia to Reading on muddy roads, sometimes in pouring rain, with as much secrecy as conditions would allow. The wagons were loaded with specie and other possessions valued, in total, in the hundreds of thousands of dollars. Wooden boxes filled with gold and silver from vaults in Stephen Girard's Bank were placed in vaults at the Farmers Bank of Reading.[28] Other goods were placed in warehouses.

The precautions turned out to be unnecessary. The British, having had no trouble in sacking Washington, made the mistake of assuming that Baltimore would also be an easy mark. Fort McHenry, guarding Baltimore and its harbor, withstood a fierce naval bombardment on September 13 and 14. The British fleet, because it could not get past the fort, was unable to reach Baltimore. A British assault by land also failed to reach the city. The British army commander, General Robert Ross, was killed. Great Britain was unable to recover from the debacle at Baltimore. The retreat down the Chesapeake was humiliating.

At almost the same time, in early September, the British suffered another damaging blow at Plattsburgh, New York, and on Lake Champlain. This, too, was a combined attack on land and water that went awry. British troops had moved south from Montreal to invade the United States, planning to proceed down the Hudson Valley to New York City and thereby sever New England from the rest of the country. Capture of Plattsburgh, on the western shore of Lake Champlain, was one of the first objectives. A British fleet on the lake was routed by American naval forces, whereupon the British army units that were amassed for an attack on Plattsburgh hastily withdrew and then kept on retreating all the way back to Canada.

Earlier in the summer, in the Niagara Falls area of Canada, American troops had won three hard-fought engagements, each of them entailing hand-to-hand combat with bayonets, in the Battle of Fort Erie, the Battle of Chippewa and the Battle of Lundy's Lane. In these and other battles in the War of 1812 the American fighting man came of age, proving that he could stand face to face and toe to toe against a highly trained British regular and win. When news of the British retreats from Baltimore and Plattsburgh reached Ghent, the negotiators for Great Britain knew they had better settle quickly on the best terms they could get. However, they still had hopes of salvaging something from the war, especially an expansion of Canada into U.S. territory.

British troops had occupied a large part of Maine, mostly wilderness, during the war with virtually no American resistance. The British negotiating team was particularly stubborn in trying to hold on to that ground as part of the peace agreement. American negotiators were in no mood to make concessions, though, and there was no need to. Great Britain, lacking recent victories in the war (except for that one wild night in Washington), had no bargaining chips at the peace table. Moreover, the British government was encountering hostility on the home front. The English people were weary of war. As one historian described the situation, there "was a growing clamor against military expenditures. As long as Napoleon was a threat, the British were willing to put up with back-breaking taxes—not only for their own forces, but their allies too. They had bankrolled the struggle for almost 20 years; now Bonaparte was gone and they wanted relief. The American war was no way to get it."[29]

Formal and final agreement on terms of peace, called the Treaty of Ghent, was reached on Christmas Eve, 1814. Then came the final irony in a strange war that had already taken many odd turns and twists. The biggest battle of the war was fought after the war was over, or, at least, after it was supposed to be over. News that a peace treaty had been signed in December did not reach America until February. In the meantime, British troops had been transported to the mouth of the Mississippi River in an armada of British ships and were defeated decisively in the Battle of New Orleans. The climactic day of the battle was January 8, 1815, following several weeks of fighting along approaches to the city. General Edward Pakenham, the British commander, was killed. General Andrew Jackson, the victorious American commander, was an instant national celebrity of the first magnitude, far and away the greatest hero to come out of the War of 1812. Thirteen years later he would be elected president.

The Treaty of Ghent had no startling provisions. Two countries tired of war agreed to end it. No changes were made in the U.S.-Canadian border, but commissions were created to resolve disputes where the precise location of the border was unclear. The end result, although not spelled out, was abandonment of British hopes to control, or at least partly control, the Mississippi River and to make all of the shorelines of the Great Lakes a part of Canada. Great Britain did not specifically agree to end impressment of American citizens into the British navy but, in fact, the practice did end. Likewise, the British did not explicitly promise to stop harassing American merchant ships on the high seas but, in fact, the practice did stop.

In February of 1815, when news of the Treaty of Ghent and the end of the war reached Philadelphia, the Delaware River was frozen solid. Thomas P. Cope described in his diary a typical scene on the river, a scene that Girard could enjoy from his wharf or his bedroom windows: "The Delaware is alive with skaters—several hundred persons moving on its smooth surface in all directions. Men, women and children are perambulating the ice, and sleds and wheel carriages cross as on dry ground. The sky is clear, the air tranquil and cold, the ice firm and smooth."[30]

Entries in Cope's diary told of several days of joyous celebration in Philadelphia as war-weary people welcomed the return of peace:

> Whilst sitting quietly at my fireside, my ear was saluted with the merry chiming of the bells, which satisfied me that something new and important had taken place .... The town is in a great bustle; joy sparkles in almost every countenance .... There was a general illumination of the city last night [February 15]. No accident, fracas or violence occurred that I have heard of. It seemed as if everybody capable of going out had by common consent agreed to perambulate the streets, peaceably to enjoy the spectacle. About 10 the lights were extinguished and all remained quiet .... The public manifestations of joy are almost unbounded.[31]

Thus the successful conclusion of the War of 1812 was a memorable and festive occasion for the American people.

In retrospect, the turning point in the conflict was Girard's bold pledge of his fortune for the war effort. When he plunked down millions in cash, inspiring others to join him in contributing within their means, he built a bridge that led from impending disaster to ultimate victory.

There is a footnote to the story of Girard and the War of 1812 that merits attention, not because it had any effect on the outcome of the war, for it had no effect at all, but because it tells something about Girard.

In May of 1813, soon after he had provided critical financing to the Treasury, Girard offered to the government the use of his fleet of ships at no charge. He also volunteered to serve personally in the war effort—without pay and in whatever capacity he might be useful. "I will lend them [the ships] and give my services gratis for the defence of our country," he said in a formal written offer to the secretary of the Treasury.[32] The offer was not accepted. Nothing could have been gained by putting Girard's ships in government service, for they were already being put to maximum use in the conduct of maritime trade despite the British blockade, and there was no need for the personal services of a captain in his sixties, long retired from sea duty.

What America needed from Girard was not his ships or himself but precisely what he gave: his money and his ringing vote of confidence in his country's ability to win the war and pay its debts. America did both. After winning the war it paid its debts, not only its war debts but all other debts as well.

Twenty years after the end of the War of 1812, in the second term of President Jackson, the national debt was reduced to zero. The United States of America was free and clear of all outstanding obligations. The country did not owe a penny to anybody. The war not only was won. It also was paid for.

In summary, it can still be argued, as it was by some in 1812, that America's second war with Great Britain may not have been wise or necessary. However, there can be no doubt about the legacy of that war. In its aftermath, America was a free and independent country with its territory intact, a country that was at peace with the world and respected by the world, a country that was fiscally responsible and financially secure. Without Girard, it is highly unlikely that America would have been all of these things. It might not have been any of these things.

CHAPTER 18

A Corpse Gets a Kiss, A Mistress Waits, A New Bank Is Born
1815-1823

Maybe money can't buy happiness, but it can buy lots and lots of love.

IN THE AFTERMATH of the War of 1812 Polly Kenton began to notice something of great significance on her regular visits to the wing for the insane at Pennsylvania Hospital. Mary Girard was not just growing older. She was also growing weaker. By 1815 she had been in the hospital a quarter of a century. Now, after all those years, she might be close to death. When she died, Stephen Girard would be free and clear to marry his mistress if he wanted to.

Polly had given Stephen her love unstintingly for nineteen years, and during that time he had become the richest person in America. She had every reason to believe that the pleasure she had lavished upon him had made a positive contribution to his business and financial success. Thus, as Mary's physical condition worsened, it was understandable that Polly may have let herself do a little dreaming. She could easily imagine, or at least hope, that she was just a heartbeat away from becoming the second Mrs. Girard and, ultimately, the richest woman in America.

During the war years Stephen had tried twice to get a divorce. However, there is no evidence to indicate that his motivation was to be free to marry Polly. Apparently his quest for a divorce was based on

financial, not matrimonial, considerations. Mary, her insanity notwithstanding, would have been entitled to at least one third of Stephen's
estate under Pennsylvania law if he died before she did, regardless of
any contrary provisions that he might write in a will. Stephen, as a
multi-millionaire in his sixties, was becoming quite concerned about
the possibility that Mary might outlive him and inherit much of his
wealth despite her incompetence. It was difficult to get a divorce in
Pennsylvania in Girard's time, all the more so if a husband was trying
to divorce an insane wife. In that case a special act of the state legislature
was required, and legislators were usually reluctant to sanction divorce
in such circumstances. Stephen had petitioned the legislature for a
divorce in 1812 and the request had not even made it out of committee.
He had tried again in 1813 and had failed again. After that, he was
resigned to the reality of his situation: He and Mary would remain
husband and wife until death claimed one of them.

It happened on September 13, 1815. Death took Mary Girard on
that date. She died in Pennsylvania Hospital twenty-five years and
thirteen days after she had been admitted on August 31, 1790. She
had been thirty-one then. She was fifty-six when she died. She and
Stephen had been married thirty-eight years, but she had been sane
only eight of those years. She had gone insane when she was twenty-six
and had lived in a state of insanity for thirty years, more than half of
her life. For twenty-eight of the thirty years that Mary was insane,
Stephen had lived with mistresses, first with Sally Bickham for nine
years, until she left him to marry another man, and then with Polly
Kenton for the next nineteen years. Those are the cold, hard numbers
in the long-running nightmare that was the insanity of Mary Girard.
They do not begin to tell the story. Statistics cannot capture the tragedy
of it all, and the underlying sadness of having an insane wife for three
decades.

Yet Stephen had steadfastly and resolutely refused to let Mary's
insanity drag him down and ruin his life. His determination to triumph
over the adversity in his marriage certainly was a major factor in his
devotion to work and his phenomenal achievements in business. His
resolve to be happy, despite the presence of an insane wife a mile away,
was largely successful. As detailed in previous chapters, he had a

well-earned reputation among contemporaries as a man who derived a great deal of enjoyment from all that he did, in his counting-house, at his bank, on his farm, in his home.

Notwithstanding appearances of contentment during Mary's long illness, there were times when Stephen's inner pain surfaced poignantly. One such time occurred when he was writing a letter to a business associate in a distant city after Mary had been insane nearly twenty years. "I note with pleasure," Stephen wrote wistfully, "that you have a large family, that you are happy, and that you enjoy an honest fortune; this is all a sensible man has a right to expect. As to me, I live like a convict, constantly occupied and often passing nights without sleep. I am entombed in labyrinths of business, and tormented by care .... You see that your position is a thousand times better than mine."[1] At the time Stephen wrote these words he was well on his way to accumulating his first million dollars and Polly was in her twenties, near her zenith in beauty. Yet, for all of that, for all of his money and for all of his pleasure, Stephen was envious of others, especially of others with large families.

Deep down, he had never stopped missing Mary. He had never stopped remembering the way she used to be. Maybe most of all, he had never stopped missing the children, sons and daughters of his very own, that he had always wanted and that he knew now he would never have. Consequently, Mary's death hit Stephen much harder than might have been expected, considering that she had been hospitalized for twenty-five years and that he had tried twice to divorce her. He was overcome emotionally when she died. He lost his customary composure, overwhelmed by the tragedy that had reduced their years of happiness together to such a precious few. There were so many might-have-beens that would never be.

The dazzling young woman who had captivated and married Stephen when she was eighteen had almost ceased to exist when she was twenty-six. Her body had lived another thirty years, but not her mind. Her quarter of a century in Pennsylvania Hospital had been almost entirely in a mental vacuum. As one nineteenth century writer summed up Mary's time in the hospital, she "had lingered through a painless blank of twenty-five years' duration" and had died "still insane."[2]

Stephen Simpson, who was an employee of Stephen Girard's Bank at the time of Mary Girard's death, recorded some of the happenings: "At the request of her husband, she was buried in the lawn of the north front of the hospital; and her grave, marked only by a simple mound of earth, is carefully preserved, and may still be seen [in 1832] .... As soon as Girard was informed of the death of his wife, he proceeded to the hospital and gave directions to have her body interred, where it now reposes, requesting to be sent for when every preparation for the burial had been completed. Towards the close of the day, after the sun had withdrawn its last beams from the tallest sycamore that shades the garden, Mr. Girard was sent for, and when he arrived, the plain coffin of Mary ... was carried forward in silence to her humble resting place .... The burial was conducted after the manner of the Friends [i.e., the Quakers], who have the management of the Institution."[3]

The usually stoic old sea captain broke down at the funeral. William Wagner, a long-time employee of Girard who worked in his counting-house and sailed on his ships, described the climactic moment: "I shall never forget the last and closing scene. We all stood about the coffin when Mr. Girard, filled with emotion, stepped forward, kissed his wife's corpse, and his tears moistened her cheek."[4]

After the coffin had been lowered into the grave, Girard turned to the hospital's manager, Samuel Coates, and said: "It is very well."[5]

The burial site was described by Henry Ingram, who interviewed Wagner and others who attended Mary Girard's funeral: "A lovelier spot could hardly have been found within the city, the smooth lawns, broken with occasional flower-beds, shaded by tall sycamores, and kept with Quaker-like simplicity and neatness."[6] The absence of a headstone to mark Mary's grave was in keeping with official policy of the hospital at that time. The beautiful and unpretentious setting appealed to Stephen Girard, so much so that, in the words of Ingram, it was Stephen's "original intention to have been buried here himself."[7] However, by the time Stephen died, the hospital had stopped issuing permits for burial on the grounds.[8]

Mary's journey to her final resting place was not a long one. She was buried about fifteen yards from the building where she had been a patient. Mary had quarters in two buildings, in one for seven years, and in the other for eighteen years, during her stay in Pennsylvania Hospital. From 1790 to 1797 she was in the hospital's original building, on the west side of Eighth Street between Spruce and Pine Streets. The mentally ill shared the structure with other patients. In 1797 she and other mental patients were moved to a new building on the east side of Ninth Street between Spruce and Pine Streets. The second building, known initially as the New House, was for mental patients exclusively.[9] It was America's first insane asylum, even though it was not formally labeled in that manner.

Both of the buildings where Mary lived as a mental patient still stand and are known today as the East Wing and the West Wing of the Pine Building. The wings remain in use as integral parts of Pennsylvania Hospital but no longer house the insane. The hospital's mental patients were relocated in the 1840s to spacious grounds on North Forty-Ninth Street in Philadelphia, where enlightened work in the development and application of care for the mentally ill was conducted under supervision of an innovative and renowned pioneer in psychiatry, Dr. Thomas S. Kirkbride.[10]

The care and treatment that Mary Girard received in Pennsylvania Hospital, although primitive by modern standards, were the most advanced in her time anywhere in America, and perhaps in the world. Her husband never had cause to regret sending her there.

In 1903 a bronze tablet in memory of Stephen and Mary Girard was given to Pennsylvania Hospital as a gift of the Board of Directors of City Trusts in behalf of the City of Philadelphia. An inscription on the tablet identifies Stephen as "a liberal contributor to the Pennsylvania Hospital."[11] Labeling him "a liberal contributor" is an understatement. In a history of Pennsylvania Hospital covering the first ninety years, from 1751 to 1841, Stephen Girard was accurately described as "by far the largest individual benefactor of the hospital."[12] He gave the institution numerous donations over a period of many years while he was living and remembered it generously in his will.

Shortly after his wife's death, Stephen gave thousands of dollars to the hospital and to individuals who had helped to care for Mary, including nurses and attendants.[13] In 1817, when artist Benjamin West donated one of his masterpieces, "Christ Healing the Sick in the Temple," to Pennsylvania Hospital, Stephen Girard was the principal benefactor in providing facilities to exhibit the famous painting, which is still on display. In the first year that it was on exhibition, thirty thousand visitors saw it. Each paid an admission fee of twenty-five cents.[14]

Polly Kenton was the odds-on favorite to become the second wife of Stephen Girard if he remarried. There were no other known contenders. Just as Stephen was sole proprietor in his bank, so Polly was sole proprietor in his bedroom. Fidelity apparently was her credo. There is no evidence to suggest that she was ever unfaithful to Stephen, or, for that matter, that he was ever unfaithful to her, during their years together in a relationship that was a marriage in all but name. She prepared his meals, or supervised their preparation by others, and she ate with him when he wanted her to. She was the hostess when there were guests. She ran the house and supervised the servants. She was the unofficial mother of Stephen's three orphaned nieces, Antoinette, Caroline and Henriette, the daughters of his brother John. Polly had raised the girls, as though they were her own, ever since they had arrived at the Girard household as small children in 1805. She had given them love and kindness and guidance. She had nursed them when they were sick. She had played with them and laughed with them, and so had Stephen. He and Polly were like a father and a mother as well as a husband and a wife.

Stephen had given the three nieces good educations in private schools. Now, in 1815, the girls had blossomed into young ladies. They were all in their teens, ranging in age from fourteen to nineteen. The oldest of them, Antoinette, had been married the year before.

Polly also raised two nieces of her own as integral members of the Girard household, and four of Polly's sisters had lived in the Girard home at various times, all of them at the same time for a while. Boys in their teens or pre-teens, serving as apprentices in the counting-house, often lived in Stephen's home, where they were fed and cared for by Polly. She was, for all intents and purposes, their mother.

In 1817 two of Stephen's nephews, sons of one of his brothers in France, came to Philadelphia. Stephen paid for their support and education. Polly mothered them also.

All in all, Polly at one time or another helped to raise more than twenty boys and girls, most Stephen's relatives and apprentices, some her own. The household at times numbered more than a dozen persons, adults and children. Stephen enjoyed the company, and so did Polly. She nurtured the extended family with abundant energy and good humor.

So Stephen had many good reasons to be in love with Polly and to be grateful to her. Moreover, it was by no means unusual, in the early nineteenth century, for a man to marry his mistress. If Stephen had married Polly, after waiting a decent interval following Mary's death, nary an eyebrow would have been raised. It would have seemed a natural thing to do. Patient Polly waited, and she waited, and she waited. Weeks turned into months, and months turned into years. Still there was no wedding. Stephen may have had several reasons for not asking Polly to marry him, reasons that had nothing to do with whether or not he was in love with her.

First of all, he had nothing to gain by marrying her. She was already doing everything for him as a mistress that she would do for him as a wife. He could reasonably expect to keep on having her companionship and her love without the complications of marriage. Additionally, there were considerations of life expectancy. He knew that Polly, being twenty-six years younger than he, almost certainly would outlive him. If that happened, and if he married her, she would inherit millions of dollars from him. Those millions probably would wind up eventually in the hands of an assortment of her relatives who would be sorely tempted to use the money to support lives of indolence and indulgence. As noted earlier, Stephen was determined to prevent his wealth from becoming a subsidy for that kind of living. Moreover, having studied Pennsylvania's inheritance laws in relation to Mary, Stephen knew that Polly, if she became Mrs. Girard, would be entitled to such a large portion of his legacy that there might not be enough left to achieve the gigantic charitable objectives he may have been starting to think about in 1815.

Meanwhile, aside from matters in his personal life, Girard was occupied with pressing business affairs. The main focus was on banking. In the aftermath of the War of 1812, with victory won and peace secure, it was apparent to President Madison and members of Congress that the country could not rely on always having Stephen Girard around to dig into deep pockets and come up with millions of dollars when the U.S. Treasury ran out of money. The same thing was apparent to Girard. He suggested that another Bank of the United States be created to replace the one that did not get its charter renewed in 1811, a circumstance that had led to Girard's entry into the banking business.

Madison, with a height of five feet, four inches (two inches shorter than Girard), was the shortest president the United States has ever had. He was the first president to wear long pants instead of knee breeches.[15] (Long pants made him look taller.) Yet this diminutive president was a man of great stature in the eyes of his countrymen in 1815. He had stood tall against the British, daring to face them down, defying formidable odds, and he had lived to tell the tale. He had been foolhardy, some had said, to lead America into war, but he had triumphed, and he had finished, once and for all, the fight that had begun at Lexington and Concord forty years earlier. Just as shots fired by the Minutemen in 1775 had been heard round the world, so had shots fired by American soldiers and sailors in the Second War of Independence been heard round the world. They gave the United States new status and prestige on a global scale in 1815. It was not only Madison who stood tall at the end of the War of 1812. So did all Americans who savored the victory.

Madison tried to capitalize on his newly earned popularity, and on fame won in earlier accomplishments, by getting new legislation through Congress to shore up the nation's financial structure. As a member of the Second Continental Congress during the Revolutionary War, he had helped to give America freedom. As the Father of the Constitution, he had helped to give America a framework of government. As a member of the First Congress of the United States, he had helped to give America a Bill of Rights. Now, as a president flush with post-war jubilation, he would try to give America a stable monetary and banking system. It would be one more achievement for a man who did not really need any more achievements to be enshrined in the pantheon of truly great Americans.

In 1815 Congress passed a bank bill that was not to Madison's liking. He vetoed it. His administration then took the lead in writing a bill that was acceptable to him. A pivotal role in this process was played by Girard's old friend Alexander Dallas, who had become secretary of the Treasury. He was one of the Philadelphia lawyers who had been hired by Girard in 1812 to advise him on the legality of his plan to operate an unincorporated bank as a sole proprietor. In 1815 and 1816 Secretary Dallas consulted with Girard on numerous occasions to get his views on provisions being considered for new banking legislation as it was being written.

A bill was drawn to create a Second Bank of the United States, to be headquartered in Philadelphia instead of Washington. The First Bank of the United States, authorized by Congress in 1791, quite naturally had been located in Philadelphia because it was the capital of the United States at that time. Selection of Philadelphia as the site of the Second Bank was a high honor, considering that Washington had been the nation's capital since 1800. Locating the Second Bank in Philadelphia was official recognition that the city was still the country's financial center. This was due in large measure to Stephen Girard's Bank and to Girard's enormous personal wealth.

John Jacob Astor, the most powerful financier in New York City, joined Girard in supporting the bill. Crucial backing in Congress came from Representative Henry Clay of Kentucky, who was Speaker of the House, and Representative John C. Calhoun of South Carolina, who was chairman of a House committee that had jurisdiction over banking legislation. Clay and Calhoun were just beginning to emerge as national figures of great influence. Their most powerful years were still ahead of them. They had initially been opposed to direct participation in the banking business by the federal government but changed their minds after being persuaded that a Second Bank of the United States, with effective management and adequate capital, could give greater stability to the nation's financial affairs.

A bill creating a Second Bank of the United States cleared Congress in early April of 1816 and was signed by President Madison on April 10. The bank was given a charter of twenty years and a capitalization of thirty-five million dollars. The U.S. government would provide seven million dollars, and the remaining twenty-eight million dollars would come from public subscriptions at one hundred dollars a share. The President appointed five people to a twenty-five member board of directors. The other twenty directors were elected by public share-holders.[16] Even before the bill was signed into law, Secretary Dallas wrote a letter to Girard asking him if he would accept appointment to the bank board.[17] He said he would. President Madison made the appointment on April 26.

The public subscription of bank shares opened on the Fourth of July in 1816 with a limit of three thousand shares allowed to any one individual, company or corporation to assure broad distribution of stock. Girard promptly invested $300,000, the maximum amount permitted. However, when the subscription closed on July 23, it was nearly three million dollars short of the twenty-eight million dollars required for full capital funding.

Girard quickly organized a syndicate of investors to subscribe to the residue. When the public subscription reopened on August 26, with the limit of three thousand shares no longer applicable, Girard immediately bought all of the remaining 29,736 shares, at a cost of $2,973,600, on behalf of himself and others in the syndicate.[18] Girard personally owned 4,500 shares, representing an investment of $450,000.[19] In the words of one commentator, Girard "astounded the financial world" with his spectacular role in making the public subscription a success.[20] The sole proprietor of Stephen Girard's Bank, occupying the building of the former First Bank of the United States, thus became a driving force in making the Second Bank of the United States a reality.

It turned out, though, that sitting on a bank board of twenty-five members was not quite the same as owning a bank and having full decision-making authority. Girard soon became disenchanted with loan policies of the Second Bank. He considered them to be overly liberal and a dangerous invitation to economic collapse. Unable to change the policies, he resigned from the board of directors on December 31, 1817. His unheeded warnings about the dangers of too-easy credit proved to be on target. Excessively rapid expansion of loans was a major cause of the Panic of 1819 and the recession that followed. There was, however, some good news in that year for the Second Bank of the United States. Its constitutionality was upheld on March 7, 1819, by the U.S. Supreme Court in a landmark case, *McCulloch v. Maryland*. The suit had been filed in the name of James McCulloch, cashier of the Baltimore branch of the bank, after the Maryland legislature had tried to put the branch out of business, or at least to inflict serious harm, by imposing a heavy tax. The Supreme Court ruled that the Second Bank was not only constitutional but also exempt from state taxation. The nation's highest tribunal was in accord with a position that had been taken by Girard, namely that the federal government had a right (also a responsibility, Girard had said) to be an active participant in the field of banking to protect the public interest.

The headquarters of the Second Bank of the United States, which was located in Carpenters' Hall in Philadelphia in its early years, moved in 1824 to a new building (it still stands) on the south side of Chestnut Street between Fourth and Fifth Streets. However, the bank did not have its twenty-year charter renewed when it expired in 1836. The decisive votes in Congress came in 1832, just a few months after Girard's death. President Andrew Jackson (the first president to be born in a log cabin) won a bitter battle against charter renewal and then sealed the victory by winning re-election to a second term as president.

Nonetheless, the basic principle advocated by Girard and opposed by Jackson, i.e., there should be direct participation in banking by the government of the United States, was revived successfully in another century. That principle was the basis for creation of the Federal Reserve System in 1913.

In the years after the War of 1812, and, in fact, while the war was still in progress and the outcome was still in doubt, Girard was involved in other banking matters even more important to him than helping to establish the Second Bank of the United States. He was in numerous battles against hostile forces, mostly competing bankers and their political allies, who wanted to put Stephen Girard's Bank out of business.

The Pennsylvania legislature waged a persistent attack against Girard's banking enterprise. A bill to impose a state tax on unchartered banks was introduced but not enacted. Another measure, designed to make it more difficult for unchartered banks to operate, was passed by one-vote margins, forty-two to forty-one in the House and fourteen to thirteen in the Senate, but was vetoed by Governor Simon Snyder.[21] Subsequently, a bill intended to outlaw unincorporated banks—including any bank owned by an individual—was enacted over Governor Snyder's veto and took effect in 1815. However, the new law failed to shut down Stephen Girard's Bank. A short-lived attempt by the state to close his bank was abandoned after Girard, citing a provision in the Pennsylvania Constitution prohibiting ex post facto legislation, argued successfully that the new law could not apply to his bank.[22]

Even after Girard had come to the financial rescue of the country in the War of 1812, Congress enacted a tax on banks that imposed the heaviest burden on those that were unincorporated. After the law was in force, an attempt was made to amend it in a way that would have put unincorporated banks on equal footing with other banks. The proposed amendment was defeated by a margin of one vote in the Senate after it had been passed by the House.[23]

It would be uplifting to think that the persistent attempts at state and federal levels to require banks to be chartered and incorporated were an early manifestation of consumer protection, but such was not the case. It was more a matter of limiting the competition. The officers, directors and stockholders of chartered and incorporated banks were the driving force behind the banking legislation; they did not want free and unrestricted entry into the banking business. They especially did not want the kind of very tough competition that Stephen Girard was giving them.

Despite all of the efforts that were made to cripple or destroy Girard's unchartered and unincorporated banking operations, they were a huge success in terms of community service, which was his main objective. As a wealthy sole proprietor with no need to pay dividends or show a profit, he concentrated on short-term loans to residents of Philadelphia to help them start or expand small businesses and to accommodate personal or family needs.[24] Even though he had loaned millions of dollars to the government in a war-time emergency, that was not his usual style as a banker. He preferred to give small loans to many borrowers rather than large loans to a few borrowers. From his standpoint, it was prudent banking policy to spread the risks. From the standpoint of borrowers, Stephen Girard's Bank acquired a reputation as the best place for people of modest means to go when they needed money. Although he gave fair consideration to all loan requests, Girard catered mainly to the working class rather than to the rich, to small business rather than to big business. He especially liked to give a helping hand to young, industrious people just starting out in a trade.[25]

In banking, as in maritime commerce, Girard outhustled the competition. He got up earlier and worked harder. He gave his thoughts about dilatory bankers and merchants in a letter to a business associate in 1817: "Our city abounds with that class of amateurs who generally breakfast at 9 or 10 o'clock in the forenoon" and spend much of the day "with what they call their friends in eating, drinking, smoking, talking of business which does not concern them, and whenever some of their commercial operations prove disadvantageous, which is often the case, they attribute it to bad luck."[26]

Even while operating his own bank successfully, Girard continued to consider the Second Bank of the United States a sound investment. For several years in the 1820s the value of his holdings in shares of the Second Bank exceeded $700,000. He became the largest individual stockholder in the Second Bank of the United States just as, earlier, he had been the largest individual stockholder in the First Bank of the United States.[27]

Although banking occupied much of Girard's time, he continued to prosper as a maritime merchant and to give a great deal of his attention to world trade matters. During the Panic of 1819, while other merchants were retrenching, he acquired another ship, the *Superb*, and assigned it to the China trade. In the early 1820s he lost two of his "philosopher" ships, the *Voltaire* and the *Montesquieu*, in wrecks off the coast of The Netherlands. As always, he accepted the losses without complaint as part of the cost of doing business. He did not just overcome adversity; he seemed to thrive on it. In his later years, having become so wealthy, he could easily absorb financial setbacks of a magnitude that might have sunk a shipowner of lesser means.

More by accident than by design, Girard acquired thousands of acres in a rural area of Louisiana, land that he would never see, during the Panic of 1819. A merchant in Baltimore, short on cash, used the acreage to settle an account. The transaction was not typical. Most of Girard's real estate investments were in Pennsylvania.

Being the richest man in America and the nation's most powerful banker did not change Girard in any substantive way. He was still, quite literally, as down to earth as ever. Besides going out to the farm on a daily basis to enjoy hard labor, he did the gardening at his bank. Regular customers, arriving to do their banking, became accustomed to seeing the owner of the bank before they entered the building. He would be toiling and sweating, keeping the grounds looking nice, taking personal pride in the appearance of his establishment outside as well as inside. "It was his custom during the spring and summer months," in the words of Stephen Simpson, "to spend an hour or two every morning ... in the garden attached to his bank. Here he employed himself in pruning his vines, nursing his fig tree, the fruit of which he was extremely fond, and dressing his shrubs. His passion for pruning was excessive, and often found no end but in the total extermination of the tree; especially when he found it obstinate in growth, or slow in bearing fruit."[28] This simple scene speaks volumes about Stephen Girard. The richest American was a little bit eccentric, yes, but he was never indolent and never pompous. He was, for all his wealth and power, humble.

After the defeat of Napoleon at Waterloo in 1815 (followed by his banishment by the British to the remote island of St. Helena, where he died in 1821) many citizens of France who were allied with him fled to America. Violence against Napoleon's supporters erupted throughout France. Hundreds were killed by mobs. A general who had served under Napoleon had his penis and testicles cut off.[29] A new French government ordered members of the Bonaparte family to leave the country.[30]

Some of the French exiles of 1815 settled in and around Philadelphia. Girard became a friend of a number of them, and they often were guests in his home for Sunday dinner. Foremost among them was Joseph Bonaparte, a brother of Napoleon and a former king of Spain. He purchased a principal residence (an estate of 211 acres, later expanded to 1,800 acres[31]) in New Jersey, near Philadelphia, and rented a house in the city from Girard, on the southeast corner of Twelfth and Market Streets.

When Bonaparte learned that his rented house was part of an entire block owned by Girard, bounded north and south by Market and Chestnut Streets, and east and west by Eleventh and Twelfth Streets, the former king could not resist trying to acquire the complete property.

According to a story that has been passed down through the years, he brought up the subject at one of the Sunday dinners at Girard's house. Bonaparte said he was prepared to pay a good price if Girard was willing to sell.

"What would you consider a good price?" Girard wanted to know.

"I will cover it with silver half-dollars," replied Bonaparte with a flourish.

"I will take that offer," Girard rejoined, his one eye twinkling, "on condition that you stand them on edge."

Bonaparte could not help laughing, knowing that he had been outmaneuvered and that he had met his match as a bargainer, but there was no deal.[32] That block, now in the heart of downtown Philadelphia, near the convention center that opened in 1993, is still owned by Stephen Girard's estate.

Bonaparte tried to sell Girard a large estate near Paris, but he was not interested. Thoroughly Americanized, and with no intention of ever again returning to France, even for just a visit, Girard had no desire to invest in real estate in his native country.

Other high-placed Frenchmen, besides Joseph Bonaparte, who became regulars at Girard's Sunday dinners included Henri and Charles Lallemand, two brothers who had been generals in Napoleon's army. They were key figures in ill-fated efforts to establish settlements of former residents of France in Alabama, which would become a state in 1819, and in Texas, which was still claimed by Mexico. Henri Lallemand married Henriette Girard, Stephen's niece, in 1817. Joseph Bonaparte was at the wedding, as were many others from France who had settled in the Philadelphia area. The ceremony was at St. Augustine's Roman Catholic Church on Fourth Street between Race and Vine Streets. The church had been built in the 1790s, with Stephen Girard and President Washington among the contributors, and it would be destroyed by fire during anti-Catholic riots in 1844. (A new church was built on the same site.)

The marriage of Henri and Henriette was tragically brief. Henriette, a bride at sixteen, was a widow at twenty-two, but she would marry again.

It is likely that Joseph Bonaparte and Girard talked secretively about the feasibility of trying to help Napoleon escape from his British captors on St. Helena. According to one historian who has written extensively about the Bonapartes, a ship owned by Girard was being prepared for a voyage to that far-away island in the summer of 1821 when word was received that Napoleon, at fifty-one, had died.[33]

There would have been huge odds against an escape by Napoleon, even with outside help, but he was never one to worry about odds. On one occasion, when told that an enemy force outnumbered his army three to one, he had replied: "I have fifty thousand men. Add myself, and you get a hundred and fifty thousand."[34]

Ironically, if an attempt had been made to help Napoleon escape from St. Helena, he might not have wanted to leave. After he had been on the island a few years, and his health was deteriorating, he began to picture himself as a martyr whose place in history—especially in the history of France—would be more secure if he died in British captivity. He once summed up his thoughts on the subject: "If Christ had not died on the Cross, He would not have become the Son of God."[35]

On October 25, 1822, the President of the United States sat down at his writing desk in the White House and penned a long letter to Stephen Girard asking for a personal loan of forty thousand dollars. James Monroe, not yet halfway through his second term, had fallen on hard times.

"My long employment in the service of my country," President Monroe said, "under circumstances which rendered it impossible for me to pay due attention to my private concerns, and in offices which, until the present one, afforded compensation inadequate to my support, has subjected me to debts for which I wish to provide, in a manner satisfactory to the parties & with the least injury to myself. To accomplish this very desirable object, it is important to me to obtain a loan of from 25,000 to 40,000 dollars, for the term of five years. For this loan I am willing to pay the usual bank interest ... and to give security on real property .... The property which I would thus pledge, is an estate in Ablemarle County, Virginia, adjoining the estate of Mr. Jefferson .... It consists of 3,500 acres ....

"I have made this proposition to you, from a belief that if in your power, you will afford me the accommodation desired, and should you do it, I can assure you that you will render me a service which I shall always recollect with much sensibility."[36]

Two days after receiving the letter, Girard granted the loan in the full amount, forty thousand dollars, for a term of five years as requested. After all, he had already bailed out the government of the United States to the tune of millions of dollars in the War of 1812. By comparison, bailing out the President of the United States was a minor transaction.

A little over a year later, on December 2, 1823, President Monroe proclaimed the famous doctrine that bears his name. He said, in the key passages: "The American continents, by the free and independent condition which they have assumed and maintain, are henceforth not to be considered as subjects for future colonization by any European powers .... We should consider any attempt on their part to extend their system to any portion of this hemisphere as dangerous to our peace and safety."

Girard was pleased by the Monroe Doctrine, of course, having been a long-time advocate of independence in the Americas, but he thought the result was likely to be war between the United States and major European powers. He expected them to challenge the doctrine rather than acquiesce to it. He sent messages to his agents, captains and supercargoes around the world, alerting them to the prospect of war and ordering them to make appropriate preparations and to take prudent precautions.

In a letter to his agent at Rotterdam, in The Netherlands, for example, Girard gave these instructions relative to one of his ships that was soon to sail to China: "Increase your present armament with four more guns of same calibre as those which are on board so to make eight mounted guns with powder, gun shot, small arms, cutlasses and all other requisite war utensils, to which you will add six or seven good seamen over and above your present complement .... While at sea, you will avoid speaking to any vessel unless compelled by unforeseen circumstances. In time of war, a constant lookout should, during the day, be kept at the masthead."[37]

As it turned out, there was no need for Girard to be concerned. No one in Europe, remembering the thrashing that had been given to the British in the War of 1812, was willing to take on the United States of America.

Thus the replenishment of an empty U.S. Treasury by Girard in 1813 was still paying dividends a decade later. America had won the war and it had won enduring respect. When the President of the United States spoke, the world listened.

CHAPTER 19

Coal and Railroads, Emeline and Jane, Twilight and Death

1823-1831

*Life is a river, starting small and weak and
steadily growing in size and strength, flowing
always forward on a one-way trip, passing each
place but once with no going back, finally
reaching death in the infinite fathoms of an ocean
called eternity.*

STEPHEN GIRARD, in his seventies, and then in his eighties, did what comes naturally to anyone who reaches milestones of old age: He began to think about, and prepare for, death. However, he never even considered retirement. "When Death comes for me," Girard said, only a month before he died, "he will find me busy, unless I am asleep in bed. If I thought I was going to die tomorrow, I should plant a tree, nevertheless, today."[1] An aging Girard's commitment to long hours of hard work was almost fanatical and never faltered, his great wealth notwithstanding. He believed that "to rest is to rust."[2]

Despite his fame he steadfastly remained modest and unassuming, persistently resisting efforts to memorialize him. When a prospective biographer (Stephen Simpson) asked Girard for an interview, he firmly declined. "My deeds must be my life," he said. "When I am dead, my actions must speak for me."[3] When a book publisher (Joseph Delaplaine) was preparing a series of volumes on famous Americans and

307

asked Girard to sit for a portrait, the reply was a polite but unequivocal refusal. "Convinced as I am that at the approach of death I will be anxious to depart this world with tranquility," he said, "I do not wish to leave behind any marks which may cause regret; therefore I must decline granting what I have uniformly refused to others."[4]

Thus there would be no portraits of Girard in his lifetime, only after his death. His persistent refusal to sit for a portrait, even in his later years, is all the more remarkable considering that he knew members of the Peale family for a long time, especially Charles Willson Peale and Rembrandt Peale.[5] On one occasion, when Rembrandt Peale embarked on a trip to France, Girard gave him a letter of introduction describing him as "one of the first painters of the United States."[6]

In the mid-1820s, it was subsequently disclosed, Girard was soliciting legal advice in regard to provisions of a will. During this period, it also was revealed later, a lengthy will was written, although it was not the final version. Meanwhile, even as he was thinking about death, Girard still had a lot of living to do.

In 1824 he had the pleasure of serving on a committee that made arrangements for a visit to Philadelphia by Lafayette. It was one stop on a thirteen-month tour of the United States by the French hero of the American Revolution. He was in Philadelphia from September 28 to October 5, eight days filled with festive occasions and much speech-making. Lafayette, who had been invited to America by President Monroe in accord with a resolution passed by Congress, began his tour in New York and then traveled through New Jersey, crossing the Delaware River at Trenton. He was greeted on the northern outskirts of Philadelphia, near Kensington, by six thousand militia, and made a grand entrance into the city in a parade with many thousands of participants. They included the governors of Pennsylvania and New Jersey and numerous other dignitaries, along with large numbers of ordinary people. Members of the Committee of Arrangements rode in carriages immediately preceding a carriage conveying the guest of honor.[7]

The line of march included 3,500 infantrymen, hundreds of cavalrymen, more than 200 artillerymen with their ordnance, 150 veterans of the American Revolution riding in carriages, 100 high-ranking officers of the army and the navy riding on horseback, 100 prominent citizens on horseback, 400 young men and 150 young boys of no particular distinction other than being representative of America's future, hundreds of printers, 700 mechanics of various trades, 300 farmers, 300 weavers, 200 cordwinders, 150 ropemakers, 150 coopers, 150 butchers, 100 shipbuilders and hundreds of cartmen with their carts.[8]

Along the parade route were many arches of triumph for the procession to pass under, including an arch across Chestnut Street in front of Independence Hall that was forty-five feet wide and twenty-four feet high.[9] A crowd believed to be in excess of 300,000, more than double the population of Philadelphia at that time, viewed the parade in the afternoon, and an estimated 160,000 were still in the streets in the evening to enjoy an illumination of the city.[10]

Lafayette expressed surprise that there was no memorial to George Washington in Philadelphia. A group of prominent citizens met with Lafayette on October 1 to discuss the situation. Girard and others were appointed to a committee to raise funds for a monument, which they did, but nothing came of their efforts until late in the nineteenth century. By then, the money they had collected, with accumulated interest, totaled more than $30,000. It was used to finance, in part, a monument dedicated by President William McKinley on May 15, 1897.[11] The $250,000 memorial, forty-two feet high, is made of bronze and granite and features an equestrian statue of Washington. Originally located at the Green Street entrance to Fairmount Park, the memorial was moved to its present location, in front of the Philadelphia Museum of Art, in the 1920s when the museum and the Benjamin Franklin Parkway were built.[12]

In the last years of his life, when he was in his middle and late seventies and early eighties, Girard correctly perceived that coal and railroads were the waves of the future. At the age of seventy-nine he was high bidder at thirty thousand dollars for sixty-seven tracts of anthracite coal lands in Schuylkill County that were sold at public auction in Philadelphia on April 17, 1830. They had been acquired many years earlier by the First Bank of the United States. He knew they were potentially of great value, but he also knew there were high risks involved because of the likelihood of defective titles and surveys.

The tracts were described at the time of the auction as totaling more than twenty-seven thousand acres, but it turned out that the true figure was a little over seventeen thousand acres.[13] Nonetheless, they were a good buy. Girard, as noted in an earlier chapter, was ahead of his time in recognizing that coal was far superior to wood as a heating fuel. He could foresee that fortunes would be made in Schuylkill County and other counties of the anthracite region in northeastern Pennsylvania. The land purchased by Girard is in the vicinity of a town that still bears his name: Girardville. Girard also bought six thousand acres of undeveloped land in Erie County, in northwestern Pennsylvania, where there remains today a town in that county named Girard.

In May of 1831, when he was eighty-one years old, Girard made a commitment to invest $200,000 in shares of the Danville and Pottsville Railroad, which planned to build and operate a rail line serving his coal lands in Schuylkill County. He became a director of the company and installed the husband of one of his nieces as chairman of the board.[14] Girard's $200,000 investment was payable in installments, which would be completed by executors of his estate after he died. This business venture, entered into in the last year of his life, dramatized his accurate perception of railroads as potentially efficient and profitable carriers of coal. He also invested thirty thousand dollars in the Mount Carbon Railroad, another prospective coal carrier that also would not yet be operating when he died.[15]

However, he did live to see the completion of yet another transportation project in which he was a major investor (more than twenty thousand dollars[16]): the Chesapeake and Delaware Canal. It connects the Delaware Bay with the Chesapeake Bay and reduces shipping distance and time between Philadelphia and Baltimore. The canal, which is still in operation, opened in 1829 with the husband of another niece of Girard as a member of the board of directors.[17]

Virtually to the end of his life Girard continued to invest shrewdly and profitably in real estate in Philadelphia, along with occasional speculations in land that was far away and he would never see, in Kentucky, for example. His ongoing acquisitions of lots in residential blocks of Philadelphia, and his almost constant employment of highly skilled craftsmen in the building trades to erect houses to rent or sometimes to sell, gained for him a steadily growing reputation as a producer of homes with workmanship of exceptional quality. He visited building sites on a daily basis to make personal inspections, his one good eye examining closely the materials used and the manner in which they were put together. He was noted for helping to beautify the city with attractive rows of brick homes, some of them three or four stories high. They were built to stand for centuries, and many of them are still being lived in. They can be seen today in prime residential blocks near Independence National Historical Park, such as on the south side of Spruce Street between Third and Fourth Streets.[18]

Girard remained active in maritime trade in the final years of his life. His standards of excellence for shipbuilding were as high as they were for home-building. As was noted in an earlier chapter, Girard's ships have been authoritatively described as "the finest merchant sailing vessels ever constructed in the United States at any time."[19] This accolade was applicable to design and materials as well as to workmanship.[20] Girard was justifiably proud of both the appearance and the performance of his ships.

To the very end of his life Girard never stopped loving the sights and sounds and smells of ships and ship-related activity. His home and counting-house on Water Street, backing up to his wharf and offering close-up views of the Delaware River and the busiest section of the Philadelphia waterfront, were in a neighborhood that became increasingly commercialized during his later years. Stephen Simpson, who knew the area well, said that Girard lived "admidst the bustle and clangor of business, ships, drays, carts and wagons: the only music appropriate to his character, and the only harmony that chimed with the current of his thoughts .... Living thus amidst the turmoil of his business, his life became devoted to labour, and labour formed the pleasure of his life."[21]

Simpson asked rhetorically how Girard, especially after he had become so rich, could enjoy living on a "narrow, dirty, and confined street ... kept in incessant and horrible noise by the everlasting din of merchandise." Simpson answered his own question: "Such, however, it did not appear to Mr. Girard, whose habits had made him familiar with the scene, and transformed all its blemishes into charms, making even the bilge-water breeze to bear the perfume of the rose, and the rude song of the mariner appear as the sweetest effusion of harmony."[22]

A story was told by Simpson to illustrate how Girard, even when he was the richest person in America and a powerful banker, well up in years, remained nonetheless devoted to hard and menial labor, loving every minute of it. A man went to Girard's counting-house one day on a business matter but was unable to talk with him "because he was cutting up his hogs for his winter provisions."[23]

Despite advancing age, there was no letup in Girard's active role at his bank, with continuing emphasis on loans and other services for small businesses and families of modest means. He had suffered a severe personal loss in 1822 when his bank's astute and industrious cashier, George Simpson, died, but Girard weathered the blow with characteristic stoicism. The cashier's son, Stephen Simpson, recalled the day after his father's death when Girard said to the bereaved young man: "Your father, Mr. Simpson, was an old man, and old men must die. It is nothing uncommon. When one man dies we must find others to do the business. The bank must not stop because one man dies."[24]

Girard promptly promoted Joseph Roberts, the first teller, to replace the deceased Simpson as cashier. Service to the bank's customers continued without interruption. Girard was sensitive to the harsh realities of death and the sorrow it can inflict on survivors, but he also firmly believed that it was a bank's responsibility to be dependable in all circumstances. The curtain closed for George Simpson, but the show went on.

Roberts got along well with Girard and turned out to be a very able replacement for Simpson. The bank continued to be well managed and to prosper. Abraham Ritter, who knew Roberts well for many years, described him as a man of "serious, sober countenance" who was "civil, respectful and gentlemanly." He had a "remarkably erect stature" and a "measured gait .... I never saw him or heard of his losing his balance of decorum. He was a gentleman of the old school."[25]

Girard, by this time, was showing his age in many ways. Stephen Simpson gave a lengthy description of Girard as he appeared early in 1823, at the age of seventy-two, soon after Roberts had taken over as cashier of the bank:

> At this period, the hearing of Mr. Girard had become so much impaired as to require a high pitch of the voice to make him sensible of the sound. The sight of his remaining eye, too, had become extremely imperfect, so that he could

with difficulty read a legible and plain hand-writing. His countenance was perfectly pallid, totally devoid of animation, and the very picture of abstraction itself; being square, full, muscular, and deeply indented with the lines of thought, even to his expansive and capacious forehead, which indicated remarkable research, meditation and capacity. When he spoke, however, a smile played round his mouth, which gave to his face a very agreeable expression, and indicated a strong original propensity to harmony and fellowship. Even at that age, there shone in his remaining eye a peculiar lustre, which told of deep passion, sagacious observation and quick perception. Without the lustre of this eye, you would have imagined the bust of some antique sage to have stood before you; but the twinkling and sparkling of that eye, I shall never forget—sometimes playful, and even sarcastic in its glance—always cunning; but at most times, and most generally, stern, fixed, and thoughtful; rather seeking the ground than steadily meeting your opposing look.

His mouth, when not relaxed by an insinuating smile, expressed unalterable determination, or what in the common affairs of life would be termed obstinacy. His high cheek-bones and breadth of face gave indication of that singular expression of head, which bespoke the extraordinary character of the man. Increasing age had given him a slight and almost imperceptible palsied tremor of the head which, added to his bald crown and his queue with here and there a few scattered grey hairs, gave him, when uncovered, an imposing air of veneration. You felt an involuntary sensation of respect and reverence for his age and would have concluded that this physical approach to the leafless era of life was attended by a corresponding fading and withering of the energies of the man, though at that period his body was not shrunk in size or impaired in vigour, but square, robust and thick-set as in the heyday of his life.

.... He had experienced no diminution of his constitutional strength and had been attacked by no obvious and serious malady. He still indulged in his wonted exercises and remitted not a jot from his accustomed and severe labour, having adopted it as a maxim never to anticipate the inroads or invite the dilapidations of age by abating any of his customary habits. He said it was time enough to give up when nature summoned him to surrender, and as for death, why, when it came, it would find him busy, if he was able to stand upon his feet, or not wrapt in his slumbers.

He held it to be a weakness almost criminal to give over labour because a man was advancing in years, so long as he retained health and strength. Industry, he maintained, had no respect for times, seasons or years, and it was the duty of every man to be useful to society through all stages of existence, the plea of age being but the pretext of idleness and the repose of a spirit which sought excuses for the non-performance of imperative duties.[26]

Not everyone in Girard's life was physically able to keep on working until death intervened. In 1827, at the age of seventy-five, Betsy Ross retired after many busy decades of self-employment as a seamstress, and also as a maker of flags for Girard and for many other shipowners, as well as for a general clientele of business, governmental and residential customers. She had been married three times, widowed three times and had given birth to seven children, all daughters, five of whom were still living. One of them carried on the seamstress and flag-making business after her mother's retirement. Betsy Ross (known as Betsy Claypoole after she married her third husband) had failing eyesight in her old age, like Girard, but she would outlive him by more than four years. She would be eighty-four and blind when she died in 1836.[27]

Sally Bickham, Girard's mistress for nine years, from 1787 to 1796, died in 1824, at the age of fifty-five, in northeastern Pennsylvania. She had moved to that part of the state with her second husband after her first husband died.[28]

Polly Kenton, having succeeded Sally as a mistress in 1796, served Girard in that capacity for thirty-one years until her retirement in 1827 when she was fifty-one and he was seventy-seven. Polly had given up all hope of ever becoming Mrs. Girard and inheriting a large part of Stephen's fortune. She was in poor health, suffering from a number of ailments, at the time of her departure from the Girard household, although she would outlive Stephen by many years. When she retired, she moved back to Whitemarsh, north of Philadelphia, in the area where she had grown up on a farm. During retirement she lived with relatives, because she wanted to, not because she was, to any degree, dependent on them. Retiring at the age of fifty-one was no problem for Polly. She was financially secure. Stephen had paid her $250 a year, plus food and clothing and shelter and other living expenses and amenities. The $250 alone, not counting the fringe benefits, was a good salary, far more than Polly could have made as a farm worker or a laundress, two lines of work in which she had experience before becoming a mistress.

Polly may have retired mainly because she no longer had to work and was tired of working. Her housekeeping duties, although supervisory, may have become more time-consuming over the years. She also may have grown weary of being a mistress for a man who was seventy-seven years old, a man who had slept with her during the best years of her womanhood but did not want to marry her. It is possible, too, that Stephen no longer found Polly satisfying and decided that, if he was going to keep on having a mistress, he ought to have one who was younger.

For whatever reason or reasons, and there may well have been more than one, Polly walked out of the house on Water Street in 1827, the house she had lived in since 1796, the year it was completed. She walked out of Stephen's life. She walked off into the sunset. From all indications the parting was amicable and by mutual agreement, but it is not known who, at first, originated the idea of a separation.

Stephen did not have to look far to find a replacement for Polly. A young and pretty woman, younger and prettier than Polly, was already living in his house and, in fact, had grown up in his house. She was Polly's niece, Emeline Kenton, who had known Stephen virtually all of her life and was very fond of him.[29] She was eighteen years old. Emeline was hired as Stephen's housekeeper, although he obviously could have found a more experienced, more mature and better qualified woman for that position. Emeline may also have been his mistress, but that is uncertain. In the early nineteenth century it was not unusual for a man in his seventies to have a mistress in her teens. It is not clear, though, whether Stephen still needed or wanted the services of a woman in his bed by the time he had reached the age of seventy-seven. If he did, there can be very little doubt that Emeline was available.

Besides being an eye-catching beauty, Emeline was beholden to Girard. He had known her since she was a little girl, and he had provided her with the comforts and the security of a rich man's house. He had watched her blossom into full-blown womanhood. She was, as a surviving portrait clearly shows, strikingly attractive in her facial features, and she had beautiful black hair.[30] Mary also had been a pretty woman of eighteen with beautiful black hair when Stephen married her, half a century earlier. Emeline may have reminded him of his wife, the way she had been, fifty years before, when their love was new.

Stephen had given bounteous gifts to Emeline when she was a child, including an expensive doll from China, and they were followed by continuing tokens of affection as she matured. After she became his housekeeper, Stephen gave her a gold watch. It is inscribed, inside the lid: "Presented to Emeline G. Kenton by Stephen Girard Aug 30

1828."[31] According to a story that has been handed down from generation to generation in the Kenton family, Emeline had pleaded with Stephen "for a watch to remember him by."[32]

In Girard's time it was customary to show respect, even reverence, for loved ones who were old, especially for an aging head of the house. It was expected of a young woman that she would express her gratitude to an elderly man who had been good to her, all the more so if he had raised her and supported her and educated her. Emeline, at the very least, must have shown her affection for Stephen with hugs and kisses and words of endearment, thereby brightening the days of an old man in his declining years. There may have been times when she went beyond hugs and kisses in saying thank you to a kind and generous benefactor. Stephen would convey his appreciation to Emeline, and the depth of his feelings about her, by remembering her quite generously in his will.

Emeline was Girard's housekeeper for about a year. Then she embarked on a life of her own. She married Richard Taylor, a nephew of Alexander Taylor, a sea captain who had worked for Girard.[33] Jane Taylor, Richard's aunt and Alexander's widow, replaced Emeline as Girard's housekeeper.

Thus Polly and Emeline and Jane, the final three women in Stephen's life, were linked by familial ties. To recapitulate, Polly was Emeline's aunt, and Jane was an aunt of Emeline's husband. To state it another way, Emeline was Polly's niece and the wife of Jane's nephew. Jane was middle-aged, in her forties or, perhaps, in her fifties, and began her service to Girard when he was seventy-eight. She was his last house-keeper, remaining in his employ three years, until he died. They developed a close relationship. She was good to him, and he was appreciative of her, as would become evident when his will was read. She may have been his mistress, but there is no evidence to confirm that she was. She apparently slept in the same room with him, although maybe not in the same bed, at least during times that he was too ill to be left alone. When an inventory of Girard's household belongings was taken soon after his death, there were two double beds in his bedroom. On a wash stand in his bedroom there were two pitchers and two bowls.[34]

In the adjoining and connecting bedroom, according to the inventory, there was no bed, nor was there a pitcher or a bowl. It is not known how long this arrangement, two beds in Girard's bedroom, existed. The second bed may have been put there just a day or two before he died, to accommodate an around-the-clock vigil by Jane. However, she most likely would have needed a second bed in his room a year earlier when she was nursing him back to health after serious injuries received in an accident (to be discussed later).

In 1829 the state government of Pennsylvania ran out of money and teetered on the brink of financial collapse, the result of years of profligate spending. Governor John Shulze made the long journey, about a hundred miles, from Harrisburg to Philadelphia to ask Girard for help. (The state capital had moved from Philadelphia to York in 1799 and to Harrisburg in 1812.) Having already come to the financial rescue of the U.S. government and a U.S. president, Girard responded readily to the governor's plea. Girard loaned him $100,000 to keep the state government afloat, with no guarantee that the money would ever be repaid. The legislature was not in session and had not authorized the loan.

Stephen Simpson, as an employee of Stephen Girard's Bank at the time, well understood both the desperation of Governor Shulze and the risk that Girard was taking. Simpson put the transaction in perspective in this account:

> When bankruptcy stared the commonwealth in the face, and embarrassed every movement of the government ... Mr. Girard stepped forward with his wonted public spirit and patriotism and furnished from his bank a loan of one hundred thousand dollars. When it is considered that there was no law to authorize this loan; that it was taken up on the personal credit of the state executive, and was merely an act of public spirit to meet a great public exigency, it must be allowed to possess something beyond the negative merit of a fiscal speculation, and to have conferred essential service upon the commonwealth. In this manner is the character of Stephen Girard illustrated by his actions, in the most unequivocal and imposing light, leaving no room to doubt his patriotism or question his public spirit.[35]

Simpson described the plight of the state: "The last cent of its credit, as well as its resources, had been expended. The public works stood still. The interest on the state loans remained unpaid .... It was at such a time that Girard contributed to uphold the system of our internal improvements and sustain the public credit from total dissolution— when others would not, on account of the panic and alarm that overspread the public mind."[36]

So it was that, in 1829 as in 1813, Girard walked in where angels feared to tread. Just as he had come to the rescue of the Treasury of the United States, so did he come to the rescue of the Treasury of Pennsylvania. His $100,000 loan to the state government, as the millions he had loaned to the federal government sixteen years before, was a desperately needed cash transfusion in the nick of time.

Throughout the 1820s, and throughout his seventies, Girard maintained a continuing interest in civic and charitable enterprises. Besides serving on committees to honor Lafayette and to raise money for a memorial to Washington, Girard was a contributor (eight hundred dollars) to the Franklin Institute when it was founded in Philadelphia in 1824.[37] From a small beginning, devoted principally "to giving young tradesmen and manufacturers instruction in the sciences applied to the arts,"[38] the Franklin Institute became a many-faceted and widely renowned educational and research institution for the advancement of science and industry. (It is best known to the general public today for its museum on the Benjamin Franklin Parkway.)

Girard served on a committee that planned the Philadelphia Merchants' Exchange, although it was not completed until after his death. The handsome structure, in Greek Revival architecture, is on the northeast corner of Third and Walnut Streets. (It is now a part of Independence National Historical Park.) The Exchange gave merchants and others, including sea captains and shipowners, a place to meet and talk and transact business, a place that was more suitable, although perhaps not more convivial, than the taverns and the coffee houses.

Throughout his years of advancing age, Girard remained active in agricultural and horticultural societies, in port and maritime associations, and in all manner of charitable enterprises for relief of the aged, the indigent, the infirm, the widowed and the orphaned. Girard derived much satisfaction, even fun, from these public-spirited and kindhearted endeavors. He genuinely enjoyed helping others, giving to others, sharing with others. As one contemporary Philadelphian told him: "No man in this town has more pleasure than yourself .... Your enjoyments are ... in accomplishing lasting good to mankind."[39]

At 4:30 in the afternoon on December 21, 1830, as dusk was arriving on the first day of winter and the shortest day of the year, Girard had an accident that came dreadfully close to ending his life then and there. The eighty-year-old pedestrian was run over by horses and a wagon in the gathering darkness while he was crossing Market Street at the Second Street intersection. Months later, when he had recovered sufficiently to resume writing letters, he described the "extraordinary accident" with "the horses of a wagon running against me, throwing me down, and one of the wheels going over my head."[40] The horses were going at full trot, according to Girard. If the wheel had passed over the middle of his head, the injuries probably would have been fatal. However, he received a glancing blow, the wheel scraping across the right side of his head and face. He suffered severe lacerations of one ear and one cheek, with considerable flesh torn away, and substantial loss of blood.

The unflappable octogenarian nonetheless was able to get up and walk home, two and a half blocks away, under his own power, brusquely declining offers of assistance, but the injuries turned out to be serious enough to keep him confined to his bedroom for two months.

"This was undoubtedly the most severe stroke of affliction that Mr. Girard had ever been subject to," Simpson said. "His anguish and sufferings must have been extreme, though endured with the uncomplaining fortitude of the stoic. The operations performed ... on his cheek [without anesthesia] would have shaken the fortitude and broke the constitution of a younger man."[41] Girard showed great courage, without flinching, as his wounds were periodically probed, cleansed and dressed. On one such occasion, when the pain was especially severe, he said: "Go on, Doctor, I am an old sailor; I can bear a good deal."[42]

At that stage in his life Girard had not been to sea in more than forty years, but he nonetheless continued to think of himself as a sailor, as he had ever since that day long ago when he had sailed out of Bordeaux for the first time, as a lad of thirteen.

A contributing factor, if not the principal cause, of Girard's mishap while crossing the street must have been the failing sight in his one functioning eye. Simpson described the deteriorating condition:

"His eyesight becoming more and more dim, he found it difficult to walk the streets with that safety that he had done a few years before. In the year 1830 I often discovered him groping in the vestibule of his bank, and feeling about for the door, without success. Still he would suffer no one to attend on or assist him."[43]

In late winter and early spring of 1831 Girard gradually recovered sufficiently to get back into a regular work routine. It was at this time, in the last year of his life, that he bought a tract of forty-five acres in the countryside about a mile north of the Philadelphia city limits (as they were located in 1831). This would turn out to be the most important real estate transaction of Girard's entire life, although the significance of the purchase would not become generally known until after his death.

By December of 1831, a year after his accident, Girard was maintaining a heavy work schedule. He was writing business letters just two days before Christmas. There was much influenza in Philadelphia during that holiday season, and Girard contracted the disease. Complications, including pneumonia, developed quickly and were fatal. At fifteen minutes past four o'clock in the afternoon of the day after Christmas, December 26, 1831, Stephen Girard died at the age of eighty-one years, seven months and six days.

Simpson described the death scene in Girard's bedroom:

A friend of his who sat in his chamber an hour in the morning of the day of his death, represents him to have been altogether unconscious of his condition, and incapable of recognizing those around him. But a short time before he died, he got out of bed and walked across the room to a chair; but almost immediately returned to his bed, placing his hand to his head, and exclaiming [in French], 'How violent is this disorder! How very extraordinary it is!' These were the last words he spoke, to be understood—and soon after expired; thus verifying the opinion, which he had always entertained, that nature would remove him from this scene of existence, as she had brought him into it, without his care, consciousness, or cooperation.[44]

Maintaining constant vigil at Girard's bedside in his final hours, in addition to others who were coming and going, were his last housekeeper, Jane Taylor, and his durable slave, Hannah. The latter was the only one present on his last day of life from his distant past. She had been owned by the Girard family for more than half a century. Hannah had spent most of her life in quiet and faithful service to Stephen, working in his kitchen or wherever else in his house she could be of help. It was appropriate that she was with him at the end, for she would soon find out that she was the first person mentioned, the first beneficiary named, in his will.

An opus of more than ten thousand words, the will was read on the day after Girard died. He had been generous in life, but he had saved the best for the grand finale. The richest person in America became, in death, the greatest philanthropist America had ever known.

CHAPTER 20

A Spectacular Funeral, An Amazing Will

1831

The end of life need not be the end of good deeds.

IT WAS less than half an hour before sundown when Stephen Girard died. The news spread quickly, first along the waterfront and then throughout the city. The flag of every ship in port was lowered to half-mast.[1] This touching tribute to an old man of the sea came straight from the hearts of those who sailed the trade routes of the world. Girard had been one of them. Others might call him a merchant or a banker or a farmer or a philanthropist, and he was, indeed, all of these, and more, but along the river he was known first and foremost as a sailor, a mariner, a salt-spray denizen of the briny deep. He had known what it was like to ride a rolling deck in the teeth of a gale, to climb a mast and straddle a yard, to tangle with canvas and rope, to haul and furl, to risk life and limb. The spontaneous expression of honor and respect in the harbor of Philadelphia, aboard all ships irrespective of nationality, was more eloquent than a eulogy in conveying the affection and admiration that were felt for Girard by the seafaring brotherhood.

Christmas had come on a Sunday in 1831 and Girard died on Monday. His will was read on Tuesday, primarily to see if it contained any instructions pertaining to funeral arrangements. It did not. However, with a reading of the will, even though newspapers did not publish it in full until after the funeral, it became generally known that Girard was giving huge sums for educational, charitable and public purposes, sums that were unapproached in the history of America up to that time.

Flags were flown at half-mast on buildings in Philadelphia, as well as on ships in the harbor, from soon after his death until after his funeral on Friday, December 30. Four days of mourning, in the traditionally festive time between Christmas Day and New Year's Day, dramatized the high esteem for Girard in the city that had been his home for more than half a century. The one-eyed Frenchman who had arrived in Philadelphia as the captain of a weather-battered schooner, virtually on the eve of America's Declaration of Independence, had emerged from obscurity to become the city's most distinguished citizen.

Municipal officials, with formal sanction by City Council, took the extraordinary step of making the funeral a major public event, essentially under city sponsorship, to assure that appropriate recognition would be shown to Girard's full range of astonishing achievements. Emphasis was given not just to his successes in the mercantile world of business and banking but also to his public service to Philadelphia and to America, especially his unending generosity throughout his lifetime, and even in death, to people and institutions and governments in need of help. The city took charge of funeral arrangements in consultation with Girard's business associates and his relatives who lived in the Philadelphia area, principally his three nieces, the daughters of John Girard.

The essence of Stephen Girard, a man so rich and yet so much a man of the people, was well expressed in a resolution adopted by City Council (formally called the Select and Common Councils), a body on which he had served:

> Contemplating the humility of his origin, and contrasting therewith the variety and extent of his works and wealth, the mind is filled with admiration of the man, and profoundly impressed with the value of his example. Numerous and solid as the edifices are, which he constructed in the city and vicinity of Philadelphia, they will contribute but a transitory record of what he was, when compared with the moral influence that must arise from a knowledge of the merits, and means, by which he acquired his immense estate. These merits and means were probity of the strictest kind, diligence unsurpassed, perseverance in all pursuits, and a frugality as remote from parsimony as from extravagance. The goodness of his heart was not manifested by ostentatious subscription or loud profession; but when pestilence stalked abroad, he risked his life to

preserve from its ravages the most humble of his fellow-citizens, and wherever sorrow, unaccompanied by immorality, appeared at his door, it was thrown wide open. His person, his home, and his habits evinced the love of what was simple, and he was a devoted friend to those principles of civil and religious liberty which are the basis of the political fabric of his adopted country.[2]

There were many tributes to Girard in the press. "Industry and frugality was his motto," one Philadelphia newspaper said, and it reminded readers that he not only was "the first merchant and the most opulent banker in this country" but also "was fond of agriculture, feeding his own cattle, curing his own beef."[3]

Another Philadelphia newspaper said: "To those who knew him in distant towns and cities as a rich banker ... his benevolent exertions in the cause of suffering humanity ... are not perhaps so familiar."[4]

Still another Philadelphia newspaper said: "He was always generous to the poor in times of distress .... His stores of wood [have] been freely distributed to the friendless and shivering. His purse, too, has been generally found ready to open for any case of real distress which was communicated properly to him."[5]

This outpouring of accolades by contemporaries was a measure of how much Girard was loved and revered in his own time.

A public notice from the city was published in Philadelphia newspapers in advance of the funeral. The line of march for the funeral procession underscored the humanitarian side of Girard and included some of the organizations and institutions he had belonged to and had contributed to. The great variety of Girard's civic and charitable interests was reflected in the makeup of the funeral procession. Every participant named in the published notice, and many more that were not named, were direct beneficiaries of Girard's personal service or monetary generosity or both. The notice read:

> The funeral of the late Stephen Girard will proceed from his late residence in North Water Street to the burial ground of the Holy Trinity Church [a Roman Catholic Church that still stands and remains active], N.W. corner of Spruce and Sixth Streets, at 10 o'clock on Friday forenoon, December 30.
>
> The Trustees of the Bank of Stephen Girard are requested to meet and proceed together as mourners, next after the relatives of the deceased.
>
> An invitation is respectfully given to public bodies, institutions and societies hereinafter named, to proceed to the funeral in the following order:

The Mayor, Recorder, Aldermen, and the Select and Common Councils, with their officers.

The wardens of the Port of Philadelphia. [Girard was one of the wardens for more than twenty years. Wardens served without pay and had various duties that included granting licenses to pilots who brought ships up and down the Delaware River and Delaware Bay, and setting rules for ship traffic and for cargo loading and unloading.[6]]

The officers and members of the Grand Lodge [Masons] of Pennsylvania, and of the subordinate Lodges. [Girard, as noted earlier, became a Mason in 1788.]

The officers and members of the Society for the Relief of Distressed Masters of Ships and Their Widows.

The officers and Contributors to the Pennsylvania Hospital.

The Controllers and Directors and officers of the Public Schools.

The officers and members of the Pennsylvania Institution for the Deaf and Dumb.

The officers and members of the Orphan Society.

The officers and members of the Societe de Bienfaisance Francaise.

The officers and members of the Fuel Saving Society [a charitable organization that supplied fuel to the poor for heating and cooking].

Other benevolent societies are respectfully invited and requested to proceed next after the Fuel Saving Society.

In a community in which Mr. Girard was as universally known as he was useful, it is not practicable to give special invitations to individuals, or is it supposed that invitations will be expected. All those who knew Mr. Girard personally or by reputation, and who revere his example and memory, are respectfully invited to attend his funeral.

It is customary to protract the time fixed for funerals for one hour beyond that designated. In the present instance the procession will positively move at 11 o'clock.

The procession will move up Water Street to Arch, up Arch to Sixth, down Sixth Street to the place of interment, at the corner of Spruce and Sixth Streets.[7]

Another notice published in Philadelphia newspapers made a request for public participation by residents of the city during the funeral:

The late Stephen Girard, Esq., having by his will left very handsome bequests to the City of Philadelphia, as well as during his lifetime very extensively contributed to its beauty and improvement, it is respectfully suggested to all citizens who are not conscientiously scrupulous to close their windows [i.e., to close their shutters or their curtains or their draperies] at least from the hours of ten to twelve o'clock as a testimony of gratitude and respect to the memory of their liberal benefactor.[8]

The funeral proceeded on schedule, and it quickly became apparent that history was being made. Philadelphia had not seen a funeral of such magnitude in more than forty years, since Benjamin Franklin had been laid to rest in 1790. Three thousand people were in Girard's funeral procession, which was so long that no one could see the beginning and the end of it at the same time.[9] Another twenty thousand lined the procession route, which was a little over a mile.[10] The throng jammed sidewalks and spilled into the streets.

According to one newspaper account the spectators consisted of "immense numbers of all ages and both sexes." Girard's body was conveyed "in a richly decorated coffin on an open hearse." Some mourners were on foot and others rode in carriages. The mayor was listed among mourners walking and wearing "broad mode hat-weepers and scarfs." Officers of the Grand Lodge of Masons of Pennsylvania and subordinate lodges "wore their collars and jewels but not their aprons."[11]

Another newspaper reported that the funeral "was conducted in a mode consistent with the character of the deceased—with solemnity and decorum unaccompanied by pomp." Spectators were seen as "persons desirous not of gratifying curiosity but of paying a lasting tribute of respect to a great public benefactor."[12]

Girard was buried in the churchyard cemetery of Holy Trinity beside the remains of General Henri Lallemand, the first husband of Girard's niece, Henriette. Girard had told his nieces that he wanted to be buried there, although that was not his first choice. As noted previously, Girard had wanted to be buried beside his wife in an unmarked grave at Pennsylvania Hospital, but by the time he died the hospital had stopped allowing burials on its grounds.

The funeral procession for Girard ended with a simple burial at the graveyard. There was no participation by a clergyman of any denomination. Girard's body was taken inside the church, accompanied by Masons, but there was no service there. When the multitudes in the entire length of the procession had reached the general area of the graveyard, clogging the streets with a surging sea of mourners, the body was taken out of the church and to the burial site. Stephen Simpson, who was there, described the final moments: "No church ritual was performed at his grave; and like his wife, after the manner of the

Friends, he was silently deposited in the final abode allotted to frail and fleeting humanity .... No man was ever buried with such unanimous public respect."[13]

Baptized a Catholic when he was one day old, Girard never renounced his Catholicism—although for most of his life he did not attend church services, and he did not receive the last rites of the Catholic Church when he was on his deathbed. He and Mary, it will be recalled, were married in an Episcopal Church. As noted earlier, he contributed generously to building funds and special appeals of Catholic churches, as well as churches of other denominations. When he made a major contribution for construction of St. Augustine's Roman Catholic Church, built in the 1790s, he was listed in church records as a Catholic. Girard attended Catholic churches on special occasions such as baptisms, weddings and funerals. He allowed his three nieces, who grew up in his home and were almost like daughters, to be raised as Catholics and to attend services in Catholic churches.[14]

Thus Girard was permitted to be buried in a Catholic churchyard and to share a plot with a Catholic niece's first husband, who was also a Catholic.

Bishop Francis Patrick Kenrick of the Roman Catholic Diocese of Philadelphia said in his diary that he allowed Girard to be buried "in consecrated ground for this reason chiefly: He had been baptized a Catholic, he never renounced (formally) communion with the Church; and, when taken sick, death stole upon him unperceived. It is right to believe that in other circumstances (if he had been conscious of approaching death) he would have asked for the ministry of a priest."[15] It was indicated in Bishop Kenrick's diary that a Catholic service had been planned for Girard, to precede his burial, but the service was cancelled at the last minute. "The body of Stephen Girard was brought to the Church of the Most Holy Trinity, with great funeral pomp," Bishop Kenrick said. "The Free Masons (commonly so called) were making a great display in honor of their (departed) brother. They wore a uniform vesture around the neck, were decked out with gems (medals or pins), and walked in public procession. When I saw them coming into the church thus adorned, I refused to go on with the (burial) rite of the Church, and the body was buried without the presence of a priest."[16]

Girard's will was more than a legal document. It was part essay, part philosophy, part personal opinion—with heavy doses of discourse on architecture, education and city planning. More than a decade after Girard died, when the will was still being contested in the courts, testimony before a committee of the Pennsylvania House of Representatives gave details on how the will was written. William J. Duane, the lawyer who assisted Girard in preparing the will, said the task took five or six weeks in early 1830, when Girard was seventy-nine, and they worked behind locked doors to maintain secrecy and prevent interruptions.

An earlier will, prepared in 1826 with assistance from a different lawyer, was modified and expanded. Duane said many sections of the 1830 will went through several drafts with heavy editing and repeated rewriting. In the process the two men had long discussions on numerous topics related directly or peripherally to the will. They included architecture, law, politics and religion. Duane emphasized that all of the ideas and wishes expressed in the will originated with Girard and that Girard did almost all of the writing in early drafts. "The outlines, the bones and the muscle of the will were all Mr. Girard's," Duane said.[17] The lawyer also indicated that Girard had written at least one will, maybe more than one, before the wills of 1826 and 1830.[18] He apparently had a fairly firm idea of what he wanted to do with most of his money long before his death, despite being almost eighty when he expressed it in final form. Duane testified that Girard had devised plans over a long period of time for a school for poor boys who had been orphaned. It was revealed by Duane that he had numerous conversations with Girard over a span of many years about creating such a school.[19] In the light of Duane's testimony it may be seen more clearly why Girard did not want to marry Polly Kenton (or any other woman, for that matter) after his wife died. If he had married again, with a second wife eventually inheriting millions of dollars, the amount left over to build and operate a school for orphans could have been quite skimpy.

Girard had been the richest American for twenty years when he died. His net worth at the time of his death was, in round numbers, seven and a half million dollars. That figure was used by two of Girard's nineteenth century biographers, Henry W. Arey and Henry Atlee Ingram, and is close to the mark. According to a calculation made by the author of this book, based on an analysis of eleven reports filed from 1832 to 1839 by executors of Stephen Girard's Will, by trustees of Stephen Girard's Bank, by commissioners of the Girard Estates, and by independent appraisers and auditors,[20] the net worth of Stephen Girard at the time of his death was approximately $7,670,000. To give some idea of how much money that was in 1831, consider this: Men working on Girard's farm were paid fifty cents a day.[21] Women doing farm work for Girard were paid three dollars a week.[22] (Hence men and women on his farm received essentially the same pay, assuming they all had one day off a week, which was generally the case except during times of planting and harvesting.) Women doing housework in Girard's home received sixty-two and a half cents a day.[23] Junior officers with day-to-day financial responsibilities in Stephen Girard's Bank, such as the first bookkeeper, the paying teller and the receiving teller, were paid twenty dollars a month or less.[24] Presidents of several major banks in Philadelphia were paid two thousand dollars a year.[25] As Ingram observed, writing from a perspective of more than fifty years after Girard died, his wealth not only was "the greatest fortune known in America" up to that time but also "was surpassed by few, if by any, of the private fortunes abroad."[26]

A precise determination of Girard's total wealth on the day he died was never made in a court of law. This was due to the unprecedented size and complexity of his estate, with some values changing constantly and with some goods beyond the jurisdiction of the United States. Exact dollar amounts were figured for portions of the estate, comprising collectively the vast majority of it, but not for the estate in its entirety. At the moment of his death Girard had accounts receivable and payable at ports scattered around the world. He had ships and cargoes on the high seas and in harbors hither and yon. Weeks or months passed before many of his captains, supercargoes and shipping agents learned that Girard had died. In the interim, goods were bought and sold as though he were still alive.

On the home front, he had loans outstanding, through his bank, totaling $3,479,961.[27] This huge sum, in itself a personal fortune almost unprecedented in size, was money owed to Girard, with interest, but not immediately available. Repayment schedules were not altered after he died. Debtors were instructed to keep on meeting their obligations under terms of their loan agreements, as though Girard were still alive. Most of the loans outstanding were for amounts less than five hundred dollars, underscoring Girard's policy of catering to the needs of small businesses rather than big businesses, and families of modest means rather than the wealthy.[28]

He owned real estate valued at $1,741,854. Most of it, valued at $1,522,143, was in Philadelphia and vicinity. Coal lands in Schuylkill County, in the anthracite region of Pennsylvania, were valued at $175,246, including extensive improvements that had been made relative to the mining of coal, which had already begun. More than 200,000 acres in Louisiana were listed at $42,681. Six thousand acres in northwestern Pennsylvania were valued at $1,784.[29]

At the time of his death Girard owned shares in the Second Bank of the United States valued at $664,715.[30]

He had another major investment of $276,484 in the Schuylkill Navigation Company.[31] That company, with Girard as the primary source of funding, had built the Little Schuylkill Navigation Railroad between Tamaqua and Port Clinton in Schuylkill County, a distance of twenty miles. The railroad had begun hauling anthracite in horse-drawn coal cars on November 23, 1831, just a little over a month before Girard died. On March 9, 1833, this railroad became the first in the anthracite region of Pennsylvania to carry coal in a train pulled by a steam locomotive.[32]

As mentioned earlier, Girard also had made large financial commit-ments to the Danville and Pottsville Railroad Company ($200,000) and the Mount Carbon Railroad ($30,000) which also became coal carriers in Schuylkill County. His funding of the Danville and Pottsville Railroad, on the installment plan, was on a schedule of ten payments of twenty thousand dollars each, and the full amount had not been paid when he died. Girard's executors continued the payments. The last one was made on September 21, 1833.[33]

All in all, Girard's investments in railroads, including payments made posthumously, surpassed the $500,000 mark. There can be little doubt that he would have become an even larger player in the pioneering era of railroad building if he had lived a few years longer.

Despite all of his other business and financial interests, Girard remained active in his first love, maritime trade, to the very end. He had a new ship under construction when he died. When his ships that had been on overseas voyages at the time of his death came back to their home port during 1832, officers and crew members were paid by the executors of Girard's will.

Payroll records show that Girard never lost his knack for running a tight ship, holding down costs and maximizing profits by carrying minimal crews consistent with safe and efficient operation. In the eighteenth century he had captained a two-masted brig of two hundred tons on trans-Atlantic runs with ten people on board, two officers and eight crew members. In the 1830s he had much larger ships, with three masts and ranging from three hundred tons to 375 tons, sailing not only across the Atlantic but as far as the East Indies and China with as few as fourteen and, at the most, nineteen people aboard, including three officers.[34]

Besides being unprecedented in size and scattered over much of the earth, Girard's wealth had a characteristic that was uniquely complex: No one had ever died before who was the owner of a bank all by himself, at least not a bank with millions of dollars in assets. The responsibility for settling Girard's estate was divided between trustees of his bank and executors of his will. It will be recalled that in 1812, when he had founded his bank as a sole proprietorship, unincorporated, unchartered, with no directors and no stockholders, he had anticipated that a potentially troublesome situation could arise when he died. To protect depositors and borrowers, he had appointed trustees and had vested in them the authority they would need to wind down the affairs of the bank in orderly fashion, after he died, without causing panic or inconvenience for customers or the public at large.

The plan worked. It may be said, with the advantage of hindsight, that Girard exercised sound judgment in keeping the executors of his will far removed from his banking business. There was no run on the bank when he died. His depositors, and holders of his bank notes, had faith in Girard's integrity. They had faith in the soundness of his bank.

They had faith in the competence of the trustees he had appointed. It was well that such faith prevailed. In 1836, five years after Girard died, auditors disclosed that the trustees of the bank found what they considered to be a disturbing situation when they took charge, immediately following his death. On-demand obligations, principally to depositors and to holders of bank notes (currency) in circulation, totaled $709,844. Yet there was only $17,530 in specie (gold and silver) in the vaults.[35] If large numbers of people had responded to the news of Girard's death by going to his bank and withdrawing their deposits in specie, and turning in their notes for specie, as they were lawfully entitled to do, the vaults would have been emptied quickly.

The trustees, as a precautionary measure, secretly applied for, and received, a credit line for $100,000 from the Second Bank of the United States.[36] From the back door of the Second Bank to the back door of Stephen Girard's Bank was less than three hundred yards. As much of the $100,000 as required, and probably additional hundreds of thousands of dollars, if needed, could have been borrowed and transported swiftly, in specie, if there had been a run on Stephen Girard's Bank. As it turned out, not one penny of the credit line was used.[37] There was no need for it. For nineteen years Girard had built a reputation as a banker who could be counted on. In death, as in life, that reputation held.

When Girard died, his fortune did not die. It continued to live and to grow. He had known that he could not take it with him, so he devised ways to perpetuate it. He demonstrated that it was possible to increase a fortune even while giving it away. He kept his executors busy not just counting and disbursing his money but doing things with it. At the time of his death he had plans in the works for massive real estate development on land he owned in what would become a part of downtown Philadelphia. Those plans were implemented as though he had not died. In a period of five and a half years, beginning in 1832 and ending in 1837, the executors of Girard's will erected seventy-eight buildings at a cost of $814,506 in the block bounded on the north by Market Street, on the south by Chestnut Street, on the east by Eleventh Street, and on the west by Twelfth Street (the same block that Joseph Bonaparte had tried, unsuccessfully, to buy). The new buildings consisted of twenty-two four-story brick stores with granite fronts and fifty-six four-story brick houses.[38] More than a century and a half later, real estate in that block would still be owned by administrators of Girard's estate, with rental income utilized to provide food, clothing, shelter and education for poor orphans enrolled at Girard College in Philadelphia. Founding and funding, forever, the school for orphans was the centerpiece of Girard's bequests that also included substantial sums for a long list of other benevolent enterprises ranging from charitable organizations to civic services and public works. He also gave generous amounts to relatives, employees and other individuals, but his wealth was so gigantic that these expenditures hardly put a dent in the total estate of $7,670,000. More than ninety-eight percent of Girard's net worth, a phenomenal and perhaps unprecedented percentage, was given away for philanthropic purposes, and most of this philanthropy was structured so that it will continue in perpetuity.

Thus Girard's will was really and truly a living will. Although he never really found a fountain of youth in his lifetime, he tapped an apparently inexhaustible fountain of money in his after-life. In the last twenty years before his death, from 1811 to 1831, he was constantly giving away significant amounts of money for charitable purposes. Yet his net worth was growing at a phenomenal pace, from two million dollars to more than seven and a half million dollars. In the first 160 years after his death, from 1831 to 1991, his fortune skyrocketed from $7,670,000 to $230,000,000, and that was after providing support and education for many thousands of orphans over the years, and after contributing funds for other charitable and civic enterprises as well. The $230,000,000 valuation of Girard's estate in 1991 included all real estate and more than $175,000,000 in other kinds of investments that were producing revenue.[39]

A century after his death, Girard's coal lands alone were generating millions of dollars a year in royalty income. By the late 1930s, when the widespread use of anthracite coal was coming to a close, Girard's estate had received $65,000,000 in coal royalties from the anthracite tracts that Girard had bought for $30,000 in 1830.[40]

Girard's imaginative use of trust funds set a standard for future philanthropists. His will defined in practical terms, not in theory but by example, how to carry on good works indefinitely from the grave. In pondering the provisions of Girard's will it is important to bear in mind that, as his lawyer said, an enormous amount of time and effort went into the writing and the rewriting. Moreover, as Duane also testified, the will was substantively the work of Girard even though the lawyer was responsible for some of the legal terminology. Thus the will tells something about Girard's innermost and carefully considered thoughts. They were articulated in his will when he was still quite active in business and very definitely of sound mind.

Girard's first thoughts in composing his will were not of Polly, the mistress who had served him for more than three decades while he was becoming a millionaire and then a multi-millionaire. His first thoughts were of two women who went even farther back in his life: Mary, his wife, and Hannah, his slave. He could leave nothing to Mary, of course, since she had preceded him in death by sixteen years, so he did the next best thing that he could do for her. His first bequest, thirty thousand dollars, was to Pennsylvania Hospital, the institution that had cared for her for a quarter of a century. His second bequest, and his first to an individual, was to Hannah. He gave his venerable slave (who was probably in her late seventies) her freedom. He also gave her financial security in the form of a lifetime income of two hundred dollars a year. To make sure that Hannah's income would be absolutely secure for the rest of her life, he linked it directly to his bequest to the hospital. He gave her first claim to the thirty thousand dollars. This is the language he used to establish the linkage:

> I give and bequeath unto 'The Contributors to the Pennsylvania Hospital,' of which corporation I am a member, the sum of thirty thousand dollars, upon the following conditions, namely, that the said sum shall be added to their capital, and shall remain a part thereof forever, to be placed at interest, and the interest thereof to be applied, in the first place, to pay my black woman Hannah (to whom I hereby give her freedom,) the sum of two hundred dollars per year, in quarterly payments of fifty dollars each in advance, during all the term of her life; and, in the second place, the said interest to be applied to the use and accommodation of the sick in the said Hospital, and for providing, and at all times having competent matrons, and a sufficient number of nurses and assistant nurses, in order not only to promote the purposes of the said Hospital, but to increase this last class of useful persons, much wanted in our City.[41]

So, in the culmination of a rather remarkable sequence of events, a slave who had given a daughter to a young Frenchman, John Girard, in St-Domingue in the 1770s, before there was a United States of America, ultimately had first claim to the first bequest in the will of the richest person in America in 1831.

Except for Hannah, no other woman had been a member of the household of Stephen Girard longer than Polly. She, too, was remembered in his will, although, perhaps, not to the extent that might have been expected. Identified in the will as "my late housekeeper," Polly was bequeathed a lifetime income of three hundred dollars a year.[42] That was enough, and then some, to provide a quite comfortable living, but it was a far cry from what she would have received if Stephen had married her.

Emeline, the pretty young niece of Polly who had succeeded her as Stephen's housekeeper, received a lifetime income in the same amount as Polly. Girard identified Emeline in the will as the "wife of Mr. Richard M. Taylor."[43]

Jane Taylor, Girard's housekeeper in his last years, was made the recipient of a lifetime income of five hundred dollars a year. She was identified in the will as "my present housekeeper (the widow of the late Captain Alexander Taylor, who was master of my ship *Helvetius*, and died in my employment)."[44]

Girard also bequeathed a lifetime annual income of five hundred dollars to Sarah Hesley, the housekeeper on his farm (and Polly Kenton's sister). He gave Sarah an additional three hundred dollars a year, for a total of eight hundred dollars annually, until her young daughter reached the age of twenty-one.[45] Additionally, Sarah's grown son received one thousand dollars in a lump sum.[46] Two of Polly's sisters who had lived in Girard's home on Water Street and had helped with housekeeping duties received lifetime incomes of three hundred dollars a year, the same amount that Polly received.[47]

Girard did not forget the captains of his ships in his will, but he found a way to keep them on their toes even after he died. To each captain who had completed at least two voyages in Girard's service and was still in his employ, the sum of fifteen hundred dollars was bequeathed "provided he shall have brought safely into the port of Philadelphia, or if at sea at the time of my decease, shall bring safely into that port, my ship or vessel last entrusted to him, and also that his conduct during the last voyage shall have been in every respect conformable to my instructions to him."[48] Always a stickler for having his orders carried out, Girard did not want any of his captains slacking off when they got word that their boss had died.

Girard's indentured servants and apprentices were rewarded with funds for clothing and education and with individual bequests of five hundred dollars in cash.[49] He gave a lifetime income of one thousand dollars a year to the widow of one of his former lawyers, Jared Ingersoll, an unexplained act of extraordinary generosity.[50] Numerous relatives of Girard were bequeathed what would normally have been considered huge amounts of money, by 1831 standards. However, there was nothing normal about Girard's wealth. Relatives who had been hoping for a million dollars or more, or at least hundreds of thousands of dollars, were disappointed when they were given just thousands of dollars. The three nieces he had raised in his home, the daughters of his brother John, received varying amounts. All three were in their thirties and married. Antoinette, the oldest of the three nieces, was left ten thousand dollars plus a lifetime income of unspecified amount in the form of interest and dividends from a trust fund of fifty thousand dollars, with the principal of the trust fund to go to her children when she died.[51] Caroline, the only one of the three nieces who had no living children in 1831 (her only child having died in infancy), did not receive any immediate bequest but was bequeathed a lifetime income of unspecified amount in the form of interest and dividends from a trust fund of ten thousand dollars, with the trust fund's principal to go to her children, if any, when she died. If she died without children, the trust fund's principal would go to the children of her sisters.[52] Henriette, the youngest of the three nieces, received ten thousand dollars in cash but no trust fund. Her daughter was the beneficiary of a trust fund of twenty thousand dollars, getting interest and dividends until she was twenty-one, and then the principal.[53] Girard did not explain why the nieces were treated differently. The variations may have reflected differences in the financial conditions of the nieces' husbands, with Girard setting the amounts according to need.

An assortment of relatives still living in France, including a brother and many nieces and nephews, received five thousand dollars each.[54]

The house where Girard was born, in Bordeaux, was bequeathed to the brother and one of the nieces.[55] A half-sister received a lifetime income of four hundred dollars a year.[56]

All told, the bequests to individuals, i.e., to relatives, employees, former employees and others, required outlays of cash totaling about $150,000 at the outset. That figure included payments in lump sums and money used to create trust funds in specified amounts. Many of the lifetime incomes to beneficiaries did not require trust funds. Girard stipulated that many of the incomes were to be financed with rents from real estate that he owned. Generally speaking, he wanted his properties that were capable of producing revenue to be retained rather than sold. (His house in Mount Holly, New Jersey, had been sold long ago.) While $150,000 was a large amount of money in 1831, it was less than two percent of $7,670,000. Girard bequeathed the remainder, more than seven and a half million dollars, for charitable and civic purposes. Rental revenue earmarked initially to provide annual incomes to individuals was converted to charitable purposes when the recipients died.

In addition to the previously mentioned thirty thousand dollars to Pennsylvania Hospital, Girard gave twenty thousand dollars to the Pennsylvania Institution for the Deaf and Dumb, twenty thousand dollars to the Grand Lodge of Pennsylvania (Masons) for "the relief of poor and respectable brethren," ten thousand dollars to create a trust fund to provide "in every year forever" fuel for distribution "amongst poor white house-keepers and room-keepers, of good character, residing in the City of Philadelphia," and ten thousand dollars to the Society for the Relief of Poor and Distressed Masters of Ships, Their Widows and Children, "of which Society I am a member."[57]

He also gave six thousand dollars to Passyunk Township, where his farm was located (now a part of Philadelphia), to "purchase a suitable piece of ground ... and thereon erect a substantial brick building, sufficiently large for a school-house, and the residence of a school-master, one part thereof for poor male white children, and the other part for poor female white children of said Township."[58]

Regarding 208,000 acres owned by Girard in Louisiana, he gave, conditionally, one thousand of them to Judge Henry Bree, a business associate in Louisiana who had managed Girard's holdings there. The will stipulated that Bree could use the one thousand acres for a "term of 20 years as if it was his own … and enjoy for his own use all of the net profits." The conditional bequest to Bree included, besides the one thousand acres, "appurtenances and improvements" and "upwards of thirty slaves now on said settlement, and their increase." It was stipulated that "no part of the said estate or property, or the slaves thereon, or their increase, shall be disposed of or sold for the term of twenty years." At the end of that time, or at Bree's death if he should not live that long, "the land and improvements forming said settlement, the slaves thereon, or thereto belonging, and all other appurtenant personal property, shall be sold" with proceeds going to the City of New Orleans for "such uses and purposes … most likely to promote the health and general prosperity of the inhabitants."[59] Thus, while Girard's will gave immediate freedom to his household slave, Hannah, there would be a continuation of the status quo for slaves he had owned but had never seen in Louisiana, and there would be slavery at birth for their children.

The conditional bequest of one thousand acres to Bree hardly put a dent in the 208,000 acres Girard had owned in Louisiana. The remaining 207,000 acres, which were undeveloped, were divided into two parts, with one part twice as large as the other. The smaller part, one third of the total, was bequeathed to the City of New Orleans with instructions that it be held for ten years and then sold "gradually from time to time" with the proceeds going, again, for "such uses and purposes … most likely to promote the health and general prosperity of the inhabitants."[60] The larger part, two thirds of the total, was bequeathed to the City of Philadelphia, also with instructions that it be held for ten years and then sold gradually from time to time, but the proceeds would go for "the same uses and purposes" as the "residue of my personal estate."[61] That "residue" was the heart and soul of Girard's estate.

Some seven thousand words of his will, about two-thirds of it, were devoted to the residue, with detailed instructions on what to do with the millions and millions of dollars that he knew would be left over after the previously enumerated individual, institutional, organizational and governmental beneficiaries had received their designated allotments.

A big piece of the residue, half a million dollars, was set aside for the City of Philadelphia to create a trust fund with the income to be used for various specified purposes, some of them tightly and narrowly defined.[62] First on the list was "to lay out, regulate, curb, light and pave a passage or street, on the east part of the City of Philadelphia, fronting the river Delaware, not less than twenty-one feet wide, and to be called Delaware Avenue, extending from Vine to Cedar Street [now South Street]."[63] Girard's objective, as he made clear, was to enhance the appearance of the waterfront and to improve public access to the river. In regard to appearance, he called upon the city "to compel the owners of the wharves to keep them clean."[64] Delaware Avenue from Vine to Cedar, passing between Girard's house and his wharves, was completed, fifty feet wide, in 1839.[65]

Second on the list of things that Philadelphia was instructed to do with income from the trust fund of $500,000 was "to pull down and remove all wooden buildings ... that are erected within the limits of the City of Philadelphia, and also to prohibit the erection of any such building within the said City's limits at any future time."[66] Third on the list was "to regulate, widen, pave and curb Water Street," a project he described in great detail through several pages of his will. He wanted the street to "be not less than thirty-nine feet wide, and afford a large and convenient footway, clear of obstructions and incumbrances of every nature, and the cellar doors on which, if any shall be permitted, not to extend from the buildings on to the footway more than four feet." He specified that the street "shall be repaved by the best workmen, in the most complete manner."[67]

Extensive improvements were made on Water Street, but many of the dwellings and offices, including Girard's, were soon torn down to make way for warehouses. Today, vehicles going north on Interstate 95 pass through space that used to be occupied by Girard's house.

Aside from the priority projects enumerated, Girard decreed that income from the trust fund of half a million dollars should be used by officials and citizens of Philadelphia "as they think proper, to the further improvement, from time to time, of the eastern or Delaware front of the City."[68]

Girard bequeathed $300,000 of the residue to the Commonwealth of Pennsylvania "for the purpose of internal improvements by canal navigation." He stipulated, however, that the Commonwealth would not get the money unless it enacted laws requiring Philadelphia to comply with his aforementioned wishes regarding Delaware Avenue, wooden buildings and Water Street. If Pennsylvania failed to enact these laws within one year after his death, Girard said in his will, the $300,000 must go to another beneficiary, "to the United States of America, for the purposes of internal navigation."[69] Pennsylvania lost no time enacting the laws that Girard had mandated. The Commonwealth received the $300,000 from the executors of Girard's will on April 19, 1832, less than four months after his death.[70]

Thus the usually humble Girard showed some flashes of arrogance when writing his will at the age of seventy-nine. However well-intentioned and worthy, the street improvements and zoning regulations prescribed for Philadelphia lost a bit of their luster when Girard made the $300,000 bequest to the state contingent on their approval. The old champion of Jeffersonian democracy, no doubt emboldened by the power of his money, allowed himself to become imperious.

Unspecified amounts of the residue of his estate, but only dividends and interest, not the principal, were authorized by Girard to be used "to enable the Corporation of the City of Philadelphia to provide more effectually than they now do, for the security of the persons and property of the inhabitants of the said City, by a competent police, including a sufficient number of watchmen, really suited to the purpose: and to this end, I recommend a division of the City into watch districts, or four parts, each under a proper head, and that at least two watchmen shall, in each round or station, patrol together."[71]

Girard also bequeathed an unspecified amount of the residue of his estate, dividends and interest only, not the principal, to enable Philadelphia "to improve the City property, and the general appearance of the City itself, and, in effect, to diminish the burden of taxation, now most oppressive, especially on those who are the least able to bear it."[72]

All of the foregoing bequests in Girard's will, as gigantic as they were, in the aggregate, would pale in comparison with The Big One: millions of dollars to build and operate a boarding school for "poor male white orphans."[73] Disgruntled relatives, wanting those millions for themselves, would fight tooth and nail to break the will.

CHAPTER 21

First a Fight in the Courts, Then an Enduring Legacy
After 1831

*If you want to see greed in its ugliest form, just
watch people contesting a rich relative's will.*

AS THE centerpiece of his will, Stephen Girard allocated two million dollars from the residue of his estate for construction of a boarding school for orphans and an unspecified number of additional millions, which in time would become hundreds of millions, to operate and maintain the school forever.

From the moment he wrote this provision in his will Girard knew that, when he died, the jackals would come. He knew that his relatives, including distant kin he had never met, would try to snatch these millions from the orphans so they could divide it up among themselves. Relatives trying to break his will would have to take aim at the school for orphans because that was where the money, the really big money, was. The only way the relatives could get millions and millions of dollars for themselves would be to take away millions and millions of dollars from the orphans. The relatives would have to kill the school, somehow and someway. They would have to block its construction and prohibit its operation. They would have to find a fatal flaw in the school or in the will. They would have to show, in some manner, that the school or the will was illegal or unconstitutional.

This had been constantly on Girard's mind as he was writing his will. William J. Duane testified that, when their many weeks of labor was finished and the completed will lay before them, Girard had asked him what he thought of it. The lawyer, knowing that his client valued candor, had answered him with a frank and honest opinion. The will, Duane told Girard, will never stand up in court.[1] Nonetheless, Girard had remained adamant. He was not going to compromise his wishes or change the wording in the will just to make it easier to defend in a courtroom.

Girard originally stipulated in his will, as it was written when he signed it on February 16, 1830, less than two years before he died, that the school for orphans must be built in the block bounded by Market, Chestnut, Eleventh and Twelfth Streets.[2] Nevertheless, the school was not located there. That was, in fact, the block where, as previously noted, twenty-two stores and fifty-six houses were built by his executors after he died.

In June of 1831, six months before he died, Girard signed a codicil to his will changing the location of the school to a newly acquired tract of forty-five acres in the country, a mile north of the city limits.[3] Girard referred to the school for orphans as a "college" in his will but said boys as young as six could be admitted. The institution, as he described it, would be a combination elementary school and secondary school, accommodating students in grades one through twelve.

The will gave minutely detailed descriptions of floor plans and supporting walls for the main building. Girard stipulated that at least four additional buildings must be erected at the outset. He said, moreover, that the school grounds had to be "enclosed with a solid wall, at least fourteen inches thick, and ten feet high, capped with marble and guarded with irons on the top, so as to prevent persons from getting over .... At each place of entrance there shall be two gates, one opening inward, and the other outward; those opening inward to be of iron ... and those opening outward to be of substantial wood work, well lined and secured on the faces thereof with sheet iron."[4]

In what would become a highly controversial provision, Girard also declared in his will:

"I enjoin and require that no ecclesiastic, missionary, or minister of any sect whatsoever, shall ever hold or exercise any station or duty whatever in the said College; nor shall any such person ever be admitted for any purpose, or as a visitor, within the premises appropriated to the purposes of the said College. In making this restriction, I do not mean to cast any reflection upon any sect or person whatsoever; but, as there is such a multitude of sects, and such a diversity of opinion amongst them, I desire to keep the tender minds of the orphans, who are to derive advantage from this bequest, free from the excitement which clashing doctrines and sectarian controversy are so apt to produce; my desire is, that all the instructors and teachers in the College shall take pains to instill into the minds of the scholars the purest principles of morality, so that, on their entrance into active life, they may, from inclination and habit, evince benevolence towards their fellow creatures, and a love of truth, sobriety, and industry, adopting at the same time such religious tenets as their matured reason may enable them to prefer."[5]

This statement is very characteristic of eighteenth century French Enlightenment thought and reinforces the view that Girard's long-running fascination with the French *philosophes*, especially Voltaire and Rousseau, continued undiminished in old age. Girard's relatives, however, were not interested in his philosophical bent. This stipulation in his will gave them the opening they were looking for. They would contend that a school for orphans that barred ecclesiastics, missionaries and ministers was in violation of constitutional guarantees of freedom of religion. The relatives saw this provision as the Achilles heel of Girard's will. Ultimately, they hired Daniel Webster, widely hailed as "the most brilliant orator in America,"[6] to argue their case before the Supreme Court of the United States.

Girard's relatives, some of them living in the United States (including the three nieces he had raised in his home) but many of them living in France, played their cards carefully. They refrained from hasty or rash action, and they bided their time. They did not contest the will until they had received their inheritances, thus making sure that, whatever the outcome of their litigation, they would at least have safely and securely in their hands whatever Girard had bequeathed to them.

After the disbursements had been made, the relatives filed suit initially for a rather small additional amount, testing the judicial waters cautiously. It was contended by the relatives, in their first suit, that provisions of Girard's will concerning real estate did not apply to properties acquired by him after the will was written. Realizing that he might be vulnerable to such a maneuver, Girard had written a codicil stating he wanted to include in his will "several parcels and pieces of real estate" he had purchased after the will was written "as well as any real estate that I may hereafter purchase." The codicil was signed on Christmas Day in 1830, one year and one day before he died. It is noteworthy that the signing of the codicil took place just four days after Girard had been seriously injured when run over by horses and a wagon. He may have felt that he might not have long to live.

The codicil notwithstanding, the Pennsylvania Supreme Court, after hearing arguments on March 29, 1833, ruled that nine properties owned by Girard at the time of his death, with purchase prices totaling $66,418, were not covered in his will and must be divided among his relatives (who could, if they wished, sell the properties and divide the money).[7] Those nine properties did not, however, include the tract of forty-five acres that Girard had bought in the spring of 1831 to be the site of the school for orphans. As noted previously, Girard had written another codicil to his will specifying that the school was to be located on that tract.

Encouraged by the court victory in the case of the nine properties, Girard's relatives and their lawyers began preparing a suit seeking to invalidate Girard's plans for a school for orphans. That suit was filed in 1836 in the U.S. Circuit Court for the Eastern District of Pennsylvania. The defendants were the City of Philadelphia and the executors of Girard's will. Besides Girard's lawyer, William J. Duane, the executors were John A. Barclay, Thomas P. Cope, Timothy Paxson and Joseph Roberts. Barclay had been the chief clerk in Girard's counting-house. Cope was the prosperous merchant who kept a diary (quoted several times in this book). Paxson, one of Philadelphia's largest dealers in flour, had his place of business on Water Street one block north of Girard's residence.[8] Roberts was the employee of Stephen Girard's Bank who became the cashier after George Simpson died.

The principal plaintiffs, acting in behalf of Girard's relatives collectively, were a niece and a nephew, Francoise Fenelon Vidal and John Fabricus Girard. They were the chief instigators of the move to break the will of their uncle. Other relatives had joined the suit, some reluctantly, to protect their interests and to be sure that, if the suit was successful, they would share fully in the booty. Hence the suit was listed formally as *Vidal et. al. v. the City of Philadelphia.* The suit was also known, more familiarly, as the Girard Will Case. An unqualified victory was won by the City of Philadelphia in the U.S. Circuit Court, which upheld Girard's will on all counts at issue. The plaintiffs then appealed to the U.S. Supreme Court. That tribunal held a preliminary hearing in 1843, followed by final arguments in 1844.

In those days, lawyers appearing before the Supreme Court did not have to boil down all they wanted to say to just one hour, as they would be required to do in a later time. Each side in the Girard Will Case was allowed five days for final arguments. The plaintiffs appeared to have achieved a significant advantage when they were successful in obtaining Daniel Webster to represent them before the Supreme Court. He was in the highest echelon of distinguished Americans of his time. Besides being widely acclaimed as the nation's greatest orator, he was also generally recognized as the "ablest lawyer" practicing before the Supreme Court.[9] Moreover, he has been appropriately described as "at the full tide of his power" in 1844.[10] He was sixty-two years old and had served in Congress, first in the House and then in the Senate, for more than twenty years. More recently, as secretary of state, he had represented the United States in negotiating the Webster-Ashburton Treaty with Great Britain, which had settled long-standing disputes over territory along the U.S.-Canadian border. He had received fourteen electoral votes for president in 1836.

More to the point, Webster had been the lawyer on the winning side in two landmark cases before the U.S. Supreme Court, *McCulloch v. Maryland* and the Dartmouth College Case. *McCulloch v. Maryland,* as discussed in an earlier chapter, upheld the constitutionality of the Second Bank of the United States and affirmed the right of the federal government to participate in banking activities, while invalidating Maryland's tax on the Second Bank and declaring that a state does not have a constitutional right to tax an entity of the federal government. The Dartmouth College Case, also known as *Dartmouth College v. Woodward,* affirmed the sanctity of institutional and corporate charters, making them equal with contracts under the law, and declared that a state does not have a constitutional right to nullify arbitrarily the provisions of a lawfully created contract or charter.

With these notches already on his belt, Webster was quite a catch for Girard's relatives as their fight to break the will entered its crucial final phase. Yet, Webster faced a formidable adversary in Horace Binney, a distinguished Philadelphia lawyer, sixty-three years old, who was engaged to defend the city and the executors before the Supreme Court. He had helped Girard write an earlier will, in 1826, and was familiar with his most intimate thoughts regarding a school for orphans.

Each side had two lawyers for the showdown. Assisting Webster was Walter Jones. With Binney was John Sergeant.

Girard's will was attacked by the plaintiffs on a broad front. They argued, for example, that the City of Philadelphia, in the absence of any lawful authority to do so, could not legally accept a bequest of real and personal property for the purpose of creating and operating a school for orphans. The plaintiffs argued, moreover, that Girard's bequest, although supposedly for charitable purposes, was intended to benefit unnamed orphans of indefinite number and consequently was too vague to be implemented under laws of Pennsylvania governing charities.

The main assault, though, was on the religious issue. In three days of highflying oratory before the Supreme Court, sixty percent of his allotment of five days, Webster devoted his attention to the religious issue exclusively. He hammered away at Girard's exclusion of ecclesiastics, missionaries and ministers from the school for orphans, even as visitors. This exclusion, Webster argued eloquently and emotionally, was fundamentally at odds with freedom of religion as constitutionally guaranteed to the people. In essence, the position of the plaintiffs was that Girard's "plan of education" for the orphans "was derogatory to the Christian religion, contrary to sound morals, and subversive to law."[11] Webster described the central objective of himself and his clients in noble terms, calling it "a defense of Christianity against the inroads of paganism and infidelity."[12]

Binney, who might have been expected to be overshadowed by Webster, rose to the occasion. Going to the crux of Webster's argument, Binney denied emphatically that Girard's will was anti-Christian or barred Christianity from the school for orphans. Moreover, Binney noted, there was no constitutional requirement in Pennsylvania or in America that Christianity be taught in a school. Girard, Binney said, "has used plain, familiar, and intelligible words. There is no ambiguity whatever in them. They have a clear, definite meaning, which any man, learned or unlearned, may apprehend; and it is one meaning, and neither more nor less. He enjoins and requires, and this is all that he has said, and all that he means, that no ecclesiastic, missionary, or minister, of any sect whatsoever, shall ever hold or exercise any station or duty whatever in the said College, and that no such person shall ever be admitted for any purpose, or as a visitor, within the premises appropriated for the purposes of the said College. This is a meaning as lawful as it is plain. We may think what we please of the injunction, as uncourteous, disrespectful, inexpedient .... But we cannot think ... that what it thus plainly means to enjoin is unlawful. In other words, no man will say that any ecclesiastic, missionary, or minister, of any sect whatever, has a *lawful* right to hold or exercise any station or duty in such a college, or to admission for any purpose, or as a visitor within the premises, *against the will or injunction of the founder of it.* If this exclusion be its meaning and end, there never was, and never can be, a more lawful injunction by the founder of a school or college, be the consequences what they may."[13]

Binney added: "All that with any semblance of truth can be charged against his Will, is that it *omits expressly to provide for the teaching of Christianity*: and if this is a fatal defect, no endowment of a school for instruction in human learning only, can ever be lawful—which is an absurdity." Binney said there was no way that Girard's will could be found unlawful unless "the law under all circumstances requires Christianity to be taught in every school, and also that it should be expressly provided for by the founder."[14]

Emphasizing, moreover, that Girard did not exclude the teaching of Christianity to the orphans in his school, Binney said: "He says expressly, that his teachers in the College must take pains to instil into the minds of the scholars the *purest principles of morality*, so that on their entrance into active life, they may evince benevolence towards their fellow-creatures, and a love of truth, sobriety and industry, adopting at the same time such religious tenets as their matured reason may enable them to prefer. Interpreting these expressions with any, the least candor, can they be understood to prohibit the Bible, from which the purest morality is drawn, or the evidences of Christianity, or such systems of Christian morals, as place them upon the sure and only basis of Christianity? I answer no .... Mr. Girard has enjoined instruction in the *purest morality.* He has given no statement of the basis on which he requires it to be taught. He has not said a word in opposition to the universal scheme of all Christian countries and seminaries."[15]

Zeroing in on the constitutional question, Binney said: "There is no law that says Christianity shall be taught in our schools, by Christian ministers. Is there any law that says it shall be taught at all? The Constitution is at the remotest distance possible, from doing the mischief to Christianity, of imposing its faith upon any one."[16]

In this context Binney was referring to the Constitution of Pennsylvania, but his argument could have been applied with equal force to the Constitution of the United States. Girard, far from being opposed to freedom of religion, was in accord with the most fundamental principle of religious freedom in America: separation of church and state.

Binney had effectively turned the tables on Webster, persuading the court that there was nothing in Girard's will that was either un-Christian or unconstitutional, and that, to the contrary, it was the plaintiffs who sought to erode constitutional protections of religious freedom by trying to prohibit creation of a school that would not admit ecclesiastics, missionaries and ministers to its premises.

The Supreme Court upheld Girard's will unanimously in 1844. Justice Joseph Story wrote the opinion. It ran nearly ten thousand words, almost as long as Girard's will. The court ruled against the plaintiffs on all of the substantive questions they had raised.

On the religious issue, Justice Story summarized in one long sentence the objection of the plaintiffs that Webster had expounded for three days:

"This objection is that the foundation of the College upon the principles and exclusions prescribed by the Testator is derogatory and hostile to the Christian religion, and is so void, as being against the common law and public policy of Pennsylvania, and this for two reasons; first, because of the exclusion of all Ecclesiastics, Missionaries and Ministers of any sect, from holding or exercising any station or duty in the College, or even visiting the same; and secondly, because it limits the instruction to be given to the scholars to pure morality, and general benevolence, and a love of truth, sobriety and industry, thereby excluding by implication all instruction in the Christian Religion."[17]

Justice Story, in the core of his opinion as it concerned the religious issue, delved into the heart of the controversy in several long and compelling paragraphs, as follows:

"The Testator does not say that Christianity shall not be taught in the College, but only that no ecclesiastic of any sect shall hold or exercise any station or duty in the College. Suppose, instead of this, he had said that no person but a layman shall be an instructor, or officer, or visitor in the College, what legal objection could have been made to such a restriction? And yet the actual prohibition is in effect the same in substance. But it is asked; why are ecclesiastics excluded, if is not because they are the stated and appropriate preachers of Christianity? The answer may be given in the very words of the Testator: —'In making this restriction, (says he,) I do not mean to cast any reflection upon any sect or person whatsoever; but as there is such a multitude of sects, and such a diversity of opinion amongst them, I desire to keep the tender minds of the orphans, who are to derive advantage from this bequest, free from the excitement which clashing doctrines and sectarian controversy are so apt to produce.' Here, then, we have the reason given ....

"Suppose the Testator had excluded all religious instructors but Catholics, or Quakers, or Swedenborgians; or to put a stronger case, he had excluded all religious instructors but Jews, would the bequest have been void on that account? Suppose he had excluded all lawyers, or all physicians, or all merchants from being instructors or visitors, would the prohibition have been fatal to the bequest? The truth is, that in cases of this sort, it is extremely difficult to draw any just and satisfactory line of distinction in a free country, as to the qualifications or disqualifications which may be insisted upon by the donor of a charity, as to those who shall administer or partake of his bounty ....

"The objection, itself, assumes the proposition that Christianity is not to be taught, because ecclesiastics are not to be instructors or officers. But this is by no means a necessary or legitimate inference from the premises. Why may not laymen instruct in the general principles of Christianity, as well as ecclesiastics? There is no restriction as to the religious opinions of the instructors and officers .... Why may not the Bible, and especially the New Testament, without note or comment, be read and taught as a divine revelation, in the College—its general precepts expounded, its evidences explained, and its glorious principles of morality inculcated? What is there to prevent a work, not sectarian, upon the general evidences of Christianity, from being read and taught in the College by lay teachers? Certainly there is nothing in the Will that proscribes such studies. Above all, the Testator positively enjoins, 'That all the instructors and teachers in the College shall take pains to instil into the minds of the scholars the purest principles of morality' .... The Testator has not said how these great principles are to be taught, or by whom, except it be by laymen, nor what books are to be used to explain or enforce them. All that we can gather from his language is, that he desired to exclude sectarians and sectarianism from the College, leaving the instructors and officers free to teach the purest morality, the love of truth, sobriety and industry by all appropriate means ....

   "It is the unanimous opinion of the Court, that the decree of the Circuit Court ... ought to be affirmed, and it is accordingly affirmed."[18]

   Thus the Girard Will Case produced a decision of the Supreme Court of the United States that was a ringing affirmation of religious freedom, but not in the way that Daniel Webster had envisioned.

   Stephen Girard, thirteen years after his death, emerged from the litigation with his integrity intact, a man who had been perceptive enough to understand, when many others did not, that freedom of religion is not truly meaningful unless it belongs to the people and not, exclusively, to religious professionals on the payrolls of churches. As for the plaintiffs, especially those who lived in France, there is no evidence that they cared one whit about religious instruction for poor orphans in Philadelphia. The objective of the plaintiffs, their one and only objective, had been to prevent millions of dollars in Stephen Girard's estate from being used to educate orphans so that they (the plaintiffs) could have those millions for themselves. The decision of the Supreme Court dashed their hopes. Even if the Supreme Court had declared the religious provisions in Girard's will to be unconstitutional, there is no certainty that the money earmarked for a school for orphans would have gone instead to Girard's relatives. The school might have come into being anyway. It is quite possible that the court, if it had nullified Girard's ban on ecclesiastics, missionaries and ministers, would have ordered the school to be built and to be operated without the ban. In that case, Girard's relatives would have been left with a hollow victory and no monetary gain.

It is significant that the relatives did not challenge the will on grounds of discrimination on the basis of race and sex. Even though Girard had specified that those admitted to the school for orphans must be white males, that was not a controversial provision in 1831. Slavery was still lawful in much of the country, and even where blacks were free, hardly anyone was saying they were equal. As for women, they continued to lack anything even remotely resembling equality in social, civil and political rights. American society was of the whites, by the whites and for the whites. It was of the males, by the males and for the males. Girard's will, in 1831, would have caused more of a stir, and might have been vulnerable to a successful challenge in the courts, if he had insisted on mixing the races and the sexes in his school for orphans.

Supreme Court approval of Girard's will in 1844 cleared the way for the school for orphans to become a reality. Work had begun more than a decade earlier and was well advanced by 1844. A Board of Directors had been created on February 11, 1833, headed by Nicholas Biddle. He was president of the Second Bank of the United States and had been a long-time friend of Girard. Ground had been broken for the main building, which would be named Founder's Hall, on May 6, 1833, and the cornerstone had been laid on the Fourth of July of that year.[19] The school had been named Girard College in honor of its founder and benefactor, although Girard did not give the school a name in his will and did not suggest that the school bear his name.

The tract of forty-five acres of farm land where Girard College was built (and where it has been ever since) was purchased from William Parker and was located on Ridge Road in Penn Township. The acreage and surrounding area became part of Philadelphia in 1854. After that, rural characteristics gave way rapidly to residential and commercial development. Ridge Road, bordering the college on the east, became Ridge Avenue. Girard Avenue, the main east-west thoroughfare in that part of Philadelphia, intersects with the walled-in campus both on the east and on the west. The college was built before the avenue.

The square block originally intended by Girard to be the site of the school for orphans was less than ten acres. The school would have been cramped on that site, and it would have been difficult to acquire additional acreage in that area because surrounding blocks were already developed by the time of Girard's death or soon after.

There is no indication that Girard ever considered locating the school for orphans on his 567-acre farm in Passyunk Township, now a part of Philadelphia. A school on that site would have had virtually unlimited potential for expansion of enrollment and facilities without congestion and while retaining large areas of open space.

Girard set forth in his will in a straightforward manner his humanitarian concerns that motivated him to found a school for poor orphans:

"I have been for a long time impressed with the importance of educating the poor, and of placing them, by the early cultivation of their minds and the development of their moral principles, above the many temptations to which, through poverty and ignorance they are exposed; and I am particularly desirous to provide for such a number of poor male white orphan children, as can be trained in one institution, a better education, as well as a more comfortable maintenance, than they usually receive from the application of the public funds."[20]

Providing for a boarding school for orphans in his will was, in a sense, an extension of what Girard had been doing much of his life. He had given room and board and education to his orphaned nieces and to apprentices in his counting-house and to relatives of his mistresses for many years. The dozens of youngsters he raised and educated while he was alive were predecessors of the students who would attend Girard College.

To fully appreciate the significance of Girard's bequest for a school for orphans, it needs to be understood that opportunities for education for poor children in Philadelphia were either nonexistent or grossly inadequate during his lifetime. There were no public schools at all in the city until 1818. Beginning in that year, there was a primitive public school system for poor children only, a system that segregated the poor and condemned them to second-class schooling. The quality of education in these early public schools was substantially inferior to the offerings in private schools. So was the quality of the physical surroundings. The impoverished pupils attended classes that typically were held in makeshift facilities in run-down buildings not built to be schools. It was a low-budget school system without teachers. Older children taught younger children with adult supervision, a form of self-education known as the Lancastrian method, named after Joseph Lancaster, who introduced the system in England.[21]

It was not until 1836, five years after Girard's death, that Philadelphia began public education with teachers, and without a requirement that the pupils be poor. Although Girard required that the pupils in his school for orphans be poor, his aim was not to discriminate against them because of their poverty. Just the opposite. His aim was to give the poor an education at least equal, and preferably superior, to education available to the affluent.

Girard stipulated in his will that the school for orphans must be "sufficiently spacious for the residence and accommodation of at least three hundred scholars, and the requisite teachers and other persons necessary in such an institution as I direct to be established." He specified further that the school must be supplied "with decent and suitable furniture, as well as books and all things needful to carry into effect my general design." He said the school "shall be constructed with the most durable materials, and in the most permanent manner, avoiding needless ornament, and attending chiefly to the strength, convenience, and neatness of the whole."[22]

He said the main building of the school for orphans must be at least 110 feet wide and 160 feet long. "It shall be three stories in height, each story at least fifteen feet high in the clear from the floor to the cornice: It shall be fire proof inside and outside. The floors and the roof to be formed of solid materials, on arches turned on proper centres, so that no wood may be used, except for doors, windows and shutters: Cellars shall be made under the whole building .... There shall be a cellar window under and in a line with each window in the first story—they shall be built one half below, and the other half above the surface of the ground, and the ground outside each window shall be supported by stout walls; the sashes should open inside, on hinges, like doors, and there should be strong iron bars outside each window; the windows inside and outside should not be less than four feet wide in the clear: There shall be in each story four rooms, each room not less than fifty feet square in the clear."[23]

Girard continued in great length and meticulous detail for page after page in his will, describing the school's main building. Entry halls at each end had to include

> a double staircase, to be carried up through the several stories; the steps of the stairs to be made of smooth white marble, with plain square edges, each step not to exceed nine inches in the rise, nor to be less than ten inches in the tread .... The first floor shall be at least three feet above the level of the ground around the building .... All the outside foundation walls, forming the cellars, shall be three feet six inches thick up to the first floor, or as high as may be necessary to fix the centres for the first floor .... When carried so far up, the outside walls shall be reduced to two feet in thickness, leaving a recess outside of one foot, and inside of six inches .... A chain, composed of bars of inch square iron, each bar about ten feet long, and linked together by hooks formed of the ends of the bars, shall be laid straightly and horizontally along the several walls, and shall be as tightly as possible worked into the centre of them throughout, and shall be secured wherever necessary, especially at all the angles, by iron clamps solidly fastened ... to prevent cracking or swerving in any part.[24]

Notwithstanding all of these details, and many, many more, regarding design and construction of the main building, Girard did not stipulate a style of architecture for the exterior. He said "utility and good taste" should be the determining factors in making decisions about aspects of the building he did not specify.[25]

It was Nicholas Biddle, who was chairman of the Building Committee as well as president of the Board of Directors, who suggested that the main edifice (Founder's Hall) be styled in the form of an ancient Greek temple. He had been to Greece and had been impressed by the beauty of the architecture he had seen there.

Thomas U. Walter, a native of Philadelphia, was selected to be the architect of Founder's Hall. He, too, went to Europe to study first-hand numerous specimens of classical architecture.[26] Founder's Hall has been called, without overstatement, "one of the finest examples of Greek Revival architecture" in America.[27] Walter later designed the dome of the Capitol of the United States.

Girard said in his will that "a competent number of instructors, teachers, assistants, and other necessary agents shall be selected" for the school, and "they shall receive adequate compensation for their services: but no person shall be employed, who shall not be of tried skill in his or her proper department, of established moral character, and in all cases persons shall be chosen on account of their merit, and not through favour or intrigue."[28]

In regard to students, Girard went into great detail about how they should be selected, cared for, and taught:

"As many poor male white orphans, between the age of six and ten years, as the said income shall be adequate to maintain, shall be introduced into the College as soon as possible; and from time to time, as there may be vacancies, or as increased ability from income may warrant, others shall be introduced ....

"If there shall be at any time, more applicants than vacancies, and the applying orphans shall have been born in different places, a preference shall be given—first to orphans born in the City of Philadelphia; secondly, to those born in any other part of Pennsylvania; thirdly, to those born in the City of New York (that being the first port on the continent of North America at which I arrived) and lastly, to those born in the City of New Orleans, being the first port on the said continent at which I first traded, in the first instance as first officer, and subsequently as master and part owner of a vessel and cargo ....

"Orphans admitted into the College, shall be there fed with plain but wholesome food, clothed with plain but decent apparel, (no distinctive dress ever to be worn) and lodged in a plain but safe manner. Due regard shall be paid to their health, and to this end their persons and clothes shall be kept clean, and they shall have suitable and rational exercise and recreation. They shall be instructed in the various branches of a sound education: comprehending Reading, Writing, Grammar, Arithmetic, Geography, Navigation, Surveying, Practical Mathematics, Astronomy, Natural, Chemical and Experimental Philosophy, the French and Spanish languages, (I do not forbid, but I do not recommend, the Greek and Latin languages) and such other learning and science as the capacities of the several scholars may merit or warrant. I would have them taught facts and things, rather than words or signs; and especially, I desire that by every proper means a pure attachment to our republican institutions, and to the sacred rights of conscience, as guaranteed by our happy constitutions, shall be formed and fostered in the minds of the scholars ....

"Should it unfortunately happen, that any of the orphans admitted into the College, shall, from malconduct, have become unfit companions for the rest, and mild means of reformation prove abortive, they should no longer remain therein ....

"Those scholars who shall merit it shall remain in the College until they shall respectively arrive at between fourteen and eighteen years of age; they shall then be bound out ... to suitable occupations, as those of agriculture, navigation, arts, mechanical trades, and manufactures, according to the capacities and acquirements of the scholars respectively, consulting, as far as prudence shall justify it, the inclinations of the several scholars, as to the occupation, art or trade, to be learned ....

"I leave, necessarily, many details to the Mayor, Aldermen and Citizens of Philadelphia, and their successors; and I do so, with the more confidence, as from the nature of my bequests, and the benefit to result from them, I trust that my fellow-citizens of Philadelphia will observe and evince especial care and anxiety in selecting members for their City Councils, and other agents."[29]

It is apparent from all the provisions in Girard's will relative to the school for orphans that he had given a great deal of thought not only to the physical appearance of the facility but also to the kind of education that would be offered. Sixteen years after his death the dream was realized. Founder's Hall, under construction for fourteen and a half years, was completed in November of 1847, as were four other buildings.[30] Girard College officially opened on January 1, 1848, with an initial enrollment of one hundred orphans. A second hundred were admitted on October 1 of that year and a third hundred on April 1, 1849.[31]

Henry W. Arey, the first secretary of the college, wrote a detailed and sometimes highly technical description of Founder's Hall and some of the techniques employed in its construction. Selected excerpts should enhance appreciation of the remarkable and painstaking workmanship that went into this magnificent building.

Arey recorded that there are

> eight columns on each end, and eleven on each side, counting the corner columns both ways, making in all thirty-four columns. The order of architecture ... is Grecian Corinthian. The columns are six feet in diameter, and fifty-five in height; the bases are nine feet three inches in diameter, and three feet two inches high, and the capitals are eight feet six inches high, and nine feet four inches wide .... The corner columns have one and one-half inches more diameter than the intermediate ones, for the purpose of overcoming the apparent reduction in their size arising from their insulated position .... The net amount of marble in each column, including the base and capital, is 1,346 cubic feet; the weight 103 tons ....

"The roof is composed of marble tiles, four and a half feet long, four feet wide, and two and three-fourth inches thick in the middle; the sides being elevated an inch and a half above the general surface, to prevent the water from running into the joints at their junction. Each of these joints is covered with a marble saddle, four and a half feet in length, ten inches in width, and six and a half inches in thickness, and hollowed out on the under side so as to embrace the ridges on two adjacent tiles. Every upper tile overlaps the one below six inches; and the under side is grooved and fitted to corresponding ridges and projections on the surface, thus preventing admission of water from beating rains or capillary attraction. At the same time their construction is such as to admit of being laid without coming actually in contact with each other, thus rendering them free to expand and contract with the various changes of temperature ....

"These tiles rest on nine inch brick walls, built four feet apart from centre to centre, across the whole building, on the upper surface of the third story arches. This plan of support affords access at all times to the underside of every tile, and facilitates examination in case of leakage."[32]

Arey also recorded that the roof has 2,046 tiles weighing 776 pounds each and 2,061 saddles weighing 214 pounds each. The roof, additionally, has marble chimney tops and cast-iron skylights weighing twenty tons, and lead and masonry gutters weighing forty-three tons. The total weight of the roof is 969 tons.[33] The total weight of the building, Arey reported, is 76,594 tons. That figure includes more than twelve million bricks weighing 27,087 tons, 13,537 tons of marble and 1,717 tons of granite.[34]

It was fitting that this behemoth of a building, Founder's Hall, was styled to look like a temple, for the students of Girard College, from the very beginning, were steeped in religion. Worship services were a mandatory part of the college routine seven days a week. From Monday through Friday the students attended two worship services a day, at seven in the morning (after breakfast) and at five in the afternoon (immediately following a very long day in the classrooms). On Saturday there was a morning service at seven but none in the afternoon. Every Sunday the students were required to attend four religious services. Two of them, at nine in the morning and two in the afternoon, were in small groups in dormitory buildings and were similar to a Sunday school, with religious reading and instruction. The other two Sunday services, at 10:30 in the morning and 3:30 in the afternoon, were worship services for the entire student body and included a sermon delivered by the president of the college or someone he designated to perform that duty. All worship services, daily and Sunday, included the singing of a hymn, the reading of a chapter from the Bible, and a prayer.[35]

So, all told, the students were required to attend fifteen religious services a week. That was a huge dose of religion, by any standard. In that context it becomes rather apparent that the relatives of Stephen Girard were being absurd when they alleged that he was trying to keep religion and the teaching of religion out of his school for orphans. Quite obviously, Justice Story had been right: There was nothing in Girard's will that would forbid religious services or religious instruction.

Discipline at Girard College was unusually benign by nineteenth century standards. As Arey described it: "Discipline ... is almost entirely administered through admonition, deprivation of recreation, and seclusion; but in extreme cases, corporal punishment may be inflicted by order of the President, and in his presence."[36] Making corporal punishment a last resort, and permissible only with the president of the college present, was in accord with the provision in Girard's will that the orphans be subjected only to "mild means of reformation." This was extraordinarily humane treatment in a time when giving a youngster a licking with a birch rod or a leather strap was so commonplace that being "taken to the woodshed" had become a part of the language. Thus in exercising moderation and showing compassion in the disciplining of students, Girard College was from the outset an institution far ahead of its time, just as Stephen Girard had so often been a man far ahead of his time.

Girard's will did not define "orphan." Dictionaries generally give the word two meanings: "a child whose father and mother are dead: sometimes applied to a child who has lost only one parent by death."[37] However, the directors of Girard College chose, in the beginning, to give the word their own definition: "a fatherless child."[38] Accordingly, persons applying for admission to the college in behalf of a prospective student had to state when and where the boy's father had died. The mother could be living or dead. Later, admission requirements were broadened. A boy who had lost his mother, but not his father, could be admitted. Sometimes a boy with both parents living was enrolled, usually when a father had deserted his family or, in some other circumstance, was not providing adequate support, or any support at all, for his child.

In the early years of Girard College, for most of its first century actually, there was very little, if any, public assistance for the poor. Waiting lists of prospective students were common. Facilities expanded and enrollment grew to one thousand and well beyond. Upon graduation the typical "Girard boy" went directly into the work force, utilizing skills he had learned at the college. All this would change later.

Three years after Girard College opened, Stephen Girard's remains were moved from the graveyard at Holy Trinity Roman Catholic Church to Founder's Hall at the college. The transfer led to a bizarre court battle, bordering on the ghoulish, over custody of the remains. In 1833, soon after City Council had approved plans for Founder's Hall, the Building Committee of Girard College had obtained permission from the Council to construct a vault "in the most suitable and durable manner" and to move Girard's body to the college at the earliest feasible time.[39] On December 30, 1850, nineteen years, to the day, after Girard was buried, the Philadelphia Health Office granted a request from the Commissioners of the Girard Estates for a permit to open Girard's grave and remove the remains, as authorized by City Council seventeen years earlier. Permission for removal also was granted by church authorities.[40]

Early in 1851—it was either January 6 or January 7; there is some question about the precise date—the remains of Stephen Girard were removed from the grave. They were taken, first, to the undertaking establishment of Simon Gartland on Thirteenth Street north of Chestnut Street. There, the lead coffin was opened in the presence of a number of witnesses, including some members of City Council. When the coffin was opened, according to one account, "a quantity of gas burst out and was exploded by the flame of a candle." The beard of a City Councilman was singed.[41] The undertaker reported that the remains consisted of "a skull and a handful of bones."[42] After the coffin had been resealed, it was placed inside another coffin.[43] Very soon thereafter, on January 9, 1851, the remains were taken to Girard College. On that same day, January 9, a memorial service was conducted at the college with the college president presiding. In attendance were students, faculty and staff of the college. Also witnessing the proceedings were the aforementioned Commissioners of the Girard Estates, who were the official custodians and administrators of assets willed by Girard to the City of Philadelphia.[44]

Immediately following the service the remains were taken to a room in the northwest corner of the third floor of Founder's Hall. The president of the Commissioners of the Girard Estates then locked the door of the room and turned the key over to the president of the college. He was to keep the remains safe until a sarcophagus—which would include a life-size marble statue of Girard, already completed—could be installed on the first floor near the building's main entrance.[45] With Stephen Girard's remains securely under lock and key at Girard College, City Council gave the Commissioners of the Girard Estates instructions to reinter the remains in a permanent location at the college in a manner that would be both "expedient and appropriate."[46]

Relatives of Stephen Girard, still smarting from their defeat in the

U.S. Supreme Court seven years earlier, filed suit in the Philadelphia Court of Common Pleas, seeking an injunction against removal of Girard's remains from the churchyard. The relatives contended that the removal was illegal because no one had asked for, or had received, their permission. The central question of the litigation became: Who owns Girard's remains? Girard's relatives claimed ownership. They declared also that neither the City of Philadelphia nor Girard College had any lawful grounds for claiming ownership.[47] In his will, Girard had said nothing about the school for orphans being his final resting place. The will did stipulate, however, that "a room [in the school] most suitable for the purpose shall be set apart for the reception and preservation of my books and papers" and that space in the school shall also be provided for "my plate and furniture."[48]

The court denied the relatives' petition for an injunction, mainly on the grounds that the remains already had been moved and, consequently, it was too late for a court to issue an order prohibiting removal. In the court's view, an order to return the remains to the grave in the churchyard could not be considered without first resolving the ownership question, and resolving that question would require a full hearing with all interested parties given ample opportunity to prepare testimony and to testify. The court invited the relatives to pursue the ownership question, if they wished, by filing a suit addressed to that issue, but they declined to do so. There was no ruling by the court as to who owned the remains of Stephen Girard.[49] Possession thus turned out to be tantamount to law. If an injunction had been obtained while Girard's remains were still in the churchyard, the burden of proof would have been on the City of Philadelphia and the Commissioners of the Girard Estates to show they had a lawful right to move the remains to the college without the consent of Girard's relatives. After the remains had been moved to the college, the burden of proof was on the relatives to show they had a lawful right to undo what had already been done.

On September 30, 1851, after more than eight months under lock and key in a back room on the third floor of Founder's Hall, the remains of Stephen Girard took their last journey, moving to their final resting place in the sarcophagus that had been installed in the front foyer on the first floor. It was a ceremonious occasion equivalent to another funeral. Officers and members of dozens of Masonic lodges in Pennsylvania were participants, along with the mayor, members of City Council and other officials of Philadelphia. They marched to the college in a procession of fifteen hundred people that began at the Masonic Hall on Third Street near Spruce, about three miles away. Services at Founder's Hall, conducted principally by Masons, included eulogies and, in closing, a solemn filing past the sarcophagus by the entire student body of the college and others in attendance. The activities were completed in the evening with a banquet at Musical Fund Hall on Locust Street west of Eighth Street.[50] (Five years later, in Musical Fund Hall, a new political entity called the Republican Party would hold its first national convention.[51])

So, exactly nineteen years and nine months after Stephen Girard had been buried in the yard of a Roman Catholic Church, his remains were entombed in a Grecian temple that, under provisions of a will unanimously upheld by the Supreme Court of the United States, had been declared off limits to any member of the clergy of any church.

In 1968—120 years after Girard College opened—the U.S. Supreme Court, in one of its many decisions knocking down the barriers of racial segregation in America, declared unconstitutional the provision in Girard's will that restricted admission to "white" applicants only. The decision came after five years of picketing and demonstrating outside the wall and near the main entrance of the college. The protests were inspired and orchestrated principally by Cecil B. Moore, a popular Philadelphia lawyer, City Council member, civil rights activist and local leader of the National Association for the Advancement of Colored People. Sixteen years later, after more litigation, the ban against admission of females was lifted in 1984.

Thus the provision in Girard's will that his school be for "poor male white orphans" has been greatly modified over the years. Today, many of the students are not male. Many are not white. Many are not orphans. However, all of them are still poor, when they arrive. They do not stay poor. They enjoy a good education, comfortable living conditions and numerous amenities. In the last decades of the twentieth century the enrollment was fluctuating in the range of five hundred to six hundred, with more than ninety percent of the graduates going on to institutions of higher learning.

By the early 1990s more than twenty thousand students had been admitted to Girard College since it opened in 1848. More than 3,800 of its graduates were still living. Talking to Girard alumni is an uplifting experience. They convey in personal terms how much Girard's generosity has meant to them. Typically, they look back on their years at the college with a combination of joyous recollection and eternal gratitude. Girard College has literally turned life around for thousands of youngsters who had previously endured poverty and despair.[52] Girard graduates know, however, that if they become an ecclesiastic, a missionary or a minister of any sect, they cannot be welcomed back to the campus of their alma mater, not officially, anyway, and not even for alumni events and class reunions. Unofficially, enforcement of this provision in Girard's will has been relaxed somewhat in recent years. As recently as the 1980s, invitations to on-campus ceremonies and festivities routinely included a reminder of the ban on ecclesiastics, missionaries and ministers,[53] and persons seeking admission to the campus as visitors without prior clearance (including the author on his first visit to do research for this book) were routinely stopped by guards at the gate and asked to sign a form affirming they were not an ecclesiastic or a missionary or a minister.

Banks, as well as the school for orphans, have given prominence to the name Girard for many generations of Philadelphians, but the banks so named were not a continuation of Stephen Girard's Bank. It died when he died, just as he had planned. Subsequent banks bearing the Girard name were not connected in any way with Stephen Girard.

After Girard's death, the building that had been occupied by Stephen Girard's Bank was rented to a new financial institution called the Girard Bank, chartered in 1832. It later became the Girard National Bank. That name disappeared in the 1920s in a merger with the Philadelphia National Bank.[54] Another financial institution, called the Girard Life Insurance, Annuity and Trust Companys when it was chartered in 1836, later became the Girard Trust Company and still later the Girard Bank.[55] That name vanished in the 1980s in a merger with the Mellon Bank.

A larger-than-life bronze statue of Stephen Girard by sculptor John Massey Rhind was donated to the City of Philadelphia by alumni of

Girard College and other contributors in 1897.[56] It was unveiled on Girard's birthday (May 20) of that year on the West Plaza of City Hall.[57] The statue subsequently was moved to the West Plaza of the Philadelphia Museum of Art.

Girard College alumni also were major donors of a life-size statue of Girard that was unveiled on June 2, 1990, in Girard Park, bounded by Shunk Street, Porter Street, Twenty-First Street and Twenty-Second Street in Philadelphia. Girard's farmhouse still stands in the park, near the statue, and serves as a neighborhood community center. The statue in Girard Park is a bronze replica of the marble statue in front of the sarcophagus at Girard College.

The statue at the sarcophagus is the first thing a person sees when entering Founder's Hall through the main entrance. The somewhat startling impression, especially for a first-time visitor, is that Stephen Girard has been standing there all these years, waiting to give you a warm welcome and show you around.

CHAPTER 22

In Retrospect

A life takes on sharper focus after it has been lived. Similarly, the story of a life acquires clearer perspective after it has been told.

NOW, looking back, it may be seen with greater clarity what made Stephen Girard such a remarkable man. It was a combination of many extraordinary qualities, a rare blend of courage, industry, tenacity and frugality seldom seen in one individual. It was his love of work and love of life. It was his enjoyment in making money, surpassed only by his enjoyment in giving it away. He was a marathon runner who went the distance in life, never tiring and never faltering. He overcame a physical handicap and personal tragedy. He was a responsible and caring citizen. He was there when his city needed him. He was there when his state needed him. He was there when his country needed him. He derived much joy from working with his hands at a time when it was considered demeaning for rich men to do manual labor. He was humble when many men of wealth were haughty. He was kind and humane in an era when it was far more fashionable to be unmerciful and cruel. He had faults, many of them, but they were outweighed by his virtues, including honesty and integrity and decency and generosity. He was "eccentric" enough to give away his wealth for the benefit of others when he could as easily have been more "normal" by spending most of it on pleasures for himself. He was a mariner, a merchant, a banker, a farmer, a one-man conglomerate. He was, when you stop to catch your breath and think about it, the kind of really exceptional person who does not come strolling down the pathway of history very often.

Reflecting on Girard's long life, with the advantage of hindsight, it may be readily seen that there were many turning points. Some came when he was young, and they had far-reaching and long-lasting results. One such turning point, perhaps the most important in terms of enduring impact on Girard, was his inability to sell at a profit in the West Indies the cargo he had acquired in France, with borrowed money, on his first voyage after getting his captain's license. As a result he went to America instead of returning to France, and he acquired a modest amount of capital that eventually grew into the largest fortune in America.

Another significant turning point, perhaps the most intriguing in the context of history, came in May of 1776 when the captain of a British warship denied Girard's request for water. That caused him, soon afterward, to take his storm-battered schooner into Philadelphia for an unscheduled and unwanted stop. One thing led to another and he became a resident of that city for the rest of his life, ultimately playing a crucial role as the financial architect of America's victory over Great Britain in the War of 1812. A little water, if it had been given to Girard on that day in May, might have made a big difference in the life of Girard, in the future of the United States, and in the history of the British Empire in America.

When all is said and done, however, there were traits in the character of Stephen Girard that defined the man and his life even more than unexpected turning points. His indefatigable capacity for work, and his inexhaustible love of work, were crucial to his business and financial success, as were his ability and resolve to overcome adversity and tragedy including his blind and deformed eye and the loss of his wife to insanity. Tightly interwoven in the fabric of his character were two threads that may have been the most admirable and the most inspirational of his traits: his unwavering courage and his unrelenting generosity.

It has been said of Girard that "his moral worth and fearless spirit shown forth like a star in the darkest night."[1] That was never truer than in 1793 when he risked everything, most of all his life, in choosing not to flee from Philadelphia but to stay and to fight the yellow fever.

It also has been said of Girard that "he ranks among the great benefactors of mankind."[2] His benefactions continue and, barring unforeseen circumstances, will never end. Although he died without offspring, the students and the alumni of Girard College—past, present and future—are his living legacy.

They are, in both a spiritual and a material sense, his children.

In His Own Words

"No one can live in this world without finding some troubles."

"I have taken a wife who is without fortune, it is true, but whom I love and with whom I am living very happily."

"As for my fortune, I do not seek for it."

"The love of work is my greatest ambition."

"To rest is to rust."

"No man shall ever be a gentleman with my money."

"My deeds must be my life."

"When I am dead, my actions must speak for me."

"Diminish the burden of taxation, now most oppressive, especially on those who are the least able to bear it."

"Go on, Doctor, I am an old sailor; I can bear a good deal."

"No ecclesiastic, missionary or minister of any sect whatsoever, shall ever hold or exercise any station or duty whatever in the said College, nor shall any such person ever be admitted for any purpose, or as a visitor, within the premises."

"I do not mean to cast any reflection upon any sect or person whatsoever, but, as there is such a multitude of sects, and such a diversity of opinion amongst them, I desire to keep the tender minds of the orphans, who are to derive advantage from this bequest, free from the excitement which clashing doctrines and sectarian controversy are so apt to produce."

"All the instructors and teachers in the College shall take pains to instil into the minds of the scholars the purest principles of morality, so that, on their entrance into active life, they may, from inclination and habit, evince benevolence towards their fellow creatures, and a love of truth, sobriety, and industry, adopting at the same time such religious tenets as their matured reason may enable them to prefer."

"When Death comes for me, he will find me busy, unless I am asleep in bed."

"If I thought I was going to die tomorrow, I should plant a tree, nevertheless, today."

Notes

GP is the abbreviation for Girard Papers. See the Preface for a discussion of the Girard Papers and their availability.

Chapter 1

1. Stephen Simpson, *Biography of Stephen Girard* (Philadelphia: Thomas L. Bonsal, 1832), 16. This biography was published four months after Girard's death. Simpson is both a primary and a secondary source. As an employee of Stephen Girard's Bank for the last fifteen years of Girard's life, Simpson observed Girard on a regular basis and had conversations with him in an employee-employer relationship. Simpson also learned much from his father, George Simpson, who for ten years preceding his death in 1822 was the cashier of Stephen Girard's Bank and during that time had almost daily contact with Girard. Additionally, Stephen Simpson obtained information from more than a dozen other people who knew Girard personally or on a business basis.
2. Ibid., 16-17.
3. Ibid., 17.
4. Henry Atlee Ingram, *The Life and Character of Stephen Girard* (Philadelphia: E. Stanley Hart, 1885), 20. Ingram was a great-grandson of John Girard, Stephen Girard's brother. In researching his biography of Stephen Girard, Ingram interviewed William Wagner, who was an employee of Stephen Girard for twenty-one years, and three nieces of Stephen Girard who lived with him for many years when they were children, adolescents and young women. One of the nieces was Ingram's grandmother.
5. Girard to John Williams, 26 April 1830, GP.
6. Henry W. Arey, *The Girard College and Its Founder* (Philadelphia: Sherman, 1852; reprinted 1866), 6-7. Arey was secretary of Girard College when he wrote this biography, published twenty-one years after Girard's death. Arey is a primary source, especially for matters related to the founding and early history of Girard College.
7. George Wilson, the author of this book, was six when his father died.
8. Arey, *Girard College and Its Founder*, 7.

Chapter 2

1. The author of this book has sailed across three oceans—the Atlantic, the Pacific, the Indian—on ships traveling alone.

2. A surgical kit that was owned by Stephen Girard is in the Stephen Girard Collection at Girard College in Philadelphia.

3. For information on crew sizes on sailing ships see: Ships' Papers, GP. See also: Jonathan Goldstein, "The Ethics of Tribute and the Profits of Trade: Stephen Girard's China Trade (1787-1824)," 1969, a scholarly research paper in the collection of the Library of the Philadelphia Maritime Museum. The name of this museum was changed to Independence Seaport Museum in 1995.

4. For information on the lengths of sailing ships and the heights of their masts see: Howard I. Chapelle, *The Search for Speed Under Sail, 1700-1855* (New York: W. W. Norton, 1967). See also: Charles G. Davis, *Ships of the Past* (Salem, Massachusetts: Marine Research Society, 1929).

5. For a comprehensive account of the development and characteristics of all kinds of ships see: Peter Kemp, *The History of Ships* (Stamford, Connecticut: Longmeadow Press, 1988). Chapters Three through Nine are devoted principally to sailing ships.

6. For a brief, nontechnical discussion of masts and sails on various categories of eighteenth century vessels, with illustrations, see: Edwin Tunis, *The Young United States, 1783 to 1830* (New York: Thomas Y. Crowell, 1969), 85.

7. Roger G. Kennedy, *Orders From France* (New York: Alfred A. Knopf, 1989), 132.

8. William F. Zeil, *A Catalogue of the Personal Library of Stephen Girard (1750-1831)* (Philadelphia: published jointly by Girard College and the American Philosophical Society, 1990), 131.

9. Henry Atlee Ingram, *The Life of Jean Girard, de Montbrun* (Philadelphia: published privately, limited edition, 1888), 13.

10. "Exercises in Navigation," Manuscripts, MS-7, 1772, GP.

11. Ingram, *Life of Jean Girard*, 15.

12. Ship's log, *Sally*, 25-26 (noon to noon) April 1773, GP.

13. For documentation and additional information relative to Girard's voyages as a *pilotin* see: Ships' Papers, 1764-1773, GP. See also: Harry Emerson Wildes, *Lonely Midas* (New York, Farrar & Rinehart, 1943), 308.

Chapter 3

1. Mercantile Papers, December 1773-June 1774, GP. See also: Wildes, *Lonely Midas*, 18-19.

2. Arey, *Girard College and Its Founder*, 9.

3. Some writers have given the name of the vessel as the *Jeune Bebe*. According to the log written by Girard, quoted later in this chapter, the correct name was *Jeune Babe*. That spelling was declared correct in 1990 after research conducted under auspices of the Girard College Committee on Stephen Girard Papers and Effects. See: Zeil, *Catalogue of Library of Girard*, 133.

4. In some writings the *Jeune Babe* has been called a sloop. Girard's log, as noted later in this chapter, indicated that the vessel had two masts. A sloop had only one mast.

5. Ship's log, *Jeune Babe*, 14-15 (noon to noon) May 1776, GP.

6. Some writers, making an erroneous translation of eighteenth century French, have concluded that Girard must have been sailing south from St-Pierre and Miquelon. The latitudinal readings in Girard's log show beyond question that he was sailing north from St-Domingue. For an explanation of how the error in translation may have been made (by assuming that a word in French meant "from" when it actually meant "to") see:

Marvin W. McFarland, *Stephen Girard: A Very Human Human Being*, an address at Girard College, 22 April 1977, published as a booklet by the college, 5. McFarland, a graduate of Girard College in 1936, developed an enduring interest in Stephen Girard and became an authority on the man and his times. McFarland was an assistant to the librarian at Girard College, working on the Girard Papers, before entering military service during World War II. After the war he had a distinguished career with the Library of Congress, becoming chief of the Science and Technology Division. He was also associated with Girard College on a part-time basis as a consultant to the college president on the Girard Papers. After retiring from the Library of Congress McFarland was curator of the Girard Papers. He died in 1985.

7. Ship's log, *Jeune Babe*, 14-15 May 1776, GP.
8. Ibid., 15-16 May 1776.
9. Ibid., 16-17 May 1776.
10. Ibid., 18-19 May 1776.
11. Ibid., 19-20 May 1776.
12. Ibid., 20-21 May 1776.
13. Ibid., 21-22 May 1776.
14. Ibid.
15. Ibid.
16. Ibid.
17. Ibid., 22-23 May 1776.
18. Ibid.
19. Ibid., 28-29 May 1776.
20. Ibid., 29-30 May 1776.
21. McFarland, *A Very Human Human Being*, 5.

Chapter 4

1. For an interesting and entertaining look at life in Philadelphia in 1776 see: David R. Boldt, ed., "Bicentennial Journal," special supplement of *Philadelphia Inquirer*, 20 October 1975.
2. Edwin B. Bronner, "Village Into Town," in *Philadelphia, a 300-Year History*, ed. Russell F. Weigley (New York: W. W. Norton, 1982), 57.
3. Robert I. Alotta, *Street Names of Philadelphia* (Philadelphia: Temple University Press, 1975), 98.
4. George Wilson, *Yesterday's Philadelphia* (Miami: E. A. Seemann, 1975), 16.
5. Ray Thompson, *The Story of Betsy Ross*, (Fort Washington, Pennsylvania: Bicentennial Press, 1975), 5-8.
6. Ibid., 6.
7. Ibid., 31-33.

Chapter 5

1. James Parton, *Famous Americans of Recent Times* (Boston: Ticknor and Fields, 1867), 229.
2. Ingram, *Life of Girard*, 33-34.
3. Parton, *Famous Americans*, 230.
4. Simpson, *Biography of Girard*, 21.
5. For a fanciful account (based on an itemized bill from Coy's Inn) see: Wildes, *Lonely Midas*, 29-30.

6. Record of Marriages, St. Paul's Church, 1777, GP.

7. Parton, *Famous Americans*, 229.

8. Ingram, *Life of Girard*, 38.

9. Simpson, *Biography of Girard*, 22-23.

10. For a discussion of different kinds of money in early America, and their relative values, see: John Bach McMaster, *The Life and Times of Stephen Girard* (Philadelphia: J. B. Lippincott, 1918), 1:12-14.

11. Donald H. Kent, *Anthony Wayne, Man of Action*, rev. ed., Historic Pennsylvania Leaflet No. 2 (Harrisburg: Pennsylvania Historical and Museum Commission, 1976), 2.

12. Wayland F. Dunaway, *A History of Pennsylvania*, 2nd ed., 1948 (New York: Prentice-Hall, 1935), 149.

13. Christine Sweely, *The Liberty Bell*, Historic Pennsylvania Leaflet No. 35 (Harrisburg: Pennsylvania Historical and Museum Commission, 1974), 2.

14. John B. B. Trussell, Jr., *The Battle of Germantown*, Historic Pennsylvania Leaflet No. 38 (Harrisburg: Pennsylvania Historical and Museum Commission, 1974), 1-4.

15. Henry C. Shinn, *The History of Mount Holly* (Mount Holly, New Jersey: Mount Holly Herald, 1959), 73.

16. George DeCou, *The Historic Rancocas* (Moorestown, New Jersey: News Chronicle, 1949), 120.

17. Shinn, *History of Mount Holly*, 61.

18. Zachariah Reed, "The History of Mount Holly," a manuscript, 1859, in the Mount Holly Library.

19. Wildes, *Lonely Midas*, 33.

20. Michael Vinson, "The Society for Political Inquiries: The Limits of Republican Discourse in Philadelphia on the Eve of the Constitutional Convention," *The Pennsylvania Magazine of History and Biography*, April 1989, 192. This magazine has been published by the Historical Society of Pennsylvania since 1877. All issues, with a consolidated index, are in the collection of the Historical Society, Thirteenth and Locust Streets, Philadelphia.

21. The pistols, made in France about 1800, are in the Stephen Girard Collection at Girard College in Philadelphia.

22. Ingram, *Life of Girard*, 41-42.

23. Henry M. Tinkcom, "The Revolutionary City, 1765-1783," in *Philadelphia, a 300-Year History*, 145.

Chapter 6

1. DeCou, *Historic Rancocas*, 121.

2. Certificate of Citizenship, GP.

3. Stephen Girard to Pierre Girard, no date, circa February 1779, GP.

4. Ibid.

5. Wildes, *Lonely Midas*.

6. Privateering is still sanctioned in America, by the Constitution of the United States, but is legal only with authorization by Congress, which has the constitutional power to "grant Letters of Marque and Reprisal, and make Rules concerning Captures on Land and Water." (Art. I, Sec. 8, Par. 11.) Letters of Marque are licenses to civilians allowing them to arm their ships and capture foreign ships and cargoes.

7. For more details, see extensive correspondence between Girard and Captain Gear Chad-

Notes

wick, and between Girard and George P. Keeports, June-Sep
was Girard's agent in Baltimore. See also: McMaster, *Life and*
8. Barbara W. Tuchman, *The First Salute* (New York: Alfred A. Knop
9. Samuel Eliot Morison, *The Oxford History of the American People* (
   University Press, 1965), 265. For a concise and authoritative accou.
   up to the Battle of Yorktown, and the battle itself, see: Ibid., 253-26
10. Tuchman, *First Salute*, 291.
11. Dunaway, *History of Pennsylvania*, 185-186.
12. Ibid., 398-400.
13. J. Robert Mendte, *The Union League of Philadelphia Celebrates 125*
    (Devon, Pennsylvania: William T. Cooke, 1987), 11.
14. Stephen Girard to John Girard, 28 August 1784, GP.
15. Abraham Ritter, *Philadelphia and Her Merchants* (Philadelphia: publishe   or,
    1860), 22.
16. Simpson, *Biography of Girard*, 169, 173.
17. Cheeseman A. Herrick, *Stephen Girard, Founder*, 5th ed., 1945 (Philadelphi   .ied
    by Girard College, 1923), 22. See also: Wildes, *Lonely Midas*, 55-56, 72-73,   ee
    also: McFarland, *A Very Human Human Being*, 7-12.

Chapter 7

1. Nancy Tomes, *A Generous Confidence, Thomas Story Kirkbride and the Art of Asylum-.
   ing, 1840-1883* (New York, Cambridge University Press, 1984), 85.
2. Stephen Girard to John Girard, 21 February 1785, GP.
3. Ibid., 21 May 1785, GP.
4. Ibid., 1 June 1785, GP.
5. Ibid., 19 July 1785, GP.
6. Ibid., 25 August 1785, GP.
7. Stephen Girard to M. Giboin, 25 August 1785, GP.
8. McFarland, *A Very Human Human Being.*
9. The portrait is in the Stephen Girard Collection at Girard College in Philadelphia.
10. Stephen Girard to John Girard, 28 April 1787, GP.
11. Ibid.
12. Ibid., 21 March 1787, GP.
13. Jonathan Goldstein, *Philadelphia and the China Trade, 1682-1846* (State College, Penn-
    sylvania: Pennsylvania State University Press, 1978), 35.
14. Ship's log, *Deux Amis*, 7 December 1787, GP.
15. Pierre Girard to Stephen Girard, 29 July 1785, GP.
16. Ship's log, *Deux Amis*, 18 December 1787, 2 February 1788, GP.
17. Ibid., 11 May 1788 to 18 July 1788.
18. Kemp, *History of Ships*, 150-151.
19. Dunaway, *History of Pennsylvania*, 590.
20. Simon Schama, *Citizens* (New York: Alfred A. Knopf, 1989), 373. See the same page
    for an illustration showing the spanking in progress. The woman was spanked after she
    had spit on a portrait of Jacques Necker, the French finance minister who had de-
    manded that taxes be reformed, that government spending be cut, and that the extrava-
    gances of Queen Marie Antoinette be curbed. It was the dismissal of Necker by King
    Louis XVI that triggered the storming of the Bastille.

21. Stephen Girard to Madame Samatan, 6 April 1795, GP.

22. Simpson, *Biography of Girard*, 177.

23. Ibid., 178.

24. McFarland, *A Very Human Human Being*, 9.

25. The author of this book has had access to confidential records in the Historic Library and Archives Collection of Pennsylvania Hospital (on microfilm in the Library of the American Philosophical Society in Philadelphia) and has examined many of those records for the years that Mary Girard was insane. Researchers requesting access to the hospital's confidential records are routinely required to sign a pledge, which states: "I agree to abide by the following regulations: To preserve the confidentiality of the archival case records and letters by refraining from making any public or private disclosure of information contained in these records which would identify any person as a subject of such records. I shall make no notation of names concerning patients or case records, nor will I reveal such names verbally or in writing, or in publications. I agree to give credit for any material reproduced, to Historic Library, Pennsylvania Hospital." Confidentiality notwithstanding, it is a matter of public record that Mary Girard was a patient at Pennsylvania Hospital, that she exhibited many manifestations of insanity, that she was diagnosed as an incurable lunatic upon entering the hospital, and that she remained insane during her entire time in the hospital. There is nothing in the hospital records that would indicate otherwise. The author of this book can make that statement, unequivocally, without violating any rules or pledges of confidentiality. To consult sources that have been on the public record for some time, concerning Mary Girard's insanity and her treatment for insanity, see: Thomas G. Morton, *The History of the Pennsylvania Hospital, 1751-1895* (Philadelphia: Times Printing House, 1895; reprinted, New York: Arno Press, 1973), 138. See also: William H. Williams, *America's First Hospital: The Pennsylvania Hospital, 1751-1841* (Wayne, Pennsylvania: Haverford House, 1976), 126. See also: Herrick, *Stephen Girard, Founder*, 21-22. See also: Wildes, *Lonely Midas*, 55-56, 72-73, 86-90. See also: McFarland, *A Very Human Human Being*, 7-12.

26. See Portrait Gallery inside main entrance of Pine Building, Pennsylvania Hospital.

27. See historical exhibit in the Pavilion, Pennsylvania Hospital.

28. J.H. Powell, *Bring Out Your Dead* (Philadelphia: University of Pennsylvania Press, 1949), 11. See also: Richard G. Miller, "The Federal City, 1783-1800," in *Philadelphia, a 300-Year History*, 180-181. See also: Historical exhibits in the Medical Library, Pennsylvania Hospital.

29. James M. Beck, *Stephen Girard, Merchant and Mariner*, an oration delivered at the unveiling of a statue of Stephen Girard on the West Plaza of City Hall in Philadelphia, 20 May 1897, subsequently printed as a book (Philadelphia: J.B. Lippincott, 1897), 12.

30. Ibid.

31. Charles E. Rosenberg, *The Care of Strangers, the Rise of America's Hospital System* (New York: Basic Books, 1987), 18.

32. Ibid.

33. Ingram, *Life of Girard*, 52.

34. Tomes, *A Generous Confidence*, 26.

35. Ibid., 30.

36. Ibid., 26.

37. Original papers conveying in detail the views of Benjamin Rush regarding care for the insane are in the Historic Library and Archives Collection of Pennsylvania Hospital.

eview of the play see: Mary Martin Niepold, "'Girard' Is Strong Drama," *Phila-
: Inquirer*, 13 August 1976.
;on, *Biography of Girard*, 40.
on, *History of Pennsylvania Hospital*, 138. See also: McFarland, *A Very Human Hu-
Being*, 10.
rick, *Stephen Girard, Founder*, picture opposite title page.

)ter 8

n Girard to Stephen Girard, 21 October 1789, GP.
)ert, Rouch & Co. to Stephen Girard, 11 September 1791, GP.
.ller, "The Federal City," in *Philadelphia, a 300-Year History*, 188.
4. Mathew Carey, *A Short Account of the Malignant Fever Lately Prevalent in Philadelphia*
(Philadelphia: printed by the author, 1794; reprinted, New York: Arno Press, 1970), 77,
94.
5. Powell, *Bring Out Your Dead*, Preface, 5.
6. Ibid.
7. Ibid., 8-11.
8. Carey, *Short Account of Malignant Fever*, 16-17.
9. Ibid., 17-18.
10. Linda Stanley et al., *Courage in the Face of Crisis: Yellow Fever Strikes Philadelphia, 1793*
(Philadelphia: Historical Society of Pennsylvania, 1989), 1. This is an unbound document prepared by the Education Department of the Historical Society.
11. Carey, *Short Account of Malignant Fever*, 13.
12. Ibid., 15.
13. Ibid., 21.
14. Ibid., 21-22.
15. Ibid., 23.
16. Ibid., 24.
17. Powell, *Bring Out Your Dead*, 109.
18. Carey, *Short Account of Malignant Fever*, 28-29.
19. Ibid., 29.
20. Ibid.
21. Ibid., 31.
22. Powell, *Bring Out Your Dead*, 59.
23. Carey, *Short Account of Malignant Fever*, 19.
24. Ibid.
25. Ibid.
26. Powell, *Bring Out Your Dead*, 61-62.
27. Miller, "The Federal City," in *Philadelphia, a 300-Year History*, 186.
28. Carey, *Short Account of Malignant Fever*, 32.
29. Powell, *Bring Out Your Dead*, 146.
30. Ibid., 152-153.
31. Ibid., 161-162.
32. Ingram, *Life of Girard*, 65-66.
33. Girard to Les Fils de P. Changeur & Co., 16 September 1793, GP.
34. Girard to Paul Bentalou, 16 October 1793, GP.
35. Girard to John Ferrers, 4 November 1793, GP.

36. Public Health Papers, 1793, GP.
37. GP. The diary of Peter Seguin was published as a booklet by Girard College in 1984, edited by William Francis Zeil and printed by the Girard College Print Shop.
38. Miller, "The Federal City," in *Philadelphia, a 300-Year History*, 188.
39. Ibid.
40. Carey, *Short Account of Malignant Fever*, 34.
41. Simpson, *Biography of Girard*, 56.

Chapter 9

1. Samuel Flagg Bemis, *A Diplomatic History of the United States*, rev. ed., 1946 (New York, Henry Holt, 1936), 68.
2. Ibid.
3. *Pennsylvania Packet and Daily Advertiser*, 2 January 1788, GP.
4. Samuel Eliot Morison and Henry Steele Commager, *The Growth of the American Republic*, 3rd ed., 1942 (New York: Oxford University Press, 1930), 1:388.
5. Girard to Bonnaffe Freres et Fils, 6 January 1794, GP.
6. Girard to Alexander Hamilton, 26 February 1794, GP.
7. For more information about the Battle of Fallen Timbers see: Kent, *Anthony Wayne*, 4.
8. The author of this book was a newspaperman for forty years. He has been a recipient of "secret" information, obtained through what is commonly called a "leak," more times than he can count. "Leaks" often serve the public interest, but the primary motivation of those who do the "leaking" usually is self-interest.
9. Morison and Commager, *Growth of the American Republic*, 1:357.
10. Ibid.
11. *Dunlap and Claypoole's American Daily Advertiser*, 28 July 1795, GP.
12. Morison and Commager, *Growth of the American Republic*, 1:358.

Chapter 10

1. Ingram, *Life of Girard*, 110-111.
2. Ibid., 111-112.
3. Ritter, *Philadelphia and Her Merchants*, 71-72.
4. Ibid., 72. Ritter did not identify the seamstress who gave him this information. It is possible to speculate that she may have been Betsy Ross or Sally Bickham, but there is no evidence to support such speculation.
5. Ibid., 75.
6. Ibid., 75-76.
7. Ingram, *Life of Girard*, 113-115. For a similar version of the same story see: Ritter, *Philadelphia and Her Merchants*, 73.
8. Arey, *Girard College and Its Founder*, 24. See also: Ingram, *Life of Girard*, 143.
9. Girard to F. Duplessis, 21 December 1804, GP.
10. Ingram, *Life of Girard*, 132-133.
11. Ibid., 133-134.
12. Simpson, *Biography of Girard*, 74.
13. Ibid.
14. Zeil, *Catalogue of the Library of Girard*, 23.
15. Ibid., 100-102.
16. Simpson, *Biography of Girard*, 13.

17. Ibid.
18. Ibid.
19. Ibid., 73.
20. Ibid., 69-70.
21. Ibid., 71.
22. Ibid., 151.
23. Ibid., 91-92.
24. Ibid., 88-90.
25. Ibid., 93-94.
26. James Mease, *The Picture of Philadelphia* (Philadelphia: B. and T. Kite, 1811, reprint, New York: Arno Press, 1970), 355-356.
27. Parton, *Famous Americans*, 223.
28. Ibid.
29. Ibid., 235-236.
30. Eliza Cope Harrison, ed., *Philadelphia Merchant, the Diary of Thomas P. Cope, 1800-1851* (South Bend, Indiana: Gateway Editions, 1978), 394.
31. Arey, *Girard College and Its Founder*, 25.
32. Ibid.
33. Meade Minnigerode, *Certain Rich Men* (Freeport, New York: Books for Libraries Press, 1927; reprint, 1970), 29.
34. Carl and Jessica Bridenbaugh, *Rebels and Gentlemen* (New York: Reynal & Hitchcock, 1942), 246.

Chapter 11

1. George R. Beyer, *Pennsylvania Roads Before the Automobile*, Historic Pennsylvania Leaflet No. 33 (Harrisburg: Pennsylvania Historical and Museum Commission, 1972), 2.
2. Alotta, *Street Names*, 53.
3. Ritter, *Philadelphia and Her Merchants*, map opposite p. 29. See also: Zeil, *Catalogue of the Library of Girard*, 77-78, 176. See also: two maps of "Girard's Real Estate on Water Street," marked M-50 and M-51, in the Stephen Girard Collection at Girard College in Philadelphia.
4. Alotta, *Street Names*, 53.
5. Kennedy, *Orders From France*, 99.
6. Ibid.
7. Ritter, *Philadelphia and Her Merchants*, 72-73.
8. Ingram, *Life of Girard*, 123-127.
9. Marvin W. McFarland, *Citizen Stephen Girard*, an address at Girard College, 19 May 1973, published as a booklet by the college, 5.
10. Accounts of Expenditures and Other Transactions, 1796, GP.
11. In the Stephen Girard Collection.
12. Mercantile Papers, 31 December 1795, GP. See also: Wildes, *Lonely Midas*, 328-329.
13. McFarland, *A Very Human Human Being*, 9.
14. Wildes, *Lonely Midas*, 184.
15. Ibid.
16. McFarland, *A Very Human Human Being*, 9.
17. Simpson, *Biography of Girard*, 191.
18. Farm Records, 1798-1809, GP.

19. Ibid.

20. Public Health Papers, 1793-1798, GP.

21. Simpson, *Biography of Girard*, 21.

22. Ibid., 44.

23. Deeds and Title Papers, 26 December 1797, GP. See also: Zeil, *Catalogue of Library of Girard*, 175-176.

24. Ingram, *Life of Girard*, 119-121.

25. Simpson, *Biography of Girard*, 95-96.

26. *The Register of Pennsylvania*, 5 February 1831. See also: Zeil, *Catalogue of Library of Girard*, 52.

Chapter 12

1. Jonathan Goldstein, *Philadelphia and the China Trade, 1682-1846* (State College, Pennsylvania: Pennsylvania State University Press, 1978), 17.

2. Ibid., 26-30.

3. Ibid., 21-22, 27.

4. For numerous discussions of general market conditions in South America see: letters received by Stephen Girard after 1800 from correspondents in South American ports, GP. See especially: letters from Edward George and Martin Bickham received by Girard in May and June, 1810, GP.

5. *Philadelphia Times*, 6 July 1879.

6. Ibid.

7. Ibid.

8. Ibid.

9. For a concise but detailed history and description of Azilum see: Norman B. Wilkinson, *A French Asylum on the Susquehanna River*, 4th ed. rev., Historic Pennsylvania Leaflet No. 11 (Harrisburg: Pennsylvania Historical and Museum Commission, 1969). The site of Azilum has been preserved and is open to the public in warm-weather months.

10. Girard to John Ferrers, 5 November 1799, GP.

11. Girard to Caleb Earl, 8 November 1799, GP.

12. Jack Shepherd, *The Adams Chronicles* (Boston: Little, Brown, 1975), 184.

13. McMaster, *Life and Times of Girard*, 1:397-398.

14. Shepherd, *Adams Chronicles*, 198.

15. Neal R. Peirce, *The People's President* (New York: Simon and Schuster, 1968), 69.

16. Ibid., 70.

17. Girard to Jean Deveze, 17 May 1800, GP.

18. Paul Bentalou to Girard, 20 February 1801, GP.

19. Ibid.

20. Resolution of Committee of Arrangements, 20 February 1801, GP.

21. Bemis, *A Diplomatic History*, 177.

Chapter 13

1. Ingram, *Life of Jean Girard*, 114-116.

2. Ibid., 118.

3. Stephen Girard to John Hourquebie, 14 December 1803, GP.

4. Arthur Preston Whitaker, *The United States and the Independence of Latin America, 1800-*

1830 (Baltimore: John Hopkins Press, 1941; reprinted, New York: Russell & Russell, 1962), 6.

5. Harrison, *Diary of Thomas P. Cope*, 10 June 1810, 252.

6. Girard to M. Curcier, 11 February 1811, GP.

7. See letter from Girard to Majastre & Tardy, 21 February 1811, GP.

8. Girard to Vincent Bolivar, 6 March 1811, GP.

9. Memorandum from Don Jose Antonio Cabrera and Don Pedro Lopez to Girard, 30 November 1811, GP.

10. Girard to Telesforo Orea, 2 December 1811, GP.

11. Girard to James Monroe, 2 December 1811, GP.

12. For a concise account of the Chesapeake Affair see: Bemis, *Diplomatic History*, 145-146.

13. Ritter, *Philadelphia Merchants*, 73-74.

14. Girard to John Hourquebie, 17 August 1798, GP.

15. Herrick, *Stephen Girard, Founder*, 119.

16. Tunis, *Young United States*, 71.

17. Zeil, *Catalogue of Library of Girard*, 88. See also: *A Report of the Trial of James Sylvanus M'Clean, Alias J. Melville, and William L. Graham, Before the Supreme Court of Pennsylvania* (Philadelphia: John Binns, printer, 1812). See also: Ingram, *Life of Girard*, 74-75.

18. For additional details of the investigation by the government of Haiti and the court case in Philadelphia see: Wildes, *Lonely Midas*, 330-331.

Chapter 14

1. Mercantile Papers, 31 December 1800, GP. See also: Wildes, *Lonely Midas*, 328-329.

2. Mercantile Papers, 31 December 1807, GP.

3. Margaret L. Coit, *The Growing Years, 1789-1829*, vol. 3 of *The Life History of the United States* (New York: Time Incorporated, 1963) 45.

4. Mercantile Papers, 31 December 1811, GP.

5. From an address in Philadelphia in 1939 at a meeting of the Historical Society of Pennsylvania. The address was subsequently published as part of a book: Charles Lyon Chandler, Marion V. Brewington, Edgar P. Richardson, *Philadelphia, Port of History, 1609-1837* (Philadelphia: Philadelphia Maritime Museum, 1976). See p. 60.

6. For the full text of the protest, dated 10 January 1806, see: *Poulson's American Daily Advertiser*, 18 January 1806, GP.

7. Bemis, *Diplomatic History*, 144-146.

8. Girard to Charles N. Bancker, 5 August 1811, GP.

9. Girard to Baring Brothers, 5 June 1811, GP.

10. Girard to Robert Thompson, 29 December 1811, GP.

11. Girard to William Adgate, 29 December 1811, GP.

12. Adgate to Girard, 10 February 1812, GP. This letter was completed 11 February.

13. Ibid.

14. Adgate to Girard, 20 March 1812, GP.

15. Thompson to Girard, 21 March 1812, GP.

16. Adgate to Girard, 27 March 1812, GP. This letter was completed 28 March.

17. George Matthews to the Collector of the Port of Philadelphia, 31 March 1812, GP.

18. Girard to Allen McLane, 20 April 1812, GP.

Chapter 15

1. Josiah Granville Leach, *The History of the Girard National Bank of Philadelphia, 1832-1902* (Philadelphia, J. B. Lippincott, 1902; reprinted New York: Greenwood Press, 1969), 17.
2. Donald R. Adams Jr., *Finance and Enterprise in Early America* (Philadelphia: University of Pennsylvania Press, 1978), 4.
3. Ibid.
4. Ibid., 14.
5. Financial Papers of Girard and His Bank, 18 May 1812, GP.
6. Ibid., 1 June 1812.
7. Ibid., 15 June 1812.
8. Ibid., 30 June 1812.
9. Memorandum of Agreement Between Girard and Trustees of the Bank of the United States, 9 May 1812, GP. For an account of the bank purchase see: Adams, *Finance and Enterprise*, 18-19. The First Bank of the United States was called simply the Bank of the United States during its existence. Historically, to avoid confusion, it has been called the First Bank of the United States ever since the Second Bank of the United States was created.
10. Legal brief from Jared Ingersoll and Alexander Dallas to Girard, 20 May 1812, GP.
11. Ibid.
12. Indenture Between Stephen Girard and Trustees of Stephen Girard's Bank, 23 May 1812, GP.
13. Ibid.
14. Contemporary quotations and documentation regarding Girard's lovemaking have already been provided. See Chapter 11 and the notes for Chapter 11.

Chapter 16

1. Donald R. Hickey, *The War of 1812* (Urbana, Illinois: University of Illinois Press, 1989), 44.
2. Ibid., 46.
3. Ibid., 77.
4. Ibid., 76.
5. Jared Ingersoll to Girard, 11 June 1812, GP.
6. Ibid. See also: McMaster, *Life of Girard*, 2:200, 2:241.
7. Girard to George Simpson, 27 July 1812, GP.
8. Adams, *Finance and Enterprise*, 30.
9. Kennedy, *Orders From France*, 254-261.
10. Henry Adams, ed., *The Writings of Albert Gallatin* (Philadelphia: J.B. Lippincott, 1879), 1:532.
11. Adams, *Finance and Enterprise*, 30.
12. Ibid., 30-31.
13. James Monroe to Girard, 5 April 1813, GP.
14. Adams, *Finance and Enterprise*, 31.
15. Adams, *Writings of Gallatin*, 1:532-533.
16. Ibid., 1:535.

Chapter 17

1. Gustavus Myers, *History of the Great American Fortunes* (Chicago, Charles H. Kerr, 1907), 1:43.
2. Harrison, *Diary of Thomas P. Cope*, 552-553.
3. Charles A. Beard and Mary R. Beard, *The Rise of American Civilization* (New York: Macmillan, 1927, reprinted 1930), 2:383-384.
4. Ibid.
5. Elizabeth M. Geffen, "Industrial Development and Social Crisis, 1841-1854," in *Philadelphia, a 300-Year History*, 327.
6. Irwin Richman, *Albert Gallatin, Master of Finance*, Historic Pennsylvania Leaflet No. 25 (Harrisburg: Pennsylvania Historical and Museum Commission, 1962).
7. Harrison, *Diary of Thomas P. Cope*, 257.
8. Simpson, *Biography of Girard*, 142.
9. David Parish and Girard to Albert Gallatin, 5 April 1813, GP.
10. Albert Gallatin to David Parish and Girard, 7 April 1813, GP.
11. Kennedy, *Orders From France*, 262.
12. Adams, *Finance and Enterprise*, 32.
13. Ibid.
14. Albert Gallatin to David Parish and Girard, 7 April 1813, GP.
15. Subscriptions at S. Girard's Bank to the Loan of XVI Millions, 15 April 1813, GP.
16. Adams, *Finance and Enterprise*, 36.
17. Ibid.
18. Some writers have said, erroneously, that Girard put up $1,191,500 of his own money for the government loan of sixteen million dollars in 1813. The writers apparently obtained that figure from the April 15 list of subscribers to the residue of the loan and failed to take into account that Girard also provided the entire $1,191,500 listed in the name of David Parish and, earlier, had subscribed to $100,000.
19. Adams, *Finance and Enterprise*, 36.
20. Kennedy, *Orders from France*, 264.
21. Adams, *Writings of Gallatin*, 1:534-538.
22. For detailed accounts of battles on land and sea in 1813 see: Hickey, *War of 1812*, 126-158.
23. Simpson, *Biography of Girard*, 160.
24. Agreement, Circuit Court U.S., Philadelphia, February Term, 1819, in the Case of Treasury Department of the United States versus Stephen Girard, GP.
25. Girard to Baring Brothers, 16 May 1815, GP.
26. Baring Brothers to Girard, 18 March 1815, GP.
27. Hickey, *War of 1812*, 183.
28. Edward George to Girard, 8 September 1814, GP.
29. Walter Lord, *The Dawn's Early Light* (New York: W.W. Norton, 1972), 310.
30. Harrison, *Diary of Thomas P. Cope*, 303.
31. Ibid.
32. Girard to William Jones, 11 May 1813, GP.

Chapter 18

1. Girard to F. Duplessis, 21 December 1804, GP.
2. Ingram, *Life of Girard*, 84.

3. Simpson, *Biography of Girard,* 39.

4. Ingram, *Life of Girard,* 85.

5. Simpson, *Biography of Girard,* 39-40.

6. Ingram, *Life of Girard,* 86.

7. Ibid.

8. Ibid., 86-87.

9. Tomes, *A Generous Confidence,* 29.

10. Ibid., 34-37.

11. Herrick, *Stephen Girard, Founder,* 23-24.

12. Williams, *America's First Hospital,* 126.

13. Simpson, *Biography of Girard,* 40.

14. Williams, *America's First Hospital,* 128.

15. Joseph Nathan Kane, *Facts About the Presidents,* 2nd ed. (New York: H.W. Wilson, 1968), 37.

16. Adams, *Finance and Enterprise,* 53.

17. Alexander Dallas to Girard, 8 April 1816, GP.

18. Adams, *Finance and Enterprise,* 55-56.

19. Ibid., 65.

20. Thomas C. Cochran, *Pennsylvania, a Bicentennial History* (New York: W.W. Norton, 1978), 75.

21. Adams, *Finance and Enterprise,* 29.

22. Ibid., 38-43.

23. Ibid., 37-38.

24. Ibid., 100-101.

25. Ibid., 108.

26. Girard to John Stoney, 9 March 1817, GP.

27. Adams, *Finance and Enterprise,* 117, 119.

28. Simpson, *Biography of Girard,* 150-151.

29. David Stacton, *The Bonapartes* (New York: Simon and Schuster, 1966), 181.

30. Ibid., 183.

31. Ibid., 208.

32. This version of the story, with some embellishment, is taken from McFarland, *Citizen Stephen Girard,* 6.

33. Stacton, *The Bonapartes,* 211.

34. Ludwig, *Napoleon,* 462.

35. Stacton, *The Bonapartes,* 211.

36. James Monroe to Girard, 25 October 1822, GP.

37. Girard to Edward George, Jr., 23 December 1823, GP.

Chapter 19

1. *American Daily Advertiser,* 1 February 1832. See also: Herrick, *Stephen Girard, Founder,* 108-109.

2. Herrick, *Stephen Girard, Founder,* 108.

3. Simpson, *Biography of Girard,* 46.

4. Girard to Joseph Delaplaine, 28 September 1818, GP.

5. Zeil, *Catalogue of Library of Girard,* 120.

6. Girard to Paul Durer and Co., 20 August 1809, GP.

7. Marian Klamkin, *The Return of Lafayette, 1824-1825* (New York: Scribner's, 1975), 75-77.

8. Ibid., 77-78.

9. Ibid., 80.

10. Ibid., 80, 84.

11. Zeil, *Catalogue of Library of Girard*, 127.

12. Roslyn F. Brenner, *Philadelphia's Outdoor Art* (Philadelphia: Camino Books, 1987), 50-51.

13. John N. Hoffman, *Girard Estate Coal Lands in Pennsylvania, 1801-1884* (Washington: Smithsonian Institution Press, 1972), 9-15.

14. Zeil, *Catalogue of Library of Girard*, 19.

15. Ibid., 17.

16. "Inventory of the Personal Estate of Stephen Girard, Deceased," filed by his Executors in the Register's Office of the City and County of Philadelphia, 31 December 1832, Supplementary Inventory 12 January 1833, 10.

17. Zeil, *Catalogue of Library of Girard*, 19-20.

18. Nicholas B. Wainwright, "The Age of Nicholas Biddle, 1825-1841," in *Philadelphia, a 300-Year History*, 281.

19. Chandler, Brewington and Richardson, *Philadelphia, Port of History*, 60.

20. Ibid.

21. Simpson, *Biography of Girard*, 188.

22. Ibid., 188-189.

23. Ibid., 171.

24. Simpson, *Biography of Girard*, 163.

25. Ritter, *Philadelphia and Her Merchants*, 170.

26. Simpson, *Biography of Girard*, 152-154.

27. Thompson, *Story of Betsy Ross*, 66-68.

28. Wildes, *Lonely Midas*, 335-336.

29. Some writers have spelled the niece's name Emmeline. The correct spelling is Emeline.

30. The portrait (an oil painting, dated 1836 and attributed to John Sartain) is in the Stephen Girard Collection at Girard College, a gift in 1987 from Edith V. Krabach, a great-granddaughter of Emeline.

31. The watch also is in the Stephen Girard Collection, also a gift in 1987 from Edith V. Krabach.

32. From information provided by Edith V. Krabach in 1987 in conjunction with her gifts to the Stephen Girard Collection.

33. Ibid.

34. "Inventory of the Personal Estate of Stephen Girard," filed by his Executors, 31 December 1832, 2-3. The inventory of furnishings and other possessions in his home on Water Street was completed 17 January 1832, twenty-three days after his death.

35. Simpson, *Biography of Girard*, 165.

36. Ibid., 165-166.

37. Zeil, *Catalogue of Library of Girard*, 117.

38. James Ronaldson to Girard, 14 July 1824, GP. Ronaldson was the first president of the Franklin Institute.

39. Wildes, *Lonely Midas*, 275.

40. Girard to Martin Bickham, 26 February 1831, GP.

41. Simpson, *Biography of Girard*, 209.
42. Ingram, *Life of Girard*, 91.
43. Simpson, *Biography of Girard*, 208.
44. Ibid., 211.

Chapter 20

1. Simpson, *Biography of Girard*, 214.
2. *American Daily Advertiser*, 30 December 1831.
3. McMaster, *Life of Girard*, 2:444.
4. *Philadelphia Gazette*, 27 December 1831.
5. *Saturday Bulletin*, 31 December 1831.
6. Mease, *Picture of Philadelphia*, 70.
7. *Philadelphia Gazette*, 29 December 1831.
8. *American Daily Advertiser*, 30 December 1831.
9. *Philadelphia Gazette*, 30 December 1831.
10. Wainwright, "The Age of Nicholas Biddle," in *Philadelphia, a 300-Year History*, 290.
11. *United States Gazette*, 31 December 1831.
12. *Philadelphia Daily Chronicle*, 30 December 1831.
13. Simpson, *Biography of Girard*, 214-215.
14. Herrick, *Stephen Girard, Founder*, 159-160.
15. Diary of Francis Patrick Kenrick, Bishop of Philadelphia, 1830-1851, 30 December 1831. A copy of Bishop Kenrick's diary entries for this date is in the files of the Stephen Girard Collection at Girard College. For commentary on Bishop Kenrick's diary entries for this date, with selected quotations, see: Herrick, *Stephen Girard, Founder*, 159, 162.
16. Diary of Francis Patrick Kenrick, 30 December 1831.
17. Herrick, *Stephen Girard, Founder*, 142-143.
18. Ibid., 142.
19. Ibid., 135-136.
20. "Inventory of the Personal Estate of Stephen Girard, Deceased," filed in the Register's Office for the City and County of Philadelphia, 31 December 1832, Supplementary Inventory filed 12 January 1833. "Accounts of the Executors of the Last Will and Testament of Stephen Girard," filed in the Register's Office for the City and County of Philadelphia, 25 May 1833. "Second Settlement of the Estate of Stephen Girard, Deceased—1833," filed in the Register's Office for the City and County of Philadelphia, 15 October 1833. "Mr. Lippincott's Report, From the Commissioners of the Girard Estates—1835," filed in the Select and Common Councils of Philadelphia, 1835, no day or month given. "Third Settlement of the Estate of Stephen Girard, Deceased—1836," filed in the Register's Office for the City and County of Philadelphia, 1836, no day or month given. "Report of the Auditors on the Trustees Account—1836," filed in the Court of Common Pleas for the City and County of Philadelphia, 17 October 1836. "Fourth Settlement of the Estate of Stephen Girard, Deceased—1836-1837," filed in the Register's Office for the City and County of Philadelphia, 6 April 1837. "Auditors' Report on Accounts, Nos. 1, 2, 3 & 4—1837-1838," filed in the Orphans' Court for the County of Philadelphia, 19 February 1838. "Fifth Settlement of the Estate of Stephen Girard, Deceased—1837-1838," filed in the Register's Office for the City and County of Philadelphia, 15 August 1838. "Auditors' Report in the Matter of Stephen Girard, Deceased—1837-1838," filed in the Orphans' Court for the County of Philadel-

phia, 13 May 1839. "Exceptions to the Auditors' Report on the Fifth Account of the Executors of Stephen Girard," filed in the Orphans' Court for the County of Philadelphia, 1839, no day or month given.

21. "Accounts of the Executors," 13.
22. Ibid., 3,
23. Ibid.
24. "Report of the Auditors—1836," 9.
25. Ibid., 14.
26. Ingram, *Life of Girard*, 155.
27. "Report of the Auditors—1836," 7.
28. Adams, *Finance and Enterprise*, 126-128.
29. "Accounts of the Executors," 41.
30. "Inventory of the Personal Estate," 12.
31. Ibid.
32. "Steam Excursion Will Celebrate Railroad Anniversary," *The Times News*, Lehighton, Pennsylvania, 15 July 1991.
33. "Second Settlement of the Estate," 5.
34. "Accounts of the Executors," 9, 15.
35. "Report of the Auditors—1836," 7.
36. Ibid.
37. Ibid.
38. "Auditors' Report on Accounts, Nos. 1, 2, 3 & 4—1837-1838," 6.
39. Annual Report, Philadelphia Board of City Trusts, 1991. See also: Ronald Glass, "Where's Girard's Money?" *The Girard News*, Girard College, Philadelphia, November 1991. See also: Leigh Jackson, "Behind the Walls at Girard College," *Philadelphia Daily News*, 23 March 1992.
40. Glass, "Where's Girard's Money?"
41. Girard's Will, Section I.
42. Ibid., Section XVIII.
43. Ibid.
44. Ibid.
45. Ibid.
46. Ibid., Section XVII.
47. Ibid., Section XVIII.
48. Ibid., Section XV.
49. Ibid., Section XVI.
50. Ibid., Section XVIII.
51. Ibid., Section XII.
52. Ibid., Section XIII.
53. Ibid., Section XIV.
54. Ibid., Sections X-XI.
55. Ibid., Section IX.
56. Ibid., Section XVIII.
57. Ibid., Sections II-VII.
58. Ibid., Section VIII.
59. Ibid., Section XIX.
60. Ibid.

61. Ibid.
62. Ibid., Section XXII.
63. Ibid.
64. Ibid.
65. Alotta, *Street Names*, 53.
66. Girard's Will, Section XXII.
67. Ibid.
68. Ibid.
69. Ibid., Sections XXIII-XXIV.
70. "Accounts of the Executors," 17.
71. Girard's Will, Section XXIV.
72. Ibid.
73. Ibid., Sections XX-XXI.

Chapter 21

1. Herrick, *Stephen Girard, Founder*, 143-144.
2. Girard's Will, Section XXI.
3. Ibid., Codicil dated 20 June 1831.
4. Ibid., Section XXI.
5. Ibid.
6. Herrick, *Stephen Girard, Founder*, 148.
7. Ibid., 146-147.
8. Ritter, *Philadelphia and Her Merchants*, 27. See also the map opposite p. 26.
9. Herrick, *Stephen Girard, Founder*, 148.
10. Ibid.
11. Ibid., 152.
12. Ibid., 154.
13. *Arguments of the Defendants' Counsel and Judgment of the Supreme Court U.S. in the case of Vidal and Another, Complainants and Appellants, Versus the Mayor, Etc., of Philadelphia, the Executors of Stephen Girard, and Others, Defendants and Appellees, January Term, 1844* (Philadelphia: Girard College Print Shop, 1929, reprinted from Philadelphia Edition, 1854), 113-114.
14. Ibid., 116-117.
15. Ibid., 118.
16. Ibid., 123.
17. Ibid., 314-315.
18. Ibid., 317-320.
19. Arey, *Girard College and Its Founder*, 30-31.
20. Girard's Will, Section XX.
21. Edgar P. Richardson, "The Athens of America, 1800-1825," in *Philadelphia, a 300-Year History*, 226.
22. Girard's Will, Section XXI.
23. Ibid.
24. Ibid.
25. Ibid.
26. Robert D. Schwarz, *The Stephen Girard Collection, a Selective Catalog* (Philadelphia: Girard College, 1980), p. IV.

27. Ibid.
28. Girard's Will, Section XXI.
29. Ibid.
30. Arey, *Girard College and Its Founder*, 31.
31. Ibid., 35.
32. Ibid., 44-45, 48.
33. Ibid., 48.
34. Ibid., 52.
35. Ibid., 42-43.
36. Ibid., 43.
37. *Webster's Deluxe Unabridged Dictionary*, 2nd ed., s.v. "orphan."
38. Arey, *Girard College and Its Founder*, 36.
39. Herrick, *Stephen Girard, Founder*, 163.
40. Ibid., 163-164.
41. *Freemasonry in Pennsylvania, 1730-1907* (Philadelphia: Grand Lodge of Pennsylvania, 1918), 365-366.
42. Ibid., 366.
43. Ibid.
44. Herrick, *Stephen Girard, Founder*, 164-165.
45. Ibid., 165.
46. Ibid., 164-165.
47. Ibid., 165-166.
48. Girard's Will, Section XXI.
49. Herrick, *Stephen Girard, Founder*, 166.
50. *Freemasonry in Pennsylvania*, 386-393.
51. Wilson, *Yesterday's Philadelphia*, 35.
52. The author of this book has talked with Girard College graduates whose recollections of their student years go as far back as the early 1920s.
53. As an example, see invitation to Founder's Day, 20 May 1989.
54. "Two Banks Named Girard," an undated pamphlet published by the Girard Bank, chartered 1836, Philadelphia.
55. Ibid.
56. Brenner, *Philadelphia's Outdoor Art*, 64-65.
57. Beck, *Girard, Merchant and Mariner*, title page.

Chapter 22

1. Beck, *Girard, Merchant and Mariner*, 14. The quotation is from an address by James M. Beck at the unveiling of the statue of Stephen Girard on the West Plaza of City Hall in Philadelphia, 20 May 1897.
2. Herrick, *Stephen Girard, Founder*, 127. The quotation is from an address by Nicholas Biddle at the laying of the cornerstone of Founder's Hall at Girard College, 4 July 1833.

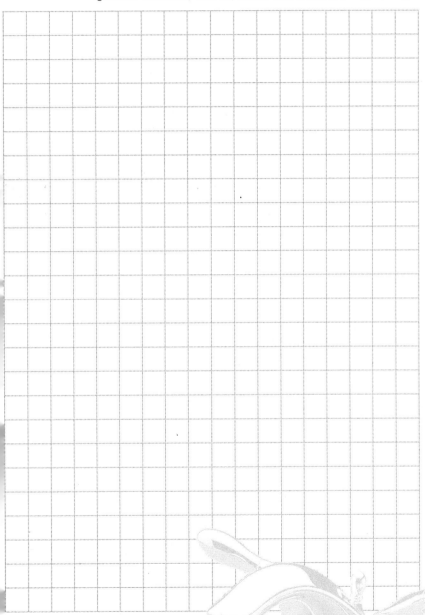

2951 Hwy. 501 East   Conway, SC   29526-9515 •   843.347.3121
Sales 1.800.944.9292 •   Fax 1.800.945.9292 • www.wolverinebrass.com

Adams

Bolt

Bibliography

Adams, Abigail, and John Adams. *The Book of Abigail and John: Selected Letters of the Adams Family, 1762-1784.* Edited by L.H. Butterfield, Marc Friedlaender, and Mary-Jo Kline. Cambridge: Harvard University Press, 1975.

Adams, Donald R., Jr. *Finance and Enterprise in Early America: A Study of Stephen Girard's Bank, 1812-1831.* Philadelphia: University of Pennsylvania Press, 1978.

Alotta, Robert I. *Street Names of Philadelphia.* Philadelphia: Temple University Press, 1975.

Arey, Henry W. *The Girard College and Its Founder: Containing the Biography of Mr. Girard, the History of the Institution, Its Organization and Plan of Discipline, With the Course of Education, Forms of Admission of Pupils, Description of the Buildings, Etc., Etc. and the Will of Mr. Girard.* Philadelphia: Sherman, 1852; reprinted 1866.

Baltzell, E. Digby. *Philadelphia Gentlemen: The Making of a National Upper Class.* Glencoe, Illinois: The Free Press, 1958.

—. *The Protestant Establishment: Aristocracy and Caste in America.* New York: Random House, 1964; republished, New Haven, Connecticut: Yale University Press, 1987.

Bartlett, Richard A. *The New Country: A Social History of the American Frontier, 1776-1890.* New York: Oxford University Press, 1974.

Beard, Charles A., and Mary R. Beard. *The Rise of American Civilization.* 2 vols. New York: Macmillan, 1927; reprinted, 1 vol., 1930.

Beck, James M. *Stephen Girard, Merchant and Mariner: An Oration Delivered at the Unveiling of a Statue to Stephen Girard on the West Plaza of the City Hall, Philadelphia, May 20, 1897.* Philadelphia: J.B. Lippincott, 1897.

Bemis, Samuel Flagg. *A Diplomatic History of the United States.* New York: Henry Holt, 1936; revised edition, 1946.

Beyer, George R. *Pennsylvania Roads Before the Automobile.* Historic Pennsylvania Leaflet No. 33. Harrisburg: Pennsylvania Historical and Museum Commission, 1972.

Birch, Thomas. *Thomas Birch, 1779-1851, Paintings and Drawings.* A catalogue for an art exhibition. Philadelphia: Philadelphia Maritime Museum, 1966.

Boldt, David R., ed. *The Founding City.* Radnor, Pennsylvania: published jointly by the Philadelphia Inquirer and the Chilton Book Company, 1976.

Bowen, Catherine Drinker. *Miracle at Philadelphia: The Story of the Constitutional Convention, May to September 1787.* Boston: published by Little, Brown and Company in association with the Atlantic Monthly Press, 1966; republished, 1986.

Brenner, Roslyn F. *Philadelphia's Outdoor Art: A Walking Tour.* Philadelphia: Camino Books, 1987.

393

Brewington, Marion. "Maritime Philadelphia, 1609-1837." *Pennsylvania Magazine of History and Biography*, April 1939.

Bridenbaugh, Carl, and Jessica Bridenbaugh. *Rebels and Gentlemen: Philadelphia in the Age of Franklin.* New York: Reynal and Hitchcock, 1942.

Bronner, Edwin E. "Village Into Town." In *Philadelphia, a 300-Year History.* See Weigley.

Burt, Nathaniel. *The Perennial Philadelphians: The Anatomy of an American Aristocracy.* Boston: Little, Brown and Company, 1963.

Burt, Struthers. *Philadelphia: Holy Experiment.* Garden City, New York: Doubleday, 1945.

Carey, Mathew. *A Short Account of the Malignant Fever, Lately Prevalent in Philadelphia.* 4th edition, improved. Philadelphia: printed by the author, 1794; reprinted, New York: Arno Press and the New York Times, 1970.

Carlyle, Thomas. *The French Revolution: A History.* No city given, no publisher given, 1837; reprinted, New York: Modern Library, no date given.

Cawley, James, and Margaret Cawley. *Along the Old York Road.* New Brunswick, New Jersey: Rutgers University Press, 1965.

Chandler, Charles Lyon, Marion V. Brewington, and Edgar P. Richardson. *Philadelphia, Port of History, 1609-1837.* Philadelphia: Philadelphia Maritime Museum, 1976.

Chapelle, Howard I. *The Search for Speed Under Sail, 1700-1855.* New York: W.W. Norton, 1967.

Chapin, Bradley. "Felony Law Reform in the Early Republic." *The Pennsylvania Magazine of History and Biography*, April 1989.

Clark, Hazel C., and Eleanor S. Rogers. *Mount Holly: A Picture Story of Its Historical Growth.* Mount Holly, New Jersey: Mount Holly Historical Society, 1975.

Cobb, Charles E., Jr. "Haiti Against All Odds." *National Geographic*, November 1987.

Cochran, Thomas C. *Pennsylvania: A Bicentennial History.* New York: W.W. Norton, 1978.

Coit, Margaret L. *The Growing Years, 1789-1829.* Vol. 3 of *The Life History of the United States.* New York: Time Incorporated, 1963.

Cope, Thomas P. *Philadelphia Merchant: The Diary of Thomas P. Cope, 1800-1851.* Edited by Eliza Cope Harrison. South Bend, Indiana: Gateway Editions, 1978.

Davis, Charles G. *Ships of the Past.* Salem, Massachusetts: Marine Research Society, 1929.

DeCou, George. *The Historic Rancocas.* Moorestown, New Jersey: printed by the News Chronicle, 1949.

Deveze, Lily. *A Brief Guide to French History.* Carcassonne, France: no publisher given, 1982.

Drinker, Elizabeth. *The Journal of Elizabeth Drinker, 1758-1807.* In the collection of the Historical Society of Pennsylvania, Philadelphia.

Dunaway, Wayland F. *A History of Pennsylvania.* New York: Prentice-Hall, 1935; 2nd edition, 1948.

Earle, Alice Morse. *Home Life in Colonial Days.* New York: Macmillan, 1898; reprinted, 1948.

Ferm, Vergilius. *Pictorial History of Protestantism: A Panoramic View of Western Europe and the United States.* New York: Philosophical Library, edition published by Bramhall House, a division of Clarkson N. Potter, 1957.

Fisher, Sydney George. *Men, Women and Manners in Colonial Times.* New York: J.B. Lippincott, 1897; reprinted, 2 vols., Detroit: Singing Tree Press, 1969.

Fitzroy, Herbert William Keith. "The Punishment of Crime in Provincial Pennsylvania." *The Pennsylvania Magazine of History and Biography*, July 1936.

Freemasonry in Pennsylvania, 1730-1907. Philadelphia: Grand Lodge of Pennsylvania, 1918.

Gallatin, Albert. *The Writings of Albert Gallatin.* Edited by Henry Adams. 3 vols. Philadelphia: J. B. Lippincott, 1879.

GALLATIN

←

WB Wolverine Brass Inc.

Geffen, Elizabeth M. "Industrial Development and Social Crisis, 1841-1854." In *Philadelphia, a 300-Year History*. See Weigley.

Girard, Stephen. The Papers of Stephen Girard, the Stephen Girard Collection, and the Personal Library of Stephen Girard. Founder's Hall, Girard College, Philadelphia. The Papers of Stephen Girard also may be seen, on microfilm, in the Library of the American Philosophical Society, Philadelphia.

Glubok, Shirley, ed. *Home and Child Life in Colonial Days*. New York: Macmillan, 1969. Abridged from *Home Life in Colonial Days* and *Child Life in Colonial Days*, both by Alice Morse Earle.

Goldstein, Jonathan. *Philadelphia and the China Trade, 1682-1846: Commercial, Cultural and Attitudinal Effects*. State College, Pennsylvania: The Pennsylvania State University Press, 1978.

—. *The Ethics of Tribute and the Profits of Trade Stephen Girard's China Trade (1787-1824)*. A manuscript in the Library of the Philadelphia Maritime Museum, 1969.

Herrick, Cheesman A. *Stephen Girard, Founder*. Philadelphia: Girard College, 1923; 5th edition, 1945.

Hickey, Donald R. *The War of 1812: A Forgotten Conflict*. Urbana, Illinois: University of Illinois Press, 1989.

Hoffman, John N. *Girard Estate Coal Lands in Pennsylvania, 1801-1884*. Washington: Smithsonian Institution Press, 1972.

Ingram, Henry Atlee. *The Life and Character of Stephen Girard*. 2nd edition, revised. Philadelphia: E. Stanley Hart, 1885.

—. *The Life of Jean Girard, De Montbrun*. Philadelphia: edition limited, no publisher given, 1888.

Inverarity, Robert Bruce. *Early Marine Navigation*. Philadelphia: Philadelphia Maritime Museum, 1976.

Jackson, John W. *The Delaware Bay and River Defenses of Philadelphia, 1775-1777*. Philadelphia: Philadelphia Maritime Museum, 1977.

Jones, Absalom, and Richard Allen (identified in book by initials: A.J. and R.A.). *A Narrative of the Proceedings of the Black People, During the Late Awful Calamity in Philadelphia, in the Year 1793: And a Refutation of Some Censures, Thrown Upon Them in Some Late Publications*. Philadelphia: printed for the authors by William W. Woodward, 1794; Afro-American History Series, Maxwell Whiteman, ed., Historic Publication No. 223, Philadelphia: Historic Publications, no date given.

Kane, Joseph Nathan. *Facts About the Presidents: A Compilation of Biographical and Historical Data*. 2nd edition. New York: H.W. Wilson, 1968.

Kemp, Peter. *The History of Ships*. Stamford, Connecticut: Longmeadow Press, 1988.

Kennedy, Roger G. *Orders From France: The Americans and the French in a Revolutionary World, 1780-1820*. New York: Alfred A. Knopf, 1989.

Kent, Donald H. *Anthony Wayne, Man of Action*. Revised edition. Historic Pennsylvania Leaflet No. 2. Harrisburg: Pennsylvania Historical and Museum Commission, 1976.

Kent, Frank R. *The Story of Alexander Brown and Son*. Baltimore: printed privately for the company by Norman T.A. Munder, 1925.

Klamkin, Marian. *The Return of Lafayette, 1824-1825*. New York: Charles Scribner's Sons, 1975.

Klein, Philip S., and Art Hoogenboom. *A History of Pennsylvania*. 2nd and enlarged edition. State College, Pennsylvania: The Pennsylvania University Press, 1980; 1st edition, New York: McGraw-Hill, 1973.

Leach, Josiah Granville. *The History of the Girard National Bank of Philadelphia, 1832-1902.* New York: Greenwood Press, 1969; originally published, Philadelphia: J.B. Lippincott, 1902.

Lord, Walter. *The Dawn's Early Light.* New York: W.W. Norton, 1972.

Ludwig, Emil. *Napoleon.* Translated by Eden Paul and Cedar Paul. New York: Boni and Liveright, 1926.

Maclean, Frances. "'We Will Confound the Calumniators of Our Race . . . .'" *Smithsonian,* October 1987.

Marion, John Francis. *Philadelphia Medica.* Philadelphia: SmithKline Corporation, 1975.

McFarland, Marvin W. "Meet Mr. Girard." *Steel and Garnet.* Girard College. May 1941.

—. "Meet Mr. Girard: His Boyhood Days in Old Bordeaux." *Steel and Garnet.* Girard College. November 1941.

—. "Meet Mr. Girard." *Steel and Garnet.* Girard College. January 1942.

—. "Meet Mr. Girard: A Family in Disintegration." *Steel and Garnet.* Girard College. April 1942.

—. "Mr. Girard Looks at War." *Steel and Garnet.* Girard College. May 1942.

—. "Meet Mr. Girard: Farewell to Old Bordeaux." *Steel and Garnet.* Girard College. October 1942.

—. *Citizen Stephen Girard.* An address at Girard College, 19 May 1973. Published as a booklet by the college, 1974.

—. *Stephen Girard: A Very Human Human Being.* An address at Girard College, 22 April 1977. Published as a booklet by the college, 1977.

McMaster, John Bach. *The Life and Times of Stephen Girard: Mariner and Merchant.* 2 vols. Philadelphia: J.B. Lippincott, 1918.

Mease, James, *The Picture of Philadelphia.* Philadelphia: B. and T. Kite, 1811; reprinted, New York: Arno Press and the New York Times, 1970.

Mendte, J. Robert. *The Union League of Philadelphia Celebrates 125 Years, 1862-1987.* Devon, Pennsylvania: William T. Cooke, 1987.

Miller, David S. "The Polly: A Perspective on Merchant Stephen Girard." *The Pennsylvania Magazine of History and Biography,* April 1988.

Miller, Randall M., ed. "Women in the Revolutionary Era." *The Pennsylvania Magazine of History and Biography,* April 1991.

Minnigerode, Meade. *Certain Rich Men.* Freeport, New York: Books for Libraries Press, 1927; reprinted, 1970.

Morison, Samuel Eliot. *Admiral of the Ocean Sea: A Life of Christopher Columbus.* Boston: Little, Brown and Company, 1942.

—. *The Oxford History of the American People.* New York: Oxford University Press, 1965.

Morison, Samuel Eliot, and Henry Steele Commager. *The Growth of the American Republic.* 2 vols. 3rd edition, revised and enlarged. New York: Oxford University Press, 1942; originally published in 1 vol., 1930.

Morris, Richard B., ed. *Encyclopedia of American History.* Revised and enlarged edition. New York: Harper and Brothers, 1961.

Morton, Thomas G. *The History of the Pennsylvania Hospital, 1751-1895.* Philadelphia: published by the Pennsylvania Hospital, 1895; reprint edition, New York: Arno Press, 1973.

Myers, Gustavus. *History of the Great American Fortunes.* 3 vols. Chicago: Charles H. Kerr, reprinted, 1911.

Nash, Gary B. *Class and Society in Early America.* Englewood Cliffs, New Jersey: Prentice-Hall, 1970.

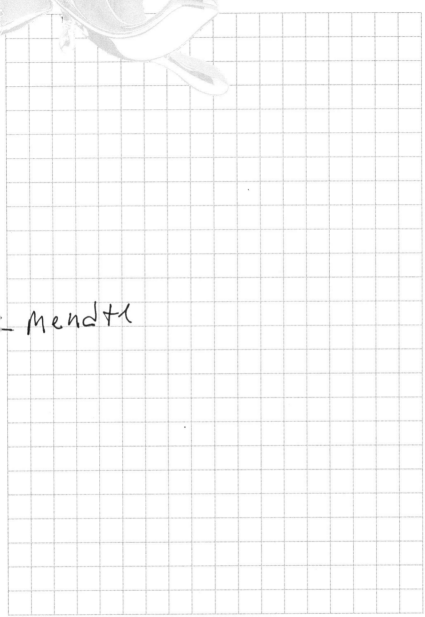

— Mendt1

Sales 1.800.944.9292 • Fax 1.800.945.9292 • www.wolverinebrass.com
2951 Hwy. 501 East Conway, SC 29526-9515 • 843.347.3121

Nunnally, Elam W., Catherine S. Chilman, and Fred M. Cox, eds. *Troubled Relationships.* Vol. 3 of *Families in Trouble.* Newbury Park, California: Sage Publications, 1988.

Papa, Joan Springer. "Dolley Madison: 'A Fine, Portly, Buxom Dame.'" In *The Founding City.* See Boldt.

Parton, James. *Famous Americans of Recent Times.* Boston: Ticknor and Fields, 1867; reprinted, New York: Johnson Reprint Corporation, 1967.

Peirce, Neal R. *The People's President.* New York: Simon and Schuster, 1968.

Pennsylvania Hospital. The Historic Library and the Archives Collection. Pine Building, Pennsylvania Hospital, Philadelphia. Portions of the Archives Collection also may be seen on microfilm in the Library of the American Philosophical Society, Philadelphia.

Pleck, Elizabeth. *Domestic Tyranny: The Making of Social Policy Against Family Violence From Colonial Times to the Present.* New York: Oxford University Press, 1987.

Powell, J.H. *Bring Out Your Dead: The Great Plague of Yellow Fever in Philadelphia in 1793.* Philadelphia: University of Pennsylvania Press, 1949.

Proud, Robert. *The History of Pennsylvania.* 2 vols. Philadelphia: printed and sold by Zachariah Poulson, Jr., 1797.

Reed, Zachariah. *The History of Mount Holly.* A manuscript in the Mount Holly Library, Mount Holly, New Jersey, 1859.

Richardson, Edgar P. "The Athens of America, 1800-1825." In *Philadelphia, a 300-Year History.* See Weigley.

Richman, Irwin. *Albert Gallatin, Master of Finance.* Historic Pennsylvania Leaflet No. 25. Harrisburg: Pennsylvania Historical and Museum Commission, 1962.

Ritter, Abraham. *Philadelphia and Her Merchants.* Philadelphia: published by the author, 1860.

Rosenberg, Charles E. *The Care of Strangers: The Rise of America's Hospital System.* New York: Basic Books, 1987.

Rowe, G.S. "Women's Crime and Criminal Administration in Pennsylvania, 1763-1790." *The Pennsylvania Magazine of History and Biography,* July 1985.

Rupp, George P., ed. *Semi-Centennial of Girard College, 1848-1898.* Philadelphia: J. B. Lippincott, 1898.

Rupp, I. Daniel. *History of Northampton, Lehigh, Monroe, Carbon and Schuylkill Counties.* Lancaster, Pennsylvania: G. Hills, 1845.

Schama, Simon. *Citizens: A Chronicle of the French Revolution.* New York: Alfred A. Knopf, 1989.

Schwarz, Robert D. *The Stephen Girard Collection: A Selective Catalog.* Critiqued and annotated by Marvin W. McFarland. Prepared under the direction of the Girard College Committee on Stephen Girard Papers and Effects. Philadelphia: Girard College, 1980.

Shepherd, Jack. *The Adams Chronicles.* Boston: Little, Brown and Company, 1975.

Shinn, Henry C. *The History of Mount Holly.* Mount Holly, New Jersey: published by the Mount Holly Herald, 1959.

Simpson, Stephen. *Biography of Stephen Girard.* Philadelphia, Thomas L. Bonsal, 1832.

Stacton, David. *The Bonapartes.* New York: Simon and Schuster, 1966.

Stanley, Linda, et al. *Courage in the Face of Crisis: Yellow Fever Strikes Philadelphia, 1793.* Philadelphia: A document prepared by the Education Department of the Historical Society of Pennsylvania, 1989.

Stephen Girard Will and Biography. No author, publisher, city of publication or date given. Probable publication date: 1832. A bound volume in Rare Book Department of Free Library of Philadelphia.

Stordeur, Richard A., and Richard Stille. *Ending Men's Violence Against Their Partners: One Road to Peace.* Newbury Park, California: Sage Publications, 1989.

Straus, Murray A., and Richard J. Gelles. "Violence in American Families: How Much Is There and Why Does It Occur?" In *Troubled Relationships.* See Nunnally.

Sweely, Christine. *The Liberty Bell.* Historic Pennsylvania Leaflet No. 35. Harrisburg: Pennsylvania Historical and Museum Commission, 1974.

Thompson, Ray. *The Story of Betsy Ross.* Fort Washington, Pennsylvania: Bicentennial Press, 1975.

Tinkcom, Henry M. "The Revolutionary City, 1765-1783." In *Philadelphia, a 300-Year History.* See Weigley.

Tomes, Nancy. *A Generous Confidence: Thomas Story Kirkbride and the Art of Asylum-Keeping, 1840-1883.* New York: Cambridge University Press, 1984.

Trussell, John B.B., Jr. *The Battle of Germantown.* Historic Pennsylvania Leaflet No. 38. Harrisburg: Pennsylvania Historical and Museum Commission, 1974.

Tuchman, Barbara W. *The First Salute.* New York: Alfred A. Knopf, 1988.

Tunis, Edwin. *The Young United States, 1783 to 1830.* New York: Thomas Y. Crowell, 1969.

U.S. Department of Commerce. *Historical Statistics of the United States: Colonial Times to 1970.* Washington: U.S. Government Printing Office, 1975.

Vinson, Michael. "The Society for Political Inquiries: The Limits of Republican Discourse in Philadelphia on the Eve of the Constitutional Convention." *The Pennsylvania Magazine of History and Biography*, April 1989.

Wainwright, Nicholas B. "The Age of Nicholas Biddle, 1825-1841." In *Philadelphia, a 300-Year History.* See Weigley.

Weigley, Russell F., ed. *Philadelphia, a 300-Year History.* New York: W.W. Norton, 1982.

Whitaker, Arthur Preston. *The United States and the Independence of Latin America, 1800-1830.* Baltimore: Johns Hopkins Press, 1941; reprinted, New York: Russell and Russell, 1962.

Wilburn, Jean Alexander. *Biddle's Bank: The Crucial Years.* New York: Columbia University Press, 1967.

Wildes, Harry Emerson. *The Delaware.* New York: Farrar and Rinehart, 1940.

—. *Lonely Midas.* New York: Farrar and Rinehart, 1943.

—. *William Penn.* New York: Macmillan, 1974.

Wilkinson, Norman B. *A French Asylum on the Susquehanna River.* 4th edition, revised. Historic Pennsylvania Leaflet No. 11. Harrisburg: Pennsylvania Historical and Museum Commission, 1969.

Williams, William H. *America's First Hospital: The Pennsylvania Hospital, 1751-1841.* Wayne, Pennsylvania: Haverford House, 1976.

Wilson, George. *Yesterday's Philadelphia.* Miami: E.A. Seemann, 1975.

Wismes, Armel de. *Genealogy of the Kings of France.* Nantes, France: Artaud Freres, no date given.

Zeil, William F. *A Catalogue of the Personal Library of Stephen Girard (1750-1831).* Philadelphia: published jointly by Girard College and the American Philosophical Society, 1990.

—, ed. *The Diary of Peter Seguin: A Young House Guest of Stephen Girard.* Philadelphia: Girard College, 1984.

Index